palgrave advances in international history

Palgrave Advances

Titles include:

Patrick Finney (*editor*)
INTERNATIONAL HISTORY

Marnie Hughes-Warrington (*editor*)
WORLD HISTORIES

Phillip Mallett (*editor*)
THOMAS HARDY STUDIES

Lois Oppenheim (*editor*)
SAMUEL BECKETT STUDIES

Jean-Michel Rabaté (*editor*)
JAMES JOYCE STUDIES

Frederick S. Roden (*editor*)
OSCAR WILDE STUDIES

Jonathan Woolfson (*editor*)
RENAISSANCE HISTORIOGRAPHY

Forthcoming:

Robert Patten and John Bowen (*editors*)
CHARLES DICKENS STUDIES

Anna Snaith (*editor*)
VIRGINIA WOOLF STUDIES

Nicholas Williams (*editor*)
WILLIAM BLAKE STUDIES

Palgrave Advances
Series Standing Order ISBN 1–4039–3512–2 (Hardback) 1–4039–3513–0 (Paperback)
(*outside North America only*)

You can receive future titles in this series as they are published by placing a standing order.
Please contact your bookseller or, in the case of difficulty, write to us at the address below
with your name and address, the title of the series and the ISBN quoted above.

Customer Services Department, Macmillan Distribution Ltd, Houndmills, Basingstoke,
Hampshire RG21 6XS, England

palgrave advances in international history

edited by
patrick finney
university of wales, aberystwyth

First published 2005 by
PALGRAVE MACMILLAN
Houndmills, Basingstoke, Hampshire RG21 6XS and
175 Fifth Avenue, New York, N.Y. 10010
Companies and representatives throughout the world

PALGRAVE MACMILLAN is the global academic imprint of the
Palgrave Macmillan division of St Martin's Press LLC and of
Palgrave Macmillan Ltd.
Macmillan® is a registered trademark in the United States,
United Kingdom and other countries. Palgrave is a registered
trademark in the European Union and other countries.

ISBN 1–4039–0436–7 hardback
ISBN 1–4039–0440–5 paperback

This book is printed on paper suitable for recycling and
made from fully managed and sustained forest sources.

A catalogue record for this book is available
from the British Library.

Library of Congress Cataloging-in-Publication Data
Finney, Patrick, 1968–
Palgrave advances in international history / edited by Patrick Finney.
p. cm.
Includes bibliographical references and index.
ISBN 1–4039–0436–7 — ISBN 1–4039–0440–5 (pbk.)
1. Historiography. 2. International relations. 3. World politics. I. Title.

D13.F4994 2005
907'.2—dc22

2004051407

10 9 8 7 6 5 4 3 2 1
14 13 12 11 10 09 08 07 06 05

Printed and bound in Great Britain by
Antony Rowe Ltd, Chippenham and Eastbourne

contents

acknowledgements

I would like primarily to thank the contributors, whose receptive, constructive and professional attitudes made the experience of editing this volume far less nightmarish than is usually the case with such collective endeavours. At Palgrave, I must thank Luciana O'Flaherty who originally suggested that I might like to put together a volume on international history for this series, and who oversaw its genesis and gestation with patience, tact and just the right amount of chivvying. I received very helpful comments on a series of draft proposals from a number of anonymous referees, to whom I am also grateful. The volume was already in train when I took up a post in the Department of International Politics at the University of Wales, Aberystwyth, one of the most historically evocative locations on the globe from which to ponder the history of international relations, and one that currently provides an exceptionally stimulating intellectual home. I am grateful to all my colleagues there, especially in the international history section, for contributing to the development of my thoughts on the field through myriad diverse interactions. Finally, my biggest debt is to Susan, who I hope may now be at least partially consoled that book projects can in fact come to an end.

Parts of Chapter 3 have previously been published in Bruce Cumings, 'The American Century and the Third World', *Diplomatic History*, 23 (2) (1999) 355–70; we are grateful to Blackwell Publishers for permission to reprint them here.

Parts of Chapter 6 have previously been published in L. V. Scott and P. Jackson, 'Journeys in Shadows', in L. V. Scott and P. Jackson (eds), *Understanding Intelligence in the Twenty First Century: Journeys in Shadows* (London: Routledge, 2004), pp. 1–28.

notes on the contributors

Mark Philip Bradley is Associate Professor of History at Northwestern University. He is the author of *Imagining Vietnam and America: The Making of Postcolonial Vietnam, 1919–1950* (2000) and is currently working on a global history of the human rights revolutions of the twentieth century.

Susan L. Carruthers is Associate Professor of History at Rutgers, the State University of New Jersey. Her area of teaching specialization is 'the United States and the World', but she writes more widely on cultural and communicative dimensions of international history. Her publications include *Winning Hearts and Minds: British Governments, the Media and Colonial Counterinsurgency* (1995) and *The Media at War: Communication and Conflict in the Twentieth Century* (2000). She is currently completing a book on captivity and the early Cold War.

Bruce Cumings is Norman and Edna Freehling Professor of History at Chicago University. His publications include *The Origins of the Korean War*, 2 vols (1981, 1990) and *Parallax Visions: Making Sense of American-East Asian Relations* (1999).

Miriam Fendius Elman is Associate Professor of Political Science at Arizona State University. She is the editor of *Paths to Peace: Is Democracy the Answer?* (1997) and co-editor of *Bridges and Boundaries: Historians, Political Scientists, and the Study of International Relations* (2001) and *Progress in International Relations Theory: Appraising the Field* (2003). Her work has appeared in the *American Political Science Review, International History Review*, the *British Journal of Political Science, Security Studies, International Studies Quarterly*, and other scholarly journals. She currently serves on the Editorial Board of *International Security* and is working on a project concerning the international context of democratic state-building.

John Ferris holds a PhD in War Studies from King's College, London, and is a Professor of History at the University of Calgary. He has published widely in intelligence, military, diplomatic, strategic and international history. Amongst other works, he has authored *The Evolution of British Strategic Policy, 1919–26* (1989), edited *The British Army and Signals Intelligence in the First World War* (1992) and co-authored (with Christon Archer, Holger Herwig and Timothy Travers) *World History of Warfare* (2002).

Patrick Finney is a Lecturer in International History at the University of Wales, Aberystwyth, and has published widely on historiography and theory, the origins of the Second World War, and international relations in Southeastern Europe. He has edited volumes on *The Origins of the Second World War* (1997) and 'Memory, Identity and War in South Eastern Europe' (theme issue, *Rethinking History*, 6 (1) 2002), and is currently writing *Remembering the Road to World War II: International History, National Identity, Collective Memory*.

Nigel Gould-Davies gained a PhD in Political Science at Harvard and taught at Oxford before joining the Foreign and Commonwealth Office. He is currently First Secretary and Head of the Economic Section at the British Embassy in Moscow.

Akira Iriye is Charles Warren Professor of American History at Harvard University. He is a past president of both the Society for Historians of American Foreign Relations and the American Historical Association. He has published very widely on international relations in the Asia-Pacific region, on American foreign relations, and on the cultural dimensions of international history. His recent books include *Cultural Internationalism and World Order* (1997), *Japan and the Wider World* (1997), and *Global Community: The Role of International Organizations in the Making of the Contemporary World* (2002).

Peter Jackson is Senior Lecturer in International Politics in the Department of International Politics at the University of Wales, Aberystwyth. He has published widely in the fields of intelligence and security studies, French strategy and diplomacy, and the origins of the Second World War. His most recent book is *France and the Nazi Menace: Intelligence and Policy-Making, 1933–1939* (2000). He is Deputy Director of the Centre for Intelligence and International Security Studies at the University of Wales, Aberystwyth.

T. G. Otte is a Lecturer in Diplomatic and International History at the University of East Anglia, Norwich. He has published widely on aspects of great power relations in the late nineteenth and early twentieth centuries. His recent publications include edited volumes on *The Makers of British Foreign Policy: From Pitt to Thatcher* (2002) and (with G. R. Berridge and Maurice Keens-Soper) *Diplomatic Theory from Machiavelli to Kissinger* (2001), and a monograph entitled *Global Transformation: Great Britain, the Great Powers and the China Question, 1894–1905* (forthcoming). He is a frequent contributor to the *Times Literary Supplement*, and is also associate editor and reviews editor of *Diplomacy and Statecraft*.

Andrew J. Rotter is Professor of History at Colgate University. His research focus is US–Asia relations during the Cold War. He is the author of *The Path to Vietnam: Origins of the American Commitment to Southeast Asia* (1987), *Comrades at Odds: The United States and India, 1947–1964* (2000), and numerous articles and review essays. He is currently writing a book on the Hiroshima bombing and its global impact.

Len Scott is Professor of International Politics at the University of Wales, Aberystwyth, where he is also Dean of Social Sciences. He specializes in intelligence and international history. Among his recent publications are *Macmillan, Kennedy and the Cuban Missile Crisis: Political, Military and Intelligence Aspects* (1999) and (with Stephen Twigge) *Planning Armageddon: Britain, the United States and the Command of Nuclear Forces, 1945–1964* (2000). He is Director of the Centre for Intelligence and International Security Studies at the University of Wales, Aberystwyth.

Glenda Sluga is Associate Professor of History at the University of Sydney. She is the author of *The Problem of Trieste and the Italo-Yugoslav Border: Difference, Identity, and Sovereignty in Twentieth-Century Europe* (2001), and co-author (with Barbara Caine) of *Gendering European History* (1999). She is currently completing a manuscript on the international history of the national idea in the early twentieth century.

Jeremi Suri is an Assistant Professor of History at the University of Wisconsin-Madison. He is the author of *Power and Protest: Global Revolution and the Rise of Détente* (2003). He has also published articles on modern international history in *Cold War History, Diplomatic History, International Society*, the *Journal of Cold War Studies*, and numerous other journals. He is currently writing an international history of Henry Kissinger's career.

list of abbreviations

AHA	American Historical Association
AIDS	acquired immune deficiency syndrome
APSA	American Political Science Association
CIA	Central Intelligence Agency
CQRM	Consortium on Qualitative Research Methods
DPT	democratic peace theory
FBI	Federal Bureau of Investigation
GCHQ	Government Communications Headquarters
GDP	gross domestic product
GI	American serviceman (colloquial, from 'Government Issue')
HUMINT	human intelligence
ICW	International Council of Women
IGOs	inter-governmental organizations
IMF	International Monetary Fund
IMINT	imagery intelligence
IOC	International Olympic Committee
IPA	Institute for Propaganda Analysis
IPB	International Peace Bureau
IR	International Relations (academic discipline)
JIC	Joint Intelligence Committee
KGB	Committee for State Security (USSR) (post-Stalinist successor to the NKVD)
Mercosur	Mercado Común del Sur (South American economic community)
MI5	British Security Service (originally a branch of the Directorate of Military Intelligence)
MNEs	multinational enterprises

NATO	North Atlantic Treaty Organization
NGOs	non-governmental organizations
NKVD	Commissariat for Internal Affairs (USSR state security apparatus)
NSAs	non-state actors
OPEC	Organization of Oil Exporting Countries
OSINT	open-source intelligence
OSS	Office of Strategic Services
OWI	Office of War Information
POWs	prisoners of war
SARS	severe acute respiratory syndrome
SHAFR	Society for Historians of American Foreign Relations
SID	Society for International Development
SIGINT	signals intelligence
SIS	Secret Intelligence Service; also known as MI6 (originally a branch of the Directorate of Military Intelligence)
SS	Schutzstaffel: Nazi elite force
SVN	South Vietnam
UN	United Nations
UNESCO	United Nations Educational, Scientific and Cultural Organization
WMD	weapons of mass destruction
WTO	World Trade Organization

introduction: what is international history?

patrick finney

Delimiting the territory of academic tribes and explaining their customs and practices are ethnographic enterprises of formidable complexity.[1] Symptomatic of this in the case of international history is the lack of consensus not only over the proper subject matter of the field but even over the very name that it should bear. When the practice of history was professionalized and institutionalized in the nineteenth century, the study of political and diplomatic relations between states lay at its very heart, so dominant that it could simply be denominated as 'history' without any adjectival qualification. As the discipline expanded and diversified, the study of statecraft came to be the preserve of a discrete sub-field known as 'diplomatic history' which flourished in the era of two total wars because it seemed that the questions it tackled were 'of fundamental importance both to the recent history and ... to the future of mankind'.[2] After the Second World War, however, diplomatic history found its privileged position within the broader discipline increasingly threatened. Perceived as unhealthily preoccupied with the arcane machinations of elite males, its explanatory strategies and concerns were deemed irrelevant and fusty compared to those of modish competitors like social and economic history. While some practitioners nonetheless continued to plough the traditional furrow, the broader field underwent a profound transformation in response to this challenge. Thus 'diplomatic history' mutated into 'international history': it remained centrally concerned with relations between states, but adopted a much more expansive view of what constituted 'international relations', paying systematic attention not only to diplomacy, but also to economics, strategy, the domestic sources of foreign policy, ideology and propaganda, and intelligence. International history has flourished ever since, even if it has been continually beset by anxieties about marginalization and decline, haunted by the spectre of its lost pre-eminence.

If the designation 'international history' has now become firmly established, it by no means commands universal assent. Many scholars, particularly in North America, still favour the term 'diplomatic history', a preference that may – though, confusingly, does not necessarily – betray an attachment to more traditional and restricted modes of enquiry. (The question of naming is, of course, as much a normative as an empirical one.) Other practitioners regard 'international history' as a descriptor so broad and imprecise as to be meaningless, and advocate an alternative such as 'foreign relations history'.[3] Yet others, conversely, are beginning to question the validity of the term because they find it too restrictive. The emergence of 'international history' was less a discrete event than an ongoing process, and its terrain has continued to expand in directions that lead ever further away from the original heartland of 'diplomatic history': witness, for example, increased focus on non-state actors and non-governmental organizations; attention to transnational concerns such as emigration or the environment; and most notably the pervasive rise of culture, especially in works concerned with processes of cultural transfer. These issues are sufficiently remote from the formal exercise of power between states that their salience raises the question of whether 'international history' is any longer an appropriate descriptor. Indeed, it may even be argued that the term is not only empirically limiting but also politically pernicious, insofar as its use tends to reinscribe norms of state sovereignty and the centrality of the nation that ought more properly to be deconstructed. For the time being, however, 'international history' remains the most generally recognized and least problematic term available to us. Hence this introduction and this volume adopt it, though with due recognition of its limitations and instability.[4]

locating international history

My purpose here is not to provide a single rigid definition or neat prescription, nor to attempt a comprehensive survey; rather, I hope simply to convey some sense of the wide plurality of practices that currently constitute the field. Even the preliminary question of where one should look to locate the essence of international history prior to describing it is, in fact, rather problematic. Obvious points of departure would be the contents of book series and leading journals in the field (such as *Diplomatic History*, the *International History Review*, and *Diplomacy and Statecraft*), the activities of specialist academic institutions and programmes (such as the Department of International History at the London School of Economics, or the International and Global History cluster at Harvard University), and the membership rosters and conference programmes of relevant professional associations (such as the British International History Group and the Society for Historians of American Foreign Relations (SHAFR)). Yet while exploring these sites would yield helpful results, it would scarcely suffice for our purpose because much relevant activity takes place outside of these discrete locales. Important work is published elsewhere, either in general history outlets or in journals focusing on specific periods (for example, the *Journal of Cold War Studies*) or particular geographical areas (for example, *French Historical Studies*). Similarly, many practitioners are not employed in specialist institutions, but work within general history departments (where they may be primarily identified as Europeanists or modernists) or in interdisciplinary units bringing together diverse specialisms under the rubric of 'international studies' or 'international politics'. Moreover, many scholars today operate with multiple identities, and a member of SHAFR may equally be a participant in the activities of the American Studies Association or the Organization of American Historians.

Tracing the relationships of international history with cognate specialist fields is a further complex matter. In the first instance, we can identify interactions with scholars in contiguous disciplines who are concerned with similar subject matter but who bring to bear their own distinctive practices. Pre-eminent here would be the political science domain of International Relations (IR), but one could equally invoke political geography or area studies (of many different geographical realms).[5] Then there are disciplines – such as psychology – which do not necessarily deal with international subjects, but which nonetheless employ tools, techniques and models that international historians can appropriate.[6] The question of the relative advantage to be gained from reaching out in this way to scholars in other disciplines – as opposed to cherishing and refining entirely distinctive approaches – is one that has long exercised international historians. (Indeed, such debates are endemic in academia, a product of the necessity for disciplines both to broadly resemble others and yet still possess a 'unique selling point' if they are to acquire and preserve legitimacy.[7] In the modern university, intellectual awareness that disciplinary boundaries are both arbitrary and potentially inimical to creative thinking often clashes with the bureaucratic exigencies and structural incentives that perpetuate them.) A minority of international historians have been inclined to 'walk the borders' between disciplines and for them these boundaries have always seemed porous, fluid and unstable.[8] More recently, the possibilities for such fruitful interchange have multiplied dramatically given the dissemination of postmodernist literary and cultural theories. These posed fundamental transdisciplinary questions about textuality, identity and culture; in so doing, they engendered new analytical approaches that had particular ramifications for historians of foreign policy-making and of international and transnational exchanges. Hence they stimulated a further series of (ongoing) conversations with scholars in literary studies, cultural studies and anthropology whose concerns might at first glance appear very distant from those of international history.[9]

In addition to such external connections, international historians also have relationships with other specialist fields within the broader domain of history. Most longstanding here are links with political and economic historians, but equally one could mention historians of imperialism, specialists in strategic history, or historians of propaganda and intelligence.[10] Some of these fields are almost as venerable as diplomatic history, and there has consequently been overlap and interchange between them for a long time. Others originated as sub-approaches within international history, but have subsequently grown to acquire autonomous status, with their own apparatus of journals, specialist posts and conferences; thus they occupy an ambiguous position, at once part of the broader enterprise of international history and yet also separate from it. To complicate matters even further, some of these specialisms have also forged their own links with scholars in disciplines beyond the borders of history, and are themselves interdisciplinary endeavours within which historical approaches are but a part (this is true, for example, of strategic, intelligence and communications studies). Typically international historians may conceive of themselves as members of several of these specialist fields, bringing one or other label to the fore depending on context and strategic purpose. Further layers of complexity could be added by bringing in the distinctive features of international history as it is practised and structured within different national contexts, or by tracing the interchange between academics and writers on military and international history who cater more squarely to the popular market. The point here, however, is simply to demonstrate that pinning down what international history is and where it is practised is no simple matter, since it involves analysing a thick tapestry of relationships and negotiations.

narrating international history

Even if it were possible to locate a distinct 'black box' within which international history existed, this would not resolve the problem of identifying an essence or core practice. This is because the nature of the subject is at any given point contested along various axes. There are constant disputes amongst scholars about what the empirical focus of our endeavours should be, and even where this is not at issue there is debate over the merits of rival interpretations of any given episode or process. Underpinning these discussions are competing views of the relative virtues – even the validity – of different methodological, theoretical and philosophical assumptions, ultimately rooted in differences of world-view or ideology.[11] It is part of the distinctive, proudly empiricist, culture of international history that debate about these assumptions is usually sublimated within discussion of specific events, and positions are predominantly defended with reference to what the evidence will warrant rather than on more abstract grounds. But it is easy enough to detect when what is actually at stake is whether particular approaches should be deemed legitimate or worthy of acceptance within the precincts of international history.[12] This becomes even clearer at those relatively infrequent moments at which international historians do engage in explicit discussion of fundamental theoretical issues: for example, when debating their relationship with their most significant other, IR;[13] or, as in the later part of the 1990s, when the virtues of postmodernist-inspired 'discourse analysis' approaches were being widely and sometimes polemically disputed.[14] Compounding the problem, of course, is the fact that these debates also have a diachronic dimension: the issue of what international history should and should not be is also debated and changes through time. Narrating the chronological development of international history offers one means of grappling with these related issues. The narrative outlined at the beginning of this piece, which traces the transformation of diplomatic history into international history through a process of thematic expansion that continues to this day, has considerable merits in providing an orientation in the history of the field, even if it cannot by itself tell the whole story.

Classical diplomatic history came into existence during the later nineteenth century, hallmarked by meticulous reliance upon the archival record and an interpretive focus on the foreign policies of the great powers, the making and breaking of treaties, and the deliberations and actions of foreign office clerks, diplomats and statesmen. Its popularity and potency rested on a number of interrelated factors. Developments in philosophy and politics combined to make the rise of the modern European nation-state (and nationalism) seem unquestionably the central drama of the age. Paul Schroeder has characterized the Rankean notion of the *Primat der Aussenpolitik* as presupposing that 'the formation of nation-states and their quest for power and independence was *the* central theme of history and the driving force behind it'; thus it was natural that statecraft and war should occupy centre stage in historical writing.[15] As D. C. Watt put it, 'to be a historian of nineteenth-century Europe and *not* a diplomatic historian was almost impossible'.[16] The growing inclination amongst governments to publish edited collections of diplomatic correspondence to justify their foreign policies to a broader (and newly enfranchised) public further facilitated such inquiry, fuelling the belief that by revealing 'the secret stratagems of monarchs and statesmen' it could uncover 'the pattern of the past which explained the present'.[17] The apparent relevance of diplomatic history only escalated in the aftermath of the First World War, when explaining that conflict's origins became a matter of enormous political significance through the interconnection of the issue of 'war guilt' with German demands for the revision of the Treaty of Versailles. This controversy was played out through the official publication of archival material and the propagation of conflicting interpretations based upon them, which were usually patriotic in cast even as they vaunted their objectivity.[18] All this ensured that diplomatic history occupied a place of unprecedented privilege in political and intellectual discourse.

After the Second World War, circumstances conspired to induce a malaise. Research and writing continued apace, but increasingly diplomatic history acquired a reputation as 'the most arid and sterile of all the sub-histories'.[19] The rise of social and economic history, the growing influence of Marxism in the academy, and the burgeoning of fertile social science approaches in a revitalized IR demonstrated that intellectual trends had turned against it. Its fixation on events, elites (almost exclusively male), and formal power, together with its predilection for narrative reconstruction, came to be regarded as both ideologically dubious and intellectually restricted. Simultaneously, changes in the structure of contemporary international relations cast doubt on the explanatory power of politics narrowly defined. The disruptive consequences of the ending of the postwar economic boom, the rise and growing influence of counter-cultural protest movements, and the increasing prominence of non-state actors such as international organizations and multinational capitalist concerns all seemed to testify that approaches limited to the formal political and diplomatic exchanges between governments could no longer adequately capture the complexity of international relations. A further impetus for disciplinary transformation came from changes in the structure of the academy, as the 1960s saw a dramatic expansion in the higher education sector across most Western societies. This entailed an influx of much new blood into an expanded historical profession that generated an internal revisionist disciplinary dynamic: in order to garner career-building kudos, scholars were compelled to generate innovative interpretations and approaches. The gradual opening of state archives pertaining to the pre-1914 and pre-1939 periods provided a final catalyst, since it made available a wealth of new materials that scholars hungrily devoured, precipitating a new international history of the origins of the First and the Second World Wars in which these new approaches were developed and deployed.

Thus emerged an international history attentive to profound structural forces, the formulation as well as the execution of policy, a wider range of actors and a host of new thematic concerns. The term 'international history' was by no means new. The Stevenson Chair in International History at the London School of Economics had first been filled in 1932, and the designation was intended by its founder Sir Daniel Stevenson to connote an idealist and internationalist form of knowledge that would counter-balance the predominance of national and nationalist historical writing. But this nuance was gradually lost after the Second World War: in his inaugural lecture on 'the scope and study of international history' in 1955, the new holder of the chair did indeed express the melancholic hope that exposing the 'follies of the past' might have salutary political effects, but he was primarily concerned to issue a call for the thematic expansion of the field.[20] Similarly in 1954 in his classic study of nineteenth-century diplomatic manoeuvrings, *The Struggle for Mastery in Europe*, A. J. P. Taylor had opined that the study of diplomacy did 'not exhaust international history', but that scholars had also to dissect the 'deep social and economic sources' of policy, the psychology and outlook of rulers and political parties, economic factors, strategy (hitherto 'strangely neglected'), and public opinion.[21] If Taylor was too often reluctant to practise what he here preached, other scholars took up the challenge. Certain portentous landmarks are readily discernible in the debates of the 1960s: witness the controversy over Fritz Fischer's writings on German policy before 1914, which precipitated a new focus on the domestic sources of foreign policy;[22] the debate on the wellsprings of Nazi German foreign policy precipitated by Taylor with *The Origins of the Second World War*, which was to develop into a sharply polarized confrontation between 'intentionalist' and 'functionalist' approaches;[23] or the revisionist challenge to orthodox understandings of the nature and morality of American foreign policy launched by William Appleman Williams and the radicals of the Wisconsin School, who prioritized economic determinants.[24] (These examples demonstrate, moreover, that even if overtly nationalistic history had declined, the debates of international historians still had definite if usually unavowed contemporary political inspirations and implications.[25]) By the 1970s, international history had clearly come of age as a mature intellectual practice, with the appropriate paraphernalia of journals, conferences, specialist programmes and professional associations.[26]

The terrain of the new field became complex and contested: new approaches proliferated without displacing more traditional practices and the volume of publications perceptibly increased. Naturally there were tensions between competing approaches and internal debate about the proper balance to be struck between different explanatory factors: for example, as Fischerite questions about domestic determinants of policy before 1914 were posed in the cases of all the major combatants;[27] as Paul Kennedy's masterly *The Rise and Fall of the Great Powers* was castigated by critics as demonstrating the follies of economic determinism;[28] or as, during the 1980s, new sub-specialisms such as propaganda – using modish source materials such as film that seemed to challenge Rankean principles – struggled to win acceptance within the field.[29] Equally, the external boundaries of the discipline continued to be policed. A scholar such as Christopher Thorne who advocated rapprochement with IR approaches would remain a somewhat isolated if influential figure;[30] more typical of the mainstream was D. C. Watt who used his own Stevenson inaugural to urge international historians to keep a safe distance from the 'mephitic unrealisms' and impersonal abstractions of social science.[31] A more nuanced example is provided by the debate amongst historians of Nazi Germany over whether 'intentionalist' or 'functionalist' explanations better accounted for its dynamic expansionism. International historians tended overwhelmingly to favour the former, prioritizing agency, conscious intention, and the realization of clearly formulated political and strategic goals. Ranged against them were the social and structural historians of the Bielefeld School, who stressed instead how policy was the outcome of structural and functional pressures in bureaucracy, economy and society, the unplanned outcome of a dynamic process of 'cumulative radicalization'. Close reading of these exchanges reveals much about international historians' default beliefs concerning philosophical assumptions, explanatory strategies, and which types of evidence should be prioritized.[32]

If international history was thus rejuvenated, it must be admitted that many in the broader discipline failed to notice or to care. Indeed, it could be said that the emergence of a distinctive sub-field of international history in effect bracketed it off in isolation: the prevailing external attitude simply varied between 'condescension and antipathy'.[33]

General surveys of the discipline often failed to make any mention of international history at all (a tendency that is still in evidence today[34]). For all its refurbishment, it continued to be regarded as a reactionary field, remote from the discipline's cutting edge, as much in the 1970s heyday of social history as during the 1990s vogue for cultural history. Even as the appearance of a 'new international history' was proclaimed, the reflective literature was hallmarked by self-flagellatory introspection and ruminations on decline.[35] International history, so it was argued, was 'marking time', too stubbornly attached to established categories of analysis and conventional modes of explanation, and lagging woefully behind theoretical advances elsewhere in the discipline. Some of the criticisms commonly advanced might be quite easily remedied: witness, for example, the claim that too much scholarship was parochial and narrowly cast, drawing on source material from only one country's archives, even as it claimed the sobriquet 'international'. But other prescriptions entailed more fundamental change, such as the adoption of even broader and systemic approaches, a shift of attention away from 'Rankean exegesis' and towards larger and imponderable questions, and a greater interdisciplinary openness.[36] Many scholars believed that such critiques understated the sophisticated achievements of recent international history;[37] one might equally wonder whether – if underpinning all this was 'an aversion to writing about elites and the powerful' – the field could possibly meet the criticisms without abandoning its *raison d'être*.[38] Little wonder, perhaps, that international historians were gripped by a 'long crisis of confidence'.[39]

In the 1990s, this ambiguous condition persisted. On the one hand, there was a further renewal. The collapse of communist regimes in the Soviet Union and beyond gave a general fillip to the field, insofar as they appeared to restate the self-evident importance of high politics; more significantly, the archival materials that began to become available from former communist states facilitated the emergence of a 'new Cold War history' of unprecedented depth and multinational reach.[40] Yet, on the other hand, a sense of crisis intensified. In the United States, particularly, acute anxiety arose at the marginalization of international history. Reports abounded of tenured posts and programmes being lost, and many scholars became thoroughly alienated from a wider profession apparently obsessed with the triptych of race, class and gender and which seemingly viewed international history's preoccupations and practitioners alike with disdain. Despair led some international historians to take a leading role in the establishment of the Historical Society as an alternative professional organization to the irredeemably 'politically correct' American Historical

Association (AHA).[41] Compounding all this was the theoretical turbulence generated by postmodernism. This was perceived, especially in the North American context, to pose a potentially fatal threat to international history: associated with votaries of gender, social and cultural history, it was judged inherently hostile to the study of politics and diplomacy and to the use of the traditional empiricist methodologies which many practitioners assumed were necessarily entailed therein. The logic behind this linkage was rather suspect, but it certainly was the case that through its various transformations, international history had never abandoned its fundamental realist epistemology and empiricist methodology. It was the combination of methodology and subject matter – the persisting disposition to prioritize the empathetic reconstruction of the thoughts and deeds of policy-makers, rather than the focus on politics *per se* – that made international history such a target for criticism, because it rendered it intensely vulnerable to a critique of its complicity with political power. In any event, through the mid and later 1990s there were very fierce debates about these fundamental theoretical issues and about the validity of the 'discourse analysis' approaches exploring issues of race, class and gender identity that they generated.[42]

contesting international history

This narrative does not purport to offer a fully satisfactory account; indeed, it can be qualified and challenged on various grounds. A first is that this reading of disciplinary history posits an artificial and exaggerated distinction between a narrow 'diplomatic history' and the more sophisticated 'international history' that supplanted it.[43] Now, it is true that it is commonplace in the historiographical literature on earlier generations of diplomatic historians to encounter vociferous denials that they did no more than reproduce the chatter of clerks: in his treatment of Gioacchino Volpe and his school in inter-war Italy, for example, Martin Clark is as keen to exonerate them from the charge of writing narrow diplomatic history as from that of being corrupted by their service to the fascist regime.[44] Similarly, D. C. Watt has argued that even if the classical diplomatic historians of the early twentieth century focused predominantly on 'the relations between states', 'rarely if ever did they ignore the legal, intellectual, social and political penumbrae of their subject matter'.[45] Certainly, the concepts and themes that were to become prominent after the emergence of international history – such as 'unspoken assumptions' or the *Primat der Innenpolitik* – had antecedents and roots in earlier practice.[46] This can be admitted, however, without the broader generalization about the emergence of a more expansive practice being called into question; after all, the very fact of the protestation rather proves that such a beast as narrow diplomatic history did exist. Indeed, an alternative qualification of the generalization might focus on the fact that in some respects it still does. There is arguably a thread of continuity in the practice of diplomatic history right up to the present day: it is still possible to find monographs and articles that deal very closely with the political and diplomatic aspects of the foreign policy of a single state, reconstructed through careful perusal of a limited range of archival materials (what one might call, in the case of British international history, the 'FO371 School').

A second and related criticism of the 'foundation myth' retailed above concerns the question of timing. Some would argue that it was actually in the inter-war period that 'the best traditions of diplomatic history' were incorporated into 'a new international history, the study of the relations between states and societies in all their aspects'. Credit is here given to those 'critics of the European social, political and economic order' who began to propagate new ideas about the social and economic origins of imperialism, the structure of the state system, arms races, and the morality of accepted modes of conducting politics and diplomacy.[47] The flourishing of such ideas in internationalist discourses on international relations in the inter-war years is undeniable, but it is a question of interpretation as to whether they fused with diplomatic history to form a new form of enquiry at this point, or remained somewhat semi-detached from it (even, indeed, opposed to it). In any event, it seems difficult to dispute the fact that a further transformation and expansion of the field occurred after the Second World War. (Similarly, the internationalist form of enquiry that Daniel Stevenson wanted to promote was hallmarked by interest in 'world politics conducted by non-State organizations' and 'movements of thought and action which are genuinely or predominantly universal or non-national', but these issues were subsequently taken up in much more systematic fashion.[48]) There are certainly good grounds in the literature for dating the decisive transformation (though with the repeated caveat that this was a process rather than an event) at some point after the Second World War: witness D. C. Watt writing in 1984 of a 'metamorphosis over the last twenty-five years'.[49]

A further problem is that the rendering offered here might be somewhat Anglocentric. Institutional factors and intellectual preoccupations vary according to national context, and this can generate alternative ways of structuring a disciplinary history. In their important collection on the history of American foreign relations, Michael Hogan and Thomas

Paterson posit as an organizing principle that the field has been split since its foundation after the First World War between two schools of thought. On the one hand, there was the 'nationalist perspective', originally associated with Samuel Flagg Bemis, that 'stressed the continuities in American diplomacy' and 'celebrated the growth of American power', and which tended to focus on 'state-to-state relations', placing American diplomacy in 'an international, usually European, setting'. On the other, there was the tradition founded by 'progressive historians' such as Charles Beard, that was primarily interested in 'the intellectual assumptions that guided American policymakers' and the 'domestic political, economic, and regional forces that shaped their diplomacy', and which tended to stress 'change rather than continuity, conflict rather than consensus'.

The history of writing on American foreign relations can be construed as a struggle between these two evolving schools of thought. Thus after the Second World War, the field was initially dominated by 'realist historians' such as George Kennan, 'concerned primarily with the state, with state policymaking elites, and with the use of state power to advance the national interest', and writing 'in prescriptive terms' about power, geopolitics and grand strategy in ways that 'made their work particularly appealing to official Washington'. In the 1960s, the revisionist school led by William Appleman Williams challenged the dominance of 'realism', by urging a new emphasis upon 'American ideas and on the American system of liberal capitalism': 'American leaders had embraced an ideology of expansionism founded on the principle of the Open Door', and in seeking foreign markets 'had forged in the process an overseas empire that violated the best principles of the nation'. This was a critical interpretation that usefully focused attention on American policy in the Third World and on the role of non-state actors such as business and financial interests, even as it underlined the fundamental importance of ideas and ideology. This view in turn, however, inspired a counter-attack, and the rise of 'post-revisionism' from the 1970s saw a resurgence of interpretive priorities of 'realism' such as the state, the national interest and the balance of power. Although debates have moved on further since then, 'ongoing differences' between the interpretive concerns of 'realism' and 'revisionism' – geopolitics versus domestic origins; national interest versus ideology; the state versus non-state actors; the international versus the national – remain salient. Hogan and Paterson's treatment therefore suggests oppositions other than that between diplomatic and international history around which disciplinary histories could be constructed, and which from an American perspective might prove more illuminating. That said, of course, these would not necessarily be incompatible with a narrative that focuses on the gradual thematic expansion of international history's terrain.[50]

The argument about national peculiarities can be extended through further cases. In France, for example, international history developed in the shadow of the historiographically dominant Annales School with its near contempt for politics and the event; this had a significant impact on the tenor of debates around the field's very perceptible 'deepening and broadening' and affected its institutional location and relations with political science.[51] In Italy, where the field originated as 'the history of treaties and international relations', diplomatic historians have long enjoyed a particularly close relationship with the state – 'they are quite openly in state service' – presiding over government archives and supervising the publication of official documentary collections, whilst also teaching in universities, often to students who plan to enter the national diplomatic service. In consequence, Italian diplomatic historians tend to be politically conservative and disinclined 'to launch too many radical attacks against Italy's behaviour on the international stage'; hand in hand with this goes a relative distaste for interdisciplinary experimentation or departing too far from the careful Rankean redaction of political and diplomatic exchanges.[52] In Germany, historians of international relations had also long been distinguished within the discipline by their conservative methodology and historicist philosophical assumptions, and this – together, of course, with the political edge that the shadow of Nazism lent to all discussions of the German past – led them into very heated debates in the 1960s and 1970s with the Bielefeld School. The political climate following German unification has encouraged a revival of venerable traditions in the writing of political and diplomatic history; some of the resulting work advances rather dubious geopolitical interpretations for avowedly nationalist purposes, whilst some of it resuscitates in far more scholarly fashion the notion of 'the primacy of foreign policy' in German history. Simultaneously, however, new generations of scholars are embarking on innovative work dealing with transnational issues, cultural transfer, the history of international systems, and the multiple intersections of the international with social history and sociology.[53] Once more, however, the undoubted specificities of different national traditions, and the fact that communication between them is too infrequent (partly, but not only, for linguistic reasons), cannot obscure fundamental commonalities. Indeed, Jessica Gienow-Hecht has recently dubbed international historians 'a global group of worriers', united by shared anxieties about theory, methodology, the proper subject matter of the field, and whether and how it should evolve to reflect the exigencies of globalization.[54]

These competing descriptions are all examples of the kinds of stories that international historians like to tell about themselves. But such accounts by no means exhaust possible ways in which the field can be analysed, and they tend to occlude certain larger questions about international history as a political and intellectual practice. For example, although the field has lately made perceptible efforts to achieve a truly global reach, it still remains dominated by European and North American perspectives and subjects, by very traditional 'Western' methodological approaches, and indeed by European and North American practitioners. Its more overt politics are also vulnerable to critique. Even though one of the purposes behind the establishment of international history was to transcend nationalist knowledge, this has only been partially achieved: thus Maurice Vaïsse's lament that French work remains 'very Franco-centric' in focus could be adapted to apply to most national cases.[55] Despite ongoing drives to produce 'supranational history', most contemporary work remains in thrall to the national paradigm, even if only through perpetuating the assumption that the nation state should be our prime unit of analysis.[56] Moreover, international history remains politically conservative in the broader sense that its preferred modes of analysis do not readily lend themselves to purveying radical interpretations: thus comparative study of the ways in which the history and the memory of the Second World War intertwined in the decades after 1945 suggests that international history writing always tended to be a vector of conservative messages.[57] Of course, this generalization does scant justice to scholars such as those of the Wisconsin School who have attempted to advance oppositional interpretations, often through bringing structural and systemic perspectives to bear and drawing on various strands of Marxist and other critical thinking; but such interventions have always found it difficult to establish a secure or enduring place for themselves at the heart of mainstream international history.[58]

Critical IR theorists approaching international history would likely find both these political issues and thematic expansion to be fairly insignificant; their concern would rather be with the theoretical underpinnings of the practice. Attempting to categorize international historians by their politico-theoretical positions does not, however, yield very fruitful results. True to its Rankean origins, the field still strongly privileges practice over theory, and adherence to a realist epistemology and empiricist methodologies is almost universal; this generalization holds fairly true across all the thematic areas of concern into which the discipline has become split. In terms of theories about the nature of international relations, it is obviously possible to make some useful distinctions between, say, Marxists (for example, those formerly practising under state socialism), the corporatist inheritors of the revisionist tradition, feminists interested in gender, or liberal internationalists writing on global society.[59] But the mainstream is basically characterized by a commitment to a 'soft' variant of what IR scholars term 'Realism' (the 'hard' version being deemed too ahistorical and reductive[60]). International historians are not particularly prone to venture into print explicitly on such issues, so these commitments usually have to be read out of the texts in which they are sublimated. Doing this suggests that a great deal of international history rests upon an implicit acceptance of the verities of 'Realism', such as the self-evident virtues of *realpolitik*, the centrality of the state and the fact of international anarchy. For many critical IR theorists, this would by itself provide grounds for critiquing the field, but the situation is exacerbated by its dominant mode of empathetic reconstruction, which tends to lead, all too often, to the unreflective reinscription of the discourses of policy-making.[61] Constraints of space and the nature of the purpose of this volume preclude any extensive discussion of these issues here.[62] But for these theoretical reasons international history is a very problematic discourse in both political and ethical terms for those adhering to strands of post-positivist IR thinking which take seriously the constitutive role of theory and representation.[63]

mapping international history

A good deal can be gleaned about both the catholicity and the limits of contemporary mainstream practice from the prospectus for the 'International History' book series published by Praeger. This aims to promote 'historical writing that is genuinely international in scope and multiarchival in methodology' (works assuming a 'parochial perspective' by focusing upon the policy of a single state are unlikely to satisfy the editors' criteria for international history 'in the proper sense of the term'). It wishes to provide an outlet for scholarship both in 'traditional subfields' – 'military, diplomatic, and economic relations among states' – and in 'topics of nonstate history and of more recent interest' – such as non-governmental organizations and cultural relations. Thus it 'happily embraces traditional diplomatic history', but refuses to see the state and policy-makers as autonomous actors; rather it is also necessary to probe 'the broader forces within society that influence the formulation and execution of foreign policies, social tensions, religious and ethnic conflict, economic competition, environmental concerns, scientific and technology issues, and international cultural relations'. It notes the recent overwhelming trend for international historians to focus on the post-Second World War period, but it also upholds the relevance and validity of 'scholarship dealing with much earlier, even classical, eras of world history'. Finally, it stresses a commitment 'to an interdisciplinary approach to international history' and an openness to appropriate contributions from the 'separate, but interrelated, disciplines' of history, political science and IR.

This tone of tolerant openness is tempered by the restatement of certain enduring core commitments, which demonstrate how the field retains its distinctiveness by guarding crucial elements of its Rankean inheritance. On the one hand, this means an insistence on making the 'careful, scrupulous, deeply scholarly examination of historical evidence' central to practice. Scholars from political science and IR are welcome if they research and write in 'the classical tradition of intellectual inquiry' which 'examines the historical antecedents of international conflict and cooperation in order to understand contemporary affairs'; but the series will be a cold house for them if they traffic in 'abstract, and abstruse, theoretical models that have little relation to historical reality' (and which, it is asserted, have no real power to illuminate the present).[64] On the other hand, it entails a fundamental faith in realist epistemology and what postmodernist critics would disparage as the naive ideal of 'truth-at-the-end-of-enquiry'.[65] Thus the editors reject the alleged 'fashionable but ultimately intellectually and morally sterile assertion that historical truth is entirely relative and therefore that all interpretations of past events are equally valid, or equally squalid, as they merely reflect the whims and prejudices of individual historians'. Rather, they reaffirm their belief that 'the principal obligation of scholarship' is 'to ferret out real and lasting truths'. It would be difficult to find a more succinct statement of the current 'eclectic, humanist' state of the art in mainstream international history.[66]

Of course, a repeated refrain of this introduction is that no single definition can be sufficient, and this prescription can be criticized from several sides. Some practitioners would find it too liberal, conceding that international history should deal with 'the entirety of inter-state relations', but limiting the list of thematic factors deemed relevant to the diplomatic, 'military, economic, ideological, and strategic'.[67] Others would contend that recent attention to structural forces has led to the neglect of the 'individual personalities', 'decisions and actions' 'of a decision-making elite, of politicians and civil servants', that should lie at the heart of enquiry.[68] Yet others would contend that it is doctrinaire to rule studies of the foreign policy-making process in single states out of court by definition, when they can be based on massive multi-archival research and profound knowledge. Conversely, other scholars will dispute the mainstream definition for its timidity. Those plying the farther waters of transnational global history might well decry its lingering state-centrism. Those interested in incorporating insights drawn from postmodern theory into practice might regret the continued attachment to 'modernist' historical representation; far from succumbing to the dreaded (but actually chimerical) relativistic nihilism, they urge experimentation with new forms of history writing 'breaking from the omniscient, single-narrative that served and was served by the [modernist] age of territoriality'.[69]

To illuminate the current contested and pluralistic condition of the field, three interlinked issues need to be discussed. The first is the phenomenal recent rise of culture as an object of study and explanatory variable.[70] This is most obvious with the emergence of a whole new sub-field devoted to 'cultural transfer', or the transmission of cultural values, ideas and products from region to region, from ally to ally, and from friends to former, or indeed current, enemies. The study of what was often previously denominated as 'cultural imperialism' has deep roots, and used to view culture primarily as a tool of foreign policy and cultural transfer as a state practice, consciously conducted for propagandistic purposes; recently, however, models of cultural 'transmission' have been heavily qualified by an emphasis upon resistance, negotiation, and appropriation. The field has also expanded to encompass a wider range of informal cultural relations among nations and peoples, involving philanthropists, tourists, intellectuals, technical experts and a range of other non-state and societal actors.[71] A further cluster of work brings culture to bear in the analysis of policy-making, specifically to explore how 'beliefs about national identity, ideology, race and ethnicity, gender, and class', together with other cultural attitudes, 'shaped the exercise of economic, political, or military power'. Typically, this involves tracing reciprocal processes and how cultural ideas – about say, the proper form of masculinity – could help to shape and were themselves simultaneously shaped by foreign policy.[72] What is at stake in this literature is identity in all its multivalent forms: those of both self and other were negotiated, contested and transformed through international encounters. Even mainstream work now also betrays the pervasive influence of culture: witness, for example, how commonly writing on Western diplomatic relations with the Middle East is now framed through the lens of 'Orientalism'.[73] Across myriad empirical fields, scholars now freely deploy concepts such as perceptual lenses and stereotypes, simply assuming that the cultural ideological filters through which policy-makers view the world matter profoundly.

This work is extremely important. In not much more than a decade it has vastly expanded the horizons of international history, and through the deployment of new source materials and new methodologies has generated an enormously fertile literature. In the view of one partisan, it has 'introduced a degree of novelty and freshness to a professional milieu whose intellectual aura ha[d] come to resemble the stuffy, cigar-laden atmosphere of a conservative men's club'. The origins of the turn to culture are complicated and, as with most such shifts, lie both in perceived changes in real world international relations and in the realm of ideas. 'The post-Cold War *Zeitgeist*' is often invoked here, as is the failure of 'power and interest-based explanations' – with their tendency to 'treat culture and ideology as misperceptions of the way things really are' – adequately to explain a world in which 'a truly global society is just beginning to become visible as a practical project'; equally important has been the impact of postmodernism, with its stress on discourse and the constitutive role of the linguistic, which naturally encouraged taking ideas more seriously.[74] The promise of culture is similarly multifaceted. Writing on cultural exchange is accelerating existing tendencies to move beyond state-centrism and helping to fulfil the promise of writing international history on a truly global level. Work on culture and policy-making has equally radical potential to transcend the 'Realist' power political paradigms that have long dominated the field, and to replace them with more nuanced appreciations of the cultural construction of foreign policy. It even perhaps promises to destabilize some of the central interpretive oppositions – such as that between 'inside' and 'outside', 'domestic' and 'foreign' – that have long structured our practice.[75] Whether this dramatic transformative potential is realized remains to be seen.

This is to assume, of course, that such a redimensioning of international history would be a positive development; but it is emphatically not the case that all scholars would agree with this proposition. Many regret the drift away from traditional modes of enquiry, and believe culturalist approaches to be a distraction from core concerns – such as national security or economic determinants – and capable of delivering only trivial insights.[76] This underlines once more that beneath the rhetoric of tolerant pluralism, fundamental politico-intellectual disagreement persists between advocates of competing incompatible approaches. There are also 'internal' problems with culturalist approaches. Frank Ninkovich, for example, has drawn attention to unanswered questions about how culture is to be related to more traditional explanatory variables, to a persistent problem of under-theorization, and to a need for more work at both micro and macro (as opposed to mid-range) levels.[77] Volker Depkat, similarly, has noted that the way culture is invoked in this work lacks precision: it is 'so broad and all-encompassing that it is no longer analytically meaningful'. Moreover, culturalist scholars 'tend to do away with foreign policy questions altogether', or at the very least fail to demonstrate 'whether there is some degree of correspondence between the interconnection of discourses that they see as important and the factual reality of decision making'.[78]

I would add one further and contrasting note of caution about the likelihood of cultural approaches realizing their potential. When 'discourse analyses' first became an object of discussion, there was a very strong sense that they offered a means decisively to transcend 'Realism' and for the first time to transform international history into a truly critical practice. This mood of excitement was largely generated by their explicit grounding in the insights and promise of postmodernist theory.[79] Today, however, a focus on culture is far more often justified on empirical grounds, as if culture is just one more aspect of 'the real' of international relations, or one more 'cause' underlying foreign policy, that needs to be incorporated into our analyses. The irony here is that rather than challenging existing theoretical assumptions, the claim often seems to be that these approaches actually just offer us a fuller picture of how things actually were, in impeccably Rankean style. Some may regard this as welcome evidence of a field maturing, as theoretical abstraction is compelled to reckon with evidential reality. But it should also be noted that something has been lost here, as cultural approaches have been shorn of their rigorous theoretical underpinning and bracing political edge. This is in line with a broader development across the discipline of history, where the turn to culture has been the means whereby the flesh wounds inflicted by postmodernism have been sutured and a return to business (more or less) as usual has been facilitated.[80] It must therefore be an open question whether culturalist approaches will fundamentally transform international history, or whether a resilient practice will succeed in absorbing and neutering them. If the only work that culture is doing is allowing us to continue to talk about 'great men' (albeit with a focus on their troubled masculinity) or the deeds of the most powerful nation on earth (albeit in the guise of charting processes of Americanization), then there are unfortunately good grounds to doubt whether revolutionary transformation is in train.

A second key issue concerns the place of international history within the wider discipline, and even across a broader culture. Here, it is arguable that the situation is now far more positive than for some decades. There is no unanimity of view, of course, and the picture is mixed. The pessimistic continue to declare that 'in most American universities, international history has gone the way of the dinosaur';[81] yet even if there is still a sense that international historians are 'a beleaguered and besieged minority' in the profession, 'self doubt and status anxiety' co-exist with 'vitality and renewal'.[82] In January 2004, the 118th annual meeting of the AHA convened in Washington, DC, to discuss the theme of 'War and Peace: History and the Dynamics of Human Conflict and Cooperation'. This conference theme symbolized how the concerns of our field were once more returning to prominence within the broader discipline: many US international historians, scarred by the culture wars of the 1990s, would scarcely have believed that sessions entitled 'Coalitions and Alliances at War, 1900–1941' or 'Naval Blockades in Comparative and International Perspective' would ever again grace the AHA programme.[83] Not all the papers presented were recognizable as international history, but for this very reason the conference provided a welcome forum for fruitful interchange between international historians of various persuasions and scholars in the discipline at large with cognate concerns.

There are various causes of this development. Amongst the more mundane are a new willingness amongst both stalwarts of the AHA and leading international historians to seek a rapprochement: thus the latter began once more to submit (properly formatted) panel proposals to the AHA instead of confining themselves to the SHAFR annual conference, and the AHA demonstrated an unwonted enthusiasm to accept them. The fact that many international historians had taken the turn to culture, and were thus able to speak in a language that the broader profession found intelligible and appealing, undoubtedly also helped. However, the key factor lay in the wider world, with the apparent tectonic shift in the structure of global international relations precipitated by the terrorist attacks of 9/11. The subsequent launch of the 'war on terror' demonstrated beyond peradventure that the traditional concerns of our field – how states and societies interact; the nature, rationale and justification for the exercise of military power; when war can be avoided and when it should be fought – were once more of vital political, intellectual and moral relevance to the wider world.[84] Moreover, international historians of all complexions could contribute to these debates. Culturalists might dilate on how to achieve mutual comprehension between far-flung societies animated by contrasting core values, or grapple with the realization that murderous terrorists were now the most salient non-state actors in international relations. Yet traditionalists could equally well address the existence, nature and legitimacy of American empire, whether in the past, present or future. At any event, international historians found themselves once more with a ready wider audience for their work.

If there is an opportunity here, however, there are also dangers. In a masterly analysis, Michael Hogan has recently warned that international historians have no patent over the concept of 'the international' and that its salience within the academy will not necessarily be to our benefit. Hogan notes initiatives of both intellectual and institutional kinds from the Organization of American Historians 'toward internationalising the study of American history and culture', in order to respond to the challenges of globalization; similarly, he explores the transformation of the field of American studies which, largely under the influence of postmodern and postcolonial studies, has taken a 'transnational turn'. But if this meant that 'other historians are turning our way', it was also apparent that 'we have not done enough to hitch ourselves to this rising star': 'to a large extent, the internationalization of American history is happening without a substantial contribution from those who actually specialize in American international history'.

Too much of this new scholarship, Hogan argues, does not engage with the work done by international historians: indeed, it almost constitutes a parallel field in terms of its concerns and its bibliographical hinterland, and is appearing in quite separate publication outlets. The real danger is that specialists in other fields might appropriate the history of US foreign relations 'while traditional diplomatic historians are losing ground, and relevance, in the academic community'. Hogan's prescriptions for remedying this problem involve further efforts 'to break down the disciplinary boundaries that separate diplomatic history from other fields of inquiry'. This would mean encouraging the decentring of 'the study of foreign relations' by looking beyond the American nation to write more truly international or comparative history; promoting further study of non-state actors and transnational forces; drawing insights from scholars of the postcolonial and the subaltern about the linkages of power and knowledge, on cultural difference, and on the significance of 'borderlands'; and structural and institutional changes to cement in place the reinvention of the field. Hogan's vision is ambitious and persuasive, but it essentially preaches the necessity of the triumph of culturalist approaches – already promising to effect 'a great renaissance' – in order to avert the marginalization of the field. For all that he is keen to stress that 'more conventional or traditional diplomatic history' 'remains a valuable form of scholarship', his implication is that it is less vital than culturalism in the light of contemporary intellectual trends and the shifting realities of international relations; thus he can only intend that it will increasingly be a minority interest in the reconfigured discipline.[85] As someone who has previously argued that without taking an interdisciplinary turn international history 'risks ossification', I might contemplate this prospect with equanimity.[86] But partisans of more traditional approaches are surely entitled to wonder whether the cure will not be worse than the disease.

The third related issue here is the dramatic and continuing thematic expansion of the field. Comparing the contents of a recent volume of the SHAFR journal *Diplomatic History* with that of the first dramatizes this point. Founded in 1977 as 'a forum for discussion of many aspects of the diplomatic, economic, intellectual, and cultural relations of the United States', this journal was never, despite its title, the preserve of narrow diplomatic history.[87] Accordingly, the first volume contained pieces dealing with the intellectual foundations of American foreign policy, the influence of non-state actors, and American cultural diplomacy; but the balance was very much skewed towards essays on more traditional subjects such as 'The Impact of the Cold War on United States-Latin American Relations' and 'Containment in Iran, 1946'.[88] By 2004, such traditional topics remained very much in evidence, but alongside were a whole new vocabulary and array of subjects: witness 'Race, Water, and Foreign Policy', 'Jimmy Carter and the Foreign Policy of Human Rights', 'Sport and American Cultural Expansion in the 1930s' and 'Negotiating National Identity on American Television'.[89] To an extent, the causes of this shadow those animating the turn to culture. Interest in themes such as women's rights, human rights, the environment or religion may on one level simply result from scholars being sensitized to the potential significance of issues in the past by their pertinence in our present. There is also an internal disciplinary dynamic at work, as the escalating competitiveness of academic life and careers compels budding scholars to push the frontiers of the field ever further back. But a central motivation remains the perception that as processes of deterritorialization and globalization transform contemporary international relations, new forms of analysis are urgently required. In a world of 'mobile populations, flexible and sometimes even disorganized capital, global networks of electronic communications, a more image-based ... culture, and transnational activists of all kinds', the centrality of the state inevitably declines: new types of explanation will be needed as 'the nation-state fades as the necessary organizing principle of all global relationships and their histories'.[90]

The empirical and conceptual richness of much of this new work can scarcely be denied. It is also striking how many practitioners here seem to be animated by an internationalist vision that harks back to the concerns of some of the idealist founders of international history and IR. For a scholar such as Akira Iriye, writing about intellectuals' promotion of cultural internationalism or the labours of non-governmental organizations is not simply a matter of expanding the thematic terrain of the field. Rather, he is animated by a coherent alternative vision of how global politics should be organized: transcending state-centrism will refocus our efforts onto 'human affairs, human aspirations, human values, and human tragedies' and thus promote the establishment of a global civil society.[91] These efforts to resuscitate the idealist strand within international history after long decades of dominance by 'Realist' pessimism are noteworthy, and confirm the truism that choices of subject matter always carry ideological freight. The proliferation of this work, which both implicitly and explicitly challenges the state-centrism of older practice, nonetheless presents difficulties for the field as a whole. In the first instance, there are practical issues here, connected to the maintenance of international history's niche within the academy (upon which funding opportunities, institutional autonomy, and so on, may continue to depend). Increasing fragmentation into incompatible approaches must surely threaten the coherence of 'international history' as an institutional as well as an intellectual project. As pioneers of culturalism continue to redefine and even deconstruct the very concept of 'the international', the demarcated borders and distinctive core concerns – and therefore the legitimacy – of 'international history' within the academy may be imperilled.

Individual attitudes towards this prospect will obviously vary. But lurking behind these practical issues may be a larger intellectual shift. Underpinning the turn to the transnational is a belief that changes in the fabric of contemporary international relations are calling forth new forms of knowledge.[92] On this reading, diplomatic and international history with their state-centrism, Rankeanism and 'Realism' were essentially products of a nineteenth- and twentieth-century 'age of territoriality' that is now on the wane. (Territoriality here defined as 'the properties, including power, provided by the control of bordered political space, which until recently at least created the framework for national and often ethnic identity'.)[93] International history was always implicated with the international system that it purported merely to describe because its modes of analysis led it ineluctably to reinforce the epistemological and political claims of the state, lending the appearance of permanence to a phenomenon that was in fact historically contingent (for example, by occluding the ways in which state foreign policies served to discipline particular social identities).[94] Thematic expansion provided a means to paper over the cracks that emerged as the assumptions of territoriality were increasingly challenged in the later part of the twentieth century, but over time both culturalist analyses of foreign policy and the drift away from state-centrism created ever more serious tensions. The claim here, then, is that the time for a further decisive mutation of the field has now come. For all one might share Anders Stephanson's sentiment that there is an enduring validity in 'the most exquisitely traditional investigations of those rarefied diplomatic moments when the future of huge tracts of land and matters of life and death are decided by a few men, very few men, in the highest of places', there is a sense that their time has passed.[95] New approaches and new forms of writing are required to help us make sense of the way we live now. Moreover, it is very doubtful that this writing could usefully bear the name of 'international history'. It may be time, in other words, to let go, and to innovate ourselves into extinction.

approaching international history

This collection aims to provide an advanced level orientation to the field in all its current ferment and transition. Some years ago, Hayden White opined that it was enormously problematic for disciplines to take stock of themselves. Either those offering the accounts would themselves be devotees 'of one or another of its sects' and would therefore be biased; or they would be outsiders and thus 'unlikely to have the expertise necessary to distinguish between the significant and the insignificant events of the field's development'.[96] This volume assumes that this danger can be minimized by making the charting of the field a collective endeavour, in which practitioners speaking from different positions, espousing diverse, even conflicting, opinions, are brought together into conversation. To this end, I have tried to gather together a diverse group of contributors with expertise ranging from the traditional through to the more avant-garde. Despite their reputation as stubbornly unreflective empiricists, international historians of various stripes have shown themselves increasingly willing to debate the merits of various approaches within the field as well as its basic presuppositions. Hence there has emerged a still relatively small yet nonetheless respectable corpus of historiographical and methodological literature, to which this volume seeks to make a further contribution.

One limitation of the leading texts in this literature is that they restrict themselves to discussing the historiography of American foreign relations rather than international history *per se*.[97] This text aims for that broader coverage, and I have tried to amass contributors who have worked on international relations in all corners of the globe and have encouraged them to range as widely as possible with their illustrative examples. That said, the volume still has something of an Anglo-American flavour both in terms of the identities of the contributors and the material discussed in their contributions. (There is, for example, not a great deal of non-English-language material mentioned in the references.) In some respects this is a matter of contingency but it also reflects the demands of the perceived market for the volume and the practical imperative to present a coherent picture in reasonable depth, even at the expense of greater breadth (pragmatic factors here, then, slightly undercut my grander ambitions of a global vision). By the same token, most of the material discussed here relates to the international history of the twentieth century, with some forays back into the nineteenth century and beyond. It is certainly regrettable to foreclose discussion of work on earlier periods, not least because there is excellent scholarship there. Moreover, this restricted focus elides crucial questions about how contemporary international history has been bound up with the modern states system, and about how that states system evolved and spread across the globe.[98] Here too, however, there were pragmatic considerations in play, because it is the twentieth century that lies at the heart of the teaching of international history in universities today and it was again necessary to narrow the focus in order to provide a picture of sufficient depth, even at an introductory level. Introductory texts must perforce be limited in what they can achieve, but hopefully this one gestures sufficiently towards the greater complexity that lies beyond to encourage further exploration.

The tack taken in this introduction should have made clear why I have organized the volume around thematic issues. (Alternative possibilities such as chapters dealing with the historiography of specific subjects or scholarship in different countries were considered, and these have been executed with profit elsewhere.[99]) The question of which themes should be selected was problematic, given that they had to be limited in number. Any practitioner would probably come up with a different list of twelve, but the roster assembled here is eminently defensible as providing a broad coverage of leading approaches. Of course, the chapter boundaries are somewhat artificial since these themes overlap and most scholars do not deal with only a single one; equally there are certain issues – such as the rise of culture – that cut across them all. Undeniably important themes have had to be either neglected or subsumed within other categories: these include sport, the environment, race, human rights, nationalism and religion. Equally, none of the chapters can provide comprehensive coverage: thus Andrew Rotter deals with culture and policy-making, but not with cultural transfer; Bruce Cumings writes about political economy on a world-systems level, and is not greatly concerned with the more mundane economic determinants of foreign policy or economic diplomacy. More could also have been said about practical matters such as evolving state policies on archival access; the impact of changes in information technology on the form of state records, our means of accessing them, and the dissemination of our findings; the diverse pressures facing new entrants into the field; and the general vicissitudes of international history's position within the academy. But even though this and much else is elided here, readers should find utility in what is present.

The ideal chapter that I sketched out for contributors was to combine historiographical and methodological/theoretical discussion. On the one hand, it would survey important recent specialist work on the thematic issue concerned and gauge its salience within international history as a whole. On the other, it would also explore the methodological and theoretical considerations that working in a particular area entailed (ranging from conceptual or epistemological problems through to source related matters), and the strengths and weaknesses of that approach to the historical study of international relations. I also encouraged contributors to argue for the virtues of one perspective over the others by explaining the particular light that it can shed. Perhaps inevitably, this brief proved somewhat difficult to fulfil in its entirety within the limited space allowed and in any event contributors interpreted it in different ways, some highlighting historiographical issues, and others offering substantive readings of particular periods in order to illustrate the contribution of their particular thematic concern. But the resulting chapters are both pleasingly diverse and focused upon a common central concern to map out the terrain of the field.[100]

The collection begins with some staunch defences of traditional practice. Thomas Otte argues for the continued necessity of a focus on the state, diplomacy and decision-makers, albeit of a sophisticated kind. John Ferris then makes the case that international historians will neglect the study of power and war – the *ultima ratio* in international affairs – at their peril. Even though the subjects of both these chapters can in fact be studied using more modish, culturalist methods, the implication here is that traditional approaches are more suitable for exploring these enduring realities of the states system.[101] Bruce Cumings then defends a focus on political economy, drawing on the critical perspectives of world-systems theory first adumbrated in the 1970s; this clearly demonstrates the very stimulating perspectives that are opened up by long-term systemic approaches that contrast with the dominant mode of close and detailed Rankean reconstruction. Nigel Gould-Davies next sheds light on the issue of ideology. Ideology has loomed very large in the recent literature, but has too often come to be simply reduced to culture. Gould-Davies attempts to rescue it from this fate, and to outline what a more rigorous approach to ideology and international history might offer. Miriam Fendius Elman then explores the intersection between international history and IR, sketching out the contrasting ways in which the two disciplines appropriate the past, defending the complexity of political science approaches, but ultimately welcoming the contrasting insights that different disciplinary perspectives purvey. Peter Jackson and Len Scott then discuss the role of intelligence, a theme that has enjoyed a dramatically raised profile in international politics in recent times. They provide an exceptionally clear outline of the origins of the field, its different dimensions and the problems and opportunities encountered in its study.

These first six chapters at times acknowledge the presence of postmodernism and the rise of culture, but it is really in the second half of the volume that these innovations are taken up systematically. The chapter by Susan Carruthers on propaganda and opinion forms a pivot in the volume since it first provides a disciplinary history of the rise of the 'propaganda paradigm' but then explores why the legitimacy of that paradigm has been increasingly called into question with the rise of culture. Jeremi Suri then explores the role of non-governmental organizations and non-state actors, demonstrating how different a narrative of contemporary international history focusing upon them looks from traditional accounts. Next Mark Bradley explores the intersection between international history and imperial history, highlighting how the whole field has been transformed by the rise of postcolonial perspectives and a new attentiveness to discourse, language and culture. Andrew Rotter continues in a similar vein, offering a nuanced account of how culture came to prominence within the field and exploring some of the key ways in which it can transform our understanding of the nature of international relations. Glenda Sluga then discusses the issue of gender, celebrating past achievements but also expressing sharp dissatisfaction with some of the directions that work is taking today. Finally, Akira Iriye provides an elegant manifesto for the transformation of international history into transnational global history, and the intellectual and political benefits that such a further mutation of the field would deliver.

advancing international history

The brief of the Palgrave Advances series requires that volumes should 'probe the boundaries of the discipline' and 'suggest the direction of future studies'. One possible future for the field has already been sketched out above, where I endorsed the ongoing march of culture (albeit with a preference for more rigorous and critical theorization), greater openness towards interdisciplinarity, and continued expansion beyond state-centrism to generate new forms of writing and knowledge. Whether this future comes to pass, of course, remains to be seen: most of the other contributors here offer their own prescriptions for the future which are by no means all compatible. But I would conclude by urging that, leaving that issue to one side, we can profit in the present by cultivating a greater awareness of the history of our discipline and the political and ideological work that international history has done, both in its imbrication with particular forms of international relations and in its implication with politics in a more quotidian sense. This is a call that has been made before and the sentiment has suffused this introduction;[102] moreover it is quite in tune with a broader intellectual climate where 'memory' is a key cultural buzzword and reflexivity is enjoined on all academics as a cardinal professional virtue. But though international historians have now begun to explore the significance of the memory of war as a phenomenon, they remain wary of forging interpretive connections between broader cultural and political discourses of memory and the work of themselves and their forebears.[103] Yet there are fascinating stories to narrate here about how international history has, for all its claims to objectivity, itself been shaped by these broader discourses and has simultaneously contributed to them. Whatever the broader future of the field, we will be richer and more self-aware if they begin to be told.

notes

1. The allusion is to the classic study, Tony Becher and Paul Trowler, *Academic Tribes and Territories. Intellectual Enquiry and the Culture of Disciplines*, 2nd edn (Buckingham: Open University Press, 2001).
2. Roger Bullen, 'What is Diplomatic History?', in Juliet Gardiner (ed.), *What is History Today?* (London: Macmillan, 1988), p. 137.
3. Frank Costigliola and Thomas G. Paterson, 'Defining and Doing the History of United States Foreign Relations: A Primer', in Michael J. Hogan and

Thomas G. Paterson (eds), *Explaining the History of American Foreign Relations*, 2nd edn (Cambridge: Cambridge University Press, 2004), p. 10.

4. This brief discussion does not exhaust the issue of naming. Others would reserve the term 'international history' for writing that is multinational and multi-archival in scope (rather than focusing on the foreign policy of a single state), regardless of its thematic breadth. Others would only apply it to the supranational or transnational approaches that have more recently emerged. Yet others would argue that the history of the foreign relations of a given state must comprise both a 'national history' – focused on 'the internal constellation of forces' within state and society that shape foreign policy –and an 'international history' – 'focused on the external forces that influence and constrain' its encounter with the wider world: Robert J. McMahon, 'Toward a Pluralist Vision: The Study of American Foreign Relations as International History and National History', in Hogan and Paterson, *Explaining the History*, 2nd edn, p. 37.

5. On IR, a good introduction is Ole R. Holsti, 'Theories of International Relations', in Hogan and Paterson, *Explaining the History*, 2nd edn, pp. 51–90; on the interface with political (and cultural) geography, see, for example, Gearóid Ó Tuathail and Simon Dalby (eds), *Rethinking Geopolitics* (London: Routledge, 1998); symptomatic of recent interactions with area – in this case American – studies is Christian G. Appy (ed.), *Cold War Constructions. The Political Culture of United States Imperialism, 1945–1966* (Amherst: University of Massachusetts Press, 2000).

6. Richard H. Immerman, 'Psychology', in Hogan and Paterson, *Explaining the History*, 2nd edn, pp. 103–22.

7. For a fascinating essay on the emergence of history as a discipline stressing this theme, see Stephen Bann, *The Inventions of History. Essays on the Representation of the Past* (Manchester: Manchester University Press, 1990), pp. 12–32 ('History and her Siblings: Law, Medicine and Theology').

8. Emily S. Rosenberg, 'Walking the Borders', in Michael J. Hogan and Thomas G. Paterson (eds), *Explaining the History of American Foreign Relations* (Cambridge: Cambridge University Press, 1991), pp. 24–35.

9. The whole substance of Hogan and Paterson, *Explaining the History*, 2nd edn, testifies to these conversations.

10. A sense of these connections can be gleaned from historiographical surveys such as Gardiner, *What is History Today?*; Anthony Molho and Gordon S. Wood (eds), *Imagined Histories. American Historians Interpret the Past* (Princeton, NJ: Princeton University Press, 1998).

11. This general point is now almost universally acknowledged in the history and theory literature: Ludmilla Jordanova, *History in Practice* (London: Arnold, 2000); Mary Fulbrook, *Historical Theory* (London: Routledge, 2002).

12. The most obvious example of this might be the disputes about the legitimacy of the New Left 'revisionist' reading of the history of American foreign relations, especially in the Cold War. This debate began in earnest in the 1960s and was at times ferociously heated, not least because as Peter Novick has observed, for Americans this was a debate 'about who we *were*' (emphasis in original): Peter Novick, *That Noble Dream. The 'Objectivity Question' and the American Historical Profession* (Cambridge: Cambridge University Press, 1988), p. 445. The literature on this is enormous: for an orientation, see

Jerald A. Combs, *American Diplomatic History. Two Centuries of Changing Interpretations* (Berkeley: University of California Press, 1983), p. 220ff.

13. Colin Elman and Miriam Fendius-Elman (eds), *Bridges and Boundaries. Historians, Political Scientists, and the Study of International Relations* (Cambridge, MA: MIT Press, 2001); Odd Arne Westad (ed.), *Reviewing the Cold War. Approaches, Interpretations, Theory* (London: Frank Cass, 2000).

14. These debates were conducted, *inter alia*, on the H-DIPLO electronic discussion list that operates under the auspices of SHAFR. Contributions are archived on the website at: www.h-net.msu.edu/~diplo/ (accessed 20 September 2004) and can be searched by author, date, or subject. The discussion in April–May 1997 on 'gendered discourse' is particularly illuminating.

15. Paul W. Schroeder, 'Does the History of International Politics Go Anywhere?', in David Wetzel and Theodore S. Hamerow (eds), *International Politics and German History. The Past Informs the Present* (Westport: Praeger, 1997), p. 17.

16. D. C. Watt, 'Some Aspects of A. J. P. Taylor's Work as Diplomatic Historian', *Journal of Modern History*, 49 (1) (1977) 22.

17. Bullen, 'What is Diplomatic History?', p. 135. The indispensable work on the publication of documents is Keith Wilson (ed.), *Forging the Collective Memory. Government and International Historians through Two World Wars* (Providence: Berghahn, 1996).

18. Annika Mombauer, *The Origins of the First World War. Controversies and Consensus* (London: Longman, 2002), pp. 2–118.

19. Arthur Marwick, *The Nature of History*, 3rd edn (London: Macmillan, 1989), p. 94.

20. W. N. Medlicott, 'The Scope and Study of International History', *International Affairs*, 31 (4) (1955) 413–26, quote at 426. Medlicott also drew attention to the paradox that in a field supposedly hallmarked by internationalism scholars in fact enjoyed a peculiarly close relationship with the state; international history would have to emancipate itself from this in order 'finally to establish itself as a subject of academic study' (423).

21. A. J. P. Taylor, *The Struggle for Mastery in Europe, 1848–1918* (Oxford: Oxford University Press, 1954), p. 575.

22. For a recent account, see Mombauer, *Origins of the First World War*, pp. 119–74.

23. A. J. P. Taylor, *The Origins of the Second World War* (London: Hamish Hamilton, 1961); on the early stages of the debate, see Esmonde M. Robertson (ed.), *The Origins of the Second World War* (London: Macmillan, 1971).

24. See note 12 above.

25. See the pioneering R. J. B. Bosworth, *Explaining Auschwitz and Hiroshima: History Writing and the Second World War, 1945–1990* (London: Routledge, 1993).

26. Zara Steiner, 'On Writing International History: Chaps, Maps and Much More', *International Affairs*, 73 (3) (1997) 531.

27. Mombauer, *Origins of the First World War*, pp. 175–220.

28. Paul Kennedy, *The Rise and Fall of the Great Powers: Economic Change and Military Conflict from 1500 to 2000* (New York: Random House, 1987); cf. the symposium on 'The Decline of Great Britain', *International History Review*, 13 (4) (1991) 661–783.

29. Philip M. Taylor, 'Back to the Future? Integrating the Press and Media into the History of International Relations', *Historical Journal of Film, Radio and Television*, 14 (3) (1994) 321–9.
30. Christopher Thorne, *Border Crossings. Studies in International History* (Oxford: Blackwell, 1988).
31. D. C. Watt, *What About the People? Abstraction and Reality in History and the Social Sciences* (London: London School of Economics, 1983), quote at p. 19.
32. The best single essay on this debate remains Tim Mason, 'Intention and Explanation: A Current Controversy about the Interpretation of National Socialism', in Jane Caplan (ed.), *Nazism, Fascism and the Working Class. Essays by Tim Mason* (Cambridge: Cambridge University Press, 1995), pp. 212–30. The broader point made here is illustrated by the rancorous exchange between Mason and Richard Overy, reproduced in abridged form in Patrick Finney (ed.), *The Origins of the Second World War* (London: Arnold, 1997), pp. 90–112. The quotation is from Hans Mommsen, 'National Socialism: Continuity and Change', in Walter Laqueur (ed.), *Fascism*, pbk edn (London: Penguin, 1979), p. 179.
33. Gordon Craig, 'The Historian and the Study of International Relations', *American Historical Review*, 88 (1) (1983) 2.
34. David Cannadine (ed.), *What is History Now?* (London: Palgrave, 2002).
35. Jon Jacobson, 'Is There a New International History of the 1920s?', *American Historical Review*, 88 (3) (1983) 617–45.
36. Charles Maier, 'Marking Time: The Historiography of International Relations', in Michael Kammen (ed.), *The Past Before Us: Contemporary Historical Writing in the United States* (Ithaca: Cornell University Press, 1980), pp. 355–87, quote at p. 357.
37. 'Symposium: Responses to Charles S. Maier, "Marking Time: The Historiography of International Relations"', *Diplomatic History*, 5 (4) (1981) 353–82.
38. Maier, 'Marking Time', p. 356.
39. Michael H. Hunt, 'The Long Crisis in US Diplomatic History: Coming to Closure', in Michael J. Hogan (ed.), *America in the World: The Historiography of American Foreign Relations since 1941* (Cambridge: Cambridge University Press, 1995), p. 93.
40. For overviews, see 'Symposium: Soviet Archives: Recent Revelations and Cold War Historiography', *Diplomatic History*, 21 (2) (1997) 215–305; Melvyn Leffler, 'The Cold War: What Do "We Now Know"?', *American Historical Review*, 104 (2) (1999) 501–24; Odd Arne Westad, 'The New International History of the Cold War: Three (Possible) Paradigms', *Diplomatic History*, 24 (4) (2000) 551–65. The publications and activities of the Cold War International History Project are central to this 'new international history': see http://wwics.si.edu/index.cfm?topic_id=1409&fuseaction=topics.home (accessed 20 September 2004).
41. Elizabeth Fox-Genovese and Elisabeth Lasch-Quinn (eds), *Reconstructing History. The Emergence of a New Historical Society* (New York: Routledge, 1999).
42. Patrick Finney, 'Still "Marking Time"? Text, Discourse and Truth in International History', *Review of International Studies*, 27 (3) (2001) 291–308.

43. This point is made in Alexander DeConde, 'On the Nature of International History', *International History Review*, 10 (2) (1988) 282–301, though he eventually concedes that current practice is 'intrinsically deeper' than that of the past (301).

44. Martin Clark, 'Gioacchino Volpe and Fascist Historiography in Italy', in Stefan Berger, Mark Donovan and Kevin Passmore (eds), *Writing National Histories. Western Europe since 1800* (London: Routledge, 1999), pp. 189–201.

45. D. C. Watt, *Succeeding John Bull. America in Britain's Place, 1900–1975* (Cambridge: Cambridge University Press, 1984), p. 2.

46. R. J. B. Bosworth, *The Italian Dictatorship. Problems and Perspectives in the Interpretation of Mussolini and Fascism* (London: Arnold, 1998), p. 89, discussing Federico Chabod, *Storia della politica estera italiana dal 1870 al 1896* (Milan: Istituto per gli studi di politica internazionale, 1951).

47. Bullen, 'What is Diplomatic History?', pp. 136–7. As Glenda Sluga points out in her chapter in this volume, these critics included many notable women whose contribution is usually marginalized in disciplinary histories.

48. Medlicott, 'Scope and Study', 414.

49. Watt, *Succeeding John Bull*, p. 1.

50. Michael J. Hogan and Thomas G. Paterson, 'Introduction', in Hogan and Paterson, *Explaining the History*, 2nd edn, pp. 1–9; in the same volume, McMahon structures his account around the divide between 'international' and 'national' approaches ('Toward a Pluralist Vision', pp. 35–50), while elsewhere Hunt has divided contemporary practitioners into three camps: 'realists', those focusing on the domestic sphere, and those focusing on the international arena ('Long Crisis', pp. 93–126). Note that in each of these accounts, it is interpretive approaches towards American foreign relations that determine the categorization.

51. Jean-Baptiste Duroselle and Maurice Vaïsse, 'L'histoire des relations internationales', in François Bédarida (ed.), *L'histoire et le métier d'historien en France, 1945–1995* (Paris: Éditions de la Maison des sciences de l'homme, 1995), pp. 351–8, quote at p. 358; Georges-Henri Soutou, 'Die französische Schule der Geschichte internationaler Beziehungen', in Wilfried Loth and Jürgen Osterhammel (eds), *Internationale Geschichte. Themen – Ergebnisse – Aussichten* (Munich: R. Oldenbourg Verlag, 2000), pp. 31–44. The absence of almost any trace of international history from an historiographical collection such as Jacques Revel and Lynn Hunt (eds), *Histories. French Constructions of the Past* (New York: New Press, 1995) is symptomatic.

52. Bosworth, *Italian Dictatorship*, pp. 82–4; see also R. J. B. Bosworth, 'Italian Foreign Policy and its Historiography', in R. J. B. Bosworth and Gino Rizzo (eds), *Altro Polo. Intellectuals and their Ideas in Contemporary Italy* (Sydney: Frederick May Foundation, 1983), pp. 65–85.

53. Loth and Osterhammel, *Internationale Geschichte*; on the politics of German international history and its place within the broader discipline, see Stefan Berger, *The Search for Normality. National Identity and Historical Consciousness in Germany since 1800* (Oxford: Berghahn, 1997); for an introduction to the resurgence of 'the primacy of foreign policy', see Brendan Simms, 'The Return of the Primacy of Foreign Policy', *German History*, 21 (3) (2003) 275–91.

54. Jessica Gienow-Hecht, 'A Global Group of Worriers', *Diplomatic History*, 26 (3) (2002) 481–91.

55. Duroselle and Vaïsse, 'L'histoire des relations internationales', p. 358.

56. This is true even of some 'global history': *David Reynolds, One World Divisible. A Global History since 1945* (London: Allen Lane, 2000).

57. This is suggested in Bosworth, *Explaining Auschwitz and Hiroshima*; it is a point that I am pursuing further in my own project *Remembering the Road to World War II: International History, National Identity, Collective Memory*, where many nuances are added to the generalization.

58. This point is made by Bruce Cumings in his chapter in this volume.

59. See, for example, the diverse views expressed in Michael J. Hogan, 'Corporatism', Thomas J. McCormick, 'World Systems', Louis A. Pérez Jr, 'Dependency', Akira Iriye, 'Culture and International History', and Kristin Hoganson, 'What's Gender Got to Do with It? Gender History as Foreign Relations History', in Hogan and Paterson, *Explaining the History*, 2nd edn, pp. 137–48, 149–61, 162–75, 241–56, 304–22 respectively.

60. Paul W. Schroeder, 'Why Realism Does Not Work Well for International History (Whether or Not it Represents a Degenerate IR Research Strategy)', in John A. Vasquez and Colin Elman (eds), *Realism and the Balancing of Power. A New Debate* (New Jersey: Prentice Hall, 2003), pp. 114–27.

61. Frank Costigliola, 'Reading for Meaning: Theory, Language, and Metaphor', in Hogan and Paterson, *Explaining the History*, 2nd edn, pp. 279–303.

62. For some further thoughts, see Finney, 'Still "Marking Time"?'.

63. Even beyond the issue of reinscribing 'Realism', there are larger arguments about the dubious ethical and political implications of conventional narrative historiography: see, for example, Jenny Edkins, *Trauma and the Memory of Politics* (Cambridge: Cambridge University Press, 2003); Dan Stone, *Constructing the Holocaust* (London: Vallentine Mitchell, 2003).

64. Erik Goldstein, William Keylor and Cathal Nolan, 'Series Foreword', in G. Bruce Strang, *On the Fiery March. Mussolini Prepares for War* (Westport: Praeger, 2003), pp. xiii–xv.

65. Keith Jenkins, *Refiguring History. New Thoughts on an Old Discipline* (London: Routledge, 2002), p. 3.

66. Goldstein *et al.*, 'Series Foreword', pp. xiv–xv.

67. School of History, University of Leeds, 'International History and its Study: A Guide for Students' (1986), p. 1. This was one of the first definitions of the field that I encountered as an undergraduate at Leeds.

68. T. G. Otte, 'Introduction: Personalities and Impersonal Forces in History', in T. G. Otte and Constantine A. Pagedas (eds), *Personalities, War and Diplomacy. Essays in International History* (London: Frank Cass, 1997), pp. 8–9.

69. Emily S. Rosenberg, 'Considering Borders', in Hogan and Paterson, *Explaining the History*, 2nd edn, pp. 191–3.

70. For overviews, see J. Gienow-Hecht and F. Schumacher (eds), *Culture and International History* (Oxford: Berghahn, 2003); Robert David Johnson (ed.), *On Cultural Ground: Essays in International History* (Chicago: Imprint, 1994); Frank A. Ninkovich and Lipung Bu (eds), *The Cultural Turn. Essays in the History of US Foreign Relations* (Chicago: Imprint, 2001).

71. Jessica Gienow-Hecht, 'Cultural Transfer', in Hogan and Paterson, *Explaining the History*, 2nd edn, pp. 257–78.

72. Susan Brewer, '"As Far As We Can": Culture and US Foreign Relations', in Robert D. Schulzinger (ed.), *A Companion to American Foreign Relations* (Oxford: Blackwell, 2003), p. 17.

73. For example, Douglas Little, *American Orientalism. The United States and the Middle East since 1945* (Chapel Hill: University of North Carolina Press, 2002); see also, Andrew Rotter, 'Saidism Without Said: *Orientalism* and US Diplomatic History', *American Historical Review*, 105 (4) (2000) 1205–17.

74. Frank A. Ninkovich, 'Introduction: The Cultural Turn', in Ninkovich and Bu, *Cultural Turn*, pp. 1–3.

75. Frank A. Ninkovich, 'No Post-Mortems for Postmodernism, Please', *Diplomatic History*, 22 (3) (1998) 451–66.

76. Robert Buzzanco, 'Where's the Beef? Culture without Power in the Study of US Foreign Relations', *Diplomatic History*, 24 (4) (2000) 623–32.

77. Ninkovich, 'Introduction', pp. 5–8.

78. Volker Depkat, 'Cultural Approaches to International Relations: A Challenge?', in Gienow-Hecht and Schumacher, *Culture and International History*, pp. 181–5.

79. For example, Emily S. Rosenberg, 'Revisiting Dollar Diplomacy: Narratives of Money and Manliness', *Diplomatic History*, 22 (2) (1998) 155–76; this point is somewhat disputed by Depkat, 'Cultural Approaches', pp. 186–9.

80. Patrick Finney, 'Beyond the Postmodern Moment?', *Journal of Contemporary History*, 40 (1) (2005) 149–65. It remains a moot point whether the rise of the new cultural history paradigm represents the defeat or victory of postmodernism.

81. Stephen A. Schuker, 'Reflections on the Cold War: A Comment', *Diplomacy and Statecraft*, 12 (4) (2001) 1.

82. McMahon, 'Toward a Pluralist Vision', pp. 36–7.

83. Sharon Tune (ed.), *American Historical Association. Program of the 118th Annual Meeting* (Washington, DC: American Historical Association, 2003).

84. Mark A. Stoler, 'Thoughts from SHAFR President', *Passport*, 35 (1) (2004) 4.

85. Michael J. Hogan, 'The "Next Big Thing": The Future of Diplomatic History in a Global Age', *Diplomatic History*, 28 (1) (2004) 1–21, quotes at 3, 6, 8, 12, 13, 17. There is a profound irony at work if international historians are more in danger of marginalization now that 'the international' is in fashion than they were in the 1990s when it was deemed of little relevance by postmodernists.

86. Patrick Finney, 'International History, Theory and the Origins of the Second World War', *Rethinking History*, 1 (3) (1997) 375.

87. Paul S. Holbo, 'Editor's Note', *Diplomatic History*, 1 (1) (1977) vi.

88. Roger R. Trask, 'The Impact of the Cold War on United States-Latin American Relations, 1945–1949', *Diplomatic History*, 1 (3) (1977) 271–84; Richard Pfau, 'Containment in Iran, 1946: The Shift to an Active Policy', *Diplomatic History*, 1 (4) (1977) 359–72.

89. Robert Rook, 'Race, Water, and Foreign Policy: The Tennessee Valley Authority's Global Agenda Meets "Jim Crow"', *Diplomatic History*, 28 (1) (2004) 55–81; David F. Schmitz and Vanessa Walker, 'Jimmy Carter and the Foreign Policy of Human Rights: The Development of a Post-Cold War Foreign Policy', *Diplomatic History*, 28 (1) (2004) 113–43; Barbara Keys, 'Spreading Peace, Democracy, and Coca-Cola®: Sport and American Cultural Expansion in the 1930s', *Diplomatic History*, 28 (2) (2004) 165–96; Andrew J. Falk, 'Reading Between the Lines: Negotiating National Identity on American Television, 1945–1960', *Diplomatic History*, 28 (2) (2004) 197–225.

90. Rosenberg, 'Considering Borders', pp. 190–2.
91. Akira Iriye, 'Internationalizing International History', in Thomas Bender (ed.), *Rethinking American History in a Global Age* (Berkeley: University of California Press, 2002), p. 60; see also Frank Ninkovich, 'Where Have all the Realists Gone?', *Diplomatic History*, 26 (1) (2002) 137–42.
92. Rosenberg, 'Considering Borders', pp. 189–93.
93. Charles S. Maier, 'Consigning the Twentieth Century to History: Alternative Narratives for the Modern Era', *American Historical Review*, 105 (3) (2000) 807–31, quote at 808.
94. On the implication of IR and international history with a historically contingent states system, with particular reference to 'Realism', see also Andreas Osiander, 'History and International Relations Theory', in Anja V. Hartmann and Beatrice Heuser (eds), *War, Peace and World Orders in European History* (London: Routledge, 2001), pp. 14–24.
95. Anders Stephanson, 'War and Diplomatic History', *Diplomatic History*, 25 (3) (2001) 403.
96. Hayden White, 'The Historical Text as Literary Artifact', *Clio* (1974), reprinted in Geoffrey Roberts (ed.), *The History and Narrative Reader* (London: Routledge, 2001), p. 221.
97. For example, Hogan and Paterson, *Explaining the History*, 2nd edn; Schulzinger, *Companion to American Foreign Relations*.
98. For a longer-term perspective, see for example Hartmann and Heuser, *War, Peace and World Orders*.
99. There are, for example, excellent essays on geographical and chronological subject areas in Schulzinger, *Companion to American Foreign Relations*.
100. Contributors were also instructed that whilst some bibliographical guidance should be given, there was no need for it to be particularly extensive, much less comprehensive.
101. For an argument that military history could also profit by turning to culture, see John A. Lynn, 'The Embattled Future of Academic Military History', *Journal of Military History*, 61 (4) (1997) 777–89.
102. In Finney, 'Still "Marking Time"?', I suggested that international history should turn towards 'discourse analysis' and 'critical historiography'; the former has now been embraced, albeit perhaps in slightly diluted form, while engagement with the latter remains limited.
103. Typical examples include Robert McMahon, 'Contested Memory: The Vietnam War and American Society, 1975–2001', *Diplomatic History*, 26 (2) (2002) 159–84; Robert D. Schulzinger, 'Memory and Understanding US Foreign Relations', in Hogan and Paterson, *Explaining the History*, 2nd edn, pp. 336–52; the best work to date in this vein, which does encompass history-writing, is Emily S. Rosenberg, *A Date Which Will Live. Pearl Harbor in American Memory* (Durham: Duke University Press, 2003).

1
diplomacy and decision-making

t. g. otte

'Do not despise the diplomatic documents'
Gilbert Murray

International history, as an institutionalized sub-discipline within the wider field of historical research, is of fairly recent vintage. It acquired only in the 1970s what Zara Steiner has called 'the contemporary attributes of adulthood', that is university departments, scholarly journals, professional bodies and conferences dedicated to the study of this subject.[1] No doubt its coming of age received a significant stimulus from, and also in turn reflected, the rise of International Relations in the cognate political science discipline. Since then the field has expanded considerably. Though welcome, this is not without problems. Diplomacy, 'the conduct of relations between sovereign states through the medium of officials based at home or abroad',[2] is increasingly replaced with other foci of research. This may well be a reflection of the contemporary decline of the traditional sovereign nation state, the classical locus of diplomatic history.[3] In a world increasingly dominated by visual images and the media, and growing global commercial and population mobility, diplomatic historians, as Anders Stephanson noted with feigned surprise, 'seem less and less interested in the history of diplomacy' as the history of relations between sovereign state actors.[4] In consequence, the term 'international history' has now become 'so broad that it loses its usefulness'.[5]

in defence of a pragmatic approach

If international history's institutional maturity and subsequent further growth are of recent date, its pedigree is nevertheless old. To Leopold

36

von Ranke historians owe, besides much else, the emphasis on relations between the great powers, combined with the first systematic articulation of the field's separate identity under the auspices of the *Primat der Aussenpolitik*.[6] Scholarship in Britain invariably lagged somewhat behind. It was not until the end of the nineteenth century that the first history of British foreign policy appeared, intriguingly written by a former naval officer-turned-Chichele Professor of Modern History at Oxford, Captain Montagu Burrows. Reflecting J. R. Seeley's contemporary precept that history was little more than the 'handmaiden of politics', Burrows' main objective was to demonstrate 'the continuity, the continuous development, of British foreign policy'. Diplomatic history was 'to act as an interpreter, as a light to illuminate the onward path of national life, and to point out by the examples of the past what future course is most free from danger, and most likely to lead to honourable peace and wholesome prosperity'.[7] In the decade before the Great War diplomatic history became firmly established in academia, though it was still driven by the desire to distil practically applicable lessons from past great power relations.[8] Since then international history has lost that drive, and much else besides. There is a profound irony about the development of international history during the latter part of the twentieth century. Despite its institutional maturing, the emergence of a solid active core of practitioners in most universities and a proliferation of dedicated scholarly journals in the field, international history has nevertheless signally failed to engage the attention of the wider historical profession. The prevailing intellectual climate has been unfavourable to it; and, as Gordon A. Craig wistfully reflected, the dominant attitude towards international, and more especially diplomatic, history has 'varied between condescension and antipathy'.[9] Indeed, at the present moment, there is only one designated diplomatic history post in the United Kingdom.

There seems little reason to revise Craig's 1983 complaint two decades on. To observe that the history of international relations has been ignored by most historians is to state the obvious; and this has given rise to much introspection.[10] The perception that foreign policy has somehow 'been done', that it is old-fashioned and lacking in the glamour associated with theory-driven deconstructions and reconstructions of identities and views of the 'other' in terms of ethnicity, gender or sexuality, is well-entrenched in the historical profession. To some extent this is a reflection of, or rather a generational reaction against, the status of diplomatic and political history for a long period as the dominant form of historical research and teaching. In part, the stalemate in this field of historical research reflects also the massive condescension of late-twentieth-century historians towards social and political elites. The fact that, by its very nature, diplomatic history is primarily concerned with international friction and state-administered violence merely heightened widespread distaste for it as an intellectual exercise. In the Anglo-Saxon world a combination of a sense of post-imperial guilt with what Charles S. Maier, with reference to the United States of America, once called a post-Vietnam 'bad conscience about the legitimacy of United States power', helped further to shunt historical studies of international relations into the sidings of academia.[11]

No doubt, some of the prejudices against the study of great power relations have palled in recent years. Nevertheless, now that Britannia's dreadnoughts that once ruled the waves at Heaven's command have been decommissioned, and the plumed hats and scarlet uniforms of her colonial officials have been mothballed, discussions of 'genderized' concepts of Britannia or representations of identity through imperial regalia and exotic finery seem to offer a safer haven from the disturbed present;[12] and to those who view the United States as the last authentic imperial power in the traditional Western mould, the exploration of ethnicity and race, or the 'enframing' of a world-view as the premise of a world order, seem preferable to examinations of the national interest.[13] Criticizing such preoccupations is easy enough. Yet these positions raise important questions that international historians ought not to ignore. Contemporary society, and with it current scholarship, have been shaped by the demise of the modernist project, with all its established verities about the past and the future, and the concomitant rise of postmodernism. For all its self-proclaimed refusal to emphasize one particular perspective on the past, in practice postmodernism privileges certain perspectives, whilst disparaging others. Its main objective is the deconstruction of mostly patrician, metropolitan metanarratives, and their replacement with alternative, usually plebeian and regional, hegemonies.[14] This raises the question of judgement, weighting and balance. Foreign policy was and, as current international events demonstrate, remains one of the most important functions of state activity. It was and is also one that reveals the operations of the political system. Historically, foreign affairs helped to crystallize thinking about contending notions of the national interest. It thus reflected and helped to articulate ideological ideas and associate them with specific political groupings.[15] Ignoring this important aspect of state activity, then, can only produce unbalanced accounts of the past. Given also that contemporaries paid taxes to enable the state to pursue the perceived national interest, and that often they were called upon to die for it, genderising Britannia or reflecting on alterity and race is, at best, unhelpful.

It is the contention of this chapter, then, that scholars would abandon the pragmatic approach to the study and writing of international history at a price. The high politics of foreign policy decision-making and diplomacy as the instrument through which decisions were carried out must remain a principal concern of international history, if it is to remain a meaningful scholarly pursuit. What follows is not meant as a call for practitioners to return to the narrow confines of diplomatic history, as practised in the first half of the twentieth century. Rather, it is meant to reaffirm certain essentials that are central to the pursuit of international history, but which have been obfuscated in recent works and debates, especially in the United States. In these debates G. M. Young's unkind and time-worn quip that 'what passes for diplomatic history is little more than the record of what one clerk said to another' is still taken to be a profound insight into the redundant nature of this branch of historical enquiry.[16] Even in its own time the phrase was nothing but a reflection of that mid-Victorian feeling of boredom with foreign and imperial affairs. Modern international history is more sophisticated than its detractors – or those who have lost sight of these essentials – comprehend.

systemic context

The reaffirmation of the centrality of decision-making, the emphasis on human agency, and the importance of diplomacy, however, ought not to be at the expense of the wider international setting. As G. W. F. Hegel wrote in his philosophy of law, 'Without relations with other states, the state can no more be an actual individual than an individual can be an actual person without a relationship with other persons.'[17] There is nothing in this that should prove unacceptable to international historians. The sovereign state is the traditional locus of international relations, and subsequently of international history also. Whenever two or more states are in such regular and sufficient contact that their respective actions form a necessary element in the calculations of the other, they act as part of a whole: they are part of a system. States may be competitors for the same objective, or strategic partners in joint pursuit of a common interest. Whether their interaction takes the form of conflict, cooperation or, indeed, neutrality, they affect each other's behaviour through the established links between states in which they participate.[18] As Hegel's contemporary Carl von Clausewitz noted, when surveying European politics at the end of the Napoleonic era, the major and minor state and popular interests affect each other in the most varied and changeable manner. Each point of intersection binds and serves to balance the thrust of one against the other. Through all these points of intersection is revealed the wider cohesion of the whole. Thus, relations between all states serve more to preserve this whole in its current form, than to effect changes within it.[19]

Clausewitz's *en passant* remark offers two important insights to international historians. Firstly, the permanent and regular linkages and interaction between states create some form of a system; and, secondly, its own preservation is one of the system's principal goals. To facilitate the former, and to achieve the latter, the statesmen of different periods strove to establish basic rules and norms of behaviour, to regulate competition and violence, in short to devise a kind of 'grammar of international politics'. None of these attempts, however, could arrest the process of transformation inherent in international relations. The changing capabilities of individual states caused the rise and fall of powers. The changing balance between them, in turn, created a dynamic of its own, in the wake of which different international systems evolved over time.

How these systems emerged, operated, developed further, and then were transformed into a new system, has been the subject of many studies. Some scholars trace the origins of the first such system to around 2400 BCE in ancient Sumer.[20] Most agree that the modern states system, with its assumption of the legal equality of all states, came into being with the Peace of Westphalia in 1648.[21] Sir Harry Hinsley's *Power and the Pursuit of Peace*, which so deservedly has become the standard text of its kind, traces the gradual evolution of internationalist theories as to how the states system ought to be regulated. Holbraad's valuable study of contending concepts of the so-called 'Concert of Europe' in the long nineteenth century pursues a similar objective, though inevitably on a less broadly defined scale.[22] Other scholars emphasize the occasionally more dramatic and profound change in the nature of the states system. Paul Schroeder, in particular, emphasizes the enabling function of the states system. In his analysis it is an instrument that makes foreign policy possible rather than a brake on states: 'Every international system, to be stable and durable, has to provide certain collective or public goods for at least the major participants – general peace, reasonable security from attack, recognition of status, sanctity of contracts, a general expectation that promises and commitments will be fulfilled and violators curbed or punished, and so on.'[23] No international history proper is possible that ignores the systemic background against which foreign policy is formulated and executed. Thus, for instance, any study of the international history of the 1850s and 1860s needs to take into account the *de facto* withdrawal from European politics of the two powers, Britain and Russia, that had previously aimed to maintain the established Vienna order. The gradual disintegration of the Crimean system, in turn, gave an opening to the ambitious revisionists, the French Emperor Napoleon III and Prussia's prime minister Otto von Bismarck, to reshape the map of Europe according to their designs and ambitions.[24]

Historically-inspired International Relations scholars, such as Martin Wight, have argued that within the states system there are structures that need to be calibrated. States align themselves in certain structural constellations or configurations. The resulting structures may be the outcome of formal treaties, institutionalized diplomacy in the shape of international conferences or congresses, or informal arrangements that are worked out over a period of years. These are all essential elements of any international system.[25] In the course of the 1970s the structure of past states systems attracted the attention of a new breed of social scientists. The insights offered by 'systems theories' suggested that there are certain discernable patterns of international behaviour. These behavioural patterns, it was suggested, formed a coherent system, the whole of which was greater than the sum of its constituent parts. 'Systems theories', according to their leading proponents, furnish an opportunity for identifying patterns in the apparently random and chaotic behaviour of sovereign states at any stage in the past.[26]

Such an approach goes against the grain of the historian's traditionally ideographic concern with the particular. As Gordon A. Craig once observed self-critically, it would require overcoming 'our congenital distrust of theory and our insistence upon the uniqueness of the historical event'.[27] Other international historians, such as the late Christopher Thorne, have advocated just that. 'History', he argued, 'is too important to be left to the historians.' They ought to accept the need for 'border crossings', intellectual journeys of discovery across 'the lines of demarcation between the various human disciplines'.[28] There is something to be said for openness to approaches developed in cognate disciplines in order to discover correlations that may have causal significance for particular developments in international history. Alexander L. George has advocated the use of case studies, applying the method of structured focused comparison.[29] George himself applied this method to an examination of the use of deterrence as a policy tool in US foreign relations, and later the use of coercive diplomacy as an alternative to military conflict.[30] His collaboration with Gordon Craig produced the classic *Force and Statecraft*, a work saturated with historically informed insights into patterns of state behaviour.[31] The 'systems theory', or at any rate a systemic, approach also informed a series of studies in the 1980s and early 1990s in the border region between security studies and international history, which focused, for instance, on the role played by deterrence in great power relations before 1914, and why it ultimately failed.[32] Choice preferences and the limits of choices were examined, as were the nature of the pre-1914 international power system or shifting alliance patterns.[33]

Suggestions are frequently made for international historians to adopt further new systemic approaches to their subject.[34] Stimulating as such suggestions and the above studies are, they raise two central questions. The first is that of the reconcilability of the underlying approaches with traditional historical method. There is after all such a thing as the historical method, a set of general rules and methodological principles that describe the work of historians. The introduction of conceptual frameworks and devices derived from the social sciences or other cognate disciplines always runs the risk of militating against understanding and reconstruction of the past in its own right and on its own terms. Establishing patterns of behaviour entails elevating certain aspects to the exclusion of others. Abstraction and construction thus reduce the multiplicity and complexity of past phenomena to a formal simplicity.[35] Quite clearly, some of the studies cited above are principally the work of social scientists applying social science devices to historical data; and, as such, they contain more than just an element of reductionism. This, then, raises the question of balance. If international historians are to borrow from the older and newer tools in the social scientists' workshop, these tools have to be carefully chosen. They have to suit the historical material upon which they are to be brought to bear. The massive bulldozer of the systemic theory-builder will always tend to bury the unique and particular that remain the chief characteristic of history. The historians' trowel, fine-hair brush and sand-sieve, by contrast, may not always allow them to discern how past phenomena related to each other. So there is no reason why the careful and controlled application of comparative methods or insights gained from the social sciences to a series of past diplomatic modalities and problems should not help historians of international relations to gain in analytical sophistication and produce significant insights. The litmus test remains that of striking the right balance.

the realities behind diplomacy

International historians ignore at their peril the economic and other domestic 'realities behind diplomacy'. As Paul Kennedy has argued, 'the interaction between economics and strategy, as each of the leading states in the international system strove to enhance its wealth and power', was an important background factor in international history.[36] That interaction also enables the historian to illuminate global connections and correlations. Thus, the effects of the end of the American civil war extended well beyond North America. The resumption of cotton exports following the defeat of the South contributed to a cotton and then a financial crisis in Egypt and on Cuba. These crises, in turn, triggered a chain of events that led first to an Anglo-French financial takeover of Egypt and eventually culminated in sole British control of the Nile. The Cuban crisis was a contributing factor in the overthrow of the first Spanish republic in 1874, but was also a longer-term cause of the Spanish-American war of 1898.[37] Finally, the war in America tempted Napoleon III to embark upon the fatal Mexican adventure, thereby demonstrating further the constraints and limitations of French power, limitations that Bismarck would exploit fully a few years later.[38] On the other hand, finance and commerce also were tools used by statesmen in pursuit of essentially politico-strategic objectives. Thus, for instance, far from reducing British diplomacy to the role of handmaiden of City of London financial interests, Britain's prime minister and foreign secretary in the 1890s, Lord Salisbury, sought to utilize 'patriotic capitalists' for his diplomatic and strategic purposes in China.[39]

In addition, international historians ought not to neglect the military dimension. Perhaps the most obvious impact of military factors upon international affairs comes with the problem of armaments, and what are usually, if often inaccurately, referred to as 'arms races'. In a competitive international environment states pursue, and are vulnerable to, a type of competition with each other in which military technology is a major independent variable. Military technology has its own historical dynamic of qualitative leaps, quantitative advances and geopolitical spread, but these can have significant political consequences. For instance, David Stevenson's excellent study of armaments and great power relations before 1914 demonstrates that, while there was clearly no simple one-way road to world war, the dynamic of military technology was in a major part responsible for generating a sense of mutual insecurity that became a critical problem in inter-state relations.[40] How such dynamics evolved, the extent to which financial muscle played an enabling or restraining role, and how policy-makers learned to deal with them, or failed to do so, is crucial to our understanding of international history. This requires of the historian the acquisition of a considerable degree of technological expertise and understanding, in some areas, such as naval or nuclear history, perhaps more than in others.[41]

International historians readily acknowledge that the strength of armed forces, financial and economic capacity, and manpower and raw material resources are key components of external relations. Interwoven with these elements of 'hard power' is a further component. It is less tangible, hardly quantifiable, but no less crucial: diplomacy.[42] In the classic definition of diplomacy by Sir Ernest Satow, an erstwhile diplomat himself, '[d]iplomacy is the application of tact and intelligence to the conduct of official relations between states'.[43] Another former British ambassador defined it 'as the machinery by which the intercourse of nations with one another is conducted and their reciprocal relations are adjusted. It is concerned to find solutions to those incidental difficulties arising between them which conflict with the permanent laws governing national interests.'[44] Finally, Harold Nicolson offered this definition: 'Diplomacy essentially is the organised system of negotiations between sovereign states.'[45] The unjustly overlooked little treatise on diplomacy and the conduct of foreign policy from an historical perspective by the Edinburgh historian and political scientist David Playfair Heatley contains wise counsel. When studying the subject it is necessary 'never [to] separate the study of policy – whether the statesman's study of policy in prospect or the historian's in retrospect – from the appreciation of the instruments on the understanding and the use of which success depends'. Mastering the subject properly, Heatley argued, was more than a question of acquiring specialist knowledge; it depended principally upon 'forming the habit of mind that is required for appreciating questions of foreign policy'.[46] This is pertinent advice for all diplomatic historians.

A number of practical conclusions can be drawn from the above definitions and from Heatley's advice. International historians will continue to speak of Russia or America, of the Wilhelmstrasse, the Quai d'Orsay or Downing Street. Yet it is clearly understood by all practitioners that such names are a designated form of shorthand. For a proper appreciation of diplomacy as an organised system the historian needs to acquire a technical mastery not just over the surviving diplomatic sources, but also over the bureaucracies that produced them. He needs to understand how these institutions, as instruments of government, were organized, what the chains of command were or the career patterns, and how these administrative tools operated and developed. The historian has to have knowledge of diplomatic hierarchies, and he needs to understand the functions and roles of foreign ministry clerks. The point is obvious. In the years before 1914 the young Robert Vansittart may have penned some of the longest minutes preserved in the Foreign Office archives. Yet these are not a reflection of his importance or seniority; rather they are indicative of a budding official who wished to be noticed by his superiors. Similarly, the considerable length of Eyre Crowe's contemporaneous comments and memoranda is suggestive more of his relative isolation and distance from the centre of power than of his importance.[47] Failure to appreciate such aspects of relative power and position within hierarchies will result in lopsided analyses. This also applies to career structures and patterns within the foreign service. As one former senior British diplomat wrote in his memoirs, there was an old Foreign Office joke, likening the diplomatic service 'to the London Underground Railway and it was said that once a man was launched on the Inner Circle (London, Paris, Berlin, Rome) it was impossible to leave the track'.[48]

It is not merely the hierarchies that need to be understood. 'Red Tape', as Sir Thomas Sanderson, a late-nineteenth century head of the Foreign Office, observed in his eponymous memorandum, 'like drill in the army, is only the means to an end. It is the method by which a huge machine is made to move – rather ponderously – but steadily and without confusion. It is our duty to make ourselves masters of it, in order that the directions of our chiefs may be carried out properly in their details.'[49] Sanderson's plea to his junior clerks to make themselves masters of the Foreign Office machine might just as well be directed to international historians. This is not to suggest that international history ought to be confined to the study of how piles of papers were shuffled from one desk to another. However, as the works of Max Weber and of Samuel Eisenstadt have shown, the bureaucratization of advanced societies in the nineteenth and twentieth centuries had major political consequences.[50] Pointing the historian's torch into the interstices of foreign ministries, then, can help to hone our understanding of the foreign policy-making processes.[51] Foreign ministries are the administrative nerve centres of foreign policy. In modern sociological parlance they are knowledge-based organizations. At different stages of their histories different information gathering and management procedures, guaranteeing a controlled information flow, were devised, maintained, and constantly revised, geared towards the needs of informed policy-making and decisive action.[52] It is a truism to argue that the quality, reliability and quantity of policy-relevant information determines the quality of political decision-making. Without an appreciation of how foreign policy bureaucracies operated as knowledge-based organizations, historical assessments of foreign policy decisions will miss an important dimension.

the workings of diplomacy and decision-making

The above deals principally with the organizational aspects of policy-framing. In terms of the execution of foreign policy, a proper grasp of diplomacy is certainly necessary. Diplomacy is the lubricant that guarantees the smooth conduct of foreign affairs. It is, to quote Nicolson once more, 'the art of creating and expanding confidence'.[53] This implies the possession of certain social and communication skills on the part of diplomatists. Their effectiveness as diplomatic agents, and consequently later assessments of their roles by historians, will reflect, to some extent, their possession of these skills. Yet, it would be wrong for students of diplomatic history to assume that an ambassador's role simply involves wining and dining at balls and cocktail parties, as televisual cliché suggests. Diplomacy is above all a means, and as such it has developed its own method: 'It seeks, by the use of reason, conciliation and the exchange of interests, to prevent major conflicts arising between sovereign States. It is the agency through which foreign policy seeks to attain its purposes by agreement rather than by war.'[54] A successful diplomat, then, not only has to analyse the interests or ambitions of foreign countries, but also needs to take into account their different cultural and historical backgrounds as well as the personalities of the statesmen he has to deal with.[55] As seventeenth-century writer Jean Hotman advised ambassadors in 1613: 'Si c'est un prince, connaître son humeur et inclination.'[56] The diplomat's function, then, is to provide necessary information for his government and to assist in the process of adjusting conflicting interests. This has implications for the historian of diplomacy, too. Technical knowledge and an appreciation of the instrumentality of diplomacy are indispensable, but they are not enough in themselves. In addition to the critical, analytical skills that every historian needs to acquire, the diplomatic historian has to develop 'a sense of the continuity of the problems in foreign affairs, the limitations set on policy, and the very feel of the diplomatic process'.[57]

There is, of course, the danger of 'overnarrow and overspecialized professionalism', a kind of *déformation professionelle* that Geoffrey Elton identified as particularly prevalent amongst diplomatic historians.[58] True, as Gordon Craig conceded with a fine sense of self-deprecating irony, all too often professional diplomatic historians might produce

> arid monographs that had been literally copied out of the bound volumes of Foreign Office papers in the Public Record Office, tricked with Latin tags (*sub spe rati, rebus sic stantibus*, and the like) and impressive footnotes (FO France/1749; from Lyons, no. 249, very

confidential, March 4, 1869), and sent forth to grace the lower shelves of university libraries.[59]

No doubt such works, if they really do exist, may reflect pedantic and pettifogging minds. Nevertheless, the diplomatic historian cannot safely dispense with the technical knowledge of diplomacy. He has to develop an almost intuitive sense for diplomatic practice, but must avoid 'going native'. In a sense, the diplomatic historian has to be able to walk and talk with the diplomats whose actions he is studying, without taking this small circle of people at their own valuation. He has to see past problems as contemporaries saw them, and yet maintain a critical distance. These skills are the cornerstones of his professional judgement.

Bureaucracies, however, do not operate themselves in some automatic, mechanistic, self-regulating, or deterministic manner. Most, though not all, contemporary practitioners of international history acknowledge the centrality of human agency to their subject. Clearly, within the eighteenth-century social and political environment the Duc de Broglie was a sufficiently eminent person and carried enough weight to be studied as an actor in his own right, as was Lord Palmerston a century later (not to mention the totalitarian dictators of the first half of the twentieth century). Given the vast expansion of the foreign policy apparatus in every country and the proliferation of posts and offices associated with the conduct of foreign affairs in the course of the twentieth century, the question might however legitimately be asked whether historians are not elevating civil servants to 'spurious eminence ... found more commonly in the parish-pump history of domestic affairs'.[60] Once again this is a question of balance. Zara Steiner once described the foreign ministries and other institutions engaged in external affairs as 'black boxes'.[61] It is within these black boxes that policy decisions were framed and formulated. These decisions, in turn, were the responsibility of a small and semi-permanent group of people, who constituted what D. C. Watt has called the foreign policy-making elite. Watt's argument arose from his study of British relations with the United States in the twentieth century, which seemed to suggest that British policy was the result of the attitudes and experiences of a relatively small group.[62] Watt's insight is germane also to earlier periods and other countries. The foreign policy-making elite is best described as multi-tiered, comprising at the top level of senior politicians and at the bottom level of public opinion formers. In between are the diplomatists, foreign ministry officials, military and intelligence officers as well as bankers, businessmen and academics.[63] Human agency within the given system and the nature of the latter reinforce each other. Whilst individuals make any system work, their conceptualization of policy issues and their decisions are shaped by the political system in which they operate. Thus, the diplomatic concepts, foreign policy goals and strategic options pursued by the foreign policy elite were linked to the particular nature of the wider political context of the period.

The foreign policy-making process, therefore, needs to be placed into the wider political environment; and this means politics at the very top. Themes, developments and events need to be anchored in the complex web of relationships and competing influences that formed the fabric of politics. Michael Bentley and John Stevenson's observation about the 'half-closed world peopled by senior politicians, civil servants and publicists' that 'perpetuated in post-Reform Britain ground rules of party government of which the masses knew little and which the coming of "democracy" did little to supplant' is pertinent also to the study of British foreign policy.[64] The high politics approach takes account of entrenched, institutionalized interests and rival centres of power, whether focused on individual political actors or Whitehall departments. Such rivalries were liable to influence decision-making. It is the function of a ministerial bureaucracy to prepare political decisions; and it does so by reducing the complexity of available policy options. In turn, this can lead to the presentation of preferred options as necessary, in the sense of being dictated by the perceived or accepted logic of any given situation. This is not merely a question of the mechanics of the governmental machinery. Historical analyses must not be confined to following the departmental paper trail, though the historian has to master those also. The manner in which politicians and civil servants react to developing situations reflects also their core belief systems.

The human actors of international history possess their own normative values that shape and animate the behaviour of both states and systems. That behaviour results from the judgements and actions of people who operate the foreign policy apparatus with particular ideas, assumptions, and beliefs about how they should act in the world. Thus, in politics, every action, be it in actual deed or as a policy recommendation, is based on a set of premises, values, and axioms. The characteristics of any age are revealed not just in political deeds, or social and economic developments. They are expressed also in the manner in which contemporaries sought to rationalize their particular situation, and perhaps even more especially in the language and concepts in which such efforts were formulated. These concepts, or 'cognitive maps', distort reality and scale, just like any other cartographical projection. However, political decisions were based on them; and they therefore require calibration.[65] Decision-formers are mostly shaped by 'their own instinctive reactions, traditions and modes of behaviour'.[66] They were the products of their times, their national traditions and social environment. Given the pressures and constraints of time placed upon politicians, the historian ought to bear in mind Henry Kissinger's observation that their core values and convictions, formed before they reach office and power, 'are the intellectual capital they will consume as long as they continue in office'.[67]

It is, then, incumbent upon the international historian to consider the social origins, education, and recruitment processes of the power elite whose actions he studies. Nineteenth- and twentieth-century foreign policy-making elites were small, though growing, and socially relatively homogeneous. This, in turn, engendered a degree of uniformity of outlook, a firm, though not always fully articulated understanding of the basic principles of foreign policy. The 'official mind', or what an anonymous writer in the 1880s felicitously called the 'Foreign Office mind', is thus the product of a historical socialization process.[68] The pathogenesis of this 'Foreign Office mind' also requires historical calibration. To some extent it was a function of ideology, defined as a flexible set of beliefs which helped to crystallize 'accepted understandings and often unexpressed assumptions', rather than a Procrustean bed rigidly providing a panacea for any given problem.[69] Of course, the historian ought to beware not to assume too large a degree of uniformity, systematic or even profound thought, and ought to make allowance for dissenting views. Policy-making, after all, may be more ragged around the edges, haphazard and less consistent than later reconstructions inevitably suggest. Closely linked to this is the need for the historian to identify and differentiate the preoccupations and perceptions of policy-makers. Perceptions may distort, but they are decisive. They are the filter through which impressions and information are received, however selectively, and then processed, however incompletely. The identification of those perceptions that influenced the policy-makers' judgement of objectives and priorities therefore forms a crucial part of the historian's task.

One further aspect of the foreign policy-making elite requires the historian's attention, that is the problem of political generations. Differences in formative generational experiences and learning informed and shaped the shifting perceptions and changing core values of the elite. Nothing is more easily recognisable than a political generation. Nothing is also more difficult to conceptualize. Unlike biological generations, political ones are characterized not by birth dates, but by consciousness of common formative experiences.[70] The rapid political, social and technological changes in the nineteenth and twentieth centuries produced significant differences in outlook between generations. A generation is not a rigidly defined chronological phenomenon; rather it is 'a social-historical location'. The real locus of any 'new generational impulse remained the generational situation, even if members of other age-groups participated in its articulation'.[71] This can lead to apparent distortions. Lord Salisbury and Joseph Chamberlain were clearly members of different political generations, even though the age difference between them was a mere six years.[72] As D. C. Watt has pointed out, Theodore Roosevelt belonged to a more senior political generation than did Woodrow Wilson, despite the fact that he was the slightly younger of the two.[73] It is for the diplomatic historian to elucidate this problem.

Finally, the pragmatic approach embraces the notion of the principal openness of all historical situations. Historians have to grapple with all the ambiguities of free choice and individual agency, with the play of the contingent and unforeseen. They have to divest themselves of preconceived notions of paradigmatic laws and structures and other rigid, quasi-cosmic patterns of *longue durée*. Supposedly minor incidents played a more significant role in the day-to-day conduct of foreign policy, as Bertrand Russell warned:

> Nor can we ignore the part played by ... chance, ... by trivial occurrences which happened to have great effects. The Great War was made probable by large causes, but not inevitable. Down to the last moment, it might have been postponed by minor events which did not take place, though nothing that we know of made them impossible; and if it had been postponed, the forces making for peace might have become predominant.[74]

The pragmatic study of international history rests on the empirical examination of written evidence, the bulk of which is to be found in the records of political transactions. These can only be made intelligible through the thorough study of the minutiae of politics and diplomacy, and the analytical narrative of their day-to-day conduct.[75] This is the only element of inevitability in history. Of course, evidence is always subject to bias and distortion, at its creation, presentation, preservation and eventual interpretation.[76] Nevertheless, these elements of bias and distortion can be filtered out only through immersion in the archives. This and the acquisition of a technical expertise on the materials and processes under examination remain *de rigueur*. It may be 'exceedingly dull to wade through mountains of drafts and despatches but, unless this is done, the historian is unlikely to offer more than the usual trite references to imperialist rivalry among the great powers stimulated by economic competition'.[77]

conclusion

The insistence on pragmatism and immersion in the minutiae of concrete political situations should not discount other background influences. If the utterances of Foreign Office clerks ought not to be neglected by the historian, they need, however, to be set against a wider network of relationships of a systemic, cultural, financial and economic nature. Human agency holds the key to history. The lock, however, will turn only if the actions of individuals are placed against the 'realities behind diplomacy'. The 'reasons why', the process by which decisions were arrived at and then implemented, what, if any, alternatives there were, and why these were rejected: all of these will only become apparent if such background influences are taken into account. The pragmatic approach accepts that thought and action, design and choice are interlinked; and that human agency is in a dynamic process of interaction with structural and background forces. As Paul Schroeder noted, 'the international system changes when enough persons change their minds about it'.[78] This gives purpose to international history, and also lends hope to its practitioners. As in its chosen subject, however, the success of diplomatic history lies in balance and good judgement.

notes

1. Z. S. Steiner, 'On Writing International History: Chaps, Maps and Much More', *International Affairs*, 73 (3) (1997) 531.
2. I am following G. R. Berridge and Alan James' succinct definition: *A Dictionary of Diplomacy*, 2nd edn (New York: Palgrave, 2003), pp. 69–70.
3. M. Horsman and A. Marshall, *After the Nation State: Citizens, Tribalism and the New World Order* (London: HarperCollins, 1994); P. Bobbitt, *The Shield of Achilles: War, Peace, and the Course of History* (London: Allen Lane, 2002), pp. 776–807.
4. A. Stephanson, 'Diplomatic History in the Expanded Field', *Diplomatic History*, 22 (4) (1998) 595. For an instructive cross-section of recent research, see M. H. Geyer and J. Paulmann (eds), *The Mechanics of Internationalism: Culture, Society, and Politics from the 1840s to the First World War* (Oxford: Oxford University Press, 2001).
5. T. G. Paterson, 'Defining and Doing the History of American Foreign Relations: A Primer', *Diplomatic History*, 14 (3) (1990) 585.
6. L. von Ranke, 'Die grossen Mächte [1833]', in *Rankes Meisterwerke*, 10 vols (Munich and Leipzig: Duncker and Humblot, 1914–15), vol. 10, pp. 423–82;

cf. E. O. Czempiel, 'Der Primat der Aussenpolitik: Kritische Würdigung einer Staatsmaxime', *Politische Vierteljahresschrift*, 4 (3) (1963) 266–87; also W. J. Mommsen, 'Ranke and the Neo-Rankean School: State-Oriented Historiography as a Stabilizing Force', in G. G. Iggers and J. M. Powell (eds), *Leopold von Ranke and the Shaping of the Historical Discipline* (Syracuse, NY: Syracuse University Press, 1990), pp. 124–40. Ranke was by no means the pioneer of diplomatic history. This accolade ought properly belong to A. H. L. Heeren and his *Handbuch der Geschichte des europäischen Staatensystems und seiner Colonien* (Göttingen: J. F. Röwer, 1809) and his earlier *Handbuch der Geschichte der Staaten des Alterthums* (Göttingen: Rosenbusch, 1799) (translated as *A Manual of Ancient History, particularly with regard to the constitutions, the commerce, and the colonies of the states of antiquity* (Oxford: D. A. Talboys, 1829).

7. M. Burrows, *The History of the Foreign Policy of Great Britain*, 2nd edn (Edinburgh and London: Blackwood, 1897), pp. viii, 287.

8. W. A. Phillips, *The Confederation of Europe: A Study of the European Alliance, 1813–1823, as an Experiment in the International Organization of Peace* (London: Longman,.1914), pp. 292–9. Lord Acton's final project, *The Cambridge Modern History*, 13 vols (Cambridge: Cambridge University Press, 1902–11), contained a series of foreign policy chapters. The first proper, broad chronological survey of British diplomatic history, however, did not appear until after the First World War in the shape of A. W. Ward and G. P. Gooch (eds), *The Cambridge History of British Foreign Policy*, 3 vols (Cambridge: Cambridge University Press, 1922–23).

9. G. A. Craig, 'The Historian and the Study of International Relations', *American Historical Review*, 88 (1) (1983) 2; see also his reflection a decade earlier in 'Political History', *Daedalus*, 100 (2) (1971) 323–38.

10. For example, S. G. Rabe, 'Reports of Our Demise are Greatly Exaggerated', *Diplomatic History*, 16 (3) (1992) 481–6; Stephanson, 'Diplomatic History in the Expanded Field', 595–603.

11. C. S. Maier, 'Marking Time: The Historiography of International Relations', in M. Kammen (ed.), *The Past Before Us: Contemporary Historical Writing in the United States* (Ithaca, NY: Cornell University Press, 1980), p. 356.

12. Most eloquently by D. Cannadine, *Ornamentalism: How the British Saw Their Empire* (London: Penguin, 2001).

13. A. Deconde, *Race and American Foreign Policy: A History* (Boston, MA: Northeastern University Press, 1992); P. Greenhalgh, *Ephemeral Vistas: The Expositions Universelles, Great Exhibitions and World Fairs, 1851–1939* (Manchester: Manchester University Press, 1988); R. W. Ryddell, *All the World's a Fair: Visions of Empire at American International Expositions, 1876–1916* (Chicago: Chicago University Press, 1984).

14. See A. Easthope, *British Post-Structuralism since 1968*, 2nd edn (London: Routledge, 1991); K. Jenkins, *Rethinking History* (London: Routledge, 1991); J. Appleby, L. Hunt and M. Jacob, *Telling the Truth about History* (New York: Norton, 1994). For an excellent, trenchant critique, see G. Himmelfarb, 'Telling It As You Like It: Postmodernist History and the Flight from Fact', *Times Literary Supplement*, 16 October 1992, pp. 12–15, and D. C. Watt's letter to the editor, *Times Literary Supplement*, 30 October 1992, p. 15.

15. J. M. Black, *British Foreign Policy in an Age of Revolutions, 1783–1793* (Cambridge: Cambridge University Press, 1994), pp. 472–518; H. W. C. Davis, *The Age of*

Grey and Peel (Oxford: Clarendon, 1929); M. Swartz, *The Politics of British Foreign Policy in the Era of Disraeli and Gladstone* (London: Macmillan, 1985); J. Charmley, *Splendid Isolation? Britain and the Balance of Power, 1874–1914* (London: Hodder and Stoughton, 1999), pp. 398–401; A. J. P. Taylor, *The Trouble-Makers: Dissent over Foreign Policy, 1792–1939* (London: Hamish Hamilton, 1957); R. Vickers, *The Labour Party and the World: The Evolution of Labour's Foreign Policy, 1900–1951* (Manchester: Manchester University Press, 2003); M. Ceadel, *Semi-Detached Idealists: The British Peace Movement and International Relations, 1854–1945* (Oxford: Oxford University Press, 2002); P. Laity, *The British Peace Movement, 1870–1914* (Oxford: Clarendon, 2001).

16. G. M. Young, *Victorian England: Portrait of an Age* (Oxford: Oxford University Press, 1936), p. 103.

17. G. W. F. Hegel, *Elements of the Philosophy of Right*, ed. by A. W. Wood and trans. by H. B. Nisbet (Cambridge: Cambridge University Press, 1991), p. 367; cf. F. Rosenzweig, *Hegel und der Staat,* 2 vols (Munich: Oldenbourg, 1920), vol. 2, pp. 172–5.

18. H. Bull, *The Anarchical Society: A Study of Order in World Politics* (London: Macmillan, 1977), pp. 8–16.

19. C. von Clausewitz, *Vom Kriege*, 19th edn, ed. by W. Hahlweg (Bonn: Ferdinand Dümmler, 1980), p. 639. Significantly, however, Clausewitz denied the existence of a 'systematically governed balance of power and interests' (p. 638).

20. The main thrust of Adam Watson's argument in *The Evolution of International Society: A Comparative Historical Analysis* (London: Routledge, 1992), pp. 24–32; also R. Cohen, *On Diplomacy in the Ancient Near East: The Amarna Letters* (Leicester: Leicester University Press, 1995).

21. D. J. Hill, *A History of Diplomacy in the International Development of Europe*, 3 vols (London: Longman, 1906–14), vol. 2, pp. 604–7; D. McKay and H. M. Scott, *The Rise of the Great Powers, 1648–1815* (London: Longman, 1983), pp. 1–6.

22. F. H. Hinsley, *Power and the Pursuit of Peace: Theory and Practice in the History of Relations between States* (Cambridge: Cambridge University Press, 1963); C. Holbraad, *The Concert of Europe: A Study of German and British International Theory, 1815–1914* (London: Longman, 1970).

23. P. W. Schroeder, '"System" and Systemic Thinking in International History', *International History Review*, 15 (1) (1993) 128; and also his eloquent appraisal of the Vienna settlement in P. W. Schroeder, *The Transformation of European Politics, 1763–1848* (Oxford: Clarendon, 1994), pp. 575–82.

24. Still the best general account is W. E. Mosse, *The Rise and Fall of the Crimean System, 1855–1871: The Story of a Peace Settlement* (London: Macmillan, 1963); see also the recent excellent study by D. Wetzel, *A Duel of Giants: Bismarck, Napoleon III and the Origins of the Franco-Prussian War* (Madison, WI: Wisconsin University Press, 2001).

25. M. Wight, *Power Politics*, 2nd edn, ed. by H. Bull and C. Holbraad (London: Penguin, 1986), *passim*.

26. For a useful survey, see R. Jervis, 'Systems Theories and Diplomatic History', in P. G. Lauren (ed.), *Diplomacy: New Approaches in History, Theory, and Policy* (New York: Free Press, 1979), pp. 212–44.

27. Craig, 'Study of International Relations', 9.

28. C. Thorne, *Border Crossings: Studies in International History* (Oxford: Blackwell, 1988), p. 12; C. Thorne, *The Far Eastern War: States and Societies 1941–45*, pbk edn (London: Unwin, 1986), p. xxii.

29. A. L. George, 'Case Studies and Theory Development: The Method of Structured Focused Comparison', in Lauren, *Diplomacy*, pp. 43–68.

30. A. L. George and R. Smoke, *Deterrence in American Foreign Policy: Theory and Practice* (New York: Columbia University Press, 1974); A. L. George, *Forceful Persuasion: Coercive Diplomacy as an Alternative to War* (Washington, DC: United States Institute of Peace Research, 1991); also T. G. Otte, 'Of Congresses and Gunboats: Military Intervention in the Nineteenth Century', in T. G. Otte and A. M. Dorman (eds), *Military Intervention: From Gunboat Diplomacy to Humanitarian Intervention* (Aldershot: Dartmouth, 1995), pp. 19–52.

31. G. A. Craig and A. L. George, *Force and Statecraft: Diplomatic Problems of Our Time* (New York: Oxford University Press, 1983).

32. S. M. Lynn-Jones, 'Détente and Deterrence: Anglo-German Relations, 1911–1914', in S. E. Miller *et al.* (eds), *Military Strategy and the Origins of the First World War*, rev. edn (Princeton, NJ: Princeton University Press, 1991), pp. 165–94; M. Trachtenberg, *History and Strategy* (Princeton, NJ: Princeton University Press, 1991), pp. 47–99; also N. Choucri and R. C. North, *Nations in Conflict: National Growth and International Violence* (San Francisco: W. H. Freeman, 1974).

33. J. S. Levy, 'Preferences, Constraints and Choices in July 1914', in Miller *et al.*, *Military Strategy*, pp. 195–225; L. L. Farrar, 'The Limits of Choice: July 1914 Reconsidered', *Journal of Conflict Resolution*, 16 (1) (1972) 1–23; T. J. Christensen and J. Snyder, 'Chain Gangs and Passed Bucks: Predicting Alliance Patterns in Multipolarity', *International Organization*, 44 (2) (1990) 137–68; P. M. Kennedy, 'The First World War and the International Power System', *International Security*, 9 (1) (1984) 7–40.

34. For example, S. Pelz, 'On Systematic Explanation in International History', *International History Review*, 12 (4) (1991) 762–81.

35. See G. R. Elton's pertinent, though perhaps rather rejectionist, warning in his *Return to Essentials: Some Reflections on the Present State of Historical Study* (Cambridge: Cambridge University Press, 1991), pp. 62–3.

36. P. M. Kennedy, *The Rise and Fall of the Great Powers: Economic Change and Military Conflict from 1500 to 2000*, pbk edn (London: Fontana, 1989), p. xv; P. M. Kennedy, *The Realities behind Diplomacy: Background Influences on British External Policy, 1865–1980* (London: Allen and Unwin, 1981). Kennedy's arguments reflect the *malaise anglaise* of the 1970s and early 1980s: one review of the latter book was revealingly, though probably inadvertently, entitled 'Sunset glow' (*The Economist*, 28 March 1981, p. 108).

37. H. Feis, *Europe, the World's Banker: An Account of European Foreign Investments and the Connection of World Finance with Diplomacy before World War I*, pbk edn (New York: Norton, 1965), pp. 382–90; R. Carr, *Spain, 1808–1975*, 2nd edn (Oxford: Oxford University Press, 1982), pp. 306–42; and recently C. A. Bayly, *The Birth of the Modern World, 1780–1914: Global Connections and Comparisons* (Oxford: Blackwell, 2004).

38. A. R. Tyrner-Tyrnauer, *Lincoln and the Emperors* (London: Rupert Hart-Davis, 1962).

39. For details, see K. Neilson, *Britain and the Last Tsar: British Policy and Russia, 1894–1917* (Oxford: Clarendon, 1995), pp. 189–97.

40. D. Stevenson, *Armaments and the Coming of War: Europe, 1904–1914* (Oxford: Clarendon, 1996). The classic study of arms races is still H. Bull, *The Control of the Arms Race* (London: Weidenfeld and Nicolson, 1961).

41. See J. T. Sumida and D. A. Rosenberg, 'Machines, Men, Manufacturing, Management and Money: The Study of Navies as Complex Organizations and the Transformation of Twentieth Century Naval History', in J. B. Hattendorf (ed.), *Doing Naval History: Essays towards Improvement* (Newport, RI: Naval War College Press, 1995), pp. 25–40; J. R. Ferris, *Men, Money and Diplomacy: The Evolution of British Strategic Policy, 1919–26* (Ithaca, NY: Cornell University Press, 1989); Trachtenberg, *History and Strategy*, esp. pp. 261–84. For an excellent recent study of nuclear problems in bilateral relations, see C. A. Pagedas, *Anglo-American Strategic Relations and the French Problem: A Troubled Partnership* (London: Frank Cass, 2000).

42. T. G. Otte, '"It's What Made Britain Great": Reflections on British Foreign Policy from Malplaquet to Maastricht', in T. G. Otte (ed.), *The Makers of British Foreign Policy: From Pitt to Thatcher* (New York: Palgrave, 2002), pp. 11–12. On the distinction between 'hard' and 'soft' power, see J. S. Nye Jr, *Bound to Lead: The Changing Nature of American Power* (New York: Basic Books, 1991), pp. 188–201, though Nye's analysis does not include diplomacy.

43. E. M. Satow, *A Guide to Diplomatic Practice,* 2 vols (London: Longman, 1917), vol. 1, p. 1; cf. T. G. Otte, 'Satow', in G. R. Berridge *et al.* (eds), *Diplomatic Theory from Machiavelli to Kissinger* (New York: Palgrave, 2001), pp. 125–50.

44. Sir R. Rodd, *Diplomacy* (London: Ernest Benn, 1929), p. 9.

45. H. Nicolson, *Peacemaking 1919* (London: Constable, 1933), p. 4; cf. T. G. Otte, 'Nicolson', in Berridge *et al.*, *Diplomatic Theory*, pp. 151–80.

46. D. P. Heatley, *Diplomacy and the Study of International Relations* (Oxford: Clarendon, 1919), pp. 4–5, 86–7.

47. Z. S. Steiner, *The Foreign Office and British Foreign Policy, 1898–1914* (Cambridge: Cambridge University Press, 1969), pp. 114–18; T. G. Otte, 'Eyre Crowe and British Foreign Policy: A Cognitive Map', in T. G. Otte and C. A. Pagedas (eds), *Personalities, War and Diplomacy: Essays in International History* (London: Frank Cass, 1996), pp. 14–37.

48. I. Kirkpatrick, *The Inner Circle: Memoirs* (London: Macmillan, 1959), p. x.

49. Memorandum by Sir T. Sanderson, 'Observations on the Use and Abuse of Red Tape for the Juniors in the Eastern, Western, and American Departments' (private), October 1891, Foreign and Commonwealth Office Library.

50. For general discussions of this topic, see G. Sutherland (ed.), *Studies in the Growth of Nineteenth-Century Government* (London: Routledge and Kegan Paul, 1972); V. Cromwell, *Revolution or Evolution? British Government in the Nineteenth Century* (London: Longman, 1977).

51. Exemplary studies include Steiner, *Foreign Office*; E. Maisel, *The Foreign Office and Foreign Policy, 1919–1926* (Brighton: Sussex University Press, 1994); and J. M. Black, *British Diplomats and Diplomacy, 1688–1800* (Exeter: Exeter University Press, 2001). More limited in scope, but nevertheless illuminating, is J. Fisher, 'The Interdepartmental Committee on Eastern Unrest and British Responses to Bolshevik and Other Intrigues against the Empire during the 1920s', *Journal of Asian History*, 34 (1) (2000) 1–34.

52. T. G. Otte, 'Old Diplomacy: Reflections on the Foreign Office before 1914', in G. Johnson (ed.), *The Foreign Office and British Diplomacy in the Twentieth Century* (London: Frank Cass, 2004), pp. 31–52. For an instructive sociological study, see N. Stehrs, *Knowledge Societies* (London: Sage, 1994), pp. 91–119.

53. H. Nicolson, 'Marginal Comment', *The Spectator*, 25 August 1950, p. 239.

54. H. Nicolson, *The Congress of Vienna: A Study in Allied Unity, 1812–1822* (London: Constable, 1946), p. 164.

55. For a general treatment of the cultural aspects, see A. B. Bozeman, *Politics and Culture in International History*, 2nd edn (New Brunswick: Transaction, 1994).

56. J. Hotman, quoted in P. Renouvin and J.-B. Duroselle, *Introduction à l'histoire des relations internationales* (Paris: Colin, 1964), p. 311.

57. Craig, 'Study of International Relations', 5.

58. G. R. Elton, *Political History: Principles and Practice* (London: Allen Lane, 1970), p. 21.

59. Craig, 'Political History', 327.

60. Elton, *Political History*, pp. 14–15; the sentiment is implicit also in Steiner, 'On Writing International History', 536–7.

61. Steiner, 'On Writing International History', 536–7.

62. D. C. Watt, *Personalities and Politics: Studies in the Formulation of British Foreign Policy in the Twentieth Century* (London: Longman, 1965), esp. pp. 1–15.

63. See the penetrating analysis of the British foreign policy elite and its role in Anglo-Russian relations before 1917, which has implications for the wider field of international history, in Neilson, *Last Tsar*, pp. 3–83. For studies of the diplomatic apparatus of other powers, see J. Baillou (ed.), *Les Affaires Étrangères et le corps diplomatique français*, 2 vols (Paris: Éditions du Centre Nationale de la Recherche Scientifique, 1984); L. Cecil, *The German Diplomatic Corps, 1871–1914* (Princeton, NJ: Princeton University Press, 1976); J. A. Treichel, 'Magyars at the Ballhausplatz: A Study of the Hungarians in the Austro-Hungarian Diplomatic Service, 1906–1914', unpublished PhD dissertation (Georgetown University, 1972).

64. M. Bentley and J. Stevenson, 'Introduction', in M. Bentley and J. Stevenson (eds), *High and Low Politics in Modern Britain: Ten Studies* (Oxford: Oxford University Press, 1983), p. 1.

65. Otte, 'Eyre Crowe', pp. 14–16; A. K. Henrikson, 'The Geographical "Mental Maps" of American Foreign Policy Makers', *International Political Science Review*, 1 (4) (1980) 498–500.

66. J. Joll, '1914: The Unspoken Assumptions', in H. W. Koch (ed.), *The Origins of the First World War: Great Power Rivalries and German War Aims* (London: Macmillan, 1972), pp. 309–10.

67. H. A. Kissinger, *White House Years* (Boston, MA: Little Brown, 1978), p. 54.

68. Anon., *Foreign Office, Diplomatic and Consular Sketches* (London: W. H. Allen, 1883), p. 3. The phrase is usually attributed to Harold Nicolson who used it in a House of Commons debate in November 1938.

69. I am following K. T. Hoppen's definition in *The Mid-Victorian Generation, 1846–1886* (Oxford: Oxford University Press, 1998), pp. 91–2.

70. The seminal text for all such studies is Karl Mannheim's essay on political generations in his *Wissenssoziologie*, ed. by K. H. Wolff (Frankfurt: Luchterhand,

1964), pp. 509–65. For a useful summary, see R. Wohl, *The Generation of 1914* (London: Weidenfeld and Nicolson, 1980), pp. 42–84.

71. Wohl, *Generation of 1914*, p. 81.

72. See my discussion of the problem in T. G. Otte, 'A Question of Leadership: Lord Salisbury, the Unionist Cabinet and Foreign Policy-Making, 1895–1900', *Contemporary British History*, 14 (4) (2000) 1–26; also Neilson, *Last Tsar*, pp. 48–50.

73. D. C. Watt, *Succeeding John Bull: America in Britain's Place, 1900–1975* (Cambridge: Cambridge University Press, 1984), pp. 25–6.

74. B. Russell, *Freedom and Organization, 1814–1914* (London: Allen and Unwin, 1934), pp. 7–8. On the relevance of 'incidents', see K. Neilson, '"Incidents" and Foreign Policy: A Case Study', *Diplomacy and Statecraft*, 9 (1) (1998) esp. 81–2.

75. G. A. Craig, 'On the Pleasure of Reading Diplomatic Correspondence', *Journal of Contemporary History*, 26 (3–4) (1991) 369–84; A. Cassels, 'Diplomats in an Age of Alien Ideologies and Bureaucratization', *International History Review*, 9 (4) (1987) 612–20.

76. On the hermeneutical problems of interpretation the key text remains H.-G. Gadamer, *Wahrheit und Methode*, 3rd edn (Tübingen: J. C. B. Mohr, 1972), pp. 256–84.

77. G. Martel, *Imperial Diplomacy: Rosebery and the Failure of Foreign Policy* (Montreal: McGill-Queen's University Press, 1986), p. ix.

78. Schroeder, '"System" and Systemic Thinking', 134.

2
power, strategy, armed forces and war

john ferris

This is a golden age for military history. Fifty years ago, the discipline had strength in official agencies and the popular market but stood in an academic ghetto. Soon, it became even less fashionable and many academics still view it as suspect. These experiences have made military historians defensive and fearful of marginalisation, yet in fact their status has risen sharply. They retain their professional audience, rank among the largest components of popular history, and have bolstered their academic base. There are more military historians today than ever before, and more good ones whose works are mature in theory and practice. New areas of the field, such as airpower history, have been established and older ones, like naval history, have been reborn. All branches of military history are significant to international history and one of them, strategic history, is fundamental to it. This chapter will assess the field, its literature, and its place in international history.

the terrain of military history

Military history has no canonical texts. The closest approximations to foundational works are those of Clausewitz and Liddell Hart, which are actually studies of strategy informed by history. Few now read the pioneering works of academic military history by Hans Delbrück or Julian Corbett.[1] Equally, outstanding modern studies tend to be seen as inspirations rather than models to be slavishly followed. Debates among specialists abound – such as that about the quality of Anglo-American and German armies in the Second World War – but the field as a whole is not dominated by any one controversy. Military historians debated the idea of the 'military revolution' largely just to prove that they could, and hence that they were really properly academic.[2] The discipline is a loose coalition of sub-disciplines, primarily national (for example, German) and thematic (for example, war and society) in nature, and bound together by a focus on power, strategy, armed forces and war, on ideas about these matters and the human experience with them. These preoccupations clearly resemble those of international and diplomatic history, International Relations and strategic studies. Yet compared to these sister fields, military history focuses more on how force is embodied and exercised. As links to these cognate disciplines enrich military history, so too do links to policy-makers. Many military historians work in service academies or for official agencies in which historical understanding guides the formulation of policy. The influence cuts both ways: since the 1980s the concerns of military institutions about doctrine, intelligence, operational art, and the revolution in military affairs have profoundly shaped scholarly research and writing.[3]

Military historians are divided into roughly equal groups of independent scholars, academics, and government officers. This balance provides enough variety in training and employment to prevent stagnation or strangulation, and to maintain a balance between creativity, scholarship and relevance. In no other field of history save local history do non-academics have such significance; thus a journalist wrote the most influential modern work of military history.[4] The field is most powerful in the English-speaking world – here, the Commonwealth remains a great power. Australia, Canada and Israel exert remarkable influence, and the discipline holds its own in Germany, France and Russia, though it remains weaker in Italy and Japan. It consists not of one international literature, but of multiple national ones, isolated from each other in striking ways. Judging from citations, English-language historians scarcely read leading French and German military journals, and vice versa. But if the Anglophone school thus suffers from a certain Anglocentrism, it nonetheless still pays considerable attention to the history and archives of other nations. The field is as multi-archival, multi-linguistic and comparative as any other branch of history, and more so than international history where most leading journals focus on 'national' international histories or a narrow range of topics. Though neither its practitioners nor detractors would like to admit it, military history can also be rather politically correct.

At the heart of war is combat. It is therefore scarcely surprising that studies of campaigns and the human experience of war remain central to military history. But neither battles nor generals using armies in a rational-instrumental fashion are the whole of war. Beyond this operational literature, there are three schools that approach military history from social, intellectual and strategic angles. The first of these is a new sub-discipline that emerged in the 1960s and which studies the relationship between war and societies: how peoples affect and are affected by armed forces and their struggles. To students of war and society, masculinity is a military issue; a characteristic topic might be Japanese attitudes toward death in battle, and how these stemmed from culture and state policy.[5] War and society is a politicized field. Some military historians advocate it to legitimize their presence in academe; their critics see it as a threat to 'real' military history. The second strand, which has been central to academic military history, comprises works of intellectual history, exploring, for example, the extent to which armies performed poorly because they thought that way. Recently, the American military's emphasis on doctrine has magnified this impulse, engendering a literature on how military services learn and incorporate knowledge into their practice.[6]

The third of these schools, strategic history, is simultaneously part of both military and international history; its practitioners come from both fields and produce works of significance to each. It is one of the most well-established and mature approaches to international history, a state of affairs that sometimes has its costs: since military muscles developed first, strategic history has militarized the study of certain other important issues within international history. Thus the literature on intelligence has tended to focus on its military role to the detriment and neglect of its diplomatic one. In any event, before 1960, when public access to archival material after 1914 was limited, diplomatic and military historians worked in separate spheres, one focusing on foreign policy in peace, the other on battles in war. These distinctions had some bearing for periods before 1914, though military and diplomatic matters were interrelated even then.[7] As the 1960s wore on, however, and scholarly attention increasingly turned to the post-1914 period, these disciplines and their documents became intrinsically linked, because power and strategy were central to them both. Strategic history examines the diplomatic role of force and the military part of foreign policy, diplomacy in war and power in peace, and the formulation of what is sometimes called strategic foreign policy. It has many foci, and these include: the nature, and the balance, of power, and how shifts in its reality and image affect international politics; how intelligence and perceptions shape behaviour; how states choose between strategies and interests and how they formulate policy and harmonize the economic, military and diplomatic components of power; what force cannot do and what war is good for.

power and armed force

Power is central to military and international history, but until recently it received little systematic study. It is a complex matter, including everything from diplomatic influence to the strength a state can deploy in total war.[8] One may divide the fundamentals of power into material, administrative and ideational factors. The first includes geography, demography and economy. The second includes the administrative capacity and the political structure of a state – its ability to command a population and tap their resources; the quality of its institutions of government; and the attitudes of the people who make its decisions. The third includes everything that shapes the image of a state in the outside world. These elements of power are linked dialectically. The relationship between the first two converts material power from crude to finished form – from demographic and economic resources to military forces. The first determines the potential power of a state, the second how much of it can be tapped, and how well. Perception complicates these concrete factors: if the reality of power governs the course of war, its image determines that of peace. A weak state which others think strong and do not challenge will be strong; a strong nation which others view as weak may thus eventually become so. The perception of power is a source of weakness or strength, and the prestige of a state reflects power, and sustains it.

The nature of power is distorted whenever any of its parts receives credit for the whole, a mistake often made by those defining economic factors as its core.[9] Power is an alloy, formed from the interaction of many elements, each of which is necessary to the whole, none of which are sufficient for it. Consider the role of geography. Between the 1860s and the 1930s, Europe was the centre of world politics and a weak state there could affect the world more than a strong one elsewhere: hence while the United States between 1890 and 1939 possessed the world's strongest economy, it yet barely matched the diplomatic importance of Italy. Similarly, the Japanese economy ranked only alongside that of Italy among the great powers, yet because Japan was the only industrialized state in East Asia, 6000 miles from the nearest other centre of industrial power, the strategic value of the Japanese economy within its region was magnified considerably. Overwhelming strength in one element of power may not a great power make, nor weakness in one destroy it. A poor state may remain a great power because of the size and skill of its armed forces, its geographical position, the stability of its political institutions, or the ability of its statesmen; such was the case with Prussia between 1740 and 1866 and Japan between 1900 and 1941. A rich state may not convert its wealth to power, and so will matter less in world affairs than it might otherwise have done: namely, the Netherlands between 1715 and 1789, Great Britain from 1830 to 1880, and Japan and most Western European states since 1960. Rich states rarely tap their resources systematically for strategic purposes, which bolsters the position of anyone willing to do so, rich or not. In power, resolve matters more than wealth.

Power is not an abstract quality but a concrete one; what is significant are the resources that a state mobilizes for strategic ends, rather than those that it possesses but never brings actively into the equation. It is both an absolute and a comparative matter, since one's own power is weighed against that of one's competitor(s). It takes different forms in, respectively, normal diplomacy, a short campaign between two countries, or a prolonged and total war of attrition involving most members of a state system. Usually, institutions have been the central factor here, because it is they that transmute raw into refined power – a hard task, in which marginal superiority can have great results. For most of history, a state able to jump from tapping 1 per cent of its potential power to 2 per cent might thereby double its military capacity. In 1509, Venice fought every other state of Italy, Spain and Germany, as Britain fought in 1782 against half of Europe and its American colonists. Venice and Britain were defeated in these wars, but their institutional superiority was nonetheless remarkable and it was striking how little they lost and how much they held. Institutional power stems from odd things. In the 1500s, Turkey created the world's best infantry – the janissaries – out of slaves recruited from its Christian population through a boy tax. Between 1670 and 1790, the Netherlands and Britain alone on earth possessed stock markets and national banks, and thus could tap their economic resources for strategic purposes better than France and Spain, which were comparable in terms of raw gross domestic product (GDP). In the great wars of the twentieth century, however, the relative value of institutional superiority declined because many states achieved a high level of quality at that level, reducing the comparative advantage it offered. In these circumstances, what mattered most was the scale of resources: the richer a state, the more powerful it would be.

When refined, raw power becomes armed forces, which have often been remarkably small in size as well as hard to maintain. At certain times, states have regularly fielded hundreds of thousands of soldiers (in China between 453 and 221 BCE; in the Mediterranean basin between 330 BCE and 380 CE; in Europe between 1660 and 1870) and in the twentieth century even millions of them. Yet these periods are unusual. In classical Greece, armies usually comprised fewer than 15 000 men and rarely more than 50 000; the same was true in Europe from 380 to 1660, or with the European empires of the nineteenth century where relatively few soldiers conquered and held vast tracts of territory. Since 1989, armies have again slipped in size: the greatest power on earth can now barely send 200 000 soldiers beyond its borders.

Navies have traditionally been even smaller and a rich man's weapon, because (like air forces) they are highly dependent on wealth and advanced industry. Expensive to build and to keep battle worthy, in antiquity wealthy powers alone could afford great navies, and then only with private help; thus Athens and Rhodes made their captains pay to maintain their vessels. Fleets vanish without a regular programme of shipbuilding and the political will to perpetuate naval power. When Carthage destroyed the Roman fleet in 249 BCE it decommissioned its own, only to be beaten when Rome raised a new navy through forced loans from its citizens. Repeatedly, states have built great fleets only subsequently to let them rot: this happened with the Hellenistic empires and with Rome in antiquity, and then with China in the 1400s, Turkey and Spain in the 1600s, and the Netherlands in the 1700s. Few states have maintained a large navy for long, and these have commanded the seas as armies rarely have the land. The Royal Navy ruled the waves less through the qualities of its steel-eyed captains and jolly tars than through its sound organization, regular procurement and the willingness to outspend any threat.[10] Sea power is the child of both wealth and resolve.

Military power has social roots, many forms, and a competitive nature – what matters is how one's own system compares to the enemy's in specific circumstances, and the possible permutations are almost endless. Numbers and technology matter, but not enough to guarantee victory every time. A belligerent willing to take heavy losses without surrendering can beat one with high technology and low willpower. Yet on other occasions, a technological edge can deliver decisive results. Politics can defeat firepower, and vice versa. Small elite forces sometimes crush large half trained ones, and sometimes they do not. Three examples will illustrate these themes, and others.

First, consider the case of Sparta.[11] Between 550 and 370 BCE, Spartan society was both savage and inefficient. The military elite, the Spartiates, lived with their comrades in military messes, defined both by birth and wealth – their status vanished if they could not pay high mess bills. The Spartiates were a small proportion of the population, but could devote their lives to war because they lived off the enslaved bulk of it, the helots. (Any serious defeat might produce a helot revolt, which would threaten the livelihood of the Spartiates and their society.) Sparta consequently produced very good soldiers, but only in very small numbers. By normal Greek standards in 371 BCE it should have had 30 000 infantrymen; instead, it had just 6500, comprised of 1500 Spartiates and 5000 allied freeman. This deficit stemmed not from battle losses but from the elitist nature of Spartan society. Moreover, over the centuries property fell into ever fewer hands and fewer males could remain Spartiates: their numbers had fallen to 1500 in 371 BCE from 5000 in 479 BCE. Demographic weakness often compelled Sparta to take the greatest risk of all – to free and arm helots. Despite the excellence of its soldiers, its power consequently rested on a knife-edge. Spartan policy was paralysed in the 420s and the 360s BCE simply because the enemy held 100 Spartiates prisoner. By killing 400 Spartiates at Leuctra in 371 BCE, Thebes shattered Spartan power.

Diplomatic strength had long countered some of this demographic weakness. Between 530 and 370 BCE, through control of the Peloponnesian League, Sparta usually managed to raise the largest army in Greece. Spartans rarely made up even 33 per cent of the Peloponnesian host, and sometimes comprised just 10 per cent of it, but their allies' strength made up for their own weakness. Even more, for centuries Spartiates, as the only trained soldiers in Greece, exploited the habits of their amateur neighbours. Hoplites tended to veer to their right as they advanced, each sheltering his spear arm in his neighbour's shield. Spartans exaggerated this move, concentrating their mass against the enemy left flank, and then wheeling as a line to strike the enemies' centre on its unprotected side. This simple tactic, successful for so long because Greek armies were so primitive, could in fact easily be countered. During the 370s and 360s BCE Theban phalanxes did so by adopting a deep oblique formation, led by a trained elite, the Sacred Band. They held back the right edge of their line and threw their weight to the left, so striking the Spartan right long before the main fronts collided. These tactics were also a form of politics by other means. Thebes avoided battle with Sparta's allies. Its forces swung like a hammer against the right flank of Spartan-led phalanxes, against a few, outnumbered and quickly overwhelmed Spartiates. Before most members of either phalanx met, the fight was over.

The armies of nineteenth-century Europe and beyond offer a second example. During this period, European armies had a crushing superiority over non-Western ones because, for centuries, their states had regularly fought major wars against each other. Only the strongest survived in a constant competition to improve military effectiveness and efficiency. This end defined state finances, administration and politics. Compromises between monarchs and nobles produced things unique to Europe: states that maintained the largest and best armies they could afford, controlled by an able but loyal officer corps. European states became the most militarized and militarily effective on earth.

If they wanted to match the foundations of Western power, non-Western states had to undergo a revolution. In Europe, countries could maintain large armies without threatening their own existence and could become stronger simply by raising more revenues and regiments. Elsewhere, raising taxes precipitated crises and strengthening armies weakened the state. Old armies were ossified, and often they had to be destroyed before new ones could be formed. Thus in 1807 the now decadent janissaries killed the sultan who sought to discipline them; his successor slaughtered the janissaries in 1826 when they again preferred revolt to reform. Asian nations could Westernize their armies only if they made that aim fundamental, but they struggled to survive the crises that modernization caused. Westernization strained their financial and administrative systems and threatened to generate popular discontent, even revolt. Yet more problematic was the issue of military and political command. Westernization must fail unless it produced a large and able officer corps that would control the armed forces; yet such a body could potentially overthrow its political masters. In every case of attempted Westernization, the officer corps were for long periods incompetent, disloyal or both, with one exception – Japan, where Westernization followed a revolution and officers were selected for loyalty to a regime. Sooner or later, however, every Westernizing officer corps overthrew the regime that created it, including the Japanese army in the 1930s.[12]

Modern Israel provides a third instructive example. The secret of Israel's battlefield success has been military administrative techniques like conscription and an efficient and quickly mobilized reserve, something that its neighbours do not possess. The Jews of Israel are outnumbered 20 to 1 by the populations of Egypt, Syria and Jordan, but unlike them Israel can tap its population to fight a total war for a week. Largely because of its hair-trigger readiness to start wars whenever it regards itself as in peril, Israel has usually outnumbered its enemies on the battlefield. (Notably, it has done least well in wars of attrition against resolute guerrillas.) Israel's military is a national and professional force, composed of well-educated citizens able to handle modern weapons, and pursuing a strategy of annihilation with only one goal in mind: winning wars for its people, who have feared that defeat might produce a national holocaust. Israeli forces have looked so good chiefly because their enemies have been so poor. Arab armies have been intensely politicized: their fundamental aim has been not to serve a people or to win wars but to keep a regime in power. Those regimes have tapped the resources of only part of their population, namely that which is deemed politically reliable: virtually all Syrian officers stem from the Alawite sect, numbering only 10 per cent of Syria's population, just as those of Iraq under Saddam Hussein predominantly came from his own clan. This cripples the power of Arab armies. Few Arab resources have been used in war, whereas most Israeli ones have. Arab regimes prefer to lose a war rather than their army, since losing the latter might destroy their control over their populations and cause their political, even physical, extinction.[13]

Armed forces are central institutions in any state, and they both reflect societies and change them. Their maintenance bankrupts governments, subverts political systems and shapes economies. Industry has long been militarized and war industrialized. Until 1945, naval construction was the greatest form of economic activity on earth, requiring large numbers of dockyards, work crews and factories, and free access to huge supplies of raw materials. From 1840, military production became the driver of industrialization, and after 1945 military needs spurred the rise of the civil aviation and computer industries. Equally, the spread of universal male conscription for military service was a central event in nineteenth-century European history. In the eighteenth century few governments could tax their populations; a century later many could make all of their men fight and risk death for them. The spread of conscription was related to the rise of the state, to the emergence of mass nationalism and its militarization, to universal literacy, and to improved public health – armies could not be effective unless conscripts could read instruction manuals, carry heavy equipment, and regard themselves as expendable tools of the nation-state.[14]

Armies are not just instruments of state, entirely dedicated to securing victory in war with foreign enemies. For one thing, war and armed force have ritual as well as rational elements; these often clash and sometimes the former prevails.[15] Armies are also required to maintain a domestic political order. Even when the Anglo-American ideal of a depoliticized military prevails, this simply means that the army supports a regime rather than a party. Most states maintain civil supremacy over military forces most of the time, but many armies intervene routinely in politics. In twentieth century Latin America and the Middle East, soldiers typically saw themselves as watchdogs over constitution and Christianity, or nationalism and modernization. Armies, alas, are not great nation builders, and when they come to dominate a state its political life will degenerate; if coups become the currency of politics, bad coin usually drives out good. The politicization of armies also damages their combat quality, since regimes often promote their loyalists at the cost of efficiency. In the 1960s, politics in Syria and South Vietnam were chaotic and the combat quality of their armies abysmal, for generals dared not risk the commands that were their political power bases in war. In the worst case, armies can become their own masters, *mafiosi* rather than soldiers, while war ceases to be a tool to achieve ends but becomes rather a business and a way of life.

strategy

Yet armed forces usually are tools of policy, and strategy multiplies their effect. The study of strategy – the rational-instrumental use of power – is central to military history, and vice versa. Corbett helped found the discipline of military history and was himself an original strategist, especially of sea power. Delbrück pioneered the division of strategy into two types: the pursuit of decision, or attrition. After 1945, military history was shaped by Basil Liddell Hart's arguments for the superiority of unconventional uses of force, particularly the 'indirect approach', and by the revival of interest in the greatest theorists of strategy, Clausewitz and Sun Tzu.[16] Scholars differ over whether (and how far) strategy involves universal principles about the use of force or is a social construct. The greatest contemporary work on strategy denies that Clausewitz and Sun Tzu advanced contradictory theories. Instead, Michael Handel holds, their arguments were directed at different levels of analysis – Clausewitz mostly operational, Sun Tzu strategic – but when like is compared to like, the two generally agree. So do other great strategists, though their disagreements over details remain significant and indicative. These theorists add to, rather than subtracting from, each other's work. Their ideas – those about which they agree and disagree, or where one has unique insight – are the corpus of strategic thought. The logic of power and war and strategy is timeless, not culture-bound, as relevant today as ever.[17]

At the same time, states do approach strategy in different ways, with varying emphasis on aggression, uncertainty, cost, and risk. This leads to the idea of strategic cultures and of national 'ways of war'.[18] The term 'culture' is vague, however, while it is easy to overgeneralize about or oversimplify strategic traditions: for example, by assuming that the views on strategy of Sun Tzu and Mao Zedong are identical and that they represent every member of a coherent strategic tradition, governing all Chinese practice and distinct from that of all others. Victor Davis Hanson claims there is a uniquely 'Western' way of war, with its armies always focused on murderous high intensity battles. Alastair Johnston, a leading modern student of classical Chinese strategists, retorts that all of them except Sun Tzu regarded ferocious battles as normal, while their armies fought them. For similar reasons, John Lynn rejects the concept of 'Eastern' or 'Western' ways of war. Carefully defined, however, the concept of strategic culture can illuminate the way states use power. If a group maintains the same body of ideas about force and interests, and the same conditions of power and enemies, for long periods of time, it may define the same range of options and make similar choices among them, create institutions of specific character and quality, use them in distinct ways, and follow a strategic style – playing for a long game of attrition, for example, as against immediate knockout. Even so, these national 'ways of war' will have variants and they will end when the circumstances do. Between 1700 and 1945, neither Britain nor Prussia-Germany always used their stereotypical 'ways of war', and these ceased to exist when their strategic positions were transformed after 1945.[19]

Strategy is paradoxical. It is a universal way to use force to achieve aims, but ends and means are human constructs. It is a competition between wills with power and freedom, whose weapons and ambitions clash in a realm of uncertainty. Strategy defines many ways to achieve ends, sometimes mutually exclusive, any one of which may defeat another, depending on circumstances, your own choices, those of the enemy, and the nature of the game. What you can do varies with the rules and pieces; strategy is illuminated by the consideration of games theory, or games like chess, poker and hearts. There are principles of strategy, but the trick is knowing how and when to apply them. Its basic aims are to play to your strengths and not to your weaknesses; higher goals are to shelter your weaknesses behind your strengths and to attack the enemy's weaknesses with your strengths; its highest forms are to turn your weaknesses into strengths, and the enemy's strengths into weaknesses. If you are strong and the enemy weak, you may press it to decisive battle, which it will seek to evade; if you wish to manage risk and uncertainty, you may prefer a strategy of attrition; if you feel yourself at a peak of strength which must decline, you may prefer a high risk/high gains approach; perhaps you can do what you want to do, perhaps the enemy may impose its will on you. The point of strategy is not just to know how to fight a war; but to know when and how not to do so. At its highest levels strategy links military and diplomatic matters, where it takes new forms, as in the dictum popularly attributed to Lloyd George: 'What you can't square, you squash; and what you can't squash, you square.' War is a high stakes and zero-sum game between two parties, where both pay a heavy price to play and one can win only if the other loses. This may be true at times of diplomacy, but usually in multilateral relations stalemate or mutual benefit are also possible outcomes. In diplomacy, force is used on a spectrum ranging from unspoken power to deterrence to coercion and then war, and these are all different games. Armed forces are pieces with different value when used to deter wars rather than to fight them.

One can apply strategy well only if one knows which games are being played. This requires intelligence: the collection and analysis of information so as to let one use one's resources in the most effective way possible, against rivals doing the same. Intelligence is not a form of power but a means to guide its use, whether as a force multiplier or by helping one to understand one's environment and options, and how to apply force or leverage, and against whom. It shows what can be understood in the context of what cannot be known. Intelligence is a function of a complex system manned by many people. It suffers from all of the things natural to humans and complex systems, including uncertainty, friction, unachieved intentions, unintended consequences, unexpected failures and unplanned successes. A good army with bad information may beat a bad army with good intelligence. Two first-rate espionage services may neutralize each other, while mediocre intelligence may give its master a decisive advantage over an incompetent adversary. Intelligence does not necessarily let one achieve the effect one intends, for it may be counterproductive. Nor does intelligence affect diplomacy exactly as it does war. It is merely one factor in a game with many actors, where intentions and effects become tangled. In a game with five players, the best stroke possible against one rival may alarm a third and lead it to bump a fourth into deflecting one's shot – perhaps toward one's own net. Diplomatic intelligence may lead statesmen to regret specific actions that they have previously carried into effect and to favour alternative policies that were never in fact realized; it may lead them not to take certain actions at all, and this may have consequences far greater than any active stroke of policy.

Intelligence rarely affects the determination of policy, although this does happen. Frequently, it shapes the background to decisions, how statesmen perceive and learn about their environment, and very often it determines the execution of policy. It affects tactics more than strategy, bargaining more than policy formulation. Intelligence is collected through many sources, each with strengths and limits and valuable not because of their secrecy or complexity but if they provide accurate, relevant and timely information for action. Even the best sources rarely tell the whole truth and nothing but the truth. The effect of intelligence depends upon its interpretation in the context of a set of conditions that govern expectation and usability. Decision-makers can understand the world, and they do affect it. They are not mere prisoners of perception, unable to learn from error, but they are reluctant to change their minds and do tend to interpret bits of information on the basis of preconception. Nor is it ever easy to assess intelligence. Intelligence generally provides background information, masses of material, often irrelevant or of unknown accuracy, read in the light of complex patterns of preconception, unconscious or unexamined. This process is dogged by problems, such as ethnocentrism, and the tendency to project one's own way of thinking onto others, producing errors like mirror-imaging and worst-case logic.[20]

Among these problems is the influence of ideology, something it is fashionable to denigrate. A recent study of Soviet policy in 1940–41 even denies that Marxism-Leninism affected Soviet assessments or actions![21] This fashion has many founts. The triumph of liberalism has made this way of thought seem natural and all others idiotic. Liberal materialists export their ideas back to the minds of decision-makers past, making it easier to understand appeasers than anti-appeasers or revisionists. Others think interests self-evident and 'realism' the natural means to understand power: statesmen must be pure realists, and anyone who applies sentiment to diplomacy is a fool. These views are wrong. Liberalism is an ideology, 'realism' is a form of 'idealism', interests are a combination of things and ideas about them. 'Realism' is essential to assessing power and means, but it cannot define values or ends. A pure realist, aiming at power and victory for their sake alone, would be a psychopath and few statesmen are. Most of them merge realism with some idea of values, which join means to ends. The word 'realism' is a noun in search of an adjective, like 'liberal' or 'Marxist-Leninist'. Ideology inevitably affects one's views of ends, means, the rules of the game, of strategy and of power.

a strategic reading of the inter-war crisis

What strategic history has to offer international history can be illustrated by a comparison of three iterations of the modern world system. In 1815, 1919 and 1945, new orders were imposed after great wars. That of 1919 died young: why?

In 1815 and 1945, the victors were satiated by exhaustion and success. They had a preponderance of power and a common interest in restraining a great, potentially revisionist, state which had just attacked them all. So to achieve this aim and bolster the status quo, they reorganized Europe on strategic grounds. Power was so broadly based that no single event except a system-wide war could destroy its structure, while at any time most of its members accepted most of the order. Even when power shifted or alliances competed, this tension did not cause system-wide wars; indeed, in some ways it bolstered the status quo. These systems therefore absorbed challenges like those that swamped the order of 1919.[22]

The system of 1815 remained stable until 1848, then survived decades of collapsing consensus, revolution, major war and redistribution of power (Germany and Italy rose while France and Austria declined), and lived on in a radically amended form to 1914. In many ways, British strength in 1815 set buffers that let Europe remain stable for 100 years despite seismic shifts in the global distribution of power. Even the Western conquest of the world stabilized the system, by diverting the energy of some states from Europe without upsetting power there. The exception to this rule was the 'Eastern question', through which developments in Asia intermittently shook politics in Europe. During the mid nineteenth century, ideology disrupted international relations, but from 1880 the explosiveness of this mixture of conservatism, liberalism and nationalism declined, except in the Balkans. Ideology shaped the politics of European states but not European politics. Even more, all statesmen played the same game. Liberals and reactionaries agreed on its rules and assessed power accurately and similarly, reducing the number of errors in estimation, though not the significance of those which occurred. Thus in August 1914 Germany proved stronger than anyone expected, because of the interplay of war plans and the overestimation of Russian power.

Compared to this, the Cold War system was less balanced: the USSR predominated in conventional military power in Europe, while Western states did so in sea power and wealth; ideological differences were acute and misreadings of power and policy common. Yet the H-bomb meant that a system-wide war would have been mutually suicidal – indeed, no war occurred even when one of the two main alliances collapsed. The bomb forced everyone to avoid high risk strategies and to play much of the game the same way, crippled the value of conventional military power, and left the power struggle to centre on economic growth and political stability – the trump suits of the West. Since the Second World War left the United States and the USSR dominating the system and wrecked the power of European states, they could lose their empires without shaking the order, though this development reshaped Africa and Asia and caused many crises there. This system survived a revolution in power to become the basis for a new one.

Compared to those of 1815 and 1945, the 1919 system was weaker in structure, consent and power. The victors agreed far less about threats to the system and how to handle them, and controlled less of its potential power. The Great War killed some powers, wounded others, created still more, fractured the world order and left a new one to be patched together. What emerged was a fragile system under stress. The global economy was also sick, though the Great Depression was not inevitable. The structure of power was destabilized, as strength drifted to Japan and the United States from Europe, and shifted within that continent. Before 1914 the division of Eastern Europe between three empires bolstered the balance of power; the destruction of Austria-Hungary and the Russian Revolution broke it. Liberal and nationalist ideology, and the way power emerged on the ground during 1919, prevented the region from being shaped in a manner conducive to the stability of the system. Eastern Europe was divided between Germany and the USSR – both temporarily impotent – and a host of weak successor states; it no longer exerted a stabilizing influence upon the system since the Balkans extended to the Baltic. France, Italy, Germany or the USSR could easily expand into this vacuum, and upset the broader distribution of power. So too Japan with China, though only in 1940–41 did this threaten the system, as against one of its parts. Again, Germany was prostrate but retained its power and the will to it: just two years of freedom to rearm would make it the greatest military power in Europe. France dominated Western Europe, but lacked the capacity to do so for the long term.

A pendulum of power would swing over coming decades, passing many tipping points and exposing many vulnerabilities. At first, France had greater strength than she had ever had since 1812; later, Germany and Russia would become more powerful than they had been even before 1914. Far more states wished to overthrow the system than had been the case between 1815 and 1914: three major powers, several smaller ones, and factions within Japan's elite, though Japan and Italy did not actually challenge the order between 1922 and 1930. Only three great powers essentially supported the status quo, and the American return to isolationism left it actively defended by just two states that controlled only 20 per cent of the collective demographic and economic resources of the great powers; nor did France and Britain always cooperate.

Yet stability reigned during the 1920s, because liberalism was armed. Liberal powers won the war and dominated the peace. Britain, the United States and France, fairly united and heavily armed, had overwhelming military power and loosely cooperated to support the status quo. Their diplomacy clashed, but their strategies coincided. Master of the seas and Europe, their strength attracted allies, stabilized Eastern Europe, deterred threats, and bound the fractures in the world order. The revisionist powers, weak and isolated, had to play by liberal rules. Desire for revisionism occurs in most systems. Often it is part of the mechanism for survival – revisionist can be played against revisionist precisely to check revisionism. The question is whether status quo powers can deter or defeat an armed challenge to the whole system, and whether the latter can absorb radical changes without collapsing. In the 1920s, the revisionists' aims were so contradictory they could not easily cooperate, while the status quo had strength. Supported to some extent by the US and Japan, Britain and France provided a breathing space of a decade in which the fractures in the international system could heal. Power gave them the initiative in diplomacy: they were the stronger players who set the pace in most interactions – determining their nature and consequences, picking the ground and the time to fight, thrusting the burden of uncertainty and the need to make the first move in bargaining onto others, who had to guess their intentions and how to influence them. This combination helped them maintain the status quo, and modify it.

Unfortunately, this system seemed so stable that liberal internationalist statesmen felt free to revolutionize it. Their first step was to attack themselves – to weaken the military power of the status quo states, with effects that were quite unintended. Far more than between 1815 and 1914, the liberal system rested on mobilised conventional forces which substituted for weakness in the system. Hence, the order was unusually vulnerable to minor fluctuations in military strength. Between 1927 and 1934, pursuit of disarmament destroyed the liberal coalition and unleashed the revisionists. The 1930 London Naval Treaty disarmed liberalism at sea. British and American strength declined, that of Germany, Italy, France and the USSR rose, while Japan became a greater sea power but no longer a liberal one – the London Treaty sparked the explosion that impelled it towards armed revisionism. Soon, Britain pursued disarmament proposals that must wreck French power.[23] Though this aim failed, the Geneva Disarmament Conference split Britain and France, and ensnared their policies in multilateral efforts to solve all the world's problems at once. This provided Adolf Hitler with disarray to exploit. The focus on disarmament prevented liberal states from countering rearmament by revisionists. Meanwhile, the depression splintered the world economy and spurred the revisionist states toward aggression. It further eroded the armed strength of all the liberal powers, while that of every revisionist swelled. Status quo and revisionist states triggered a revolution in power. Revisionists armed and cooperated; liberals disarmed and divided. Alone, either depression or disarmament would have rocked the system, but together they wrecked it.

From 1933, the liberal order became less cohesive and strong as the beneficiaries of the status quo declined to support it or each other. The balance of power ceased to work because no one tried to make it do so: only the revisionists played power politics and they aimed to wreck the balance. They grew in strength and number – Germany, Italy, the USSR, Japan. Though the revisionists did not work closely together, when one shook the status quo, all gained. It was easier for them to shake the system than for other states to cooperate in its support. To a rare degree, last seen in Europe between 1856 and 1870, all states played a lone hand and even mere alignments were rare and weak. The system ceased to shelter its members, offering little support to any defender nor counterweight to any strength or aggression. The power of the stronger party in any bilateral relationship or the multilateral whole was multiplied, because weaker parties stood alone. That was doubly so because Hitler struck first at Central Europe, where local states were weakest and over which the powers were most divided.

The revisionists' policies could be simple – they might use the most opportunistic of tactics, pursue any bilateral relationships they wished or abandon them, wilfully manufacture incendiary situations, because they wished to destroy the system. The status quo powers did not and so their tactics were constrained and their policies were tangled. They searched for a diplomatic solution to the revisionist challenge when none existed; there was only a strategic solution, the creation of power and its use. As the liberal countries pursued their policies, they first ceded the initiative to the revisionist powers and danced to their tune, defending their own individual interests against two or three states while jettisoning those of the system, feeling themselves a vulnerable party in interactions, merely guessing at their adversaries' aims and the means to influence them. The systematic relationship between power and strategy made confusion and conflict likely. Power shifted radically away from states that supported the status quo, but then slowly back to them. They sought to rebuild their power and to deter states that had acquired a military advantage that was now in dispute or decline. The revisionist states pursued aggressive strategies involving great risks, rewards, and bluff. Minute changes in military power, perceptions or anticipations of them, dictated diplomacy: the sense of German superiority shaped the policies of Britain, France, Italy and Germany itself in 1938, as did the feeling the tide was shifting against Hitler in 1939.[24]

Decision-makers everywhere misunderstood each other's policies and power. German and Italian strength was exaggerated: that of everyone else, especially the Japanese, Soviets and Americans, underrated. Intelligence of a statistical sort on GDP or order of battle was easy to collect, but the same was not true as regards qualitative issues, or how far and fast a state could rearm. The French overestimated the size of the German army because they misconstrued the calibre of its paramilitary formations, as the British did the rate of Luftwaffe expansion and its operational doctrine because they assumed it must act like the Royal Air Force.[25] The British and French misread the evidence on the German army's operational ideas and intentions because they could not believe Germans would wish to fight in such a way or that such an approach could defeat them; the Germans did much the same with Fighter Command. The politicisation of intelligence had an ironic systematic effect. Hitler and Benito Mussolini had a more faulty perception of the relative military balance than any other statesmen. They did not understand the strength of their own forces because their underlings systematically deceived them, as well as foreigners; the Italian military misled Mussolini into exaggerating Italian strength, even though it privately overestimated French and British power![26] British and French commanders overestimated their own weaknesses and German power, which reinforced Axis miscalculations. The greatest victim of the overstatement of German power was the Axis. Mussolini and Japanese decision-makers took the decisions that ruined their countries because they believed Germany too strong to lose; so too did Hitler.

Some of these problems stemmed from ideology, and the struggle between liberal forms in Britain, France and the United States, variants of social Darwinism, militarism and racism in Italy, Germany and Japan, and Marxist-Leninist and militarist ideas in the USSR. Here the rules of the game were in dispute. Liberals conceptualized international relations as law, others as force; liberals thought war bad, others did not. When analysing the power of peoples, liberals used concepts of national and institutional character, Marxist-Leninists applied notions of economic determinism and crude class analysis, racists deployed social Darwinism and generalizations about 'races'. Power is not self-evident and people often get it wrong. Germans, Italians and Japanese fetishised willpower, assuming their races had both and that their opponents had neither; but they underrated the value of economics and organization and so misunderstood American and Soviet strength. Adolf Hitler, intellectually a mixture of social Darwinist, classical racist, Wagnerian, and vulgarized Nietzschean, assessed power in terms not of blood and iron, or gold and steel, but of race and soil. In 1940, he refused to focus on smashing Britain when it stood alone but instead chose to start a second front against the USSR because of beliefs – derived from racist theory and personal memories – that Britons were most deadly when at bay, while Russians were cattle herded by Jews into a rotten barn which would collapse with one blow.

The fundamental issue – the clash between the aims of states – would have occurred even with mutual understanding, but as it was errors about policy and ignorance of power triggered profound miscomprehension. These circumstances were deadly for people pursuing policies of bluff or deterrence and delicate forms of diplomatic manipulation and influence, which hinged on the precise delivery and comprehension of signals. Deterrence works only if one understands how other polities act, and how their leaders view the balance between you and they. Fallacious comprehension of each others' world-views clouded that understanding and deterrence failed; but so too did bluff. Statesmen viewed and played the game differently, in a dialectical and multilateral system, an atomized one, with many actors affecting each other in unpredictable ways. Statesmen thought the state system a machine where all one needed to do to create an effect was to pull a lever. In fact, the machine was baroque and broken. There were more levers to be pulled than in 1914, but with less certain outcome and more people pulling to opposite effect. People thought they knew how to get what they wanted but failed to do so, because they did not understand the system. They thought they were all playing a game with one set of rules, when each was playing a different game with the same pieces. These circumstances led to uncertainty in Paris and London and to aggression and bluff in Rome and Berlin between 1935 and 1938. They also determined the manner in which, in 1939, Germany and Britain and France and, in 1941, Germany and the USSR, and Japan and the United States and Britain, misconstrued each others' intentions and power and so entered wars of a kind none expected. Ultimately this led to the destruction of the system and the defeat of almost all its members.[27]

The Versailles system was too brittle to absorb a revolution in power, while miscalculations about policy increased the scale and frequency of clashes. Yet the Yalta system had equal weaknesses – arguably, only the existence of the H-bomb made it stable and long-lasting – while between 1854 and 1871 the Vienna system was fundamentally revised by force. Why can some systems survive greater stress than others? A system is powerful when it is supported by most of the power within it most of the time, and when its members share a common sense of the rules of the game and of their own power and prerogatives. Such a powerful system can survive any single event except a system-wide war, which it can deter. A system gains strength from the issues it can ignore, as well as those it can solve. Power is central to systems – marginal changes trigger bigger ones, by attracting friends or causing them to flee. Power is always distributed, not necessarily balanced – between 1815 and 1932 when it was most stable, the European system normally rested on a preponderance of power behind the status quo. Systems are more stable under hegemony than in a condition of balance. In a multilateral competitive system, power constantly fluctuates as do perceptions of it. Periods of transition in power – when a preponderance collapses, or several states race to maximize their strength, in a pattern of challenge and response – are conducive to crisis and war. Tipping points exist, but usually their location is unknown. Intentions cannot always be effected and unintended consequences can never be avoided.

notes

1. For Clausewitz, see Carl von Clausewitz, *On War*, ed. by Michael Howard and Peter Paret (Princeton, NJ: Princeton University Press, 1976); amongst Liddell Hart's many and varied publications, see, for example, his early volume, Basil H. Liddell Hart, *The Decisive Wars of History: A Study in Strategy* (London: Bell, 1929); Delbrück's key work is now available in English, Hans Delbrück, *History of the Art of War within the Framework of Political History*, 4 vols, ed. and trans. by Walter J. Renfroe (Westport, CT: Greenwood Press, 1975–85), a translation of the 1920 German edition; for Corbett, see, for example, Julian S. Corbett, *England in the Seven Years' War: A Study in Combined Strategy*, 2 vols (London: Longman, Green, 1907).
2. Clifford J. Rogers (ed.), *The Military Revolution Debate* (Boulder, CO: Westview Press, 1995).
3. Allan R. Millet and Williamson Murray (eds), *Military Effectiveness*, 3 vols (London: Allen and Unwin, 1988), and *Military Innovation in the Interwar Period* (Cambridge: Cambridge University Press, 1996); Michael Handel (ed.), *Intelligence and Military Operations* (London: Frank Cass, 1990).
4. John Keegan, *The Face of Battle. A Study of Agincourt, Waterloo and the Somme* (London: Cape, 1976).
5. The classic treatment is Ivan Morris, *The Nobility of Failure: Tragic Heroes in the History of Japan* (New York: Holt, Rinehart and Winston, 1975); a recent account is Naoko Shimazu, 'The Myth of the "Patriotic Soldier": Japanese Attitudes Toward Death in the Russo-Japanese War', *War and Society*, 19 (2) (2001) 69–89.
6. The most influential modern work in this vein is Timothy Travers, *The Killing Ground: The British Army, the Western Front, and the Emergence of Modern Warfare, 1900–1918* (London: Allen and Unwin, 1987); an excellent recent example is Tami Davis Biddle, *Rhetoric and Reality in Air Warfare: The Evolution of British and American Ideas about Strategic Bombing, 1914–1945* (Princeton, NJ: Princeton University Press, 2002).

7. For recent studies, see Keith Neilson, *Britain and the Last Tsar: British Policy and Russia, 1894–1917* (Oxford: Clarendon, 1995); David Stevenson, *Armaments and the Coming of War: Europe, 1904–1914* (Oxford: Clarendon, 1996).
8. For different views, cf. Paul Kennedy, *The Rise and Fall of the Great Powers: Economic Change and Military Conflict from 1500 to 2000* (New York: Random House, 1987); and the symposium on 'The Decline of Great Britain', *International History Review*, 13 (4) (1991) 661–783.
9. Kennedy, *Rise and Fall*; Christopher Price, *Britain, America and Rearmament in the 1930s* (London: Palgrave, 2001). Good examples of how to marry economic and strategic history include Mark Harrison, *Accounting for War: Soviet Production, Employment, and the Defence Burden, 1940–1945* (Cambridge: Cambridge University Press, 1996); Richard Overy, *Why the Allies Won* (London: Pimlico, 1995); Philip Pugh, *The Cost of Seapower. The Influence of Money on Naval Affairs from 1815 to the Present Day* (London: Conway, 1988); Sebastian Ritchie, *Industry and Airpower: The Expansion of British Aircraft Production, 1935–41* (London: Frank Cass, 1997).
10. For an excellent account, see Andrew Lambert, *The Last Sailing Battlefleet. Maintaining Naval Mastery, 1815–1850* (London: Conway, 1991).
11. Useful accounts of classical Greek warfare, and the Spartan state, are J. K. Anderson, *Military Theory and Practice in the Age of Xenophon* (Berkeley: University of California Press, 1970); Victor Davis Hanson, *The Western Way of War: Infantry Battle in Classical Greece* (London: Hodder and Stoughton, 1989); J. F. Lazenby, *The Spartan Army* (Warminster: Aris and Phillips, 1985); and Paul Cartledge, *The Spartans: The World of the Warrior Heroes of Ancient Greece, from Utopia to Crisis and Collapse* (New York: Overlook, 2003).
12. Christon Archer, John Ferris, Holger Herwig and Timothy Travers, *World History of Warfare* (Lincoln: University of Nebraska Press, 2002), pp. 440–82.
13. Michael Handel, 'The Evolution of Israeli Strategy: The Psychology of Insecurity and the Quest for Absolute Security', in Williamson Murray, MacGregor Knox and Alvin Bernstein (eds), *The Making of Strategy: Rulers, States, and War* (Cambridge: Cambridge University Press, 1994), pp. 534–78; Kenneth M. Pollack, *Arabs at War: Military Effectiveness, 1948–1991* (Lincoln: University of Nebraska Press, 2002).
14. A classic argument is Eugen Weber, *Peasants into Frenchmen: The Modernization of Rural France, 1870–1914* (London: Chatto and Windus, 1977). Useful longitudinal studies of conscription in recent history can be found in Lars Mjøset and S. Van Holde (eds), 'The Comparative Study of Conscription in the Armed Forces', theme issue, *Comparative Social Research*, 20 (2002).
15. For anthropological approaches to war, see Joanna Bourke, *An Intimate History of Killing: Face-to-Face Killing in Twentieth Century Warfare* (London: Granta, 1999); and John Keegan, *A History of Warfare* (London: Hutchinson, 1993). Bourke has been widely criticized for errors of fact, and Keegan for ignorance of Clausewitz.
16. The standard editions are Clausewitz, *On War*, and Sun Tzu, *The Art of War*, ed. by Ralph Sawyer (New York: Barnes and Noble, 1994). The best modern assessments of the strategic views of Corbett, Delbrück and Liddell Hart are Michael Handel, *Masters of War. Classical Strategic Thought*, 3rd edn (London: Frank Cass, 2001); Gordon A. Craig, 'Delbrück: The Military Historian', in Peter Paret (ed.), *Makers of Modern Strategy from Machiavelli to the Nuclear Age*

(Oxford: Clarendon, 1986), pp. 326–53; and Brian Bond, *Liddell Hart. A Study of His Military Thought* (London: Cassell, 1977).

17. Handel, *Masters of War*.
18. For a rare effort to test the validity of ideas about national ways of war, see David French, *The British Way in Warfare, 1688–2000* (London: Unwin Hyman, 1990).
19. Victor Davis Hanson, *Carnage and Culture: Landmark Battles in the Rise of Western Power* (New York: Doubleday, 2001); Alastair Iain Johnston, *Cultural Realism: Strategic Culture and Grand Strategy in Chinese History* (Princeton, NJ: Princeton University Press, 1995), esp. pp. 93–108; John A. Lynn, *Battle. A History of Combat and Culture from Ancient Greece to Modern America* (Boulder, CO: Westview Press, 2003).
20. John Ferris, 'Intelligence', in Robert Boyce and Joseph Maiolo (eds), *The Origins of World War Two: The Debate Continues* (London: Palgrave, 2003), pp. 308–29.
21. Gabriel Gorodetsky, *Grand Delusion: Stalin and the German Invasion of Russia* (New Haven: Yale University Press, 1999).
22. Useful commentaries on power in the international system are Hedley Bull, *The Anarchical Society. A Study of Order in World Politics* (London: Macmillan, 1977); and the symposia on 'Paul W. Schroeder's International System', *International History Review*, 16 (4) (1994) 661–757, and 'A. J. P. Taylor's Struggles for Mastery', *International History Review*, 23 (1) (2001) 1–124.
23. For accounts of these events, see John Ferris, '"It is our Business in the Navy to Command the Seas": The Last Decade of British Maritime Supremacy, 1919–1929', in Greg Kennedy and Keith Neilson (eds), *Far-Flung Lines. Essays on Imperial Defence in Honour of Donald Mackenzie Schurman* (London: Frank Cass, 1997), pp. 124–70; James Morley, *Japan Erupts: The London Conference and the Manchurian Incident, 1928–1932* (New York: Columbia University Press, 1984); David R. Stone, *Hammer and Rifle: The Militarization of the Soviet Union, 1926–1933* (Lawrence: University Press of Kansas, 2000).
24. For different views on power in the state system during the late 1930s, see Williamson Murray, *The Change in the European Balance of Power, 1938–1939. The Path to Ruin* (Princeton, NJ: Princeton University Press, 1984); Joseph Maiolo, *The Royal Navy and Nazi Germany, 1933–39* (London: Macmillan, 1998); and the essays in Boyce and Maiolo, *Origins of World War Two*.
25. The classic in the field of intelligence estimates is Ernest R. May (ed.), *Knowing One's Enemies: Intelligence Assessment before the Two World Wars* (Princeton, NJ: Princeton University Press, 1984); see also Williamson Murray and Allan R. Millett (eds), *Calculations: Net Assessment and the Coming of World War II* (New York: Free Press, 1992). The best study of assessment in any single country is Peter Jackson, *France and the Nazi Menace* (Oxford: Oxford University Press, 2000).
26. Robert Mallett, *The Italian Navy and Fascist Expansionism, 1935–40* (London: Frank Cass, 1998), pp. 180–1.
27. This discussion of the inter-war period draws extensively on the treatment in Ferris, 'Intelligence'.

3
political economy
bruce cumings*

Examining the role of economics within international history is difficult, because of the flawed assumptions that scholars too often bring to the table and the disciplinary boundaries and biases that impede enquiry. This is particularly true in the United States. The ascendancy of economics within the social sciences there has led department after department to drop economic history as a field, in favour of abstract, mathematical approaches that trumpet their lack of interest in non-quantifiable history. The history profession, under the influence of its own disciplinary fashions, also deems economic history unappealing. Moreover, dominated by Americanists, it tends to view anything international as the exclusive concern of 'diplomatic history', an arid sub-discipline with little relevance to the sacred triptych of race, class and gender, and best left to those who like to bury themselves in State Department documents. Matters do not necessarily improve among diplomatic historians, who tend to see a focus on economics as smacking of politically motivated 'revisionism' or some sort of determinism.

Perhaps these attitudes derive in part from the very success of the Wisconsin School of Fred Harvey Harrington, William Appleman Williams, Lloyd Gardner, Walter LaFeber and Thomas McCormick, scholars who always took economic forces seriously. These now departed or very senior practitioners set an exemplary standard for scholarship at the intersection of international history and political economy – Harrington's *God, Mammon, and the Japanese*, Williams' *Tragedy of American Diplomacy*, LaFeber's *New Empire*, Gardner's *Economic Aspects of New Deal Diplomacy* and McCormick's *China Market* are all classics in the literature[1] – but the influences of the Cold War and McCarthyism led other scholars, hoping to appropriate the mainstream, to brand this work 'revisionist', 'Marxist', even 'Leninist'.[2] This prejudice is a clear indication of the provincialism of American diplomatic history, but that does not make it any the less pronounced, pervasive or influential. Consequently, in the new century it is hard to argue that successors to the Wisconsin School have significant presence in the profession, or that many new practitioners work at the boundary between international history and political economy. Rather than simply survey a small literature that does not heavily impact the history profession, therefore, this chapter will think through the difficult questions of *how* political economy influences international history, whether historians like it or not, or pay attention to it or not.

world economy and global systems

The starting point must be the world economy, and the starting point for any analysis of the world economy should be Karl Polanyi's *The Great Transformation*.[3] I have taught this book for 25 years, usually as the first reading in my international history seminar, because it not only offers a comprehensive analysis of 150 years of the world economy but also explores so many difficult questions – what *is* the global system? what are its basic mechanisms of operation? how do we analyse international relations within the world system? what is the role of the state in the economy (both domestic and global)? what is required of the leading nation in the world economy? – from both an historical and a theoretical standpoint. As against the 'fiction' of Adam Smith's self-regulating market, Polanyi set an ever-expanding world economy with distant beginnings in the sixteenth century: 'the true starting point is long-distance trade, a result of the geographical location of goods, and of the "division of labor" given by location'.[4] Here was the origin of the idea of a global market, abhorring national boundaries and eventually carrying everything before it – internal tariffs, recalcitrant peasantries, and nation-states that resisted its logic. A 'circulationist', Polanyi defined capitalism as production for profit in a world market.[5] For Polanyi long-distance trade, like Smith's market, 'involved no less [than] an act of faith. Its implications were entirely extravagant'; ultimately it implied 'some vaguely conceived world unity of the future'. That is, the world market was not self-regulatory, it needed political leadership: 'the centralized state was a new creation called forth by the Commercial Revolution'.[6] The functioning of the system required a nation of last resort to intervene with loans, a central banker to control credit, a global mechanism to adjust currencies – in other words this 'vaguely conceived unity' would perform a hegemonic function. Throughout the nineteenth century, its name was Great Britain and its key mechanism was the gold standard.

Using his theory of world economy, Polanyi offered a fundamental reinterpretation of the origins of the Second World War. 'To comprehend German fascism, we must revert to Ricardian England', he wrote at the beginning of the book. The four pillars of nineteenth century civilization were the balance of power system, the gold standard, a global market and the liberal state; among them, the world market was paramount.[7] 1914 may have been widely proclaimed as the point when the nineteenth century system crumbled, but the First World War was an accidental war that weakened the pillars without yet destroying the system or Britain's global leadership. The world economy remained fundamentally intact after the war, even if Britain's leadership slowly flagged, and it was the later irruption of the Great Depression that actually precipitated systemic breakdown. Thus 'the snapping of the golden thread was the signal for a world revolution',[8] as the British and everyone else went off the gold standard in the early 1930s, leaving each nation to fend for itself, to go it alone, and to manufacture New Deals or New Orders amid the complete collapse of the world economy. The world system spun out of control, fundamentally, because Britain could no longer lead and the United States was not yet ready to do so – an insight from Polanyi that Charles Kindleberger later turned into an excellent book.[9]

In some respects, and no doubt partially, Polanyi's *Great Transformation* fulfilled the ambitions of what Karl Marx had sketched out as his unfinished final work: an examination of the mechanisms of capital on 'the grandest terrain' of the world market. In a little known but brilliant essay, 'Bastiat and Carey', Marx outlined an analysis of America in the world economy, circa 1857. After the war in Mexico brought Texas and California into the union and a host of new technologies – the steam engine, railways, the telegraph – propelled industry and commerce, Marx depicted the continental United States as poised on the advanced horizon of global capitalism. But its industry got started late, so we would expect a period of protectionism (or *nationalekönomie*) to incubate industry and hold off superior British products, followed by a victory of British economic thought – Friedrich List giving way to Adam Smith. The most famous American economist at the time was Henry Carey: 'Carey is the only original economist among the North Americans'. Except that Carey was not so original: he was a follower of List and liked high tariffs. Carey thought that this protected political economy which Marx found so exceptional, creating itself *de novo* before his eyes, was the natural economy: Carey happily regarded it 'as the eternal, normal relations of social production'; that is, 'Carey's generality is Yankee universality'.[10]

The unnatural and the abnormal to Carey was the British doctrine of free trade, which he saw as a form of highway robbery: 'Carey sees the contradictions in the economic relations as soon as they appear on the world market as *English* relations'.[11] And further:

> Originally [for Carey], the English relations were distorted by the false theories of her economists, internally. Now, externally, as the commanding power of the world market, England distorts the harmony of economic relations in all the countries of the world. ... Having dissolved this fundamental harmony in its own interior, England, by its competition, proceeds to destroy it throughout the world market. ... The only defence lies in protective tariffs – the forcible, national barricade against the destructive power of large-scale English industry. Hence, the state, which was at first branded the sole disturber of these *'harmonies économiques'*, is now these harmonies' last refuge ... with Carey the harmony of the bourgeois relations of production ends with the most complete disharmony of these relations on the grandest terrain where they appear, the world market, and in their grandest development, as the relations of producing nations.[12]

It would demean Marx's argument to cast it in our contemporary terms of 'free trade' versus 'protection'. But it is a humbling argument, for it reveals precisely what shapes our debates: the self-interest of our corporations, the myopia of our economists, the fatuity of our politicians and the provincialism of our discourse.

There is also an implicit theory of the state here. First, the state under conditions of international competition becomes the 'national barricade' – *nationalekönomie* again. But elsewhere Carey had branded it the disturber of the domestic economy. Therefore he must think the state is good for some things (protection), but not good for others (intervention in the 'free market' at home). Exactly so: historically this is nothing more than Republican Party political economy (Smoot-Hawley plus J. Edgar Hoover plus *laissez-faire*), but analytically it means the state is not simply a domestic expression, it is also shaped from without by something else: national competition ('the grandest development') in the world market ('the grandest terrain'). *Nationalekönomie* is not just for Germans but for everyone; the state should regulate competition by opening and closing within the grand terrain of the world market. This is very close to Karl Polanyi's theory of the state. The state in the milieu of the world becomes a guarantor of Polanyi's 'principle of social protection' against the ravages of world market competition.[13]

Immanuel Wallerstein is said to have taught Polanyi's *Great Transformation* for many years before working out his own 'world-system theory'. Wallerstein published the first volume of *The Modern World-System* in 1974, marking an influential watershed in historical understanding of the world economy.[14] Also a circulationist, Wallerstein united Latin American dependency theory with Polanyi, and added to it a sociology (this, after all, was his discipline). He sought the origin of the modern world-system in the 'big bang' of the 'long sixteenth century', when a capitalist trading system arose that was based not on preciosities like tea and spices but on integrated production and consumption at both ends of a long commodity chain. Coffee-drinking in European cafes had something to do with the rise of the intellectual class, but at the other end of the chain were coffee plantations employing thousands of migrant labourers; the plantations transformed Latin American agrarian societies, but did not 'modernize' them. Instead they represented 'the development of underdevelopment', as Andre Gunder Frank had put it.[15] As this global system developed, it created polar opposites: a core of advanced industrial states with every rapidly-multiplying advantage, and a periphery locked into nearly permanent stagnation. In between was the 'semi-periphery', a realm like the middle class in domestic society that provided an arena of potential upward mobility. The biblical phrase 'many are called but few are chosen' well captures the dynamic here, which refutes modernization theory's assumption that every country can do well if it leads from comparative advantage.

Getting into the hallowed realm of the core would prove as difficult as threading a camel through the eye of a needle, because for every semi-peripheral entity (Wallerstein disdained to call them countries) going up, another would be on the way down. It is a cogent argument: a century ago there were a handful of countries with comprehensively developed industrial bases (the UK, the US, France, Germany, Italy, and on the way, Japan and Russia) and today there are no new entrants, and one drop-out (Russia, its economy equivalent in size to that of the Netherlands). On a recent visit to Argentina I was overwhelmed with a sense of lost possibilities, as Argentine friends scratched their heads as to how their country, clearly on the march toward core status a century ago, got leap-frogged by the likes of South Korea.

It took a long time for historians to take notice of Wallerstein's work. The *American Historical Review* waited until 1991 to run two feature articles (predictably, in oppositional 'pro' and 'con' format) on 'the new international history', which predominantly focused upon

Wallerstein's *Modern World-System*. In the lead article Ian Tyrrell argued that a transnational or world-system perspective could help American historians overcome their addiction to exceptionalism – not a bad point in my view – but Michael McGerr responded that he was absolutely mistaken.[16] Today many historians and social scientists seem to think that Wallerstein's ideas are passé, redolent of the radicalism of the 1960s and 1970s, and indeed his prescribed remedy for people drawing the short straw in the world economy – that is, to retire from it and develop self-reliantly – seems as antique as North Korea's industrial base (and Wallerstein often lauded Kim Il Sung's 'Juche idea' of self-reliance in the 1970s). (Polanyi did not make the mistake of proposing a non-systemic remedy for the systemic world economy; in the epilogue to his book he extolled the virtues of a new world order that would subject the forces of the market to intelligent human control, that is, some kind of global democratic socialism.[17]) If we still clearly have a core and a periphery in the world, and if it seems logically necessary to have something in the middle of the system to keep it from polarizing, it has never been apparent quite how this 'semi-periphery' might be firmly grasped, understood and analysed. Certainly, no Wallersteinian would have predicted in the 1970s that 'semi-peripheral' South Korea, supposedly locked into an American system of dependency, would vastly outstrip North Korea and become the eleventh-ranking industrialized nation in the world within a mere 25 years.

But if some aspects of Wallerstein's sociology seem deficient, his and Polanyi's focus on the world economy under the hegemonic leadership of the most advanced or 'core' power still has enormous explanatory and predictive power. Since the beginning of China's reforms in 1978 and the fall of Western communism after 1989, hundreds of millions more people have given themselves up eagerly to Smith's famed propensity to truck and barter. China's transformation over the past 25 years is nothing short of remarkable. After joining up with the Soviet bloc in the 1950s and then pursuing a frank go-it-alone strategy in the 1960s and early 1970s, China chose to link up with the American-led world economy, and its trajectory since then has been a textbook example of how to bring a huge, recalcitrant country into general international commerce, to get it captured by the gravity of the world market and then watch the latter slowly work its will on the domestic society. Armed with Polanyi's insights, it was quite possible back in the late 1970s to have predicted that despite fears and promises that China would 'shake the world', it would be far more likely that the world economy would shake China.[18]

the world-system during the cold war

Although Polanyi himself believed that class interest was a fairly crude heuristic device, he observed that, despite their opposing viewpoints, 'liberals and Marxists stood for identical propositions' on the nature of economic and class interest.[19] Perhaps this congruence of fundamental assumptions explains why the global concerns of Polanyi and Wallerstein can so often be found in the papers of prominent diplomats, or why an understanding of political economy is so essential for grasping the world-views of prominent statesmen. Dean Acheson provides a good example; later to become Harry Truman's Secretary of State, he shared many assumptions with a man like Polanyi – although, of course, without Polanyi's critical bite.

Acheson was arguably the most important American policy-maker in the 1940s, embodying the fullness of American ambition in a world come apart at the seams and a quite conscious understanding that the US must be the hegemonic successor to the UK. He expressed his views concisely in a speech entitled 'An American Attitude Toward Foreign Affairs', delivered at Yale in November 1939, shortly after Germany had conquered Poland. Reflecting back on this speech many years later, Acheson recalled that he had really been seeking to 'begin work on a new postwar world system'. 'Our vital interests,' he declared at Yale, 'do not permit us to be indifferent to the outcome' of the wars in Europe and Asia; nor was it possible for Americans to remain isolated from them – unless they wished a kind of eternal 'internment on this continent' (only an Anglophile like Acheson would liken North America to a concentration camp). He located the causes of the war and the global depression that preceded it in 'the failure of some of the vital mechanisms of the Nineteenth Century world economy' that had led to 'this break-up of the world into exclusive areas of armed exploitation administered along oriental [sic] lines'. In its time, 'the economic and political system of the Nineteenth Century … produced an amazing increase in the production of wealth', but for many years it had been in an 'obvious process of decline'.

Reconstruction of the foundations of peace would require new global mechanisms: the means to make capital available for industrial production, the removal of tariffs, 'a broader market for goods made under decent standards', 'a stable international monetary system', and the removal of 'exclusive or preferential trade arrangements'. The world economy was his main emphasis, but in good *realpolitik* fashion he also called for the immediate creation of 'a navy and air force adequate to secure us in both oceans simultaneously and with striking power sufficient to reach to the other side of one of them'.[20] In memoirs written 30 years after this Yale address, Acheson began again with a fond reprise of the 'century of international peace' after Waterloo and the Congress of Vienna in 1815: 'Economically, the globe was indeed "one world." The great empires of Europe, through their colonies and spheres of influence, spread authority, order, and respect for the obligation of contract almost everywhere; and where their writs did not run, their frigates and gunboats navigated.'[21] He proceeded in the rest of this lucid book to describe the emergence of an American-led world system after 1945. Acheson was in an ideal position to craft such a narrative, since he had had the opportunity to implement his vision, first at Bretton Woods, then with the Marshall Plan and the Truman Doctrine, and finally with NSC-68; he is the person who comes closest to being the singular architect of American strategy from 1944 to 1953.

A short few years after Acheson gave this speech and Henry Luce claimed the twentieth century as 'the American century', both men seemed like visionaries: the United States accounted for half of the industrial production of all the world, emerging from the war as the single unscathed and emboldened superpower.[22] The United States had in fact already been the most productive industrial economy in the world at the turn of the nineteenth century, and everyone knew this by the early 1920s as American firms pioneered mass production and consumption and its banks became the effective centre of global lending and commerce. But it had a laughably small military, and neither the political will nor the domestic political base for global hegemony. The years from 1914 to 1941 were thus not so much part of an American century as years of hegemonic interregnum, as Polanyi had argued, in which Britain was increasingly unable any longer to lead and the United States was not yet in a position to do so. The aggression of the Axis powers, beginning with the German invasion of Poland and culminating at Pearl Harbor, changed all that, finally committing the United States to global leadership at a time when economic collapse, total war, and the attendant chaos required the construction of the new world system that Acheson had envisioned in 1939.

The moment when the baton of world leadership finally and definitively passed from London to Washington came on 21 February 1947, when a British Embassy official informed Acheson that Britain could not provide Greece and Turkey with the hundreds of millions of dollars in military and economic aid that they required, and indeed that all British assistance to those powers would have to cease within weeks. Acheson, walking to lunch with a journalist friend, subsequently mused aloud that 'there are only two powers left', the United States and the Soviet Union. Acheson was not simply suggesting that an era of bipolarity had dawned, although that was indeed true; he meant something much deeper – the substitution of American for British leadership.[23]

Acheson was present at this creation and unabashedly 'hegemonic', and he did not mistake the opportunities and perils of America's new position in the world. His problem was to be pregnant with an idea that he could not articulate, lest Harry Truman lose the next election (and announcing that the United States had now replaced Britain as the power with all the burdens of last resort in the world economy would scarcely have enhanced Truman's electoral prospects). To put it differently, the internationalist forces in American politics still lacked a strong domestic base, particularly in Congress, but also throughout a parochial body politic. George Kennan provided the solution to this dilemma with an elegant metaphor: containment. Imagine, America could march outward and inherit Britain's role of global leadership, and yet present it as a defensive play. Imagine, a doctrine defining hegemony by what it opposes, obviating the necessity to explain the nature of that hegemony to the American people, or what its consequences would be for them. It is only today, long after the fall of the Berlin Wall and the collapse of the Soviet Union, that Americans can perceive this obscured, underlying system that persists in spite of the disappearance of its ostensible *raison d'être*.

No one expressed the synthesis between the overt containment policy and the obscure but more important world economy imperatives better than Henry Luce. In a June 1947 *Fortune* editorial entitled 'The US Opportunity', Luce wrote that Americans must become 'missionaries of capitalism and democracy' and used as his 'classic current example' the archetypal multinational corporation – the American oil firm. The Arabian American Oil Company, he wrote, not only developed Middle Eastern oil but built schools, water works, even whole cities where there had only been desert. In the past American business had been content to exploit 'the world's greatest free trade area', that is, the American national market; now, however, big corporations constituted the 'front-line soldiers and battalions in the battle of freedom'. Among these 'great corporations', Luce listed exclusively high-technology, competitive firms with large international markets: Standard Oil, General Motors, General Electric, ITT, Pan American Airlines, Westinghouse, IBM, and Coca-Cola, which (Luce said later) was pursuing the 'Coca-colonization' of the world. Here 'at the top', American business was 'already international'. And so it was 'no longer the case that we can lie in the sun without having to worry about the Koreans and the Azerbaijanis'.[24] Although widely ridiculed for his effervescent rhetoric and his diehard support of Chiang Kai-shek, Luce symbolized better than anyone else the interventionist compromise that grew out of the domestic clash of the old isolationist and the new internationalist forces. He was an early avatar of what is now called 'globalization'.

In the late 1940s the struggle with communism was thus but one part, and the secondary part, of a project to revive the world economy from the devastation of the global depression and the Second World War – just as Acheson had originally suggested in 1939. At first the problem seemed to be solved with the Bretton Woods mechanisms elaborated in 1944, but when by 1947 these had not worked to revive the advanced industrial economies, along came the Marshall Plan for Europe and the 'reverse course' in Japan that removed controls on its heavy industries. When by 1950 the allied economies were still not growing sufficiently rapidly, NSC-68 (a document mostly written by Paul Nitze but guided by the thinking of Acheson – by then Truman's Secretary of State) hit upon military Keynesianism as a device that did, finally, prime the pump of these advanced industrial economies. (It is interesting that one of the most cogent analyses of this fundamental process came from a student of the Wisconsin School, who subsequently could not find an academic job and left the profession.[25])

The Korean War, seen by the North Koreans as a war of national liberation in the face of American attempts to re-stitch South Korea's economic linkages with Japan, turned into the crisis that built the American national security state and pushed through the money to pay for it: the vast procurements for this war constituted a veritable second Marshall Plan that worked for Western Europe and especially Japan (whose industrial takeoff began in the early 1950s). From June to December 1950 the defence budget quadrupled (from roughly $13 billion to $56 billion), but it did so in the midst of a massive crisis over China's intervention in the Korean peninsula: only with the opening of Sino-American war did Congress finally begin to fund the national security state at the lavish levels to which it has since become accustomed. It was the repositioning of Japan as a major industrial producer in the context of a raging anti-imperial revolution on the Asian mainland that explains much of East and Southeast Asian history for the next three decades (until the Indochina War finally ended in 1975). And the war in Korea was the lever ('Korea came along and saved us', in Acheson's famous words[26]) through which Washington finally found a reliable method that would pay the bills for cold and hot wars on a global scale: military Keynesianism, which floated economic boats not so much at home, but in Japan and Western Europe. This system, developed on a North–North axis running from Washington and New York through London, Paris, Berlin and Tokyo, remains the bedrock of the world economy today. And in the early years of the twenty-first century Japan and Germany remain firmly within this postwar settlement: still encouraged to produce and grow, they are still military and political midgets.

nothing is automatic: how contingency, agency, and politics shape hegemony

Our account so far produces a simple narrative: following Karl Polanyi, the world system broke down in the middle of the Great Depression because London could no longer bear the burden of leadership – symbolized by its inability even to maintain the gold standard – and Washington was not yet ready to do so. By 1939, Dean Acheson was ready, and in the period 1944–51 he and his allies worked out the new system. But if the world order shaped in the 1940s sprang mostly from the minds of American leaders, their task was immensely difficult – overshadowed by its very newness, its first-time quality (Acheson may have thought he was following precedent, constructing hegemony on the British model, but the simultaneous demise of formal empire made this a quite different affair), the always opaque future, and the particular experiences of the leaders themselves. No recent book better exemplifies what a student of politics and political economy can teach to historians than Robert Latham's *The Liberal Moment*. Readily admitting that he has done almost no archival research himself, Latham uses a generation's historical scholarship on the early years of the Cold War to take us through that point of origin not simply to explicate it for history (which he does as well as anyone else) but to instruct the present – and above all, the experts themselves – about the extraordinary complexity of world order-building in a time of crisis. He painstakingly constructs a theory of international order that effortlessly transcends existing debates and illustrates the manifold uses of theory in explaining both the 'big bang' of system-building after 1945 and its overriding salience for our time.[27]

The order was to be a liberal one, as Acheson had said in 1939, but in 1945 hardly anyone knew what that meant, since the world had been so illiberal for so long. It might mean a Wilsonian quest to make *this* brave new world safe for democracy, once and for all. It might mean the creed of the Anglophile internationalists, like wartime Secretary of State Cordell Hull, that free trade would create the greatest good for the greatest number, form the preconditions for representative democracy on a world scale, and thereby yield peace among nations. It might mean an extension of Franklin Roosevelt's New Deal to the world, as a kind of regulated open door. It might even mean the libertarianism of a Robert Taft, with its emphasis on the fullest extension of the market, minimal government and fiscal austerity. Whichever understanding of liberalism one might choose, the question of how to implement a liberal order in a world that had never experienced one would still remain.

The postwar order took shape through positive policy and through the establishment of distinct outer limits, the transgression of which was rare or even inconceivable, provoking immediate crisis (witness, for example, the response to Soviet pressures upon the status of West Berlin in 1948). The typical experience of this hegemony, however, was a mundane, benign and mostly unremarked daily life of subtle constraint, in which the United States kept allied powers in a state of defence, resource, and, for many years, financial dependency. This penetration of allied nations was most visible in the front line semi-sovereign states like Japan, West Germany and South Korea, and it was conceived by people like Kennan as the means to create an indirect, outer-limit control on the worst possible outcome, namely, orientation to the other side.[28] After the Cold War ended and until the manifold pressures of the war in Iraq, these American allies could almost imagine that the presence of American troops on their national territory did not make much difference, that the many American bases dotting their territory could almost be forgotten.

Latham sees this security structure as essential, however, calling it the American 'external state' and viewing it as a central element of liberal order building. This insight leads him to examine the vast global militarization of this same liberal order (eventually encompassing 1.5 million American troops stationed in hundreds of bases in 35 countries, formal security commitments to 43 countries, the training and equipping of military forces in 70 countries), a phenomenon too often treated as merely an unfortunate result or by-product of the bipolar confrontation.

In Latham's rendering, structure, contingency, and agency interacted in the making and remaking of the postwar order.[29] The structure was the global order-in-making, which he calls a 'constitutive presence'. Contingency was the historicity of a unique world crisis, namely the depression and the world war, but also the potency and essential indeterminacy of their lingering effects. Acheson, John McCloy, Robert Lovett, Kennan and the others were the agents. They had ideas, of course, and for the most part all of them were liberal-modernist ideas. The most prominent goal was to create institutions that would prevent any repetition of the domestic and international disasters of the 1930s (the folly of isolationism or the emergence of autarchic and antagonistic New Orders abroad), and especially ones that could remedy the imbalances and worst tendencies of the market. The old rules did not work and new ones had not been invented: what to do? At first, the Bretton Woods agreements appeared to be the answer, and they certainly represented a planned, logical outcome of internationalist presuppositions. Unfortunately, as we have seen, the International Monetary Fund (IMF) and the World Bank just did not work to resuscitate the industrial economies or solve the problems of the 1940s and so something else had to be done (witness the Marshall Plan, and so forth). (Indeed, one Bretton Woods institution, the International Trade Organization, never got off the ground, or at least not until the 1990s in the shape of the World Trade Organization (WTO).) Thus, 'conditions change, the unexpected happens, and agents react and change their policies.'[30]

But another critical part of the subsequent global order was unplanned, illogical, and it *did* work. This would be Latham's 'external state', the global archipelago of military bases that complemented the proliferation of advisory groups, transnational planning through bodies like the Agency for International Development, and the activities of the IMF and World Bank. Here is the true 'Archimedean point' from which we can discern what was at stake in the making and remaking of American hegemony, how the conjuncture of agency and contingency brought about an enduring structure, and the emergence of utterly unanticipated consequences (a far-flung and theoretically unlimited militarized global space, necessitating unprecedented expenditures to service it).[31] Moscow's critical role, of course, was to co-author the strategic boundaries of the two geopolitical realms, a process that was mostly complete by the end of 1947. In many ways Moscow did the West a huge favour with this parallel and coeval line-drawing, since it enabled planners to concentrate on building strength in several advantageous nodal positions (the larger part of Germany, Japan, France, Britain, Italy). From that point onward (but only from that point), a *realpolitik* logic increasingly operated in world affairs – and largely ended when the Soviet Union collapsed.

hegemony in the postwar system

How can we characterize the American-fashioned postwar world system? It has not been an empire of exclusively controlled territories. It has not been neo-imperial, exploiting the economies of its members as if they were colonies, and it has not created onerous or inescapable dependencies. It has not remorselessly subordinated its constituent members. It has established boundaries of inclusion, but it has not necessarily punished exit, if that exit is to a middle ground of neutrality or irrelevance. But this order has been a hegemonic one, and it has had – and must have – a hegemonic leader. But what is hegemony?

When I used this term in a lecture to a room full of small-college faculty a while ago, the first question that came was this: why do you indulge in conspiracy theory? Another knee-jerk response is to assume that the bearer of the term 'hegemony' must be a Marxist. But beyond the usual purview of diplomatic historians, we can find intelligent help in grasping the nature of this phenomenon. Canadian scholars have done well here, particularly those writing in the tradition of Robert Cox, the scholar most known for joining political-economic conceptions of hegemony with Gramscian-influenced cultural notions.[32] Stephen Gill, for example, redefines hegemony in terms of paramount international influence, bringing together national and international social forces, international organizations, and norms, and moving his definition away from *realpolitik* emphasis on the power of states; realists think of power primarily in coercive terms, but for Gill, 'a successful hegemony is one where consensual aspects of the system come to the forefront, although coercion is always potentially in the background'. The most important form of structural power for Gill is 'internationally mobile, large-scale capital', a global economic and social force; here Gill's views are not so very far from those of Polanyi or Wallerstein.[33]

Hegemony means, to Wallerstein, the simultaneous and temporary 'productive, commercial, and financial preeminence of one core power over other core powers'; the critical element is 'productive advantage', which conditions the other two (commerce and finance). This conception assumes that the world market is the primary mechanism and arena of hegemony – even if it also may encompass empire, colonies, 'neo-colonialism', and what is sometimes called 'informal empire'. Military advantage, conventionally thought by realists to be essential to hegemony, merely locks it in after the fact. But there are two senses of 'temporary' in the theory, which is why I emphasized this element: an abnormal first phase of enormous competitive advantage against all others, which is brief, and the normal, long phase of 'temporary' hegemony in which a core state is *primus inter pares*.[34] In this crucial sense, the US has never been in decline, in spite of much 1980s commentary to the contrary, but is merely in the middle age of hegemony, with many more decades left of relative predominance.

Hegemony is most effective when its structural power is hidden or indirect, and when it is inclusive, plural, heterogeneous, and consensual

– less a form of domination than a form of legitimate global leadership. In another rare sophisticated discussion of the concept, Robert Latham departs very sharply from the many analysts who have sought to define American hegemony in *realpolitik*, Weberian or Marxian terms (such as Robert Gilpin, Robert Keohane, Immanuel Wallerstein and Kenneth Waltz). Using a diffuse conception of power informed by Michel Foucault, Paul Ricoeur, Albert Hirschman and others, Latham gives us a spreading, undulating, seductive liberal hegemony, constructed through 'the permeation of values and understandings throughout the global system'.[35] This hegemony is potent, and it has a message: in the 1940s it crushed one form of statist empire and in the 1980s it destroyed another. In the 1990s it eroded if it did not entirely erase the last formidable alternative system, the Japan–Korea model of state-directed neo-mercantilism. (This was undermined and made vulnerable by its inclusion in the postwar world system, and when the Second World of communist countries, blocs, and iron and bamboo curtains unexpectedly disappeared, so did American indulgence for its East Asian allies' neo-mercantilism, which had always been a function of the Cold War struggle with their opposites. Yet that same system is now spreading to China, not only a rapidly growing power but also one uniquely independent of the US 'external state'.)

This almost boundless global power, immanent in the peculiarly American moment of 1945, came to express itself as a historical structure of ongoing political practice, social action, and economic exchange – a liberal moment giving way to a global structure based in, and the outgrowth of, the maturing of liberal modernism. Because of the Other – Soviet communism, old-world imperialism, national liberation movements – the boundaries of the system were policed by naval task forces, the nuclear delivery capabilities of air forces, and, above all, the archipelago of American military bases. But when the Other disappeared, the structure continued in place and, in the 1990s, achieved the full florescence that its planners had imagined in the 1940s.[36] That is, the 'New World Order' that George H. W. Bush and many others cast about for after 1989 was both the same old order and the ongoing fulfilment of the liberal moment. Unified Germany does not dominate Europe, Japan has not gone nuclear, China discovered the market, France is experiencing a world-historical predicament of national identity, and American hegemony continues apace.

middle-range theory

If we shift our attention for a moment from Polanyi or Latham's grand global level to a kind of middle-range analysis, we can see how international historians might also learn a great deal from other political economists of a variety of persuasions. The late and mostly unlamented Walt Rostow had a second, scholarly, career largely unknown to those who remember him from the John F. Kennedy and Lyndon Johnson national security team. His big tome on the world economy is a fascinating and learned study of global industrial growth, business cycles, product cycles and 'late' industrialization, by a person who might best be called a Schumpeterian – after the great political economist Joseph Schumpeter, an original analyst of the business cycle who once had (and perhaps still should have) towering influence. Rostow makes a host of fascinating comparisons across time and space, on the global and regional level, and tells us much about the differences between those nations that have successfully industrialized and kept on going, like Japan, and those that industrialized and then stagnated, like Argentina.[37] His analysis and data throw up lots of interesting questions that an historian could easily take into the archives (when I first encountered his book I was particularly impressed by his charting of the major industrial growth spurt that occurred in Japan, Korea and Manchuria in the late 1930s).

With solid work coming out on the history of the 1960s and 1970s now that so much of the diplomatic archival record is available, accounts of that period offer considerable food for thought. David Calleo produced a revealing and cogent analysis of the relative American decline that occurred as West Germany, Japan, France and the UK recovered from the Second World War, and as successive administrations struggled to pay for far-flung hegemonic commitments. 'Economic analysis lacking a sense of history or politics must expect many surprises', Calleo aptly wrote; his book covers foreign economic policy from the administrations of Kennedy through Ronald Reagan, but focuses on 'the decline and fall' of the dollar in the 1960s, the raging inflation that had its origin in the Johnson years, 'Nixon's Revolution' through the 'New Economic Policy' announced on VJ-Day 1971 – which Calleo calls 'the new mercantilism', – and the oil shocks of 1973 and 1979. He emphasizes relations with Europe and growing trade conflict between the industrial nations, and argues that relations among these powers were at the lowest point since the Second World War when Jimmy Carter left office.[38]

The 1970s themselves also witnessed, at least in the US, an outpouring of literature in political economy, much of it written by political scientists and sociologists rather than economists or historians. It is far too voluminous to survey here, but some landmark studies still serve as guides to how to think through the crosscutting of political economy and international history. Robert Gilpin, a political scientist, provided one such, in an early neo-mercantilist account of 'outsourcing' and its problems that remains current today. He particularly emphasized the deleterious effect on the American national interest of multinational corporations sending jobs abroad; he memorably raised the specter of America turning into a white-collar nation in a blue-collar sea. He argued that US foreign economic policy depended far too much on the decisions of major multinational corporations that had their own very particular interests, quite different from those of the US as a nation, or Americans as a people.[39]

The oil shocks of the 1970s profoundly affected the world system (as they do again today, with oil nudging $50 a barrel in 2004), and two seminal books stand out for their analysis of those episodes and their understanding of a global petroleum regime that continues to exercise huge influence on the world economy and nearly all nation-states. Gregory P. Nowell provided a fine analysis of the formation and functioning of the world oil cartel, which before the Second World War pioneered a coherent strategy of transnational regulation on behalf of a handful of large multinational oil firms, requiring various nations (including France, Japan and Italy) to react and respond. This is a study of the international distribution of market power and technology, which deeply affected relations between nations. Instead of focusing on single countries or companies, Nowell examines world strategic and oil policy as an ensemble, and challenges realist, national and state-centric approaches. Although Nowell is a political scientist, his book is based on deep archival research in the US and France.[40] In a very different book, John Blair breaks the global oil regime into its constituent parts and focuses on the daily imperatives of the industry (oil has to move; it is expensive to store; supply fluctuates dramatically while demand is generally stable, and so forth), to show how the so-called 'seven sisters' of leading oil companies established their global dominance, and then how that dominance was finally broken by the OPEC (Organization of Petroleum Exporting Countries) cartel in the 1970s. Blair's brilliant and indispensable portrait of this world-spanning industry – concise, to the point, utterly lacking in cant – is the first place I turned when war broke out in Kuwait in 1990, and in Iraq in 2003; in my view it is one of the great works of political economy and is fruitful for thinking through the history of any decade since the oil cartel was founded.[41]

Finally, at this middle-range level, let me urge international historians to read any book by Albert Hirschman. *Exit, Voice, and Loyalty*, *The Passions and the Interests*, his very early 1945 account of the trade dependencies that Nazi Germany established in Eastern Europe, his work on Latin

American industrialization and its problems – all of this is heuristic food for thought, for how political economy influences the international.[42] Hirschman should have won the Nobel Prize in economics long ago, and with his deep knowledge of political economy and his fine sense of history, he is in my opinion the best political economist writing in the United States.

empire?

Empire is a subject of seemingly perennial interest amongst historians, and the locus at which they most often examine the intersection of political economy and international history. It also offers a useful means for us to resume our consideration of both global systems and our current predicament. Thanks to George W. Bush, the subject has again become fashionable in the early years of the new century: so many books with 'empire' in their titles have appeared in the US that one imagines there can be few if any pundits yet to be heard on the subject; in 2004 a racehorse named 'Imperialism' even placed in the Kentucky Derby.[43] One recent authority is Niall Ferguson, arrived from England to instruct Americans to embrace the imperial mission, arguing, first, that empire is really just another name for spreading democracy and the free market (employing the British empire as an instructive example), and, second, that Americans do not make very good imperialists, lacking the necessary love of the game, patience and persistence. Chalmers Johnson, once by his own admission a spear-chucker for empire, argues the opposite: that the US is vastly overextended, and likely to suffer a major catastrophe if we fail to bring the boys home forthwith.[44]

Imperialism is clearly a useful concept for understanding, say, the history of the successive bureaucratic dynasties that ruled China until 1911, or a capitalist empire like that of Great Britain, resting on exclusively-held territories known as colonies. It is not a useful concept if we mean it to denote the United States and its position in the contemporary world, without any qualification or amplification. To do so instantly runs afoul of the classic construction of imperialism as some form of direct or monopoly control of another nation or of mechanisms of the world economy.[45] That characterization rules out use of the term by definition, for no one argues that the US runs a set of territorial possessions lacking the attributes of sovereignty or possesses monopoly controls in the world economy. A redefinition might be accomplished through the accretion of various 'post-' or 'ultra-' or 'neo-' tags, but these also beg the question. If imperialism means direct or monopoly control and neo-imperialism does not, perhaps we need a different term. At the very least, we need a careful explication of the differences between classical and contemporary imperialism.

Michael Hardt and Antonio Negri have, in their recent contribution to the debate, eschewed the term 'imperialism'.[46] Instead, they define current configurations of power in terms of 'globalization', the buzzword phenomenon of the 1990s, where the territorial realm knows no limit and the mechanisms of empire include the United Nations (UN), the IMF, the World Bank and the WTO, a multitude of non-governmental organizations (such as the nuclear inspection arm of the UN, human rights groups, commercial banks and other multinational corporations), and other groups that share a common agenda of setting the rules for a new globalized world. The US plays a critical and often determining role in this, but it is not the sole seat of empire. I think this broad-brush definition that equates empire with globalization does not work, because it encompasses every organization, everybody and everything that traces its beginnings back to post-Second World War arrangements like Bretton Woods. This makes it impossible to determine what is in and what is out of this empire (did China become part of it when it joined the WTO?). Globalization is nothing new, except to twenty-something protesters around the world; instead it is the outcome and ultimate fulfilment of American planning going back six decades, its origins visible in Dean Acheson's prescient oration of 1939.

So what, then, of an American 'empire'? We can begin again with the issue of territorial control. If the US has run an empire since 1900 or so, that empire has been non-territorial (except for the Philippines). But then what are the boundaries of this empire? How do we rule one nation or area of the world in, and another out? Simply to pose the question is again to denote the differences between an empire (it is territorial, whether in its traditional or its capitalist types), and the post-1945 American realm of action in the world. This realm is bounded by the reach of the world market, since, as Polanyi emphasized, 'market' means 'world market': the market continuously expands, carrying before it settled societies, national boundaries, even the formerly impervious structures of 'actually-existing socialism'. Or as Marx put it in *The Communist Manifesto*, the world market 'batters down all Chinese walls'.[47] The limit on the market is society: human collectivities that strive ceaselessly to subordinate the imperatives of the market to human control. Society often acts through the state, as a gatekeeper between domestic society and the backwash of the world market. Thus the fundamental global dynamic is production for profit in a world market, limited and constrained by human collectivities: and from this we derive a name for it – the world-system.

The only way in which the term 'empire' applies to the US, it seems to me, is in its archipelago of military bases: what military parlance has come to call American 'lily-pads' across the globe. The collapse of the USSR threatened to turn this vast network into a dinosaur but rather quickly it got a new lease of life, and the troops never came home. Indeed, when one thinks about it, US troops hardly ever have since 1945. Win (as in the Second World War), lose (as in Vietnam) or draw (as in Korea), the troops do not come home. Tens of thousands remain in Germany, Japan and South Korea half a century after open warfare ended. (Granted, there are no US troops in Vietnam, but they remain in the broader region.) In the aftermath of the wars in Afghanistan and Iraq, this archipelago was propelled to its furthest limit in history, a clear case of imperial overstretch where the armed forces of the US, pinned down in Iraq by a few thousand insurgents, cannot meet the other contingencies that are part of annual Pentagon planning (such as a war in Korea). US armed forces occupy many former Soviet military bases in Afghanistan, Kyrgyzstan and Uzbekistan, and are now projected into a strategic region (Central Asia) that has never been of direct interest to Washington but where the interests of four nuclear powers (China, Russia, Pakistan and India) converge. Thus Latham's 'external state' has metastasized beyond any point that American Cold War planners would recognize.

Other parts of this military territory are harder to specify. Panama, for example, was in for a long time, whether by virtue of the many American military bases there or the ease and frequency (13 or 14 times) with which the marines came ashore since the turn of the century. But today the Panama command is gone. Is Panama therefore independent? Perhaps not, but it is outside the territorial realm of the 'lily-pad' archipelago. Japan and Germany, now America's primary economic competitors, remain part of the archipelago with American bases dotting their homeland; each suffers protracted agonizing at the mere thought of exercising military force abroad. Countries like Brazil or Poland are outside of the empire, but within the realm of hegemony.[48] Both have recently suffered from severe debt burdens, both eventually succumbed to the zealous ministrations of the IMF, and both remain firmly ensconced in the semi-periphery (it is now of merely 'historical' interest that one was communist and one capitalist at the turn of the 1980s). From this sketchy outline I would conclude that 'empire' is the relative and contingent, historically bound term, whereas 'hegemony' is the name of the realm.

conclusion

In this chapter we have moved from the apparently simple principles of Polanyi's world economy to a complex narrative that helps us grasp the nature of the world system that we all live in and where we are going. Various analysts and pundits predicted over the past 15 years that the end of the Cold War would yield a return to the national rivalries and great power politics of the pre-1945 period (John Mearsheimer), a 'clash of civilizations' (Samuel Huntington) or even the 'end of history' (Francis Fukuyama).[49] But *realpolitik* does not govern the contemporary actions of the big powers; regional clashes of older civilizations in places like Bosnia and Iraq mask the burgeoning triumph of modern civilization (to which they are also – and ineffectively – reactive); and the triumph of the liberal programme does not mean 'the end of history' because in the post-Cold War era the liberal system of the 1940s realized its full, one-world dimensions, and because modern liberalism is itself a heterogeneous, contested and perpetually unfinished business.

Perhaps most striking today, however, is the utter collapse of a central tenet of the postwar liberal order, namely the idea of development and 'modernization'. Leaving aside China's rapid development, which will pose many interesting conundrums for the rest of this century, the Third World is dominated by the advanced countries in ways unprecedented since the colonial era and is for the most part decisively outside the loop of recent prosperity. It is therefore the prime source of war, instability and class conflict – but it has no convincing anti-systemic model to follow. All the systemic alternatives to the One World of multinational capital have collapsed: above all the Eastern bloc and the Soviet Union in 1989–91, but also the neo-mercantile model of East Asian development. But the least noticed collapse of our time is that of the Third World itself, the site of revolutionary nationalism and anti-imperial wars for three decades after 1945, the self-constituted alternative to both blocs in the Cold War that lasted from Bandung through the Non-Aligned Movement and into the late 1970s demands for a New International Economic Order. Today we have a collection of failed states running from Zambia to North Korea, an enormous if amorphous population of stateless people from Kosovo to Sudan, and the recurrent televised spectacle of millions of human beings starving to death, from Sudan to North Korea (again). The Third World moves not up the developmental ladder, but from statehood to catastrophe.

Today there appears to be one dominant global civilization, the American, and several atavisms masquerading as civilizational challenges

– Islamic fundamentalism, Balkan mayhem, the (not very) Confucian East, the obsolescing economic nationalism of Japan and South Korea, the declining Chinese Communist grip on a rapidly growing capitalist China, and a Russia that finds economic power only in its extractive industries, as if it had become a Third World country. Understanding how this came about is impossible unless political economy occupies a secure place at the heart of international history.

notes

*   Portions of this chapter have previously been published in my 'The American Century and the Third World', *Diplomatic History*, 23 (2) (1999) 355–70, and 'Is America an Imperial Power?', *Current History*, 102 (November 2003) 355–60.

1. Fred Harvey Harrington, *God, Mammon, and the Japanese* (Madison: University of Wisconsin Press, 1944); William Appleman Williams, *The Tragedy of American Diplomacy* (Cleveland: World Publishing, 1959); Walter LaFeber, *The New Empire: An Interpretation of American Expansion, 1860–1898* (Ithaca: Cornell University Press, 1963); Lloyd C. Gardner, *Economic Aspects of New Deal Diplomacy* (Madison: University of Wisconsin Press, 1964); Thomas J. McCormick, *China Market: America's Quest for Informal Empire, 1893–1901* (Chicago: Quadrangle, 1967).

2. Bruce Cumings, '"Revising Postrevisionism", Or, The Poverty of Theory in Diplomatic History', in Michael Hogan (ed.), *America in the World. The Historiography of American Foreign Relations since 1941* (Cambridge: Cambridge University Press, 1995), pp. 20–62.

3. Karl Polanyi, *The Great Transformation: The Political and Economic Origins of Our Time* (Boston: Beacon Press, 1957). Polanyi's classic was first published in 1944.

4. Polanyi, *Great Transformation*, p. 58.

5. 'Circulationist' connotes an approach that places the exchange of commodities, rather than their production, at the heart of theorizing about capital and class relations.

6. Polanyi, *Great Transformation*, pp. 138, 65.

7. Polanyi, *Great Transformation*, pp. 3–30, quote at p. 30. 'Ricardian' refers to David Ricardo, the influential British political economist of the early nineteenth century.

8. Polanyi, *Great Transformation*, p. 27.

9. Charles Kindleberger, *The World in Depression, 1929–1939* (Berkeley: University of California Press, 1973).

10. Karl Marx, 'Bastiat and Carey', in Karl Marx, *Grundrisse: Foundations of the Critique of Political Economy*, ed. and trans. by Martin Nicolaus (London: Penguin, 1973), pp. 884, 888.

11. Marx, 'Bastiat and Carey', p. 887.

12. Marx, 'Bastiat and Carey', p. 886.

13. Polanyi, *Great Transformation*, p. 132; see also Fred Block and Margaret R. Somers, 'Beyond the Economistic Fallacy: The Holistic Social Science of Karl

Polanyi', in Theda Skocpol (ed.), *Vision and Method in Historical Sociology* (Cambridge: Cambridge University Press, 1984), pp. 47–84.

14. Immanuel Wallerstein, *The Modern World-System. Vol. 1: Capitalist Agriculture and the Origins of the European World-Economy in the Sixteenth Century* (New York: Academic, 1974).

15. Andre Gunder Frank, *Latin America: Underdevelopment or Revolution. Essays on the Development of Underdevelopment and the Immediate Enemy* (New York: Monthly Review Press, 1970).

16. Ian Tyrrell, 'American Exceptionalism in an Age of International History', and Michael McGerr, 'The Price of the "New Transnational History"', *American Historical Review*, 96 (4) (1991) 1031–55 and 1056–67 respectively.

17. Polanyi, *Great Transformation*, pp. 249–58b.

18. Bruce Cumings, 'The Political Economy of Chinese Foreign Policy', *Modern China*, 5 (4) (1979) 411–61, and *Parallax Visions: Making Sense of American – East Asian Relations* (Durham: Duke University Press, 1999), ch. 6.

19. Polanyi, *Great Transformation*, p. 151.

20. Dean Acheson, *Morning and Noon* (Boston: Houghton Mifflin, 1965), pp. 216–17, 267–75.

21. Dean Acheson, *Present at the Creation: My Years in the State Department* (New York: Norton, 1969), p. 7.

22. Henry R. Luce, 'The American Century', *Life*, 17 February 1941, reprinted in *Diplomatic History*, 23 (2) (1999) 159–71.

23. Thomas J. McCormick, *America's Half-Century: United States Foreign Policy in the Cold War and After*, 2nd edn (Baltimore: Johns Hopkins University Press, 1995), p. 72. It is typical that this passing of the hegemonic baton should receive major emphasis from a scholar like McCormick but be passed over by many other diplomatic historians.

24. Henry R. Luce, 'The US Opportunity', *Fortune* (June 1947); for 'Coca-colonization', see Henry R. Luce, editorial, *Fortune* (February 1950).

25. William Borden, *The Pacific Alliance: United States Foreign Economic Policy and Japanese Trade Recovery, 1947–1955* (Madison: University of Wisconsin Press, 1984), pp. 12–14. Here I also rely on William Borden, 'Military Keynesianism in the Early 1950s,' unpublished conference paper (1994).

26. Dean Acheson, quoted in McCormick, *America's Half-Century*, p. 98.

27. Robert Latham, *The Liberal Moment: Modernity, Security, and the Making of Postwar International Order* (New York: Columbia University Press, 1997).

28. See, for example, Bruce Cumings, *The Origins of the Korean War. Vol. 2: The Roaring of the Cataract, 1947–1950* (Princeton, NJ: Princeton University Press, 1990), pp. 57–8.

29. Latham draws on the work of many scholars here, mentioning Franz Schurmann, Gabriel Kolko and myself among others; less obviously, perhaps, his approach is informed by the recent work of Friedrich Kratochwil, Alexander Wendt and other International Relations (IR) scholars of the 'constructivist' school.

30. Latham, *Liberal Moment*, p. 81.

31. Latham, *Liberal Moment*, pp. 65–70, quote at p. 68.

32. For an introduction, see Robert W. Cox with Timothy J. Sinclair, *Approaches to World Order* (Cambridge: Cambridge University Press, 1996).

33. Stephen Gill, *American Hegemony and the Trilateral Commission* (Cambridge: Cambridge University Press, 1990), pp. 54–6.
34. Terence K. Hopkins, Immanuel Wallerstein *et al.*, 'Patterns of Development of the Modern World-System', in Terence K. Hopkins, Immanuel Wallerstein *et al.* (eds), *World-Systems Analysis. Theory and Methodology* (London: Sage, 1982), pp. 41–82, quotes at pp. 52, 63; Immanuel Wallerstein, *Historical Capitalism* (New York: Verso, 1983), pp. 58–60.
35. Latham, *Liberal Moment*, pp. 57–65, quotes at pp. 60–1.
36. Bruce Cumings, 'The End of the Seventy-Years' Crisis: Trilateralism and the New World Order', *World Policy Journal*, 8 (2) (1991) 195–222.
37. W. W. Rostow, *The World Economy: History and Prospect* (Austin: University of Texas Press, 1978).
38. David P. Calleo, *The Imperious Economy* (Cambridge, MA: Harvard University Press, 1982), quotes at pp. 6, 45, 62, 65.
39. Robert Gilpin, *US Power and the Multinational Corporation: The Political Economy of Foreign Direct Investment* (New York: Basic Books, 1975).
40. Gregory P. Nowell, *Mercantile States and the World Oil Cartel, 1900–1939* (Ithaca: Cornell University Press, 1994).
41. John Blair, *The Control of Oil* (New York: Pantheon, 1976).
42. Albert O. Hirschman, *Exit, Voice, and Loyalty: Responses to Decline in Firms, Organizations, and States* (Cambridge, MA: Harvard University Press, 1970); Albert O. Hirschman, *The Passions and the Interests. Political Arguments for Capitalism before its Triumph* (Princeton, NJ: Princeton University Press, 1977); Albert O. Hirschman, *Journeys toward Progress: Studies of Economic Policy-Making in Latin America* (New York: Twentieth Century Fund, 1963); and Albert O. Hirschman, *National Power and the Structure of Foreign Trade* (Berkeley: University of California Press, 1945).
43. See, for example, Andrew Bacevich, *American Empire: The Realities and Consequences of US Diplomacy* (Cambridge, MA: Harvard University Press, 2002); Wesley K. Clark, *Winning Modern Wars: Iraq, Terrorism, and the American Empire* (New York: Public Affairs, 2003).
44. Niall Ferguson, *Colossus: The Price of America's Empire* (New York: Penguin, 2004); Chalmers Johnson, *The Sorrows of Empire: Militarism, Secrecy, and the End of the Republic* (New York: Metropolitan, 2004).
45. See, for example, Anthony Giddens, *The Nation-State and Violence* (Oxford: Polity, 1985), pp. 80–1, where the boundaries of traditional empires connoted nothing so much as a distant unstable realm of endless skirmishes with barbarians; in this sense the empire was coterminous with the only known world-system, with all else placed beyond the pale.
46. Michael Hardt and Antonio Negri, *Empire* (Cambridge, MA: Harvard University Press, 2000).
47. Karl Marx and Friedrich Engels, 'Manifesto of the Communist Party', in Karl Marx and Friedrich Engels, *Selected Works in One Volume* (London: Lawrence and Wishart, 1968), p. 39.
48. It was reported as this piece went to press, however, that Washington was in discussion with an enthusiastic Polish government about the possibility of building American military installations for the National Missile Defense Programme – radar stations, or even possibly missile interceptor bases – on Polish soil: Ian Traynor, 'US in Talks over Biggest Missile Defence Site in

Europe', *The Guardian*, 13 July 2004; available at: http://www.guardian.co.uk/usa/story/0,12271,1260037,00.html (accessed 16 July 2004). The Bush administration also recently announced the withdrawal of large numbers of troops from Europe and Asia, but this global redeployment by no means signifies the end of the 'lily-pad' archipelago: Michael P. Noonan, 'Reform Overdue: The Geopolitics of American Redeployment', Foreign Policy Research Institute E-Note, 23 August 2004; available at: http://www.fpri.org/enotes/20040823.military.noonan.redeployment.html (accessed 3 September 2004).

49. John Mearsheimer, *The Tragedy of Great Power Politics* (New York: Norton, 2001); Samuel Huntington, *The Clash of Civilizations and the Remaking of World Order* (New York: Simon and Schuster, 1996); Francis Fukuyama, *The End of History and the Last Man* (New York: Free Press, 1992).

4
ideology

nigel gould-davies*

All states are alike in possessing basic institutions of sovereignty, above all a monopoly of force over their territory. They are unlike in the values which legitimate that force and guide its use in shaping a state's domestic political, economic and social institutions. This chapter explores the role of ideology in international relations. It argues that this role is systematically understated, for reasons deeply rooted in International Relations (IR), but that the significance of ideology has, in fact, grown steadily over the past two centuries.[1] It suggests a way of 'bringing ideology in' to the study of international relations by developing a concept of ideological agency; explores the distinctive features of ideological foreign policy and their consequences for international order; and suggests how ideology and other sources of behaviour may be synthesized into a more satisfactory account of state conduct. Finally, it sketches a brief outline of recent international history to suggest what a more fully 'ideological' approach might look like.

the importance, and neglect, of ideology

There is an enormous literature on the concept of ideology, and an agreement on its definition is unlikely to be reached.[2] For the practical purpose of exploring the influence of ideology on international relations, it is sufficient to delineate the features that distinguish ideologies from other forms of ideas. Like culture, belief systems and *mentalités*, ideologies can provide identity and meaning embedded in a shared discourse.[3] Unlike these, ideologies aspire to systematic, rationalized knowledge and to varying degrees rest on explicit principles that are universal in scope. These have a philosophical character but, unlike philosophies, ideologies include not just theories but commitments. The principles they avow constitute both a critique of the existing order and a programme for its reform or transformation. And unlike religions, which in other respects they closely resemble, the ultimate referent of ideologies is the constitution of earthly things rather than divine command. In short, an idea-system can be said to be ideological to the extent that it comprises secular, universal principles prescribing collective human arrangements.

Ideology, then, is one form of ideational system. But it is the dominant one of modernity, the characteristic intellectual response to the profound societal transformations that eroded traditional bases for authority, raised new questions about the legitimate foundations of political, economic and social order and the purposes of state power, and created growing numbers of literate, thinking people seeking answers to them. Those answers have been few in number, though there have been many hybrids of them as well as variations within each. Liberalism defines individual freedom and rights as the basis for legitimacy; socialism stresses state ownership and control of the means of production as the guarantor of justice and equality; nationalism advocates collective membership of an independent state; fascism, especially in its Nazi form, defines race as the key criterion for membership (and even physical survival) in a political community.

There are important differences of type as well as content between ideologies. In particular, liberalism and socialism are inherently more rationalist and universal – products of the Enlightenment – than nationalism and fascism. The latter have a more ambiguous relationship with modernity, being at once a response to and reaction against it, reviving (and sometimes inventing) tradition and historical memory even as they harness modern techniques to the prosecution of their ambitions. They are less theoretically grounded and less universalist. It might be said that nationalism, in particular, arises at the intersection of ideology and culture. Its inherently more local orientation means that its impact on international relations is usually limited to the redrawing of borders, gathering in of *irredenta*, and growth of state assertiveness. Nationalists seek a bigger stake in the international system rather than its transformation. Since it shares fewer core attributes of a political ideology, nationalism will be less fully treated here.[4]

Ideologies prescribe the use of power for collective political purposes. They are in the first instance guides for domestic policy. Foreign policy is an inherently different, and far more difficult, activity. It is one of constraint rather than domination. Here, the monopoly of force within the state is now just one among many competing centres of power. It

this key point is emphasised by all Realist thinkers. Hans Morgenthau defines the rational goal of a state as 'the national interest conceived as power', and simply assumes that ideology is a mask or justification of it. Kenneth Waltz argues that rational states must maximize security rather than power. Drawing a comparison between the states system and market competition, he sets out the constraining logic of competition. While paying lip service to the range of goals a state can pursue, he insists that the imperatives of security will overwhelm them.[7]

There are variations on the Realist theme. For large states, the international system can better resemble oligopoly than perfect competition, and a margin of safety can allow some pursuit of ideas. Whether defensive or offensive technology dominates can also make a difference. But the central fact remains the search for security under anarchy. Any other goals are pursued only on sufferance. The Realist tradition is deeply antithetical to the proposition that values or other ideas, except those which reinforce the pursuit of national interest, can or should have a place in foreign policy.

Liberal arguments offer a range of familiar challenges to Realism. Against the assumption of a unitary rational actor, state policy is held to be a resultant of domestic interests refracted through a political process. Against the assumption of insecurity and competition, states are held to be capable of engaging in sustained and significant patterns of mutually-beneficial cooperation. And against the assumption of autonomous state behaviour, international institutions are held to be capable of constraining or shaping that behaviour.

Liberal criticisms of Realism are important and telling. But it is important to see how much they share. Both are theories of policy as interest-pursuit: the state interest of power and security or the domestic actor interest of economic welfare. One might also add the now neglected Marxist view of international relations as the conflict of transnational class interests. In all cases, the ends of politics are understood as the self-aggrandisement of the actors engaged in it, whether of power or plenty. They are all denominated in the coin of interests.

It is worth noting how limited this understanding of agency is. It excludes any goal that is not self-interested. Values, principles, commitments and other ideational motives – that is, non-self-regarding goals – have no place. It is true that some Liberal scholars use the generic term 'preferences', rather than 'interests', to describe an actor's ends without imputing the conferral of a benefit. But the term is used in only the most general and content-less way. When a specific theory or explanation is elaborated which requires substantive assumptions about the character of an actor's preferences, these are nearly always assumed to be security or welfare.[8]

International Relations does not ignore the existence of ideas altogether. Rather, it offers a range of arguments to account for them within the terms of interest-centred explanation. The Realist tradition characteristically depicts ideology as a means of manipulation: as a mask concealing true motives from adversaries, or a way of legitimating and mobilizing support in the eyes of a domestic population. Political scientists offer similar ways of seeing ideas as 'hooks' for hanging interests upon, as 'glue' for binding coalitions of interests, and so on. These are all variants of the classic interpretation of ideology as superstructure, resting on and reflecting underlying material interests. The purpose of such argument, perhaps Marxism's most enduring intellectual legacy, is to explain away rather than explain the role of ideas.[9] More recent functional approaches only embellish this by suggesting that ideas can aid the rational pursuit of interests.[10]

But in all such explanations, the role of ideas is marginal, if not epiphenomenal. It cannot be otherwise, for they are all efforts to transpose ideas into non-ideational terms of explanation, whose foundation is the axiom of interest-pursuit. Ideas, it seems, can do anything except be believed and pursued for their own sake. This inherently limited treatment of them will inevitably remain until we begin to develop a concept of political agency that renders intelligible the pursuit of values, ideals and principles *as ends in themselves*, and so challenges the dominant assumption of politics as interest-pursuit.

The growing interest in 'sociological' approaches to International Relations suggests a way forward. These approaches serve as a salutary counterpoint to the 'economic' methodology of rational maximisation that now dominates political science.[11] They draw attention to the role of shared norms and values in shaping relations between states, rather than that of individual self-interested actors. The English School of international relations lays stress on the common rules and institutions that help preserve order in the 'anarchical society' of the states system. Such order is held to be not a result of the pursuit of security or power by constituent states, but of a conscious and shared commitment to that order and the mechanisms that sustain it.[12] And the recent emergence of a 'constructivist' school suggests (in ways that are sometimes elusive) that the shared meanings imputed by constituent states to the international system can shape the way the system functions.[13]

A rare example of a theory about the role of shared values which is well specified and empirical rather than abstract and general is that of the democratic peace. The literature here has cast light on the distinctive behaviour of democratic regimes. One strand focuses specifically on the role of common norms. It argues that democratic states share a sense of community with one another and recognize the lack of threat they present to each other. This norm-based argument is a better explanation of the democratic peace than arguments about the role of democratic institutions. These suggest that self-interested populations, who bear the costs of war, will translate a pacific preference into foreign policy via democratic mechanisms of accountability. But such arguments argue for a generically pacific disposition of democracies, and cannot explain why democracies are willing to initiate war against non-democracies.[14] An explanation in terms of shared democratic values is more discriminating. But even this is limited to one feature – war-proneness – of democratic foreign policy; it is thus similar to Cold War debates about the inherently expansionist nature of totalitarian foreign policies. Neither offers a comprehensive approach to the impact of values on behaviour.

While sociological approaches can offer insights into the influence of ideas in international relations, they suffer two limitations. Firstly, it is not clear how much they explain. They often tend to 'thick description' rather than explanation. For example, the English School case would be stronger if it could show that the presence or absence of shared norms materially affected the degree of order.[15] As it is, its proponents find it hard to explain change and variation; there is a static quality to their analysis. Similarly with constructivism: it is not clear what, specifically, this approach can actually explain. Such statements, for example, that the Cold War ended because superpowers 'decided to end it' beg all the interesting questions about how shared interpretations of the world change.

Secondly, sociological approaches deal in *shared* ideas among groups of states. They find a role for ideas, but only at the cost of losing sight of the individual actor. States can hold competing as well as common values, and these can produce disorder and conflict rather than order and stability. It may be argued that this is at least as important in shaping international relations. Which has been the greater influence on twentieth-century history: shared beliefs in institutions of international order, or the ideological clashes between fascism, communism and democracy?

Beyond these specific limitations, there is a more general lack of robustness to arguments about the causal role of ideas. Even those who advance them typically feel obliged to show first that interest-based arguments are not on their own an adequate explanation. Realism is treated by advocates and critics alike as the default option, departure from which must be specially justified before recourse to an alternative form of explanation.[16] Ideational arguments are used to fill the gaps left by more familiar ones, rather than presenting a clear interpretation denominated in its own terms that may be compared with interest-centred ones on an equal footing.

In sum, we are all familiar with propositions about the role of ideas in international history. There is nothing exotic or obscure about them. But the study of international relations, while offering some important insights, furnishes no way of thinking systematically about this role, no account of what it means for states to pursue valued ends, what this looks like, and what it consequences are. The lacuna between empirical concerns and conceptual underdevelopment is simply enormous. A set of clear and distinct ideational terms of explanation is therefore needed, one that will redress the massive bias in favour of interest-based approaches. This, to repeat, is not only a theoretical issue. Much diplomatic history is underwritten by an implicit Realism that fits evidence about motives into the template of national interest, and makes assumptions and judgements about the primacy of interests over ideology that are rarely scrutinized. To redress the balance we need an approach that treats ideological *differences* (not only shared norms) as *autonomous* (not derivative or epiphenomenal) and *systematic* (not *ad hoc* or case-based) influences on behaviour.

towards an understanding of ideological states

Self-interested behaviour seeks goals of power, security or welfare that directly benefit the actor pursuing them. Value-directed behaviour seeks to change the actor's external environment in accordance with a given set of principles. As argued above, the distinctive feature of an *ideological* actor is its commitment to spread the values and structures of its regime-type to other states. To the extent that there remains a discrepancy between some existing societal arrangements and the values of the ideology, there will be a permanent latent impulse to extend those values into areas not under its domain. Of course, this latency is by no means always manifested and in practice it will be affected by the interaction of values and other influences, such as interests, in ways that will be touched on below. But the logic of ideology, being universal rather than local in scope, decrees a permanent dissatisfaction with its incomplete sway. Ideological goals produce distinctive foreign policies, patterns of international relations and implications for international order. These are most clearly seen by considering cases where ideological goals have been most radical in extent and comprehensive in pursuit. This is the experience of revolutionary states. In them we see the concentrated expression of ideological values, the fullest commitment to transform the international system in their own image.

One of the very few scholars to give deep and sustained thought to the experience of revolutionary states in international relations is Martin Wight. He was fully aware of their historical significance. He pointed out that, in chronological terms alone, revolutionary periods have been at least as common as non-revolutionary ones.[17] But it is his account of the impact of revolutionary states, and the deep underlying causes of their behaviour in structures of revolutionary thought, that remains unsurpassed. Revolutionary doctrines, he writes,

> transpose the melody of power politics into a new key. They introduce passion and fanaticism into calculations of political utility, and doctrine sometimes overrides or reinterprets interest. They blur the distinction between domestic and foreign policy; they transform diplomacy; and they transform war.[18]

Wight elaborated the 'Kantian' tradition embodying the key features of revolutionary international thought.[19] Revolutionaries, he held, do not accept a principled distinction between domestic and foreign policy. The domestic arrangements of other states are their intense concern. Revolutionaries will seek to interfere in them not just to influence the sources of foreign policy in other states but because reordering other social systems is the ultimate object of revolutionary aspirations. They dream of establishing international unity founded on common ideological values. The existing order and the institutions that sustain it are, in the eyes of revolutionaries, illegitimate and destined to be swept away. This is not to say that they will not use elements of this order for their own purposes. Cooperation to buy time, gain a disproportionate benefit or deceive adversaries is entirely consistent with a longer-term strategy of undermining that order. It should not be mistaken for acceptance of it. Indeed, the revolutionary approach to the current order is the opposite of that taken by Grotian, or rationalist, members of international society. Such states profess commitment to the shared principles and institutions of international order, but sometimes violate these on pragmatic grounds. Revolutionaries, by contrast, harbour a principled rejection of the international society, but may sometimes make pragmatic use of its practices.

At a minimum, revolutionary states will seek to propagate their values across borders. Where feasible, they will use not just the force of ideas but force itself to impose these values on (or as they have it, 'liberate') other peoples. *Conversion* and *crusading* are the distinctive modes of a revolutionary foreign policy. More general conditions typically conduce to such methods. Great revolutionary ideas rarely arise in one country alone. From the first, they find traction in other countries. This is often because they are a response to larger forces, or even a general crisis, of international systemic significance. They may erupt in one state, but simmer in many others. There is thus a constituency, or at least a potential one, of believers for the revolutionary state to cultivate – as it were, an ideological diaspora. As a consequence, revolutionary states characteristically develop a 'dual foreign policy' comprising two complementary arms. State-to-state relations preserve the formalities and confer the privileges of traditional diplomatic representation. Revolutionary states very often display a strong initial distaste of traditional diplomatic forms, and are tempted to reject them entirely. With time, though, they accommodate themselves to these as they recognise the usefulness of claiming the rights conferred by membership of the international system.[20] Simultaneously, 'people-to-people' or 'class-to-class' relations are conducted across state borders, without the consent (and sometimes even the knowledge) of the authorities in the target countries. Through these the revolutionary state inspires, organizes and coordinates co-ideologists within other countries, directly and systematically interfering in the internal affairs of other states. Sometimes the one supports the other in the most direct ways, as when in March 1918 Trotsky's policy of 'no war, no peace' was used to try to buy time for an uprising in Germany (and to spread communist literature among the German front lines); or when in the 1927 Arcos affair, the Soviet trade mission in London was found to be storing seditious material. More usually, the two arms will operate in discrete but complementary ways, diplomatic relations being used to claim and exploit the rights that come with recognition as a member of the international system, and ties of ideological affinity being used to work for that system's long-term transformation.[21]

While revolutionary foreign policies are often seen as irrational and unsustainable, the availability of ideological loyalties that cross-cut state borders confers on them a special advantage. It is a form of power that orthodox states do not normally enjoy. It is one of the ways in which revolutionaries challenge the principles and practices of international order. For them, the basic dynamic is not the fluid interaction of sovereign states, but an absolute, polarized conflict between allegiances which run horizontally through states, not vertically between them. While temporary, tactical truces may arise between states belonging to opposing camps, the underlying ideological forces driving international relations are irreconcilably opposed. A *de facto* state of war necessarily exists as long as the two sides continue to do so. It is a conflict conducted within states as much as between them. Indeed, in extreme cases civil war with external support and intervention breaks down the distinction between inter-state and intra-state relations completely.

In ideologized international systems, success and failure are understood in geoideological rather than geopolitical terms, measured by the expansion or decline of regime-types – what might be termed a 'balance of faith' rather than of raw power. More than this, a total calculus of the relative strength of camps – what the Soviet Union called the 'correlation of forces' – adds up forces within states as well as states themselves. Alignments between states are similarly conceived in terms of the affinities or antagonisms between the regimes that control them. Unlike Realists, ideologues do have perpetual allies and eternal enemies, their orientation fixed on the basis of political values, not fluid and shifting on the basis of self-interested alliance.

What would an ideological interpretation of international relations look like? Realism focuses on the distribution of power among states and the self-interested responses to this. The big stories it tells are of bids for great power hegemony that provoke countervailing coalitions to restore a balance of power and preserve the independence of member-states.[22] Liberalism focuses on shifting comparative advantages and the globalization of productive forces. Its big stories concern the interaction of economic interdependence and political control, and the way that the rise and decline of successive economic hegemons affects this.[23] An ideological perspective puts at the centre of attention the rise and decline of the great political idea-systems. It narrates a history of successive challenges to the principles of international order, conflicts between contending belief-systems, and struggles for the hearts and minds of the uncommitted. Table 4.1 outlines the key features of Realism, Liberalism and an 'Idealist' perspective on international relations.

A clear concept of ideological agency is an essential first step to a proper evaluation of the role of political values. It provides a way of interpreting ideological behaviour in its own terms, rather than fitting it into other categories. But a full account of the experience of ideologies must show how the imperatives and commitments of political values interact with the constraints and demands of interests. For interest-based and value-based approaches are not alternatives but complements. They imply different kinds of behaviour with different consequences. But they are all likely to be present in any situation of any complexity. The vectors of power,

Table 4.1 Key Features of IR Paradigms

Paradigm	Actor	Goal of actor	Characteristic relationship between actors	Key explanatory variable	View of history
Realism	State	Security/power	Zero-sum coercion (war)	Relative power; polarity of international system	Balance of power; hegemonic challenges
Liberalism	Individual and group economic interests	Economic welfare	Positive-sum exchange (trade, investment)	Distribution of comparative advantages	Global expansion of productive forces
'Idealism'	Political regime	Preservation, propagation, implementation of values	Conversion (crusades, propaganda)	Relationships between ideational systems	Rise and decline of ideational systems

plenty and principle pull in different directions, and the behaviour of an actor will be the resultant of all three. Indeed, they virtually presuppose one another. Political-military power requires material resources to sustain it; the pursuit of economic gain requires coercive power to protect agents and enforce agreements; and the pursuit of values requires a set of military and economic capabilities for doing so. Finally, and most importantly, while it is possible to pursue power or wealth as ends in themselves, in practice – and this has become progressively truer over the past two centuries – states acquire these capabilities at least in part because of what they wish to do with them; and this in turn is shaped by the principles they embody as political regimes.

It is easy and unsatisfying to say that the truth will always lie in a stew of 'ideas-and-interests'. For purposes of analytical clarity we will want as far as possible to suggest how the two sources of behaviour interact, and the possible outcomes or hybrids that can emerge. We can think of a state that seeks to incorporate political values in its foreign policy as simultaneously inhabiting two worlds, each with its own imperatives. The external world imposes constraints and exerts pressures on the actor, weathering away beliefs inconsistent with the world 'out there' and goals incompatible with the imperatives of security and welfare, so working to compel the routinization of ideas around the rational pursuit of interests. The internal world impels the agent to change the external one. It directs the mobilization of military and economic power in the service of valued ends. The two worlds are locked in a reciprocal struggle, each trying to conform the other to itself. Here an ideological gain will be made, an element of the existing order altered or undermined; here the prevailing order imposes itself, a belief will be abandoned or doctrine revised. Neither wholly succeeds and neither wholly fails, at least in the short term: the struggle gives rise rather to mutual adjustment.

The actor who occupies these worlds must balance the contradictory pressures to maximize its power and position in the international system, and to maintain its commitment to change that system. Six characteristic resolutions of the tension may be suggested. The first three favour the ideational world, and signify the actor's success in changing its external environment in accordance with its own beliefs and values:

1. *Resistance.* The actor may override elements of the existing order by refusing to be bound by established principles and assumptions. In international relations, institutions as important as customary law, diplomatic immunity and even aspects of sovereignty have been subject to attack by ideological states. Such states may even achieve reform of the system by successfully introducing new norms that embody, or help

to further, their own values, such as 'national self-determination' or 'limited sovereignty'.

2. *Manipulation*. The actor may manipulate aspects of the existing order, which cannot yet be changed, to its advantage. One way this can arise is if the actor claims the privileges and protection afforded by membership of the system, while seeking its reform or transformation. Another way is if the distinctive interpretation of the world furnished by the actor's ideology actually confers advantages on it, enabling it to identify factors and forces overlooked by the prevailing assumptions within the system. The early Soviet concessions policy, and its use of 'capitalist contradictions' to achieve recognition on favourable terms is an example.

3. *Innovation*. The actor may release new forces into the system, which it may also be better placed than others to exploit. It may cultivate and exploit horizontal ties of allegiance with groups and movements in other countries, which bypass and subvert the traditional vertical divisions of the states system. International relations thus begin to work in new ways, and the revolutionary state will develop new techniques and instruments to make use of them. It may find itself significantly stronger in the new categories of power than its adversaries.

Other outcomes, however, favour the external world, compelling the radical state to modify its beliefs:

4. *Compromise*. The actor acknowledges that external circumstances demand a redefinition of its goals and strategy. This typically arises when the durability of existing international arrangements requires prolonged coexistence with them, though without abandonment of commitment to their reform. It can take two forms. *Tactical compromise* involves accommodation or even cooperation that is intended only to be temporary. An example is the Leninist policy of seeking a 'breathing space' *(peredyshka)* in the 1920s. *Selective compromise* involves long-term accommodation in areas of relative weakness, while the broader conflict between principles is pursued in areas of relative strength. The post-Stalinist Soviet acceptance of the need to avoid general war in the nuclear age is an example.[24]

Compromise is not, as often assumed, tantamount to deideologization. It signifies rather the adaptation of values and beliefs – and, especially, the way they are implemented – to new circumstances, the more effectively to pursue them. There is certainly no warrant for taking policy change to be *prima facie* evidence of apostasy, as if authentic ideological agents were not permitted to adjust their thinking in the light of experience and conditions. Some analysts seem to think the only genuine revolutionary policy is one of immediate and total war against all adversaries, with any consideration of state interests signifying the creeping betrayal of revolutionary values. In fact, taking into account the interests of the primary repository and vehicle of revolutionary values is an entirely legitimate consideration. It would be reckless to disregard them. The most sustained and compelling argument for caution and compromise, especially from a position of short-term weakness, in the ultimate service of radical ends was made by Lenin, a leader of unquestioned revolutionary pedigree. Against those in the Bolshevik party who wanted to maintain a posture of unmitigated confrontation with the West, he argued forcefully that such a position actually constituted a betrayal of revolutionary values by putting into jeopardy the only state where revolution had been achieved. He pointed out how, again and again, such tactics had served the party before the revolution. Indeed they had, and contributed to the improbable triumph of the tiny Bolshevik against far more powerful adversaries. They were to do so again in the service of Leninist foreign policy. It is in his genius for political strategy and tactics that Lenin's enduring significance may be said to lie.[25]

This is not to deny that ideological actors may face stark contradictions between what their principles impel and their environment compels, and must choose between values and interests. Such dilemmas are a characteristic part of their experience, and there are two possible behavioural responses to it:

5(a) *Acceptance of costs*. The actor acknowledges the incompatibility of values with interests, and that pursuing the former rather than the latter will incur costs (possibly including a lower level of security), but nonetheless chooses to do so. After all, as Raymond Aron once posed the issue: who prefers life to the reasons for living?[26] The sternest test of belief is precisely the willingness to forgo other goods in its pursuit. Irrefutably irrational elements of Nazi wartime policy exemplify this: the use of railway networks for transport of Jews rather than *matériel*; the reluctance to let women work in factories; the treatment of Ukrainians who greeted them as liberators, and so on.[27]

5(b) *Acceptance of constraints*. The actor instead submits to the imperatives imposed by the international system, or to domestic interests. Ideological values are eroded away or so revised that they come to legitimate state power rather than drive its uses. The state gradually abandons its efforts to transform the existing order and instead pursues orthodox interests within it. It is socialized into the international order. A residue of revolutionary rhetoric and ritual may remain, but underneath lies the practice of power politics by any other name. Universalist aspirations decompose into mere expansionism. Hence Barrington Moore's persuasive depiction of the post-revolutionary Soviet polity in which the means had finally eaten up the ends.[28]

Understanding the condition of the ideological state as a dialectical relationship between a world of principles and commitments and a world of interests and constraints offers insight into its behaviour. Above all, it suggests this condition is defined by a series of choices about how to reconcile competing imperatives. This takes us beyond the tired and familiar polarities of 'ideology or interest'. Yes, these make differing demands on policy, and in the long-run chart alternative trajectories of behaviour. But it is not a matter of one or the other, but rather of how the tensions between them are managed. Debates always arise among revolutionaries about the best way to do so. These are frequently fierce because the stakes are so high. It is the central problem of revolutionary strategy. A situation of any complexity will yield a mix of partial outcomes. Some aspects of an ideology will prove successful and sustainable, others will undergo adaptation and compromise in response to external circumstances, and others still, cutting sharply across the grain of international politics, will either be discarded or retained only at palpable cost. There will be no determinate solution; resolution in any particular case will depend, among other things, on the flexibility of the ideology and its capacity to adapt to circumstances without sacrificing core values; on the severity of the constraints imposed by the international system; and the crucial and contingent role of leadership in making choices and seeking syntheses between competing demands.

This way of looking at the problem points the way to a richer conception of agency. As the study of international political economy springs up at the confluence of Realism and Liberalism, exploring the interaction of wealth creation and sovereign power, so we can conceive of a branch of International Relations that would analyse the interactions between the universal scope and unlimited ambition of values, and the local orientation and limited resources of interests. It would map out the range of tensions, affinities and resolutions between these two imperatives, and the factors that would tend to produce particular outcomes in specific cases.

This has far-reaching implications. While revolutionary ideas distil the logic of ideological agency into its purest form, most modern states – and especially the most powerful ones – have typically legitimated themselves with clearly-articulated political values, and these have been part of the discourse of their foreign policy. Indeed, I will argue below that the trend has been for ideologies to grow in international significance over time. One might say that, in the modern world, the pure, interest-pursuing state is a limiting case and very much the exception. It should not be thought to constitute an approximation of typical state behaviour any more than the extreme revolutionary should. These constructs should be thought of as ideal-types rather than paradigms. Most real cases lie somewhere in between. The practice of principle is a fundamental theme in international relations.[29]

Concepts and categories bring clarity and coherence to a subject. But their value lies in their contribution to concrete questions. On their own they cannot resolve them; they can only contribute to the empirically detailed and theoretically disciplined examination of evidence that is the domain of the historian. The big interpretative questions may still defy final resolution, but the debates will be better and it will be clearer what a good answer would look like.

Systematic study of the influence of ideology, and of other forms of ideas, on international relations is an enormous undertaking that has barely begun. Here I can suggest only the broadest outlines of an 'ideological' view of recent international history.[30] There is much more to be said on every aspect. But it will at least bring out some key themes: the recurrence of characteristic choices and dilemmas for ideological actors; the evolution of, and interaction between, ideological forms; the role of contextual factors in influencing the impact of ideologies; and the consequences of all this for international order.

the rise of ideology

Before ideologies there were religions. Many of the features attributed to revolutionary ideologies are shared by the great monotheistic religions. Religious conflict had helped plunged Europe into war in the late sixteenth and early seventeenth centuries. The 1648 Peace of Westphalia recognized the ruinous consequence of competing claims of religious allegiance. The principle of *cuius regio, eius religio* (whereby a ruler had the right to decide his subjects' religion) enshrined in the treaty amounted to a necessary truce that imposed practical limits on the universalist aspirations of faith. On it the modern states system was founded.

The century that followed saw the decline of religion as an active factor in intra-European relations, though it was important in defining Europe's relationship with the Ottoman Empire. In its place a relatively pure and fluid form of power politics was practised, epitomised by the diplomatic revolution of 1756, where four major powers swapped alliance partners. It was in this period, too, that theories of the balance of power were formulated. These invoked metaphors of mechanical or celestial movement that emphasized a state's relations to other states as the key determining factor in its behaviour, rather than any internal properties or values it might possess.

From Alexis de Tocqueville on, observers have been struck by the similarities between religion and ideology. The structures of thought and the commitments they demand have led many to conclude that they are functional equivalents, meeting a common need for universal meaning and value. In this sense the decline of religion paved the way for the rise of ideology, which has been described as a 'political religion'.[31] The first ideological values to have a dramatic international impact were forged in the crucible of the French Revolution; indeed, the very term 'ideology' was coined in this period. Debates on the interpretation of the French revolutionary wars, and on the relative importance of ideological and power-political factors, remain live. But it would be hard to argue that the introduction of radical ideas did not create new patterns of international relations, generate new forms of power, and release forces of long-term change into the international system.[32] The overthrow of the French monarchy in the name of principles of liberty and popular sovereignty very quickly extended into an open challenge to other states whose authority was not founded on them. As with subsequent revolutionary ideologies, by asserting the right to determine the regime-type of other states French leaders mounted a secular challenge to the Peace of Westphalia, which they denounced by name. They made a clear distinction between states and their peoples, and appealed directly to the latter. As a consequence, orthodox inter-state relations increasingly assumed the form of relations between the bearers of idea-systems, transcending national borders. Foreign radicals flocked to Paris, while aristocrats fled abroad to seek support for intervention. Foreign states in turn pronounced revolutionary developments in France a matter of general concern, and took measures against radical groups on their own territory.[33]

While revolutionary leaders were acutely and proudly aware of the universal scope of their principles, they differed in their foreign-policy calculus. Some believed it prudent to protect the revolution by avoiding antagonism with powerful neighbours – by not, for example, intervening in response to radical appeals for intervention abroad. More radical figures, notably the Girondin foreign minister Brissot, advocated wars of liberation and developed a fully ideologised concept of security which held that even a single remaining monarchy would present a permanent threat to France. (In his last years, Stalin was to formulate an analogous position with respect to capitalist states and Soviet security).

A growing polarization set in, a kind of ideological action–reaction spiral whereby declarations of revolutionary aspiration mobilize international reaction which in turn harden suspicion and hostility.[34] The state of permanent potential war that characterises relations between antithetical ideologies broke out into military conflict from 1792. Soon thereafter revolutionary values became increasingly transmuted into a form of political nationalism, a key component of the identity of the new French state legitimating policies that increasingly resembled traditional imperial expansion. This 'nationalization' of universal principles provoked a corresponding nationalist reaction in many of the territories that France came to occupy, which helped to mobilize populations against it. But even as fidelity to universal principles dwindled, the elemental energies awakened by them endured and were harnessed to the new goals of French imperialism. The *levée en masse*, the mobilization of an entire population's resources, transformed the conduct of war and gave France an enormous advantage. Only after 20 years of intermittent warfare, and the disastrous invasion of Russia, was France finally defeated.

Despite the restoration of the Bourbon monarchy in 1815 the forces released by the revolution were to long outlive it. They profoundly shaped the development of the international system during the nineteenth century. This system became ideologically heterogeneous, creating divisions both within states and between them. No revolutionary or doctrinaire powers emerged but, to a degree without precedent in the previous century, political developments within states shaped relations between states. The growing power of political ideas, which was to exert its greatest influence in the twentieth century, was fostered by the complex of processes that constitute modernization – urbanization, industrialization, mass literacy, education – which swept east across Europe, creating populations (or sometimes cultural elites speaking in their name) uprooted from traditional ways of life, receptive to new ideas, and able to read, write, debate and organize.

After the long struggle with French hegemony, the Concert of Europe was established to better manage great power relations. At least as significant were the growing divisions among those powers along broadly ideological lines. Britain resisted the early attempts of conservative powers to use the Congress system to legitimate intervention against revolution, and went so far as to withdraw from the system for this reason. After the 1830 revolution, which removed the Bourbons for good, France inclined towards Britain's more liberal policy, while Austria, Russia and Prussia periodically expressed their conservative solidarity by declarations, treaties and sometimes direct support (as when Russia suppressed the

1848 Hungarian Revolution on Austria's behalf).[35] Britain's liberalism generated domestic debates about the proper policy towards revolutions, but the dominant outcome was a non-intervention that meshed with its detached geographical position, rather than active intervention in support of liberal values. Only poor Napoleon III conducted a quixotic policy of active support for national self-determination, hopelessly mixed up with French power ambitions, which ended in comprehensive defeat.

Meanwhile, nationalism exerted a growing influence on the shapes of states. It unified Italians and Germans into major powers. Conversely, it threatened the gradual erosion of the multinational Austro-Hungarian empire. The relationship between nationalism and liberalism evolved in ways that were to have fateful long-term consequences. Until 1848, they seemed natural allies, complementary expressions of a desire for freedom against the old order. Liberal nationalism seemed a workable synthesis, culminating in a vision of harmonious coexistence between free nations of free peoples. But as nationalism grew in vigour, they increasingly pulled in different directions. By glorifying a particular culture, and even asserting its superiority, more 'integral' forms of nationalism became a force that ran across the grain of liberal ideals, and that of their more radical cousin, socialism. It could also be co-opted by states to mobilize populations behind traditional foreign policy goals. The assertion of national greatness naturally and easily complemented and augmented the advancement of state interest.

The rise of ideology in the nineteenth century played an important role in shaping international developments. It influenced state alignments and orientations and helped redraw the map of Europe. But it operated within a larger and older context of great power politics which it modified and complicated, but could not displace. On the contrary, for all its influence, ideology was decisively trumped by the logic of multipolar power politics at the outbreak of the First World War. The Franco-Russian alliance, the key first stage in the formation of the prewar alignments, joined together regimes at opposite ends of the political spectrum against the common German threat.[36] The effect was truly dramatic within states. Socialist parties who had vowed at successive congresses of the Second International to oppose war supported their respective capitalist governments unswervingly. The ties of fraternal solidarity dissolved swiftly and completely on contact with national security.

The war was a general *levée en masse*, more fully a conflict between peoples and not merely states than any that had preceded it. The ferocious national energies it released and harnessed, especially on the Western Front, gave a sharp and vengeful edge to the peace-making that followed, leading to a severely punitive treatment of Germany that contrasted with the reintegration of France into the international system after 1815. It also met the characteristically ideological demand for what is now known as 'regime change' in the defeated power. This meant not just the removal of a war leader, but a reordering of the structures and values underpinning his rule. In different ways regime change was to be closely associated with the ending of all three major conflicts of the 'short' twentieth century (1914 – 1989): the two world wars and the Cold War.

This was but one expression of the larger truth that this century marked the high tide of political ideas and of conflicts between them. It was the age of ideology. The nineteenth century had seen the slow diffusion and growing influence of the values released by the French Revolution. Now ideas were to capture state power and use this to try to transform the international system. And this challenge came not from one but several ideologies simultaneously, greatly weakening the status quo and accelerating its evolution.

This began in 1917 on two fronts. In April Woodrow Wilson brought America into the war. In October Lenin and the Bolsheviks seized power and took Russia out of the war. Both men fundamentally rejected the established institutions of international relations and sought to replace them with a new vision, though these visions were themselves fundamentally opposed. Lenin had developed an extreme variant of revolutionary Marxism, tempered by tactical acuity, which had not succumbed to the failure of the Second International on the outbreak of war. Marxism-Leninism was perhaps the most total of all ideologies, offering a comprehensive account of mankind's political, economic and social development which would culminate in the inevitable global triumph of communism. Lenin's initial vision of politics was inherently international. He believed that the Russian Revolution would trigger both similar revolutions across Europe and intervention by the threatened ruling classes of the old bourgeois order. An international civil war of classes would supplant that between states. He was partly right. The Bolsheviks worked furiously in the first years after 1917 to secure power against domestic adversaries and half-hearted interventions from abroad, and to aid revolutionary forces in Germany, Hungary, Finland and elsewhere. The failures of both intervention and revolution, and the growing stabilization of the postwar order after 1923, led to a reappraisal of Bolshevik strategy that acknowledged that temporary ebb of the revolutionary tide and the opportunity to buy time to build up Soviet power in advance of the next inevitable crisis of capitalism. Familiar debates arose about the correct tradeoffs between the protection of Soviet interests and revolutionary activism abroad. Certain tactical adjustments of methods and timing were made in Soviet policy, but the changes should not be exaggerated. In particular, the Stalinist doctrine of 'socialism in one country' should not be construed as an abandonment of revolutionary commitments. Subsequent developments, both before and after the Second World War, were to show that the essential elements of the Bolshevik world-view – above all, the irreconcilability of capitalism and socialism, and the inevitability of conflict between them, as the basic motive force of world politics – remained unchanged.

The new Soviet state had truly revolutionary goals, but its weakness and the waning of postwar instability meant its power could not match the scope of its ambitions. The United States had been in a similar position after its own revolution. But under Woodrow Wilson the latent radicalism of America's self-image was formidably unleashed by the country's decisive intervention in the First World War. His motives for doing so, and for his subsequent attempts to shape the postwar order, were extraordinarily ambitious. He sought nothing less than to remake international order on the basis of the universal principles of democracy and the rule of law. With striking clarity he rejected, even denigrated, self-interest as a basis for American policy. Indeed, he sometimes sought to *define* America's interest in terms of the spread of its values – the most radical possible position for an ideological foreign policy.[37]

Wilson's idealism was not revolutionary in the sense that Lenin's was. He sought to reform rather than overthrow the international system, and to work with other states in doing so. Nonetheless, his prescriptions were radical and discomfiting to status quo powers like Britain and France. Rejection of the balance of power in favour of a League of Nations; repudiation of secret diplomacy; anti-imperialism and self-determination: all of this challenged the old European way of doing things. Wilson was capable of compromises at Versailles, notably of the principle of self-determination he otherwise sought to implement. And he intervened with troops 17 times in Latin America. But his larger ambition for international order remained remarkably idealistic, and specifically ideological insofar as it associated a specific regime-type with creation of a secure and just international order. The war had been fought 'to make the world safe for democracy', and the peace would be secured by a permanent alliance of democratic states united in a League of Nations.

Though one authentic expression of American principles in foreign policy, there was nothing inevitable about this remarkable internationalist idealism. Wilson's leadership was decisive. Other responses to America's rise to world power status, other amalgams of principle and interest, were possible and some had been practised.[38] Against a background of domestic disillusion and Congressional resistance, Wilson's vision faltered. But his ideological legacy has outlasted him, and become an enduring and influential current of American foreign policy thinking. And it may be argued that the inherently ideological identity of the United States, founded on a political creed rather than a distinctive national or ethnic base, powerfully reinforces the Wilsonian synthesis and ensures its continuing influence.[39]

Lenin and Wilson were conscious that they represented rival alternatives to traditional principles of international order. They issued competing appeals over the heads of governments to populations. The two countries were not to clash in systemic rivalry until after 1945. But these early developments offered a brief glimpse of that future struggle. In ideological terms, the roots of the Cold War could be said to lie in 1917. Only when antithetical values were harnessed to global power would this potential be unleashed.

The rise of fascism in the inter-war period presented a third ideological challenge, one that was, in many ways, different in kind. Unlike democratic idealism and Marxism-Leninism, it was not rationalist in origin, not founded on a coherent theory or clear philosophical principles. Like nationalism, of which it was in some ways a hypertrophied version, fascism was a reaction against modernization that fostered premodern, sometimes pastoral, nostalgia. But it readily used modern methods of industry, organization and propaganda to build up its power. Like Soviet communism it aspired to a totalitarian degree of control over the individual that effaced the distinction between the public and private spheres. And like communism it established a transnational movement of parties whose ideological solidarity cross-cut state boundaries – though fascism never established anything approaching the degree of control and coordination of the Comintern.

The three corners of the inter-war ideological contest tussled in complex ways. As is characteristic of ideological politics, cleavages ran through as much as between states. Stalin disastrously misjudged the character of fascism as a final and extreme culmination of capitalism that presaged the final stage of the class conflict. He accordingly prevented, until too late, the cooperation of communist with social democratic parties that might have prevented Hitler coming to power. Conversely, the belief of many conservatives in France in 'better Hitler than Blum' inhibited an effective national response to the growing Nazi revision of Versailles.[40] The *Historikerstreit* (historians' controversy) has raised the question of whether Nazism was a reaction to Bolshevism, borrowing totalitarian techniques from, and mobilizing against, the ideological threat to the East.[41] Whether or not one accepts this argument, it seems clear that ideological conflict imparted a special intensity to the growing crisis of the 1930s, and helped to make this period a 'European civil war' and not merely a conflict between major powers.

While fascist states did not have a coherent regime-model to export, their emphasis on 'action' and the cult of violence made them inherently prone to war-like foreign policies.[42] And Nazi racial theory imparted a revolutionary dynamic to German policy by seeking to remake Europe and ultimately the world along racial, rather than political or economic, lines. Hitler was capable of making temporary, tactical compromises – most importantly, the Ribbentrop-Molotov pact of 1939, which was no more a renunciation of his hatred for 'Jewish Bolshevism' than it was a repudiation of socialism by Stalin. But his central drive was an extremist ambition of unlimited scope to exterminate 'inferior' peoples. The irrationalities this produced, from the perspective of any conceivable German national interest, piled up until they destroyed the regime.

The Cold War saw the fullest and most sustained period of ideological conflict for several reasons.[43] Firstly, the ideological bipolarity of capitalist democracy and Marxism-Leninism both complemented and sharpened the geopolitical bipolarity of superpower confrontation. Until the Sino-Soviet split there was no jostling between poles to complicate patterns of ideological alignment. Secondly, mutual nuclear deterrence sharpened the incentives to avoid direct military hostilities, thereby displacing the conflict into manifold indirect forms. Thirdly, the character of the ideologies themselves had a stabilizing effect. Both sides felt time was on their side. Belief in the inevitability of the global triumph of communism instilled patience into Soviet leaders, especially after Stalin (who understated the significance of nuclear weapons and saw the post-war period as a new prewar one).[44] The American strategy of containment was also premised on the long view: it was necessary to be firm, but the West could afford to wait until the Soviet regime was undermined by its internal weaknesses.[45] By contrast, Hitler's belief that time was working against Germany, which could therefore not afford to delay war, had been inherently destabilising. Fourthly, the capacity of both sides to project power spread this conflict around the globe. Almost no part of the world remained untouched by the clash of ideologies. Finally, both ideologies were fully universalist. Their appeal was extendable to all. Nobody was excluded from membership of either, as nationalism and fascism had excluded through ascriptive criteria of ethnicity or race. Every individual was a potential convert. The very names of the chief protagonists – the

United States and the Soviet Union – described political structures and were devoid of any reference to nation or history.

This highly-developed ideological character of the Cold War manifested itself in many ways that help explain the peculiar features of this era of international history. Both sides saw the world primarily as a struggle between two social systems. Each saw its goal not as the direct acquisition of territory against the other, but as the spread of its own system to new territory. Indeed, ideology could actually define territoriality, as with the division of Germany, China, Korea, Vietnam and Yemen along ideological lines. And the ultimate goal of each side – their concept of victory – was defined not as the defeat, destruction or occupation of the adversary, but as the overthrow of the political system within it.

The means each side developed were consonant with the ideological character of their goals. They used military intervention where this did not risk nuclear escalation, often to remove regimes that belonged to, or threatened to move into, the adversary camp. Short of this, they sought to make use of indirect, transnational sources of influence. The Soviet comparative advantage lay in the 'organizational weapon' of communist parties and front organizations. The Western advantage lay in exploiting the growth of globalizing technologies that made even Soviet bloc borders less impermeable with time. While each sought to influence the other's core population, much of the contest for 'hearts and minds' took place in the emerging Third World (where the ideology of nationalism had the same corrosive effect on maritime empires as it had had on land empires in the late nineteenth century).

The ideological basis of relations created some peculiar alignments, such as the Soviet-Cuban and US-South Vietnamese relationships. It also led to distinctive superpower-led formations. These are sometimes described as alliances and sometimes as empires, but a better term would be bloc. They were not fluid and temporary arrangements but exceedingly long-lived. They were defined not only (or, sometimes, even primarily) by the common interests of their constituent states, but by commonality of regime-type. For much of the Cold War the superpowers did not exploit bloc members in any traditional imperial sense, but found rather that bloc leadership imposed military or economic costs. What they did do was influence bloc domestic politics. So extensive were the Soviet Union's mechanisms for regulating the internal affairs of Eastern Europe that these states could be considered at best semi-sovereign. Stalin had said in April 1945 that 'war is not as in the past; whoever occupies a territory also imposes on it his own social system'.[46] Both sides thereafter defined security in these highly-ideologized terms.

Ideology was, of course, never the only influence on the Cold War. As was stressed earlier, even the most dedicated ideologue must work with, and in a world of, state power and interests. More traditional forces inevitably complicated the picture. Many Third World states sought to manipulate rather than commit to their patrons. The Sino-Soviet split led to a period of triangular diplomacy. Communist regimes in the Far East fell upon one another in the late 1970s. The West sometimes found itself supporting anti-communist but highly authoritarian regimes.

Nonetheless, ideological conflict remained the underlying dynamic, the larger reality that underlay tactical shifts and diplomatic manoeuvres. Furthermore, the interaction of values and interests did not exhibit a secular decline of ideological confrontation yielding to great power rivalry. Rather, both sides saw periodic renewal of ideological conviction. Thus after Stalin's death Khrushchev presided not only over doctrinal revision but a revivalism that saw a dramatic upsurge in confidence that the global correlation of forces was accelerating inexorably towards socialism. The most sustained American attempt, under Nixon and Kissinger, to conduct a Realist policy of accommodation with the Soviet Union on the basis of state interests, was soon followed by the far more uncompromising views of Ronald Reagan who, especially in his first term, renewed the concept of victory as regime-change by reviving a policy of active 'rollback' of communism.[47]

The way the Cold War ended in 1989 also highlights the decisive role of ideology. The inadequacies of Realist explanations for Soviet behaviour under Gorbachev are familiar and compelling.[48] The conflict ended not when the world ceased to be geopolitically bipolar – in some respects it remained so until the break-up of the Soviet Union in 1991; and the decline of Soviet power in the late 1980s was as much a consequence as a cause of Gorbachev's policies. Rather, the Cold War ended with the dissipation of *ideological* bipolarity as Gorbachev laid aside the doctrinal shibboleths of Marxism-Leninism.[49]

the end of ideology?

A broad survey, then, suggests a story of evolving ideological forms interacting with contextual circumstances, their synthesis mediated through the contingent choices of key individuals (a Wilson, a Lenin, a Reagan, and so on). As a consequence, the role of ideology in international relations grew for 200 years. 1789 saw its eruption, 1989 its effacement. Is there ideology after the Cold War? Francis Fukuyama's careful, though much misunderstood, 'end of history' thesis argued that history, understood as competition between forms of political and economic organization, is now over.[50] In this sense, history is the history of ideology – and ideology is now history. This is not to say that conflict, including conflict between values, will cease. But in a postmodern age they no longer take the form of struggle between entire systems of thought. The 1990s saw an upsurge of ethnic strife and even genocide. The possibility of a 'clash of civilizations' was debated. Western military intervention was undertaken not to change a regime but for the specific moral purpose of stopping human rights abuses.

Then there was 9/11. This has transformed thinking about international relations in ways characteristic of ideology: a conception of polarization between two sides locked in permanent war in which accommodation is impossible. But distinctive features of this conflict suggest that it may be taking an even purer form. While past ideological conflicts took place between states but had an important transnational dimension, the 'war on terror' is conducted only against a transnational movement. This means there are no state interests to modify or complicate the calculus of those who pose a radical threat to international order. For this reason, the threat is likely to be more extreme than that previously posed by revolutionary states. And the basis of this threat is not political but religious, its ultimate referent not temporal but eternal. The stakes are higher.

History, then, may not so much have ended as come full circle. The decline of religious conflict in the eighteenth century paved the way for the rise of ideology. Now the end of ideology has seen the re-emergence of religion as a driving force in international relations. Even if ideological conflict in international relations is largely over, conflicts of ideas assuredly are not.

notes

*   The views expressed here are the author's own, and not those of the Foreign and Commonwealth Office.

1.   I follow convention by using International Relations (capitalized) to denote the academic study of international relations.

2.   For a recent comprehensive discussion, see Michael Freeden, *Ideologies and Political Theory: A Conceptual Approach* (Oxford: Clarendon, 1996).

3.   Andrew J. Rotter, in his contribution to this volume, also notes that ideology is sometimes treated like culture.

4.   The ambivalent and distinct nature of nationalism as an ideology is widely recognized. Freeden's comprehensive study of *Ideologies and Political Theory* does not cover nationalism at all; cf. John Schwarzmantel, *The Age of Ideology* (London: Macmillan, 1998).

5. Martin Wight, 'Why Is There No International Theory?', in Herbert Butterfield and Martin Wight (eds), *Diplomatic Investigations: Essays in the Theory of International Relations* (Cambridge, MA: Harvard University Press, 1966), pp. 17–34.

6. For a discussion of the varieties of Realism, see Michael W. Doyle, *Ways of War and Peace* (New York: Norton, 1997), pp. 41–201.

7. Hans J. Morgenthau, *Politics Among Nations: The Struggle for Power and Peace*, brief edn (New York: McGraw-Hill, 1993), especially pp. 99–102; Kenneth N. Waltz, *Theory of International Politics* (Reading, MA: Addison-Wesley, 1979), especially pp. 63, 81–8, 128.

8. For an attempt to put some flesh on the bones of 'preference', see Andrew Moravcsik, 'Taking Preferences Seriously: A Liberal Theory of International Politics', *International Organization*, 51 (4) (1997) 513–53.

9. For a classic non-Marxist treatment of ideology as group interest – first published in 1936 – see Karl Mannheim, *Ideology and Utopia* (San Diego: Harcourt Brace Jovanovich, 1985).

10. For example, Goldstein and Keohane suggest that ideas can serve the functions of 'focal points', 'road map' and 'institutionalization': Judith Goldstein and Robert O. Keohane, 'Ideas and Foreign Policy: An Analytical Framework', in Judith Goldstein and Robert O. Keohane (eds), *Ideas and Foreign Policy* (Ithaca: Cornell University Press, 1993), pp. 3–30. Theories of bounded rationality also suggest ideas can help to efficiently economize on information.

11. For a classic statement of this distinction, see Brian Barry, *Sociologists, Economists and Democracy* (London: Collier-Macmillan, 1970).

12. The *locus classicus* is Hedley Bull, *The Anarchical Society: A Study of Order in World Politics* (London: Macmillan, 1977).

13. See, especially, Alexander Wendt, *Social Theory of International Politics* (Cambridge: Cambridge University Press, 1999).

14. See, especially, Bruce Russett, *Grasping the Democratic Peace. Principles for a Post-Cold War World.* (Princeton, NJ: Princeton University Press, 1993).

15. There was some recognition that the extension of international institutions to the decolonizing world would erode their effectiveness: Hedley Bull and Adam Watson (eds), *The Expansion of International Society* (Oxford: Clarendon, 1984).

16. Defensiveness by proponents of an ideational approach is pervasive. Daniel Philpott's recent work – one of the most ambitious and wide-ranging attempts to integrate ideas into accounts of major international change – gives a detailed explanation in each case of why Realism on its own is not adequate: *Revolutions in Sovereignty: How Ideas Shaped Modern International Relations* (Princeton, NJ: Princeton University Press, 2001). See also Paul Kowert and Jeffrey Legro, 'Norms, Identity and Their Limits: A Theoretical Reprise', in Peter J. Katzenstein (ed.), *The Culture of National Security: Norms and Identity in World Politics* (New York: Columbia University Press, 1996), pp. 451–97.

17. Martin Wight, *Power Politics*, rev. edn, ed. by Hedley Bull and Carsten Holbraad (London: Penguin, 1979), p. 92.

18. Wight, *Power Politics*, p. 88.

19. Martin Wight, *International Theory: The Three Traditions*, ed. by Gabriele Wight and Brian Porter (Leicester: Leicester University Press, 1991). Other fine studies include David Armstrong, *Revolution and World Order: The Revolutionary State*

in International Society (Oxford: Clarendon, 1993); and Mark N. Hagopian, *The Phenomenon of Revolution* (New York: Dodd, Mead, 1974), pp. 106–17.

20. See Armstrong, *Revolution and World Order*, ch. 7.

21. For an incisive study of the Soviet case, see Gerhard Wettig, *High Road, Low Road: Diplomacy and Public Action in Soviet Foreign Policy* (London: Brassey's, 1989).

22. See Paul M. Kennedy, *The Rise and Fall of the Great Powers: Economic Change and Military Conflict from 1500 to 2000* (New York: Random House, 1987).

23. See, for example, Charles Kindleberger, *The World in Depression, 1929 – 1939* (Berkeley: University of California Press, 1973); and Robert Gilpin, *War and Change in World Politics* (Cambridge: Cambridge University Press, 1981).

24. This was expressed with unconscious humour in the Soviet Communist Party's famous open letter of July 1963, responding to the critique of Soviet conduct during the Cuban Missile Crisis mounted by its Chinese counterpart: 'the atomic bomb does not draw class distinctions' (Central Committee of the Communist Party of China (ed.), *The Polemic on the General Line of the International Communist Movement* (Peking: Foreign Languages Press, 1965), p. 542).

25. Lenin set out these arguments most fully in *Left-Wing Communism, An Infantile Disorder* (London: Communist Party of Great Britain, 1920).

26. Raymond Aron, *Peace and War: A Theory of International Relations* (New York: Doubleday, 1966).

27. As Reinhard Heydrich put it, 'in dealing with the Jewish problem, economic necessities are to be ignored in principle': quoted in John H. Hertz, 'Power Politics or Ideology? The Nazi Experience', in George Schwab (ed.), *Ideology and Foreign Policy: A Global Perspective* (New York: Cyrco Press, 1978), p. 22.

28. Barrington Moore, *Soviet Politics: the Dilemma of Power* (Cambridge, MA: Harvard University Press, 1950).

29. Kissinger characterizes the basic choice for American foreign policy as whether to serve as a beacon or a crusader – that is, whether to attract other states to its values by perfecting them at home, or to actively spread them abroad: Henry Kissinger, *Diplomacy* (New York: Simon and Schuster, 1994), pp. 17–18, 803–35.

30. For a useful overview, see Alan Cassels, *Ideology and International Relations in the Modern World* (London: Routledge, 1996).

31. The comparison is pervasive. The classic treatment is Jacob Talmon, *Political Messianism* (London: Secker and Warburg, 1960). For a discussion of the theme, see Michael Burleigh, *The Third Reich: A New History* (London: Pan, 2000), pp. 5–14.

32. For accounts of the French revolutionary impact on international relations, see Kyung-Won Kim, *Revolution and International System* (New York: New York University Press, 1970); and T. C. W. Blanning, *The Origins of the French Revolutionary Wars* (London: Longman, 1986).

33. Most specifically, in the Declaration of Pillnitz in August 1791, but there were many other expressions of concern from individual states.

34. Here, as in subsequent cases of revolutionary ideology, misperception played some role: see, for example, Stephen M. Walt, 'Revolution and War', *World Politics*, 44 (3) (1992) 321–68. It is important to note, however, that these

conflicts ultimately arose from objective incompatibilities of basic values, which were often perceived very clearly.

35. On British-French affinities after 1830, see Harry Hinsley, *Power and the Pursuit of Peace: Theory and Practice in the History of Relations between States* (Cambridge: Cambridge University Press, 1963), pp. 216–17, 234.

36. The German-Austrian Dual Alliance preceded it, but by pulling Russia further away from the other conservative powers and ending France's isolation, this was a decisive development. However, the efforts to revive a Russo-German rapprochement as late as the 1905 Björkö meeting reveal the continuing influence of monarchical ties.

37. See, for example, Wilson's statement that 'There is nothing so self-destructive as selfishness … . Whereas the nation which denies itself material advantage and seeks those things which are of the spirit works … for all generations, and works in the permanent and durable stuffs of humanity': quoted in Robert E. Osgood, *Ideals and Self-Interest in America's Foreign Relations* (Chicago: Chicago University Press, 1953), p. 178. Similarly, in campaigning for the League of Nations Wilson insisted that America had entered the war not because its interests had been threatened, but because 'free people everywhere were in danger and we had always been, and will always be, the champion of right and liberty' (p. 298).

38. Kissinger, *Diplomacy*, pp. 29–55, 218–45.

39. On this 'creedal passion', see especially Samuel Huntington, *American Politics: The Promise of Disharmony* (Cambridge, MA: Harvard University Press, 1981).

40. Léon Blum was the socialist leader of the Popular Front government that came to power in France in June 1936.

41. On the *Historikerstreit*, see R. J. Evans, *In Hitler's Shadow. West German Historians and the Attempt to Escape from the Nazi Past* (New York: Pantheon, 1989).

42. Robert O. Paxton, *The Anatomy of Fascism* (London: Allen Lane, 2004).

43. For the role of ideology in the Cold War, see, *inter alia*, John Lewis Gaddis, *We Now Know: Rethinking Cold War History* (Oxford: Clarendon, 1997), especially ch. 10; Mark Kramer, 'Ideology and the Cold War', *Review of International Studies*, 25 (4) (1999) 539–76; Nigel Gould-Davies, 'Rethinking the Role of Ideology in International Politics During the Cold War', *Journal of Cold War History*, 1 (1) (1999) 90–109.

44. David Holloway, *Stalin and the Bomb: The Soviet Union and Atomic Energy 1939–56* (New Haven: Yale University Press, 1994), chs 8 and 12; Robert C. Tucker, 'The Stalin Heritage in Soviet Policy', in Robert C. Tucker, *The Soviet Political Mind*, rev. edn (London: Allen and Unwin, 1972), pp. 87–102.

45. This was explicit in George Kennan's original formulation of containment. Witness his statements that 'the United States has it in its power to increase enormously the strains under which Soviet policy must operate … and in this way to promote tendencies which must eventually find their outlet in either the breakup or the gradual mellowing of Soviet power'; 'the possibility remains … that Soviet power … bears within it the seeds of its own decay, and that the sprouting of these seeds is well advanced'; 'Soviet Russia might be changed overnight from one of the strongest to one of the weakest and most pitiable of national societies': 'X' [George Kennan], 'The Sources of Soviet Conduct', *Foreign Affairs*, 25 (4) (1947) 580–2.

46. Stalin, quoted in Milovan Djilas, *Conversations with Stalin* (New York: Harcourt Brace and World, 1962), p. 114.
47. For discussion of the strange mix of ideological militancy, utopian idealism and hard-headed Machiavellianism that underpinned Reagan's foreign policy, see Kissinger, *Diplomacy*, pp. 762–803; John Lewis Gaddis, *The United States and the End of the Cold War* (Oxford: Oxford University Press, 1992), pp. 119–32.
48. See, for example, Richard Ned Lebow, 'The Long Peace, the End of the Cold War, and the Failure of Realism', in Richard Ned Lebow and Thomas Risse-Kappen (eds), *International Relations Theory and the End of the Cold War* (New York: Columbia University Press, 1995), pp. 23–56.
49. For a discussion of many related issues, see John Mueller, 'When Did the Cold War End?', unpublished conference paper (2002).
50. Francis Fukuyama, *The End of History and the Last Man* (New York: Free Press, 1992).

5

international relations theories and methods

miriam fendius elman

This chapter provides a brief overview of some recent trends in International Relations (IR) theorists' attention to historiography.[1] My main focus is on the American academy, and how political scientists who study international security using qualitative case study methods have learned from international historians who study statecraft, military strategy and international wars. I have noted elsewhere that these two scholarly communities start with a shared subject matter, some common methodological leanings, and a mutual belief that they are under-appreciated in their own disciplines.[2] At least for political scientists, this last point now seems less pressing, and IR theorists' increasing attention to historiography is now best viewed as part of a larger renaissance of qualitative methods in political science;[3] a resurgence that is reflected in institutional developments in the American academy.[4] Despite these welcome changes, however, IR theorists still engage historiography as members of their own sub-field. Given their deep and durable disciplinary roots, it is unlikely that either history or political science will ultimately disappear as distinct intellectual projects – a recommendation recently made by Ian Clark in his fair and intelligent critique of my previous work.[5] Rather, we should aim to be separate, but not separated – with a mutual appreciation for our respective central tendencies and of the different strengths we bring to scholarly enquiry on international relations.

ir theorists and history

There is much truth in the widely held belief that IR theorists' view of history is very strongly influenced by their social science training. Much of their scholarship places a heavy stress on model building at the expense of historical context. It should be noted, however, that some of the usual suspects for this critique (including some of IR's most influential texts) are not wholly representative of the sub-field. Most famously, Kenneth N. Waltz's seminal *Theory of International Politics* has been the subject of considerable criticism for attempting to explain law-like regularities in a way that buries historical nuance.[6] But Waltz's book is unusual in following an explicit division of labour, only seeking to develop and not to *test* theory. Historical examples are included as illustrations, not tests. It has been left to other scholars to derive hypotheses from the theory, sometimes amending it in the process, and to run these propositions against the empirical record. For example, Thomas Christensen and Jack Snyder change the theory to explain how the First World War resulted from great power allies being chain-ganged into conflict, while the Second World War was the product of buck-passing from one great power to the next. Similarly, Joseph M. Grieco tests Waltz's proposition that concerns with relative gains act as a barrier to cooperation.[7]

It is not that the typical qualitative monograph in the IR sub-field is egregiously ahistorical, but rather that the emphasis is on using evidence to support or undermine an explicitly (and usually separately) stated causal argument. In political science, historical narratives are generally divided up and parcelled out into distinct chapters. These are typically packaged between several history-free analytical chapters, which are ideally to be used by other scholars in replications of the argument using different empirical evidence. The political scientist's arguments about international relations are separated from narratives.

Consequently, instead of belabouring the claim that IR theorists produce work devoid of history, it makes more sense to criticize them for using history as a vehicle for corroborating or challenging theoretical models. IR theorists do not disregard history; rather history is both expendable and essentially replaceable. Particular historical episodes are used (or not used) to the extent that they aid in theory-building and testing, and the historical evidence that is brought to bear is far less important than the theory that is being developed and examined. The historical 'case' is not vital for its own sake, and one gets the sense in much political science writing on IR that historical evidence is easily interchangeable. Like bees to blossoms, political scientists are content to buzz off from one historical event to the next, never dwelling for very long on any particular episode, and rarely becoming a true expert on any. Indeed, since political scientists aim for broad generalizations, viewing any particular war, crisis, or alliance as an instance of a larger phenomenon, they do not really *care* about the 1879 Dual Alliance between Austria-Hungary and Germany, the Fashoda Crisis of 1898, or the First World War.[8]

Just as IR theorists are sometimes incorrectly censured for being entirely ahistorical, so too international historians are critiqued with the parallel charge, of being atheoretical 'storytellers', carefully culling archival material merely for a descriptively complete narrative. To be sure, international historians view complex historical events as important in their own right, and as more than simply evidential material to prove or disprove a free-standing causal argument. Moreover, international historians are also less likely to pick and choose historical evidence from a wide range of cases, tending to specialize in particular historical periods and geographical regions – usually for their entire careers. That being said, historical narratives do offer assertions about the possible causes of the events they describe and hence rely on (albeit sometimes implicit) causal theories. As Edward Ingram puts it,

> The distinction between the political scientist's theory-based analysis and the historian's evidence-based description is false. The historian's description is a form of analysis (it explains); likewise, narrative (which has nothing to do with chronology) is applied theory, an analytical test of a proposition: each presupposes the other, and without the other, neither can be carried out.[9]

It would be difficult to argue, for example, that the writings of the eminent international historian Paul W. Schroeder, ranging from eighteenth and nineteenth century European politics to the 2003 US war on Iraq, are devoid of theory. His view of the history of great power international relations as a transformative process from war and unilateralism based on realist power strategies to union, association, and international peace premised on a 'managerial and societal' alternative – a movement that is the product of normative change, human agency, and technological development – is reflected in his writings.[10]

While international historians are apt to weave theory into their narratives, they are less likely to provide causal arguments that float freely to other contexts. By contrast, the political science sub-field of IR tends to reward scholarship that is theoretically innovative, generalizable, replicable and parsimonious. All other things being equal, books and journal articles that cover multiple empirical data points are preferred over those that provide a comprehensive, theoretically-informed analysis of a single case. Yet as Robert Jervis notes, parsimony comes at a heavy price, since the construction of a 'grand overall view' means that individual historical cases and particular events will not be fully explained.[11]

The upshot is that while scholars from both disciplines use history and theory, the central tendency in the respective sub-fields is to use them very differently. Political scientists see it as their purpose to identify recurring patterns of behaviour and to make generalizations about why such classes of events reoccur. They are much less concerned with explaining why an event unfolded as it did in that particular instance; and they are more likely to use general theories to show how the evidence all fits together. Unlike international historians, they expect that the argument for a particular case will be consistent with explanations for a wider range of similar phenomena. For the most part, IR theorists are willing to explain individual cases less fully in order to construct a grand theory that will explain the basic parameters of many cases with only a few causal factors. They tend not to view historical events as too complex to be easily classified with other events.

The ways in which political scientists and historians have assessed the Second World War provide a useful illustration of these predispositions. In his recent work, *The Tragedy of Great Power Politics*, John J. Mearsheimer argues that Nazi Germany did not represent a sharp break with the past and that German Chancellor Adolf Hitler 'behaved like German leaders before him'. From 1862 to 1945, Germany sought opportunities to expand its power through conquest, but its power capabilities determined the extent to which it could expand against the weakness of its rivals, or was compelled to pull back and pursue a defense-oriented strategy. What is important, for Mearsheimer, is not whether Germany was led by Hitler, Kaiser Wilhelm or Otto von Bismarck: 'what matters for the theory is how much relative power Germany possessed at the time'. According to Mearsheimer, Germany's foreign policy represents a case from a class of events – behaviour encouraged by the constraints and opportunities of an anarchical international system. Nazi Germany's aggression is consistent with the foreign policy that we would expect from a great power given structural conditions: the distribution of power capabilities in Europe. Yet in order to demonstrate that Germany's behaviour from the late 1930s to 1945 was to be expected given the European power structure – that is, that Nazi Germany and its behaviour is an instance of a general pattern of great power behaviour – Mearsheimer must play down the idiosyncratic features of Hitler's aggression that were motivated by his racist ideologies. As Mearsheimer notes, 'Even without Hitler and his murderous ideology, Germany surely would have been an aggressive state by the late 1930s.'[12]

Mearsheimer's position that Nazi Germany's foreign policy can be read as one example of a larger phenomenon stands in sharp contrast to historian Gerhard L. Weinberg's focus on Hitler's racism as the cause of the Second World War. Weinberg insists that the Second World War cannot be compared to other international conflicts, or to Germany's previous foreign policies, because under Nazi rule the German state and its war aims were unique. For Weinberg, the Second World War is a class by itself, not a case for a generalizable theory of great power politics. Rather than explain Nazi Germany's foreign policy as an illustrative example of a larger theory of state behaviour, Weinberg delves deeply into Germany's domestic politics and links them with its international behaviour. Thus for Weinberg, Nazi Germany's policies are unique historical events – Germany in this period is decidedly not acting as just another great power jumping through a window of opportunity.[13]

The point here is not only that Mearsheimer and Weinberg explain the origins of the Second World War differently, but that disciplinary norms guide the two scholars in different directions. Political science 'guild rules', which reward theories that transcend time and place, compel political scientists to treat Nazi Germany as a case from a class of events, and they are thus less likely to look for Germany's atypical behaviour. Operating under a different set of guidelines, historians are likely to be more sensitive to the peculiarities of a historical situation. This is not to say that IR theorists and international historians are wedded to different levels of analysis, since both sets of scholars have employed structural, domestic and individual causal factors in their narratives. However, while for Mearsheimer the Second World War is an illustrative case for a structural theory of war initiation, even political scientists less wedded to parsimonious structural theorizing tend to use the war as a means for constructing and testing general theoretical propositions.

A comparison of Weinberg's reading of the war with two recent analyses by political scientists Peter Liberman and Barbara Farnham is instructive in this regard.[14] Like Mearsheimer, Liberman argues that Nazi Germany's behaviour was driven by structural constraints. But for Liberman these constraints included trade dependence and a defensive military advantage. He thus accounts for Germany's expansionism as a means of providing for self-sufficiency for an anticipated lengthy war of attrition. Yet here too the Second World War is an instance of a broader phenomenon: expansion by trade-dependent states. Liberman tests his argument against other cases which he codes as of the same type (for example, Japan in the 1930s), and pits these historical examples against those where states were dependent on trade but where future war was expected to be short and decisive (for example, Germany and Japan prior to the First World War). Thus, in typical political science fashion, Liberman varies his dependent variable (expansion and conquest), and identifies patterns of covariation between the outcome and his explanatory variables (trade dependence and the offence–defence balance).[15] To be sure, Liberman's analysis is more in sync with Weinberg's since his broader conception of external constraint enables him to differentiate Hitler's Germany from Wilhelmine Germany, and to incorporate Hitler's racial policies into his explanation. Nevertheless, Liberman's analysis does not read like international history – it is not meant to increase our understanding of the Second World War as a particular historical episode; rather, its purpose is to offer some general conclusions about the effects of defence dominance.

Barbara Farnham's investigation of one aspect of the war's origins – President Franklin D. Roosevelt's assessment of Hitler as a threat to the US in the aftermath of the September 1938 Munich crisis – also places emphasis on Hitler's war aims and the ways in which they were perceived, but this particular fragment of history is used to illustrate and test theory. Farnham devotes the lion's share of her attention to how the Munich case study challenges both realist and liberal theory. Contra realism, Farnham argues that Roosevelt did not base perceptions of the German threat on its power capabilities for war fighting, but rather on the basis of Hitler's intentions. Germany's power mattered, but would not have prevented Roosevelt from cooperating with Hitler had the latter not exhibited an utter disregard for peaceful accommodation and compromise ('the diplomatic adjustment of legitimate grievances') at Munich. Following Munich, it was the dramatically revised expectation of how Nazi Germany would use its power potential, and not its military capabilities *per se*, that influenced Roosevelt's thinking. Yet contra also to the expectations of liberalism, Roosevelt did not link threat perception to Germany's regime type; the nature of Germany's government mattered less than did the fact that Hitler had shown at Munich that he was a leader who would not abide by the rules of the game: 'Before Hitler demonstrated his contempt for the norms relating to the peaceful settlement of disputes, Roosevelt did not assume that he would violate those norms simply because he was a dictator.'[16] As in international historian Gerhard Weinberg's reading, Farnham's explanation places Hitler, a decision-maker with unlimited war aims, at centre stage. But for Farnham, this aspect of the war is important primarily because it carries with it implications for generalizable theories of war and peace.

Political scientists' interest in categorizing the events of history into pre-existing theoretical frameworks extends beyond realism to other paradigms. For example, liberal IR theory, particularly work on the democratic peace, exhibits this characteristic. The literature on the democratic peace theory (DPT) draws on historical events as discrete facts to prove or disprove its fundamental proposition, namely that democracies do not wage war against each other.[17] The democratic peace theory links international peace to certain kinds of states. As Kalevi J. Holsti notes, 'it is not so much the system of states that is the fountain of conflict and war, but the nature of the individual states'.[18] Democratic peace theorists argue that factors internal to the state affect how foreign policy makers interpret the external environment. Domestic political norms and ideologies and/or governing institutions determine how decision-makers assess international threats and influence the propensity to wage war.

Much of the research on the democratic peace proposition has been based on quantitative methods – the focus has been on operationalizing a definition of both democracy and war, followed by a statistical analysis of large data sets that demonstrate the correlation between democracy and international conflict. IR theorists who favour qualitative methods have tended to be more critical of the proposition. By analyzing particular historical episodes, these critics have attempted to show either that democratic wars are more common than proponents believe, or that instances of peace between democracies can be explained by factors other than domestic regime type.[19]

As Colin Elman argues, in addition to parsing more restrictive definitions of both democracy and war to recode cases that might have contradicted the finding, DPT proponents:

> diluted the absolute claim ... that democracies *never* go to war with one another, in favour of the probabilistic claim that democracies are *less likely* to go to war with one another. No single case could contradict this weaker claim, as it could be said to be one of the few wars between democracies that occasionally occur.[20]

Sceptics claim that DPT proponents have stretched their definitions in order to omit historical cases that would otherwise provide evidence against their argument.[21] Britain is categorized as non-democratic in 1812, even though the US was not appreciably more democratic at this time. Spain is considered a non-democracy in 1898 because half the members of its legislature's upper house held hereditary office or were appointed by the Crown. Britain is coded as a democracy in the same year, even though the membership of its House of Lords was similarly undemocratic. In the same fashion, Imperial Germany is considered insufficiently democratic for the First World War to be considered as a case that disconfirms the democratic peace argument. In the 1940s, Britain bombed territory belonging to democratic Finland, but DPT proponents suggest that this is not a counter-example because it was not a war – 1000 troops did not lose their lives in direct conflict between those two states. Israel is labelled a non-democracy in 1948 (at a time when it fought democratic Lebanon), even though there had been over 20 years of contested democratic elections in the Jewish *Yishuv*.[22] The result is a product that risks privileging theory through doing 'bad' history. DPT proponents try too hard to fit the historical evidence into predetermined theoretical boxes, and they wind up playing fast and loose with history to arrive at a preferred theoretical conclusion.

Critics of DPT also argue that historical examples used by the theory's supporters in effect confirm plausible competing explanations for the events in question. For example, Susan Peterson suggests that, contrary to the expectations of the democratic peace proposition, democracies have sometimes come to the brink of war because of the public's pressures for a hard-line policy (as with the Franco-British conflict over Fashoda in 1898).[23] Peterson argues that a belligerent public and a powerful legislative branch can often push a more moderate executive towards war; the fact that the diplomatic crisis at Fashoda ended peacefully has less to do with shared democratic values than with France's inability to fight a militarily superior power. In fact, in this case democratizing influences exacerbated the conflict and made matters worse. It was the balance of power and not democratic politics that ultimately saved the peace.

Interestingly, some international historians are also sceptical of DPT, although for reasons that better fit with their own disciplinary guild rules. According to historians Paul W. Schroeder and John Lewis Gaddis, the key problem with the proposition (and other realist and liberal IR theories) is that it attempts to apply static concepts – democracy and war – across various historical eras 'regardless of how much the concrete, historical definitions and practical components of the terms "democracy" and "absolutism" have changed over historic time'.[24] To be sure, several DPT proponents are aware that 'democracy' does not have an equivalent meaning across centuries and cultures, and they have been quick to eschew objective indicators in favour of subjective views of democratic governance that are sensitive to time and place. For example, in an ambitious study that covers 100 years of US diplomacy in the eighteenth and nineteenth centuries, John M. Owen IV argues that even if two states can be categorized as liberal democracies according to objective criteria determined by the analyst, they may still go to war if foreign policy-makers do not perceive each other as liberal. Owen's reliance on subjective indicators of democratic states' affinity highlights that liberal peace is far from an iron law: he considers the War of 1812, the Spanish-American War and the US Civil War to be wars between liberal states, though contemporary foreign policy-makers did not regard each other's regime as such.[25]

Yet analyses like Owen's merely beg the question: how much mileage is achieved from a theory that fails to 'unpack' the concept of democracy, treating it instead as a unified category? Recent work that rejects the democracy/non-democracy dichotomy by differentiating among democracies has resulted in both richer explanations of international historical episodes, as well as in contingent theories that underscore the conditions and circumstances under which the democratic peace theory might break down. For example, David P. Auerswald shows that the propensity of democracies to use force varies based on executive accountability and its control over the agenda: 'war among democracies may be possible when an executive facing relatively low accountability has total agenda control and threatens the survival of another democracy'.[26] Indeed, as international historians contend, democracy does not constrain leaders in every case – much depends on factors that are country-specific (and specific to certain time periods within a given country), such as the delegation of war powers and the balance of power between executive, legislature and judiciary.[27]

bridging the gap:
trends in the international history/ir theory nexus

Political scientists are becoming more sophisticated consumers of international history. They recognize that historians do not produce 'an unproblematic background narrative from which theoretically neutral data can be elicited for the framing of problems and the testing of theories'.[28] Because historians weave their causal accounts into their narratives, they necessarily give prominence to those facts which figure significantly in those causes. If IR theorists rely on secondary sources without acknowledging the multiplicity of accounts for any given historical episode, in effect they are cherry-picking facts that support a preferred theory or undermine a competitor.

International historians have traditionally been much more comfortable than political scientists with complex causation, and the notion that any particular outcome can be produced by multiple causal pathways. International historians are comfortable detailing the sequence of actions leading up to an outcome, providing a detailed reconstruction of the actual process and contingencies (as well as the roads not taken). With this type of 'particularizing' research strategy, competing explanations, each specifying a different set of causal variables, cannot be ruled out because multiple factors typically converge, with each playing an integral role in the outcome. While in retrospect historical outcomes can be squared with a particular IR theory, the forces allegedly driving the events that political scientists see as inevitable may not have been those that mattered at the time to the decision-makers involved. Actors at the time were unsure of what was going to happen; consequently, different choices could have been made which would have resulted in different outcomes. Furthermore, general theories of war and peace are problematic, because it is impossible to control for chance occurrences and catalytic events.

IR theorists have begun to grapple with notions of complex causation, and are now less fixated on making universal generalizations that can be automatically reproduced across space and time. As political scientist Jack Levy notes:

> a particular condition might be necessary for one sequence to operate, and that sequence may be sufficient for a particular outcome to occur, but there may be other sequences that also lead to the same outcome but that do not involve the key condition in the first sequence. The impact of some variables may be contingent on the values of other variables, so that simple additive models will not work, and the analyst must examine the combinations or interaction effects of different sets of factors.[29]

While IR theorists are more sensitive to equifinality, they have nevertheless tried to square this with their guild's preference for establishing causal inferences through comparative analysis. The sub-field continues to be preoccupied with identifying effective strategies for appropriate historical case selection. Since theory testing is prized, historical evidence must be chosen in such a way that competing theories can be pitted against each other. This involves teasing out what each theory would lead us to expect empirically and then checking the evidence against these sets of expectations – the consistent argument wins; the inconsistent one is disconfirmed as a plausible alternative explanation. It also entails choosing cases that are hard for preferred theories to pass successfully (that is, crucial and least-likely cases); investigating anomalous cases for a theory that can suggest its scope conditions; and explicitly specifying whether causal variables are necessary or sufficient for the outcome under investigation.[30] As David Dessler suggests, IR theorists who adopt these methodological techniques tend to subscribe to a generalizing strategy, where what gets explained is an instance of a certain type of event, 'which is then shown to accompany or follow regularly from conditions of a specified kind'.[31]

Political scientists have made it clear that they want to incorporate causal complexity, but they nevertheless want to use research designs that make clear inferences and follow disciplinary norms. For example, political scientist Richard Ned Lebow suggests that historian John Lewis Gaddis' writings on the Cold War are problematic because they do not explicitly identify whether causal factors are necessary or sufficient. In his most recent book, *We Now Know: Rethinking Cold War History*, Gaddis argues that the Cold War was a function of Stalin's personality and ideology. Stalin's gratuitous use of violence and his reliance on brutality and coercion, influenced by the limitations of the political and economic features of the Soviet regime, made the Cold War inevitable.[32] But for Lebow, this reading of the superpower conflict merely begs the question: would Stalin have adopted the same policies in the absence of an over-arching Marxist ideology? Would a different Soviet leader have pursued different policies in Eastern Europe and Asia? In Lebow's words:

> Historians who offer multilayered explanations need to identify what kind of multiple causation they mean ... distinguish *between* competing causes ... and rank order those that could be reinforcing (for Gaddis, regime capabilities, ideology, and personality). They also need to describe whatever relationships exist between or among these causes. Failure to do this makes the overall argument impossible to sustain or falsify.[33]

Despite this caveat, several recent studies by political scientists on the origins of the First World War demonstrate how IR theorists are fashioning more complex causal narratives. Arguing that complexity, multiple causation and variation across time hinder theorists' ability to construct general theories of war, Lebow argues that the First World War resulted from happenstance – without the 1914 assassinations of Austro-Hungarian Archduke Franz Ferdinand and his spouse in Sarajevo, the war would not have occurred. Although Lebow recognizes that there were underlying causes for the war that created a conflict-prone environment, he is adamant that these structural features did not make the war inevitable. The chance coincidence of Sarajevo mattered because it changed the Austrian and German leaders' willingness to risk war. In the absence of this catalyst, there would have been several more years of peace, which most likely would have altered the strategic interests and domestic politics of the European great powers, and which in turn would have forestalled war. Had Franz Ferdinand not been murdered, a very different twentieth century would have been possible.[34]

In an exchange with Lebow, William R. Thompson maintains that international structure – namely a series of entrenched rivalries – *can* account for the First World War. But Thompson goes further than simply reading the events of 1914 off of a particular underlying structural cause. He does not view the outbreak of the war as an inevitable product of the division of Europe into two hostile camps with tight alliance commitments, or the German military's belief that offence had the advantage, that war was inevitable, and that Germany consequently had to take the initiative before 1917.[35] Like Lebow, Thompson eschews monocausal theorizing, where one factor is viewed as *the* key to explaining the First World War, in favour of a complex argument about how various elements combine to increase the probability of the war. Thompson argues that the war was highly contingent, resulting from a confluence of structural developments that converged. While Thompson does not ascribe as much causal weight to the Sarajevo assassination as Lebow does, he also considers multiple unexpected interactions, namely European rivalries (for example, the Anglo-German power transition; the Austro-German-Russian competition in the Balkans; Franco-German rivalry resulting from the anti-German coalition) that predated the outbreak of the war. To be sure – true to the guild rules of political science – Thompson views the First World War as a case that can be usefully compared to a sample of other systemic wars that involve 'ripe' rivalries; Lebow is more interested in reconstructing the unique path to a war that has no comparable universe of events. Nevertheless, Lebow and Thompson's understandings of the First World War are not as distinct as their spirited exchange would have us believe.[36]

Finally, Jack Levy's recent reading of the First World War also involves the intersection of multiple casual chains. Levy argues that Germany's expectation of British neutrality was a necessary condition for the war, while the German 'blank cheque' to Austria-Hungary was a necessary condition for the Austrian ultimatum and the attack on Serbia. These two necessary conditions were linked in a chain of events that led to the outbreak of a general war: without the expectation of British neutrality, Germany would not have supported Austria-Hungary's use of force. Germany did not want a world war, but it was willing to risk a local one to split the Entente. Here it is Germany's view of British behaviour that is the catalyst – remove this particular factor and alternative causal paths quickly open up.[37] In short, implicit in Levy's understanding of the First World War is a sense of what might have happened; his conclusions about what did happen involve an explicit consideration of the roads not taken.

In addition to methodological synergies, theoretical developments in IR are also bringing political scientists and international historians closer together. Specifically, the revival of neo-classical realism and the emergence of constructivism as two vibrant research agendas in the sub-field signal new areas of convergence in substantive arguments. As I have suggested elsewhere, this convergence owes much to the end of the Cold War and the break-up of the Soviet Union, events which motivated IR theorists to reconsider the explanatory power of the dominant approaches in the field (neo-realism and neo-liberalism) and opened up new space for competing approaches that emphasize the role of ideas, culture, statesmanship and the possibility of change.[38]

Constructivism eschews notions of fixed state interests or constant international structures. Rather than identify uniform state motivations and identities across historical time, recurring patterns of conflictual international relations, or the similarity of state behaviour under particular structural conditions, constructivists allow for an increased role for agency and they demonstrate how decision-makers can often change their environment – for better or for worse. Thus international relations are viewed as historically contingent – specific international structures created in certain periods of history (such as the current system of sovereign states) are potentially alterable in later periods. Just as international historians are interested in identifying decisive changes in international relations over time, so too are constructivists aware that international norms, structures and relationships are not given and fixed, but made and remade.[39]

Not only was the end of the Cold War and the demise of the Soviet empire a catalyst for the constructivist approach, but it also raised substantial dissatisfaction among realists over the adequacy of structural approaches that emphasized anarchy and the distribution of military power at the expense of state motives and intentions. As a result, many realists have taken a decidedly 'classical realist' turn. In contrast to neo-realists, classical realists – and the neo-classical realists of today – are more likely to emphasize decision-makers' perceptions and particular foreign policies rather than repeatable international patterns of behaviour. They suggest that the relationship between power and outcomes is mediated by the ways in which decision-makers think that power should be used. The central tenets of neo-classical realism – that the distribution of power is only one factor affecting threat perceptions, and that the goals and purposes for which material power will be used are equally important – are premises that resonate well with the way many international historians understand international relations.

William C. Wohlforth's explanation for the end of the Cold War and Fareed Zakaria's analysis of US expansionism in the late nineteenth century are good examples of how neo-classical realists combine domestic political factors – such as the state's capacity to extract resources for waging wars – and leaders' perceptions of the balance of power, to explain historical episodes and foreign policy decision-making. Wohlforth argues that the Cold War's end cannot be categorized as an example of an established general pattern or a type of event. Instead, different causal factors (the balance of power, Soviet domestic politics, the personality of leaders) came together to produce the end of the Cold War. The relative decline and overextension of the Soviet Union accounts for the change in Soviet behaviour and interests that was a necessary condition for superpower détente and the adoption of perestroika; the sufficient condition was the Soviet leadership's decision to refrain from resisting its decline violently.[40] Zakaria suggests that the emergence of the US as a world power is linked to an expansion of American power capabilities as well as to the increasing strength of the American state. He argues that between 1865 and 1889 the US had the power capabilities to expand but lacked the state apparatus to extract resources from society for war fighting. By the end of the nineteenth century, however, the increasing power of the presidency and the growth of the federal bureaucracy made international expansion possible. Zakaria's understanding of US foreign policy in the late nineteenth century is clearly realist: states that have more capabilities will have more international interests. But like Wohlforth, Zakaria shows that there is no direct relationship between power and international relations; in this case, the US could not maximize its influence until the American state became stronger internally.[41]

cave! hic dragones:[42]
towards a non-disciplinary international relations?

In his critique of *Bridges and Boundaries*, Ian Clark insists that IR theorists and historians must do more than 'agree to join hands and sing songs around the campfire'. Specifically, Clark challenges scholars who work on international relations to put away their distinct disciplinary baggage and construct a non-disciplinary (or perhaps anti-disciplinary)

International Relations.[43] I am strongly in favour of increasing dialogue, and in looking for opportunities for synthesis and cross-fertilization. For example, it has been heartening to see both international historians and IR theorists engaging in the same policy debates, and often reaching the same conclusions – from the expansion of NATO (North Atlantic Treaty Organization) to the 2003 war in Iraq. On NATO expansion compare, for example, historian John Lewis Gaddis' critique of the decision to expand NATO to include Poland, Hungary and the Czech Republic with that of political scientists, Bruce Russett and Alan Stam. All three scholars employed the same IR theory – balance of power theory – and drew on the same historical evidence (the precedent of including former adversaries in the postwar reconstruction of 1945–48) to question the wisdom of the policy.[44] On the decision to use force against Iraq, the writings of international historian Paul W. Schroeder and political scientist Robert Jervis read similarly. Both relied on deterrence theory to make the case against war. In addition, both referenced Cold War history to bolster their claims that the US can live in fear without jeopardizing its survival.[45]

While I welcome these, and other, examples of dialogue, I worry that Clark's well-meaning suggestion to merge the disciplines risks throwing the baby out with the bathwater. In Clark's view, the virtues of a new non-disciplinary IR would be the elimination of international/domestic or external/internal categories that merely hinder study. In my opinion, political scientists are already well aware of the need to integrate global/local politics, as evidenced by the many calls for integrating the political science sub-fields of IR and Comparative Politics. There are a number of studies that look at the international dimensions of domestic governance, civil war and military organization, and there is a long tradition in both sub-fields of addressing both domestic and international levels of analysis.[46] Even Kenneth N. Waltz, the supposed archetype of structuralism, wrote a book on domestic politics and foreign policy![47]

What is implicated in Clark's suggestion is more than the notion that political scientists should do better at integrating global/local phenomena (which in any case I would argue IR theorists are already fairly adept at doing). Rather, his advice is that scholars from both disciplines can achieve a better intellectual product by not only continuing and deepening their dialogue, but by moving beyond the disciplines themselves. The counter-argument will be obvious, if not popular: political science and history make unique contributions to the study of IR and, consequently, that study will be facilitated by preserving the distinctiveness and integrity of the disciplines. At a time when it seems that everyone from funding agencies to university presidents are heralding a new era of post-disciplinary enquiry, such a view may well fall on deaf ears. Yet I would argue that, unless it is done carefully, transdisciplinary or post-disciplinary endeavour – at least in the area of global studies – runs the risk of forfeiting the insights that both disciplines bring to bear.

One of the most important contributions that the discipline of political science makes to the study of international relations is a self-conscious attention to conceptualizing, and assessing the effects of, the international system. Students of the discipline are trained to think of international relations as an anarchic system where the whole is greater than the sum of its parts. Political scientists are trained to view international relations as an arena where units co-act, and in their interaction produce results that are frequently unanticipated, unintended, and unexpected. States coexisting in an anarchic international system face uncertainty about the intentions of other states and their likely future behaviour. As a result, international history is full of instances where security-seeking states initiated war or crises at least partly because they were unsure about other states' motives and the consequences of looming shifts in power, and there are just as many historical cases where states misjudged the status quo preferences of their adversaries. Moreover, because states exist in such a system, outcomes are produced by something more than a simple aggregation of individual states' behaviours or motives – there is thus usually a gap between what decision-makers want and what they get. Andrew Moravcsik puts it well:

> At the heart of the two leading contemporary IR theories, realism and institutionalism, is the belief that state behavior has *ironic* consequences … What states do is primarily determined by strategic considerations – what they can get or what they know – which in turn reflect their international political environment.[48]

In sum, one of the most enduring insights of IR theory is the tragedy of international relations: international war can occur even if no state really wants one; a state's attempts to increase its security can end up decreasing it; efforts to contain or to deter an enemy can create new and different adversaries; stability and peace can result even if all the states in the system are revisionists and dissatisfied with the status quo. Of course, all this is not to say that international historians are insensitive to unexpected and unwanted consequences or to the tragic and ironic nature of international relations. But insofar as the discipline of international history rewards work that renders moral judgements, holding actors accountable for their actions, and prizes work that explains international outcomes by reconstructing decisions, motives and purposive intentions, then studies of how external, non-human (and essentially non-manipulable) factors shape historical developments across time and place, and that model unintended conflict spirals and security dilemmas, are likely to be sidelined.

The growing and welcome cross-fertilization between the disciplines should not overshadow the real and enduring epistemological and methodological differences that divide the two groups. I would go further, and argue that there is great value in recognizing – even maintaining and honouring – those distinctions. Although it may be construed as such, my position does not signal parochial chauvinism or any attempt to have political science serve as the gatekeeper for the study of global affairs. I simply see it as extraordinarily helpful to have international history analysed by two groups of scholars who 'own' their expertise, and who are each trained (and train newcomers) to see international relations in a certain way. As I argued elsewhere, the challenge for political scientists and historians is to chart a course that avoids either outright mimicry or rejection, and that continues to build the institutional bridges to support productive interchange.

To illustrate the increasing openness to dialogue with historians in the IR sub-field, I conclude with a discussion of a superb recent work on the early Cold War years by historian Marc Trachtenberg, *A Constructed Peace: The Making of the European Settlement, 1945–1963*. The volume reads as a monograph by a Cold War historian from its prefatory pages.[49] It does not compare this great power conflict to others of its kind; the case evidence is not sandwiched between introductory and concluding 'theory' chapters; and the Cold War is clearly viewed as important in its own right. The book also employs (in characteristic implicit fashion) historical modes of enquiry: process tracing, path dependence and narrative. Trachtenberg is interested in how the fluid post-Second World War environment developed into a 'long peace' which today is seen as inevitable but which at the time was anything but. Trachtenberg's book reconstructs the early Cold War years as a series of interconnected 'stories': intra-alliance wrangling over Germany's future; debates over US nuclear policy; and the possibility of a showdown with the Soviet Union. By carefully tracing the process of decisions across these three causal chains, and showing the ways in which catalytic events moved the US and the Soviet Union along certain paths, Trachtenberg explains why a spheres of influence arrangement in Europe morphed into the Cold War.

A Constructed Peace has been rightly hailed by historians as a brilliant addition to the canon, winning both the American Historical Association's

George Louis Beer Prize for European international history since 1895, and the Paul Birdsall Prize for European military and strategic history since 1870. However, its reception by political scientists is especially interesting from the perspective of an observer on the overlap between the disciplines. Trachtenberg, a professor of history at the University of Pennsylvania from 1974 to 2001, has now moved to the Department of Political Science at the University of California at Los Angeles. While illustrative of the sub-field's openness to dialogue with international historians, this is not a sign of any impending disciplinary meltdown. Political science will continue to value work on the Cold War and other international conflicts that uses history to evaluate social-science theory.[50]

Political scientists are not international historians (and vice versa), and nor should they be. But there has been a weakening of some of the disciplinary boundaries, and this should be encouraged and rewarded. As evidenced by the works discussed in this chapter, many political scientists have taken the 'cure of history' and they increasingly acknowledge that they would benefit from a better understanding of historians' technical skills, especially by improving their own ability to do primary research. IR theorists now also have a greater appreciation of the contingent nature of historical claims, and the recent writings of scholars in both disciplines demonstrate increasingly convergent understandings of process tracing, path dependence and causal mechanisms. Yet IR theorists' preference for understanding international relations through general theoretical lenses, and for finding similarity in international relations in diverse times and places, remains ingrained and deep-rooted. Nor, contra Clark, is this continuing diversity to be regretted. Robert Jervis puts it well:

> Communication might be easier if we all approached questions in the same way. But this is not only unlikely, it would also represent a great loss of diversity. Our collective understanding of the world would be much poorer if political scientists or historians were to convert the other to their way of seeing the world. A dialogue in which neither party would benefit by converting the other is a bit odd, but it provides the basis for a constructive conversation, and one without an end.[51]

notes

1. Earlier works where I addressed a similar question include Colin Elman and Miriam Fendius Elman, 'Diplomatic History and International Relations Theory: Respecting Difference and Crossing Boundaries', *International Security*, 22 (1) (1997) 5–21; and Colin Elman and Miriam Fendius Elman (eds), *Bridges*

and Boundaries: Historians, Political Scientists, and the Study of International Relations (Cambridge, MA: MIT Press, 2001).

2. Colin Elman and Miriam Fendius Elman, 'Introduction: Negotiating International History and Politics', in Elman and Elman, *Bridges and Boundaries*, pp. 2–5.

3. For a useful overview, see Jack S. Levy, 'Qualitative Methods in International Relations', in Michael Brecher and Frank P. Harvey (eds), *Millennial Reflections on International Studies* (Ann Arbor: University of Michigan Press, 2002), pp. 432–54. See also Barbara Geddes, *Paradigms and Sand Castles: Theory Building and Research Design in Comparative Politics* (Ann Arbor: University of Michigan Press, 2003); Gary Goertz and Harvey Starr (eds), *Necessary Conditions: Theory, Methodology and Applications* (New York: Rowman and Littlefield, 2002); Alexander L. George and Andrew Bennett, *Case Studies and Theory Development* (Cambridge, MA: MIT Press, forthcoming); Henry E. Brady and David Collier (eds), *Rethinking Social Inquiry: Diverse Tools, Shared Standards* (Lanham: Rowman and Littlefield, forthcoming); Tim Buthe, 'Taking Temporality Seriously: Modeling History and the Use of Narratives as Evidence', *American Political Science Review*, 96 (3) (2003) 481–93; Richard Ned Lebow, 'Contingency, Catalysts, and International System Change', *Political Science Quarterly*, 115 (4) (2000–01) 591–616.

4. The American Political Science Association (APSA) has recently added organized sections on International History and Politics and on Qualitative Methods. Both sections field multiple panels at the APSA annual convention and present awards for exemplary research. In a separate development, over 20 political science departments and research centres have joined the Consortium on Qualitative Research Methods (CQRM). The Consortium runs an annual instructional workshop, and also provides a forum for the presentation and critique of new (or, at the very least, newly imported) methods of enquiry. For more on the important differences between American and non-American IR, see Ole Waever, 'The Sociology of a Not So International Discipline: American and European Developments in International Relations', *International Organization*, 52 (4) (1998) 687–727.

5. Ian Clark, 'International Relations: Divided by a Common Language?' *Government and Opposition*, 37 (2) (2002) 271–9.

6. See Paul W. Schroeder, 'Why Realism Does Not Work Well for International History (Whether or Not It Represents a Degenerate IR Research Strategy)', in John A. Vasquez and Colin Elman (eds), *Realism and the Balancing of Power: A New Debate* (New Jersey: Prentice Hall, 2003), pp. 114–27. For a comprehensive overview of Waltz's structural realism, see Jack Donnelly, *Realism and International Relations* (Cambridge: Cambridge University Press, 2000). For useful discussions of realist IR theory in general, and Waltz's impact on the realist canon, see Stephen M. Walt, 'The Enduring Relevance of the Realist Tradition', in Ira Katznelson and Helen V. Milner (eds), *Political Science: The State of the Discipline* (New York: Norton, 2002), pp. 197–230; Colin Elman, 'Introduction: Appraising Balance of Power Theory', in Vasquez and Elman, *Realism and the Balancing of Power*, pp. 1–22; Keith Shimko, 'Realism, Neorealism, and American Liberalism', *Review of Politics*, 54 (2) (1992) 281–301; Joseph M. Grieco, 'Realist International Theory and the Study of World Politics', in

Michael W. Doyle and G. John Ikenberry (eds), *New Thinking in International Relations Theory* (Boulder, CO: Westview Press, 1997), pp. 163–201.

7. See Thomas J. Christensen and Jack Snyder, 'Chain Gangs and Passed Bucks: Predicting Alliance Patterns in Multipolarity', *International Organization*, 44 (2) (1990) 137–68; Joseph M. Grieco, *Cooperation Among Nations: Europe, America, and the Non-Tariff Barriers to Trade* (Ithaca: Cornell University Press, 1990); and Joseph M. Grieco, 'The Maastricht Treaty, Economic and Monetary Union and the Neo-Realist Research Programme', *Review of International Studies*, 21 (1) (1995) 21–40.

8. IR theorists tend to ask 'What is this a case of?' For the argument that a persuasive explanation of a particular historical event must demonstrate how the event fits into a larger pattern, see James Lee Ray, *Democracy and International Conflict: An Evaluation of the Democratic Peace Proposition* (Columbia: University of South Carolina Press, 1995), ch. 4. For representative examples of work by political scientists on each of these historical events respectively, see Patricia A. Weitsman, *Dangerous Alliances: Proponents of Peace, Weapons of War* (Stanford, CA: Stanford University Press, 2004); Susan Peterson, 'How Democracies Differ: Public Opinion, State Structure, and the Lessons of the Fashoda Crisis', *Security Studies*, 5 (1) (1995) 3–37; and H. E. Goemans, *War and Punishment: The Causes of War Termination and the First World War* (Princeton, NJ: Princeton University Press, 2000).

9. Edward Ingram, 'The Wonderland of the Political Scientist', *International Security*, 22 (1) (1997) 53.

10. See, for example, Schroeder, 'Why Realism Does Not Work Well for International History', quote on p. 121.

11. Robert Jervis, 'International History and International Politics: Why Are They Studied Differently?' in Elman and Elman, *Bridges and Boundaries*, p. 391.

12. John J. Mearsheimer, *The Tragedy of Great Power Politics* (New York: Norton, 2001), quotes at pp. 182, 11.

13. Gerhard L. Weinberg, 'World War II: A Different War', in Elman and Elman, *Bridges and Boundaries*, pp. 169–79.

14. Peter Liberman, 'The Offense–Defense Balance, Interdependence, and War', *Security Studies*, 9 (1–2) (1999–2000) 59–91; Barbara Farnham, 'The Theory of Democratic Peace and Threat Perception', *International Studies Quarterly*, 47 (3) (2003) 395–415.

15. Liberman's research takes the form of a most-similar system design. Longitudinal comparisons of German and Japanese foreign policies over the course of the twentieth century enable Liberman to hold a number of variables constant while identifying the few factors that vary with the dependent variable of interest. As Jack Levy notes, this type of research design is particularly powerful: Levy, 'Qualitative Methods in International Relations', p. 440.

16. Farnham, 'The Theory of Democratic Peace and Threat Perception', 396.

17. For overviews of the democratic peace theory, see James Lee Ray, 'The Democratic Path to Peace', *Journal of Democracy*, 8 (2) (1997) 49–64; Miriam Fendius Elman, 'Introduction: The Need for a Qualitative Test of the Democratic Peace Theory', in Miriam Fendius Elman (ed.), *Paths to Peace: Is Democracy the Answer?* (Cambridge, MA: MIT Press, 1997), pp. 1–57; and Miriam Fendius Elman, 'International History and the Democratic Peace',

International History Review, 19 (4) (1997) 866–85. Seminal statements include Bruce Russett, *Grasping the Democratic Peace: Principles for a Post-Cold War World* (Princeton, NJ: Princeton University Press, 1993); Michael E. Brown, Sean M. Lynn-Jones and Steven E. Miller (eds), *Debating the Democratic Peace* (Cambridge, MA: MIT Press, 1996); John M. Owen IV, *Liberal Peace, Liberal War: American Politics and International Security* (Ithaca: Cornell University Press, 1997).

18.   Kalevi J. Holsti, *The State, War, and the State of War* (New York: Cambridge University Press, 1996), p. 9.

19.   Quantitative scholars tend to dismiss case study analysis on the basis that one or a few anomalous cases cannot falsify a probabilistic theory. While the democratic peace theory's ability to explain a particular historical event may say little about its general scope, however, cases that pose strong tests (that is, most likely cases) for the democratic peace proposition should influence our confidence in the theory. Examining cases where the central claims of the democratic peace argument do not hold up or appear to be irrelevant to the outcome can also facilitate the development of contingent generalizations that better account for when the democratic peace argument will explain best – and worst. For an extended discussion, see George and Bennett, *Case Studies and Theory Development*; and Elman, 'Introduction: The Need for a Qualitative Test', pp. 42–7.

20.   Colin Elman, 'Introduction: History, Theory, and the Democratic Peace', *International History Review*, 23 (4) (2001) 760 (emphases in original).

21.   See, for example, Christopher Layne, 'Kant or Cant: The Myth of Democratic Peace', *International Security*, 19 (2) (1994) 5–49; Raymond Cohen, 'Pacific Unions: A Reappraisal of the Theory that "Democracies Do Not Go to War with Each Other"', *Review of International Studies*, 20 (3) (1994) 207–23; Thomas Schwartz and Kiron Skinner, 'The Myth of Democratic Pacifism', *Hoover Digest*, (1999) no. 2, available at: http://www.hooverdigest.org/992/schwartzskinner. html (accessed 15 June 2004).

22.   For a discussion of these and other 'jarring contradictions', see Christopher Layne, 'Shell Games, Shallow Gains, and the Democratic Peace', *International History Review*, 23 (4) (2001) 801–2; and Elman, 'Introduction: The Need for a Qualitative Test', pp. 21–3.

23.   Susan Peterson, *Crisis Bargaining and the State: the Domestic Politics of International Conflict* (Ann Arbor: University of Michigan Press, 1996).

24.   Paul W. Schroeder, 'History and International Relations Theory: Not Use or Abuse, but Fit or Misfit', *International Security*, 22 (1) (1997) 72; see also John Lewis Gaddis, 'History, Theory, and Common Ground', *International Security*, 22 (1) (1997) 80.

25.   Owen, *Liberal Peace, Liberal War*.

26.   David P. Auerswald, 'Inward Bound: Domestic Institutions and Military Conflicts', *International Organization*, 53 (3) (1999) 499; see also David P. Auerswald, *Disarmed Democracies: Domestic Institutions and the Use of Force* (Ann Arbor: Michigan University Press, 2000). For a similar argument, see Miriam Fendius Elman, 'Unpacking Democracy: Presidentialism, Paliamentarism, and Theories of Democratic Peace', *Security Studies*, 9 (4) (2000) 97–135.

27.   Although not specifically devoted to war initiation, Norrin M. Ripsman's study of British, French and American policies toward German rearmament

following the Second World War also questions the common tendency to treat democracy as a unified category suited for all times and places. Ripsman argues that it makes more sense to consider the organization of the state for foreign policy-making (that is, unitary or divided executives, and varying degrees of executive autonomy from the legislative branch) than the overall political structure of the state: while the magnitude of public opposition to German rearmament was high in all three countries, US and British leaders could pursue this unpopular policy while the French government could not: see Norrin M. Ripsman, 'The Curious Case of German Rearmament: Democracy, Structural Autonomy, and Foreign Security Policy', *Security Studies*, 10 (2) (2000–01) 1–48; Norrin M. Ripsman, *Peacemaking by Democracies: The Effect of State Autonomy on the Post-World War Settlements* (University Park, PA: Pennsylvania State University Press, 2002).

28. See Ian Lustick, 'History, Historiography, and Political Science: Multiple Historical Records and the Problem of Selection Bias', *American Political Science Review*, 90 (3) (1996) 605–18. For the argument that international historians largely reject the notion that there can be definitive accounts of any historical episode, see John Lewis Gaddis, 'In Defense of Particular Generalization: Rewriting Cold War History, Rethinking International Relations Theory', in Elman and Elman, *Bridges and Boundaries*, pp. 301–26.

29. Levy, 'Qualitative Methods in International Relations', p. 441.

30. For an example of a study based on the logic of the least-likely case design, see Miriam Fendius Elman, 'The Foreign Policies of Small States: Challenging Neorealism in its Own Backyard', *British Journal of Political Science*, 25 (2) (1995) 171–217. Because small states are highly vulnerable to structural pressures, I argue that the foreign security policies of these states (as opposed to the great powers) should be consistent with the expectations of neorealism, and least likely to be explained by rivalling liberal arguments. An analysis of US foreign policy from the late 1700s through the 1850s, however, shows that domestic political explanations are quite robust, thus undermining our confidence in neo-realism while buttressing the validity of competing liberal claims. On how an outlier case can aid in theory testing and theory generation, see Ronald Rogowski, 'The Role of Theory and Anomaly in Social-Scientific Inference', *American Political Science Review*, 89 (2) (1995) 467–70. For an excellent recent example of the use of most-likely cases to test a general theory, see Michael C. Desch, 'Democracy and Victory: Why Regime Type Hardly Matters', *International Security*, 27 (2) (2002) 5–47.

31. David Dessler, 'Explanation and Scientific Progress', in Colin Elman and Miriam Fendius Elman (eds), *Progress in International Relations Theory: Appraising the Field* (Cambridge, MA: MIT Press, 2003), p. 387.

32. John Lewis Gaddis, *We Now Know: Rethinking Cold War History* (New York: Oxford University Press, 1997).

33. Richard Ned Lebow, 'Social Science and History: Ranchers versus Farmers', in Elman and Elman, *Bridges and Boundaries*, pp. 125–6.

34. Lebow, 'Contingency, Catalysts, and International System Change'.

35. See Scott Sagan, '1914 Revisited: Allies, Offense, and Instability', *International Security*, 11 (2) (1986) 151–75; Stephen Van Evera, 'The Cult of the Offensive

and the Origins of the First World War', *International Security*, 9 (1) (1984) 58–107.

36. William R. Thompson, 'A Streetcar Named Sarajevo: Catalysts, Multiple Causation Chains, and Rivalry Structures', *International Studies Quarterly*, 47 (3) (2003) 453–74; Richard Ned Lebow, 'A Data Set Named Desire: A Reply to William R. Thompson', *International Studies Quarterly*, 47 (3) (2003) 475–8.

37. Jack S. Levy, 'Necessary Conditions in Case Studies: Preferences, Constraints, and Choices in July 1914', in Goertz and Starr, *Necessary Conditions*, pp. 113–45. Ironically, these three studies by political scientists on the origins of the First World War read more like 'history' (in my view) than have recent works by international historians. Many historians now assign the lion's share of the blame for the war to Austria-Hungary (for exploiting the assassination of Franz Ferdinand as an excuse for war with Serbia) and to Germany (for pushing Austria into using force in order to secure Germany's position in Europe). They thus reduce the war to a linear and single causal chain – the chain of events set in motion by Austria-Hungary and Germany. For an important exception, see Samuel R. Williamson, 'The Origins of World War I', *Journal of Interdisciplinary History*, 18 (4) (1988) 795–818; Samuel R. Williamson, *Austria-Hungary and the Coming of the First World War* (London: Macmillan, 1990). Williamson's argument is similar to Lebow's: the assassination transformed the situation since it shifted the balance of power in Vienna toward those that favoured war.

38. Elman and Elman, 'Introduction: Negotiating International History and Politics', pp. 32–3.

39. Useful overviews of constructivist IR theory include Dale C. Copeland, 'The Constructivist Challenge to Structural Realism: A Review Essay', *International Security*, 25 (2) (2000) 187–212; Ted Hopf, 'The Promise of Constructivism in International Relations Theory', *International Security*, 23 (1) (1998) 171–200; Theo Farrell, 'Constructivist Security Studies: Portrait of a Research Program', *International Studies Review*, 4 (1) (2002) 49–72.

40. William C. Wohlforth, 'Realism and the End of the Cold War', *International Security*, 19 (3) (1994–95) 91–129. See also Stephen G. Brooks and William C. Wohlforth, 'From Old Thinking to New Thinking in Qualitative Research', *International Security*, 26 (4) (2002) 93–111; Randall L. Schweller and William C. Wohlforth, 'Power Test: Evaluating Realism in Response to the End of the Cold War', *Security Studies*, 9 (3) (2000) 60–107.

41. Fareed Zakaria, *From Wealth to Power: The Unusual Origins of America's World Role* (Princeton, NJ: Princeton University Press, 1998). Zakaria's central claim is that states expand when their relative capabilities increase. For an application of this argument to contemporary US foreign policy, see Fareed Zakaria, 'Our Way: The Trouble with Being the World's Only Superpower', *The New Yorker*, 14 October 2002, available at: http://www.newyorker.com/fact/content/?021014fa_fact (accessed 15 June 2004).

42. Borrowed from Susan Strange, 'Cave! Hic dragones: A Critique of Regime Analysis', in Stephen D. Krasner (ed.), *International Regimes* (Ithaca: Cornell University Press, 1983), pp. 337–54. It translates as 'Beware! Here be dragons'.

43. Ian Clark, 'International Relations: Divided by a Common Language?', 277–9.

44. See John Lewis Gaddis, 'History, Grand Strategy and NATO Enlargement', *Survival*, 40 (1) (1998) 145–51; Bruce Russett and Allan C. Stam, 'Courting Disaster: An Expanded NATO vs. Russia and China', *Political Science Quarterly*, 113 (3) (1998) 361–82.

45. See Paul W. Schroeder, 'Iraq: The Case Against Preemptive War', *The American Conservative*, 21 October 2002, available at: http://www.amconmag.com/2002_10_21/iraq.html (accessed 15 June 2004); Robert Jervis, 'Understanding the Bush Doctrine', *Political Science Quarterly*, 118 (3) (2003) 365–88.

46. See Manus I. Midlarsky, 'The Impact of External Threat on States and Domestic Societies', *International Studies Review*, 5 (4) (2003) 13–18; Michael C. Desch, 'War and Strong States, Peace and Weak States?' *International Organization*, 50 (2) (1996) 237–68; Joao Resende-Santos, 'Anarchy and the Emulation of Military Systems: Military Organization and Technology in South America, 1870–1930', *Security Studies*, 5 (3) (1996) 193–260; Michael E. Brown (ed.), *The International Dimensions of Internal Conflict* (Cambridge, MA: MIT Press, 1996); Peter B. Evans, Harold K. Jacobson and Robert D. Putnam (eds), *Double-Edged Diplomacy: International Bargaining and Domestic Politics* (Berkeley: University of California Press, 1993).

47. Kenneth N. Waltz, *Foreign Policy and Democratic Politics: The American and British Experience* (Boston: Little, Brown, 1967).

48. Andrew Moravcsik, 'Taking Preferences Seriously: A Liberal Theory of International Politics', *International Organization,* 51 (4) (1997) 521–2.

49. Marc Trachtenberg, *A Constructed Peace: The Making of the European Settlement, 1945–1963* (Princeton, NJ: Princeton University Press, 1999).

50. For a recent example, see James McAllister, *No Exit: America and the German Problem, 1943–1954* (Ithaca: Cornell University Press, 2002). Published in a leading outlet for political scientists specializing in international security studies, McAllister expertly utilizes archival documents to flesh out US interests vis-à-vis Europe as the Second World War came to an end. Specifically, McAllister considers US decision-makers' evolving policies concerning the 'German question', including the potential paths that might have been taken – such as keeping West Germany disarmed, or preventing Germany's division – and possible missed opportunities – such as reaching a cooperative settlement with the Soviet Union. As is typical for political scientists, McAllister uses these historical processes as evidential material for theory development, in this case as a set of facts with which to illustrate the validity of a neo-classical realist reading of IR. McAllister suggests that Kenneth Waltz's *Theory of International Politics* cannot help us to explain either US foreign policies in the aftermath of the Second World War or the broad patterns of international politics that emerged during the early Cold War era. What was crucial to both the US and the Soviet Union was not the balance of power between them (as Waltz's structural theory would predict) but the future orientation, and alignment, of the European states – something that at the time was less than clear. Consistent with the assumptions of neoclassical realism, McAllister's argument is not that power was irrelevant, but that it is vitally important to look at how power was used: US decision-makers used America's power resources not to balance against the Soviet Union unilaterally and thus to

ignore potential allies (as Waltz would lead us to expect) but to devise a mutlilateralist agenda that devoted considerable resources and attention to Europe. How this agenda shifted over the course of a decade into a permanent American military presence in Europe is the central historical question that McAllister takes up, but the central goal of the book is to use this historical puzzle in order to challenge Waltz's neo-realist theory in general, and his hypotheses on bipolarity in particular.

51. Robert Jervis, 'International History and International Politics', p. 402.

6
intelligence

peter jackson and len scott*

The first years of the twenty-first century have witnessed a transformation in the role of secret intelligence in international politics. Intelligence and security issues are now more prominent than ever before in both political discourse and the wider public consciousness. Public demands and expectations of intelligence have never been greater, and these demands include much greater disclosure of hitherto secret knowledge. Yet the adage that espionage is 'the second oldest profession' reflects the fact that the conduct of intelligence can be traced back to antiquity, if not indeed biblical scripture and mythology. Reflection on the theory and practice of intelligence can be found in the writings of Sun Tzu in the fifth century BCE, and the historiography of intelligence in war and statecraft attests to its longevity and significance in political affairs.

Yet it is only some five decades since intelligence first emerged as a subject of serious academic study with the publication of Sherman Kent's *Strategic Intelligence for American World Policy*.[1] And while specific events such as the American intelligence failure at Pearl Harbor have generated considerable scholarly enquiry, it is still only 20 years since two eminent British historians invoked Sir Alexander Cadogan's description of intelligence as the 'missing dimension' in the study of the history of international relations.[2] For many years there was a pervasive belief that serious academic enquiry into the role of intelligence in international relations faced insurmountable obstacles.

The development of intelligence studies as a distinct sub-field in the study of international relations has continued to gather momentum in recent years. Initially the terrain of political scientists, the role of intelligence in domestic and international politics now attracts the attention of an ever-larger number of historians. The key journal in the field, *Intelligence and National Security*, was founded in 1986, and has been followed by other international journals: notably the *International Journal of Intelligence and CounterIntelligence, Cryptologia*, and, more recently, the *Journal of Intelligence History*. The subject is firmly established in centres of teaching and research in both Europe and North America. As a result, the study of international politics has been increasingly influenced by a better understanding of the role of intelligence in policy-making. But much research remains to be done. The long-time doyen of intelligence history, Christopher Andrew, has observed that the role of intelligence 'is still denied its proper place in studies of the Cold War'. In particular, the specific and potentially crucial subject of signals intelligence remains wholly neglected in Cold War historiography.[3]

what is intelligence?

A necessary starting point in exploring the history and historiography of intelligence is to pose the question: what is intelligence? The way intelligence is defined necessarily conditions approaches to research and writing about the subject. With much contemporary analysis, intelligence is understood as the process of gathering, analysing and making use of information. Yet beyond such basic definitions there are divergent conceptions of exactly what intelligence is and what it is for. This is perhaps because, as James Der Derian has observed, intelligence is the 'least understood and most undertheorized area of international relations'.[4] David Kahn, one of the most eminent scholars in the field, similarly laments that '[n]one of the definitions [of intelligence] that I have seen work'.[5] A brief survey of various approaches to the study of intelligence illuminates the difficulties inherent in any search for an inclusive definition.

Many scholars and practitioners tend to understand intelligence primarily as a tool of foreign and defence policy-making. Some focus on its role in domestic security. Others concentrate on the role intelligence services have played as mechanisms of state oppression.[6] One interesting divergence of views pertains to the basic character of intelligence. Michael Herman (a former practitioner) treats it as a form of state power in its own right and this conceptualization is at the heart of the analysis in his influential study *Intelligence Power in Peace and War*.[7] John Ferris (an historian) proffers a different view, judging that 'intelligence is not a form of power but a means to guide its use, whether as a force multiplier, or by helping statesmen to understand their environment and options, and thus how to apply force or leverage, and against whom'.[8]

Sherman Kent's classic analysis of intelligence covers the 'the three separate and distinct things that intelligence devotees usually mean when they use the word'.[9] These are: knowledge; the type of organization that produces that knowledge; and the activities pursued by that organization. As a fundamental task of all intelligence services is to collect information, this points us toward the question of sources. Observers have traditionally distinguished between two types of intelligence: 'open' and 'secret'. Open source intelligence is information that is freely available and can be acquired without resorting to clandestine methods of collection. Typical 'open' sources include the media, published official statistics, and, recently, material available in cyberspace.[10]

Intelligence from secret sources, conversely, is usually information that targets wish to remain secret and which must therefore be obtained by clandestine means such as espionage, electronic eavesdropping and the acquisition of covert images. There are three standard means of acquiring intelligence from secret sources. The first and oldest method is to gather information from agents (commonly referred to as human intelligence, or HUMINT). The second key source of secret information comes from monitoring the signals generated by communications between other actors (signals intelligence, or SIGINT). These signals are often encoded or enciphered, but SIGINT also includes monitoring the flow of communications even when the precise meaning of messages cannot be divined. A final means of collecting secret information is to obtain photographic imagery of the object of enquiry (imagery intelligence, or IMINT). This method includes aerial reconnaissance and satellite surveillance. Together these sources make up what are commonly described as the three intelligence 'collection disciplines'.[11] But the relatively clear distinctions between 'open' and 'secret' sources were blurred with the arrival of 'spy' satellites in the early 1960s. The intelligence provided by satellites is more difficult to categorize because, although it is often information that targets would prefer to keep secret, it is obtained without violating their sovereignty in any current legal sense.[12]

The existence of different types of sources presents additional difficulties for any attempt to define intelligence activity. Should one categorize obtaining information from open sources as intelligence work? What distinguishes the intelligence process from the information gathering activities of other government agencies? Michael Herman has offered a solution to this problem by identifying 'government intelligence' as 'the specialised organisations that have that name, and what they do and produce'.[13] This distinction is also problematic, however. A central aim of the intelligence communities of the post-1945 period had been to analyse all incoming information together and to produce assessments that are based on the collective expertise of a wide range of officials. This aim has evolved along with the realization that intelligence analysis must integrate information from all sources into broader appreciations that are based on careful corroboration and set available material within the larger political and strategic context.[14] Pursuit of collaborative assessment and 'all-source analysis' means that intelligence estimates are almost always based on a combination of secret and open source information, very often drawn from government departments that have no direct involvement in secret intelligence. It therefore remains difficult to make confident judgements about exactly what intelligence is and precisely how it influences decision-making. And this problem is only exacerbated by the secrecy that inhibits and frequently prohibits scholarly enquiry into decision-making.

A good illustration of the difficulties inherent in defining intelligence is the controversial question of secret intervention in other societies (most commonly referred to as 'covert action'). Scholars have frequently ignored covert action in their analyses of intelligence. As Elizabeth Anderson has argued: 'the specific subject of covert action as an element of intelligence has suffered a deficiency of serious study'.[15] There is a clear need to locate 'covert action' within the study of international relations in general and within intelligence in particular. This may also pose an interesting challenge for theorists of intelligence. Considering covert action as intelligence work means that intelligence might be better understood as a tool *for the execution* of policy rather than a tool *to inform* policy. Since the events of 9/11, the political context for these activities, both national and international, has changed.

In sum, formulating a clear definition of intelligence and intelligence activity is far from straightforward. Much of the difficulty derives from the dual nature of intelligence. Intelligence is both a process and the information that is produced by that process. A very brief survey of the historical evolution of intelligence illustrates the dynamic relationship that has always existed between the collection of information about the world on the one hand, and the structures and processes that have evolved to better understand and use this information on the other.

the development of intelligence

The emergence of permanent intelligence services, like so much of the machinery of the modern state, was driven to an important extent by the engines of European war. As late as the mid nineteenth century none of the great powers possessed permanent organizations tasked with the collection and analysis of information on the military and political situation in other states. While political communities had long engaged in espionage and code-breaking, there were no bureaucratic organs responsible for combining this secret information with other sources of intelligence or for providing political and military leaders with intelligence assessments to guide decision-making. Modern intelligence services evolved slowly in Europe over the period from 1792 to 1918. Prior to the French Revolution, systems for managing intelligence had scarcely evolved at all since antiquity.

The earliest recorded theorizing on the nature of intelligence and its usefulness in war and politics is that of Sun Tzu. Writing around 500 BCE, Sun Tzu repeatedly emphasized the importance of intelligence to waging war. 'What is called foreknowledge,' he wrote, 'cannot be elicited from spirits, nor from the gods, nor by analogy with past events, nor from calculations. It must be obtained from the men who know the enemy situation.'[16] Signals intelligence also dates from antiquity. The Spartans are reputed to have developed a cipher system to provide for secure communications between political leaders and military commanders as early as the fourth century BCE. There is also evidence of code-breaking activity in India during the same period. The Romans used secret writing regularly, particularly during military campaigns: Julius Caesar describes the use of a sophisticated cipher system in *The Gallic War*. The first code-breaking manual on record was written by the Arabs in the ninth century CE.[17]

From the fall of Rome through to the first industrial revolution, little progress was made in developing systems for collecting and exploiting intelligence. During this entire period there were no genuine revolutions in communications technology. The swiftness with which information could be transmitted was limited to the speed of horse and sail. In fact, long-distance communications deteriorated after the fall of Rome. The fragmentation of the western half of the empire undermined the vast network of roads and sea lanes that had constituted its nervous system. Long-distance communication was further undermined by the concurrent breakdown in political stability and the rise of hundreds of independent or semi-independent feudal polities in Western, Central and Northern Europe.[18]

The situation did not improve significantly until the emergence of powerful city-states in the early modern period created the conditions necessary for the development of modern forms of diplomacy. Of particular importance for the evolution of foreign intelligence was the development of the resident ambassador as a more or less permanent institution in relations between the Italian city-states in the early fifteenth century.[19] The post of the ambassador was established as a means of acquiring information on the political, commercial and military situation abroad. Indeed, it can be argued that the diplomatic system that emerged across Europe during the Renaissance was a response to the need for information. Ambassadors inevitably used both legitimate and clandestine means to gather this information for their reports. By the mid sixteenth century most embassies recruited spies.[20]

The development of the diplomatic mail service to support ambassadors led just as inevitably to the interception of messages, the use of increasingly complicated codes and ciphers, and the evolution of 'Black Chambers' for cryptanalysis. The first 'golden age' of European secret writing and code-breaking occurred, not surprisingly, in Italy, with the appearance of celebrated masters such as Alberti of Florence, Porta of Naples and Cardan of Milan. By the mid 1600s the Geheim Kabinets Kanzlei in Vienna, the Cabinet Noir in Paris and the Deciphering Branch in London were all at work intercepting foreign communications and breaking codes and ciphers.[21]

The Revolutionary and Napoleonic Wars between 1792 and 1815 provided the stimulus for the creation of larger and more comprehensive systems for the management of information. This was because of the explosion in the size and complexity of what were for the first time truly national armies. The French system under Napoleon Bonaparte was the first to concentrate both long-term strategic intelligence and operational and tactical information within one organization, the Emperor's Cabinet. Strategic intelligence on the political and economic situation in Europe, obtained from such diverse sources as agent networks, police informants, ambassador's reports, code-breaking and the systematic study of foreign newspapers, was combined with operational and tactical information gathered by reconnaissance patrols and local sources in a system of unprecedented scale.[22]

The Napoleonic system marked a major step forward in the evolution of modern intelligence. The institutional mechanisms established to manage incoming information and to integrate it into the decision-making process were the first to strive for what would now be described as 'all-source analysis'. Yet the sheer scale of information available created formidable difficulties. This was mainly because the concept of an *analyst*, responsible for the systematic exploitation of incoming information, had yet to evolve. These mechanisms were responsible for collection and collation rather than analysis, a responsibility that Napoleon assumed himself. This system proved increasingly unworkable given the size of European armed forces along with the far-flung theatres in which they operated.

It was not until the development of the general staff system in Prussia that a permanent service was charged with the *analysis* of incoming information. In 1809, in response to crushing defeats at the hands of the French, the Prussian military system was reorganized. A special division within the war ministry was charged with preparing for war in peacetime. This inevitably generated a demand for intelligence on the political and military situation abroad. But during this period the kinds of information necessary for effective planning also expanded dramatically, with the creation of railroads and steam-powered ships. Another factor was the emergence of the telegraph, which made it possible to transmit information in something approaching 'real time'. To deal with these challenges the Prussians created the military attaché system, army or naval officers accredited to foreign governments and tasked with preparing reports on the political and military situation in the state to which they were posted. All other great powers eventually followed suit.[23] A secret intelligence service, the Nachrichtenbureau, was also founded and attached to the army staff. The key end product of this system was the 'estimate of the situation', the immediate ancestor to the modern 'net assessment', which would be integrated into strategic and operational plans.[24]

The Prussian staff system was a response to the changing nature of conflict and the need to manage effectively the ever-increasing volume of information relevant to waging war. Only permanent institutions charged specifically with the ongoing task of information gathering, analysis and planning, in peacetime as well as during war, could cope with the challenges of strategy in the modern era. Equally importantly, the Prussian system also recognized that it was no longer possible to concentrate assessment at the level of decision. It was necessary to provide for analysis at the lower levels of planning. All of these were crucial innovations which gave the Prussian army important advantages during the wars of German unification between 1864 and 1871. The success of the Prussian system thereafter made it a model for most of the other great powers. By the outbreak of the First World War every major European power possessed a permanent organization responsible for gathering intelligence from open and secret sources and for preparing assessments for decision-makers.[25]

The experience of the first 'total war' changed the practice of intelligence assessment forever. The dimensions of the conflict transformed approaches to understanding power, as armies numbering in the millions were locked in a four-year struggle for national survival. Mass industrialized warfare affected virtually every level of belligerent societies. No longer were the chief categories of military power limited to numbers of ships or sizes of standing armies. Industrial strength, access to raw materials, and levels of social and political cohesion became just as important as indices of a state's capacity to wage war. The 'Great War' also marked a revolution in signals intelligence as for the first time radio messages became central targets for interception and decryption. In a trend that would continue through the rest of the twentieth century, this led to ever larger and more sophisticated organizational structures to gather and exploit this increasingly lucrative source of political and military intelligence. In sum, the First World War entrenched intelligence as a permanent feature in both political and military decision-making. Developments in organization and communication made it possible to analyse and use information more quickly than ever before. It is difficult to disagree with the judgement that '[t]he modern age of intelligence began in 1914'.[26]

Virtually all of the great powers entered the inter-war period with larger and better organized intelligence and counter-intelligence services than they had possessed before 1914. In particular, intelligence services functioned as crucial mechanisms of political control in the totalitarian dictatorships that emerged out of the social, political and cultural crises of these years. In Nazi Germany, the Gestapo and the Sicherheitsdienst were far larger and more effective than the army's foreign intelligence service, the Abwehr. In the USSR, meanwhile, foreign intelligence was integrated into the state security and intelligence machinery (the Commissariat for Internal Affairs, or NKVD) that also controlled the sprawling empire of slave labour established by the Stalinist regime.[27] Intelligence became such a central component of political life in these regimes that it is impossible to imagine the functioning of either Nazism or Stalinism without the work of their secret services. This was another trend that characterized twentieth-century politics.

Despite the developments of the First World War and the inter-war period, intelligence as a major tool of war and foreign policy only truly came of age during the Second World War. All of the trends outlined previously, from the evolution of communications technology to the increasing size and sophistication of intelligence bureaucracies, were accelerated during this conflict. Four interrelated trends came together to underpin what one scholar has described as an 'intelligence revolution' over the course of the war.[28] The first was the advent of machine cryptanalysis and cipher-breaking by computer. This facilitated the second feature: the collection of intelligence on an industrial scale world-wide. The third was the development of a fast and efficient network for communicating this information across distances, which made it possible to exploit 'real time' intelligence on a global scale. The fourth component was the vast expansion of intelligence services in general and American secret agencies in particular. By 1945 vast intelligence bureaucracies had emerged at the very centre of the British and American war efforts. And the largest and most sophisticated of these bureaucracies were those responsible for signals intelligence. Decrypted radio messages and telegrams became a central component of virtually all strategic decision-making. Sources such as 'Ultra' and 'Magic' provided crucial information on the political intentions and military capabilities of both enemy and friendly powers.[29] By the end of the Second World War large and well-funded intelligence services had become central tools of decision-making within the government establishments of all of the important powers.

The trends and processes that characterized the evolution of intelligence during the Second World War were accelerated and amplified during the Cold War. This was largely because the nature of the superpower stand-off after 1945, and in particular the immanent (and occasionally imminent) danger of nuclear war, created a new political and strategic environment in which intelligence and intelligence services played a more prominent role than ever. There were three central reasons for this. Firstly, intelligence provided a means through which cold warriors, frustrated by the straitjacket of mutual nuclear deterrence, could fight one another. As a result, secret operations mounted under cover of plausible deniability became a key political tool in the global confrontation. Secondly, the propaganda function that all major secret services had acquired during the Second World War proved equally effective in the ongoing struggle between Soviet communism and Western free market liberalism. A key battleground of the Cold War was the hearts and minds of the world's populations. Intelligence activity, from secret propaganda operations to bribery to covert political manipulation, was ubiquitous in virtually every theatre of the Cold War. Intelligence services therefore played a fundamental role in shaping the character of the struggle by speeding its transformation from 'an old-fashioned conflict between states into a subversive competition *between societies*'.[30] Thirdly, the strategic stakes had been increased. For both sides, information about the intentions and capabilities of adversaries was more vital than ever because a successful surprise attack could mean national annihilation. One observer has noted that the Cold War was 'peculiarly an intelligence war', where intelligence services exercised unprecedented influence on decision-making and secret service work had 'an almost wartime intensity'.[31]

The result was larger and ever more expensive and complex intelligence bureaucracies using ever more powerful and comprehensive techniques for the collection of information. Supercomputers and satellite imagery transformed intelligence practice, producing vast quantities of raw information at hitherto incomprehensible speeds. And these trends have only continued into the post-Cold War era as computer power continues to expand and new possibilities of gathering and communicating information have emerged with the rise of the World Wide Web. Nor is there any sign of intelligence becoming less of a factor in world politics.[32] Indeed, at the outset of the twenty-first century, the problem of terrorism has arguably led to intelligence being more important than ever as a form of state power.

approaches to the study of intelligence

There are substantial, if rarely articulated, divergences in the way scholars have approached the study of intelligence. It is possible to identify three relatively distinct lines of attack. One approach conceives of the study of intelligence primarily as a means of acquiring new information in order to explain specific decisions made by policy-makers in both peace and war. This is favoured by international historians, but it is also characteristic of theoretical approaches that seek to explain the relationship between organizational structure and policy-making. Close attention is paid by these scholars to the process of intelligence collection, to the origin and nature of individual sources of intelligence, and to the precise use that is made of intelligence as it travels up the chain of decision. A thorough understanding of the organizational structure of government machinery, and of the place of intelligence within this machinery, is important for this approach. Also crucial is access to as much documentation as possible in order to track the way intelligence information is interpreted and used. This literature overlaps with journalistic endeavours that focus on particular cases of espionage and biographies of individual officials and agents.

A second approach strives to establish general models that can explain success and failure in the intelligence process. Characteristic of political science approaches to the discipline, it focuses almost exclusively on levels of analysis and decision. Decisive importance is attributed to structural and cognitive obstacles to the effective use of intelligence in the policy process. The aim is to identify and analyse the personal, political and institutional biases that characterize intelligence organizations and affect their performance in the decision-making process. The emphasis is on the role of preconceptions and underlying assumptions in conditioning the way intelligence is analysed and used. Studies of this type are not typically based on extensive research using primary source material. The tendency is instead to formulate general models and then to test these models against the existing historical literature as well as the memoirs and diaries of participants. The result has been a range of insights into the nature of perception and misperception, the difficulty in preventing surprise, and the politicization of the intelligence process.[33]

A third approach focuses instead on the political function of intelligence as a means of state control and, in the realm of international politics, the clandestine projection of state power. The past decade, in particular, has seen the appearance of a range of historical and political science literature on state control. If the Gestapo has long been a subject of historical study, recently released archival material has enabled scholars to explore the role of state security services in political and social life in the USSR and Eastern bloc states after 1945. A new wave of scholarship on state control since 1789 has gathered momentum. Historians are now working on a wide range of topics, from the role of British and French intelligence services in maintaining imperial control overseas to the activities of domestic security services such as MI5 or the Federal Bureau of Investigation (FBI), including their impact on political culture in, respectively, Britain and the United States.[34] Many of the scholars engaged in this research would not consider themselves as contributing to 'intelligence studies'. The interests of most lie primarily in using the records of intelligence services to better understand the role of ideology and state power in political, social and cultural life. Yet there are strong arguments for embracing this scholarship under a broader definition of 'intelligence studies' and no reason to remain confined by disciplinary boundaries that are in fact porous and arbitrary.

While much of the literature incorporates all these approaches, there are invariably differences in emphasis even in the seminal works that have been crucial in pushing research forward. At the heart of these divergences, arguably, is disagreement concerning the extent to which political assumptions and political culture shape the intelligence process at all levels. Few would deny that the process of identifying threats is inextricably bound up with political choices and assumptions. The same can be true for the gathering, assessment and dissemination of information on these threats. While it is crucial to understand political processes, scholars vary in the importance that they attribute to political culture and to ideology. Christopher Andrew, for example, argues that, 'for the conceptual framework of intelligence studies to advance further, it is essential to make a clearer distinction than is usually made at present between the roles of intelligence communities in authoritarian and democratic regimes'.[35] One notable area where differing approaches converge is research into the role of Soviet and other communist intelligence organizations, whose study has been facilitated by (some) declassification in former communist states. One especially fascinating area that has begun to be illuminated is nuclear threat perception. It now seems clear that in the early 1960s and in the 1980s Soviet authorities became genuinely concerned about the prospect of imminent American nuclear attack.[36] The role of Soviet intelligence in generating these perceptions was crucial, and study of this issue offers fertile ground for exploring the role of cognitive, bureaucratic and ideological obstacles to the effective assessment of intelligence. Moreover, such revelations have cast new light on the nature of the Cold War in general and the danger of inadvertent nuclear war in particular.

Another crucial set of questions concerns the methodological and epistemological assumptions underpinning the way the subject is studied. There has been insufficient consideration of these issues on either side of the Atlantic. The distinguished intelligence historian Richard Aldrich has cautioned against interpreting official records in national archives as 'an analogue of reality'.[37] He has argued persuasively that British archives, in particular, are highly manipulated sources of evidence for historians. The British government's long success in controlling knowledge of its wartime achievements in signals intelligence and strategic deception offers a good example of how official policy shapes the parameters of historical enquiry. There are almost certainly other such cases that have yet to come to light. One does not need to embrace a conspiratorial view of contemporary politics to appreciate the ramifications of this state practice for the generation of knowledge. These questions are especially important to consider in the light of the criticisms levelled at studies of Soviet security and intelligence services that have been based on partial and controlled access to Soviet records.[38] When advancing such criticisms, we are obliged to consider whether recent archive-based histories of British or American intelligence are based on a more comprehensive and reliable sample of the documentary record.

Focus on the limitations (and positive potential) of archival records invites comparisons with other sources, in particular oral testimony and interviews. Many journalists have written authoritative and well-researched accounts of intelligence-related issues, which rely on extensive contacts with officialdom.[39] Are these accounts more or less reliable than those based on the written archival record? Are they more or less prone to manipulation? And what of memoirs? Or the memoirs of defectors or whistle-blowers? The veracity and integrity of these sources may vary, though there are generic questions to be posed about the agendas and intentions of those who provide us with information about the world of intelligence.

intelligence and the study of international relations

Intelligence has attracted limited interest from scholars of political philosophy and International Relations (IR) theory, a fact that reflects and reproduces the attitudes of some of the canonical founding thinkers of these intellectual traditions. For while Sun Tzu may be much quoted for the importance he attaches to military intelligence, later thinkers on war were less interested and less impressed. Clausewitz, for example, may have held that knowledge of 'the enemy and his country' was 'the foundation of all our ideas and actions'; yet he also argued that much of the knowledge or 'information' obtained in war was 'false, and by far the greatest part is of a doubtful character'. How the information was acquired and processed did not much detain Clausewitz, who simply looked to officers with a 'certain power of discrimination' to guide their analysis of it.[40]

Clausewitz's lack of interest was shared by many classical realists. Machiavelli, for example, demonstrates understanding of, and enthusiasm for, what the twentieth century would come to know as strategic deception: 'Though fraud in other activities be detestable, in the management of war it is laudable and glorious, and he who overcomes an enemy by fraud is as much to be praised as he who does so by force.' Yet elsewhere in the *Discourses*, when reflecting on conspiracy, he shows no understanding of the opportunities for espionage and counter-espionage in dealing with the conspiracies of coup plotters.[41] On the other hand, Thomas Hobbes, writing in the seventeenth century, understood the potential importance and value of espionage. 'Reliable intelligence agents,' Hobbes asserted more than 300 years ago, 'are to those who exercise sovereign power like rays of light to the human soul.'[42] So intelligence is by no means entirely absent from classical thinking about the nature of international politics.

Contemporary IR theorists have nonetheless often been reluctant to incorporate intelligence into their study of world politics. Writing in 1994, Michael Fry and Miles Hochstein observed that there was a noticeable 'failure to integrate intelligence studies, even in a primitive way, into the mainstream of research in international relations'.[43] In Britain, the academic study of intelligence has developed overwhelmingly within international history, and thus reflects the methodological predisposition toward archive-based research characteristic of this sub-discipline both there and in North America. In North America, however, political scientists have played at least as prominent a role as historians in the study of intelligence in international relations. Their contributions have provided a range of theoretical reflections on the nature of intelligence and its role in decision-making. But interest in intelligence within the political science community has been confined mainly to those scholars working on theories of decision-making.[44] Intelligence is all but absent in the work of most IR theorists, and does not figure in the key debates between realist, liberal institutionalist, constructivist and postmodernist approaches. It is interesting to note that, while there exists an implicit (and sometimes explicit) assumption that the study of intelligence should fall within the realist camp, contemporary neo-realist writers have in fact largely ignored intelligence in their reflections.

If IR theory has shown limited interest in intelligence, to what extent have students of intelligence engaged with IR theory? It seems clear that different theoretical perspectives are beginning to permeate the sub-field of intelligence. The journal *Intelligence and National Security* has carried important theoretical contributions which reward Fry and Hochstein's optimistic assertions that IR and intelligence studies can fruitfully search for common ground. One notable example is Andrew Rathmell's essay on the potential importance of postmodern theorizing to the practice of intelligence.[45] Rathmell posits that existing state-based intelligence agencies are products of modernity, but that the political and economic conditions of the modern era are disappearing. Threat, he argues, is fragmenting. Different conceptual approaches to understanding the nature of security threats are therefore necessary, as are radical changes in the way intelligence agencies collect and process knowledge on these threats. The epistemological assumptions of postmodernist theory are, however, wholly at variance with trends in, for example, American military thinking, where the quest for perfect battlefield knowledge is the messianic goal of those who proselytize the revolution in information warfare.[46] Obvious questions arise about how postmodernist approaches might be implemented in practical terms. But Rathmell's prescription is intriguing, not least because it seeks policy relevance even in the most abstract (and often inaccessible) of theoretical perspectives.

If it is worthwhile engaging constructively with postmodernist thinking on security, it is also true that there are areas where postmodernists themselves need to reflect more carefully on existing approaches. The history of intelligence before the onset of the Cold War, for example, is often neglected. One resulting misconception is that open sources have only recently risen to prominence. The reality is that open sources have nearly always provided the majority of information for intelligence services during peacetime.[47] It is also misleading to describe the emergence of 'globalized' threats as a 'postmodern' phenomenon. Imperial intelligence services faced such challenges throughout the nineteenth and twentieth centuries. Information technology has changed many aspects of intelligence work, but the intellectual challenges of dealing with security problems across immense spaces and over different cultures are by no means exclusively 'postmodern'. This is admirably demonstrated by the fascinating recent work of Martin Thomas.[48] It is also the case that the threat from non-state actors did not arrive with the end of the Cold War, as the history of the Anarchists and the Fenians well testifies.

Other theoretical innovations may well have something to offer. Recent constructivist theorizing about the importance of identity and political culture in shaping both elite and public perceptions of international politics is a case in point. Its focus on identity as a central factor in the process of threat identification has obvious relevance to the study of security and intelligence. The same is true with the emphasis on cultural-institutional contexts of security policy. Intelligence services certainly have their own institutional cultures and a focus on the rules and norms that govern intelligence work in different national contexts has much to offer intelligence studies.[49] Reluctance to engage with this and other currents in IR theory will not help efforts to expand the conceptual parameters of intelligence studies. In addition, a reluctance to engage with different strains of social theory may also comply with the intentions of those who seek to configure and inform public understanding of intelligence through the control of information. The way we choose to study the subject informs our analysis and our conclusions. As Aldrich warns, taking the archive as analogue of reality is a methodological and epistemological trap that can inadvertently legitimize activities that merit a much more critical approach.

speaking 'truth unto power' or 'power unto truth'?

Much of the study of intelligence concerns the relationship between power and knowledge. A sophisticated exponent of this view has been Michael Herman, writing on the basis of 25 years' experience at Government

Communications Headquarters (GCHQ) and the Cabinet Office. Herman has received wide acclaim for his expositions of the process of intelligence and has been described as 'a historian and philosopher of intelligence'.[50] Although an advocate of broadening the scope of the subject, Herman's primary aim is to promote greater public understanding of intelligence. Yet it is also undeniable that in engaging with critical issues about the practice of the intelligence process, Herman seeks to legitimize that process. The same goals of education and legitimization may also be ascribed to other intelligence mandarins who have written about intelligence after their retirement, notably Sir Percy Cradock, former Chairman of the Joint Intelligence Committee (JIC).[51] The work of both Herman and Cradock epitomizes the prevalent self-image of the British intelligence mandarin as providing objective, 'policy-free' analysis to decision-makers.

The role of the intelligence official in the British context is therefore represented as 'speaking truth unto power'. This self-image, so central to the identity of the public servant, has been the cornerstone of both the structure and the culture of British intelligence. It is represented as the fundamental safeguard against the politicization of intelligence, which is often alleged to be a defining characteristic of autocratic and totalitarian regimes. Yet an uncritical acceptance of official or semi-official representations of the intelligence process as singularly free of ideological assumptions and political biases leaves the intelligence scholar open to the familiar charge that she or he is merely legitimizing and perpetuating the ideology of the state. These issues are of central concern to those influenced by the reflections of Gramsci and Foucault, who both have much to say about the relationship between power and knowledge. Again it seems clear that intelligence studies and IR theory would both benefit from greater engagement with one another.

The idea of speaking truth unto power also has clear relevance to debates over the proper relationship between government and academia.[52] Among academics, notions and theories of truth and power are more explicitly contested. Claims of objectivity run counter to concern with developing multiple rather than unitary narratives of the past. This, of course, is the very antithesis of Whitehall's immaculate conception of a Joint Intelligence Committee. At the same time, official practice and academic study exercise an undeniable attraction to one another. Yet there are obstacles in the way of sustained engagement between the government and the academy. Intelligence is probably the field of academic enquiry over which the British government has been most anxious to exert control. Despite a recent trend toward more openness, particularly on the part of MI5, access to archival material remains

constrained, though the National Archives (formerly the British Public Record Office) and the Lord Chancellor's Advisory Council on Public Records have endeavoured to engage British historians in the development of declassification policy. Nevertheless, it should be noted that although the Freedom of Information Act will be fully enacted in January 2005, the intelligence agencies are specifically exempt from its provisions.[53]

In the United States the relationship between academics and government has always been much more porous. Since the formation of the first centralized American intelligence agency, the Office of Strategic Services (OSS), during the Second World War, academics have played a prominent role in the evolution of American intelligence. The study of intelligence is often informed by quasi-official links, and the Central Intelligence Agency (CIA) has been keen to promote the academic study of the subject. Both the National Security Agency and the CIA each employ their own team of full-time professionally trained historians. Each has also invited 'scholars in residence' to spend extended periods working within the agencies. Such links have at times generated debate about the proper limits and intellectual integrity of such endeavours.[54]

In Britain it has long been difficult to discern any comparable relationship, and a greater distance has generally been maintained between 'academics' and 'practitioners'. Moreover, as Wolfgang Krieger points out, the situation in Germany as elsewhere in Europe is one of even less engagement.[55] There have been important exceptions to this general trend, most notably the scholars who were given privileged access to official records in order to write the official histories of the Second World War. Another notable exception is Christopher Andrew, whose collaborations with Soviet intelligence service defectors Oleg Gordievsky and Vasili Mitrokhin have illuminated the activities of the Committee for State Security (or KGB, the post-Stalinist successor to the NKVD) as well as British (and particularly Secret Intelligence Service (SIS)) successes in the espionage war. But it is only recently that a culture of greater openness has led to greater engagement between Britain's intelligence community and its universities. A good illustration of this trend was the willingness of Sir Stephen Lander, then Director-General of MI5, to attend academic meetings and conferences on the study of intelligence over the past few years. Further evidence of greater openness, at least on the part of the Security Service, is MI5's recent appointment of an academic historian, Christopher Andrew, to write its centenary history. Yet there are those that would argue that this kind of engagement is not without costs. For some academics the ivory tower should remain a sanctuary from the compromises of officialdom and provide a panorama

(or a camera obscura) on the world outside. For others, academics are there to tell the world about the world. Yet while many academics aspire to policy relevance, intelligence is one area where European officialdom may remain on the whole sceptical about the value of engagement with the academy.

dark sides of moons

Reflecting on the work of the Joint Intelligence Committee, Sir Percy Cradock has observed that 'it has a predilection for threats rather than opportunities, for the dark side of the moon'.[56] Certainly the issues of strategic surprise and of intelligence failure have loomed large in the evolution of the study of intelligence. This is unlikely to change significantly. Providing warning against surprise is central to both official and public perceptions of the fundamental role of intelligence services, and the events of 9/11 have clearly reinforced this trend.

Recent developments in the study of security in international politics have nevertheless attempted to broaden predominant conceptions to provide a more sophisticated understanding of the problems of instability and injustice in international society. The study of intelligence, with its focus on the identification and interpretation of threat, and on the architecture of threat perception, has much to offer and much to gain from greater engagement with such new approaches to security. Yet at the same time, few intelligence scholars have exhibited great enthusiasm for incorporating a broader definition of security into their research and writing.

Other traditional concerns nevertheless remain a necessary focus. Recent systematic declassification of American files dealing with covert action has made a significant contribution to understanding the origins and dynamics of the Cold War. The declassification of CIA records has more clearly revealed the scope and scale of operations from Cuba to Chile to Indonesia to Guatemala. Indeed, in the view of some scholars, the history of covert action compels revision of the historical and political accounts of the Cold War, and fatally weakens the view that American policy was simply concerned with containment.[57] These issues have not received the attention they deserve in the study of British intelligence so far. Although recently published studies by Richard Aldrich and Stephen Dorril have illuminated a great deal, British covert action in both Cold War and post-imperial contexts is an area that requires further study.[58] Here the endeavours of senior intelligence mandarins to divert the focus to the sanitized and cerebral contexts of Whitehall analysis may reflect

a conscious (or unconscious) attempt to divert attention away from the more dramatic and controversial issue of covert action.

popular culture, fictional representation and intelligence

At least since the aftermath of the Franco-Prussian War in 1871, popular culture has often played an important role in shaping both official and public attitudes towards intelligence. Michael Miller has demonstrated the way fears of foreign espionage and national insecurity gripped the French imagination during this period. The Dreyfus Affair, which had such grievous consequences for French intelligence, unfolded in an atmosphere of spy mania over the machinations of an imaginary army of German spies in France controlled by the notorious spymaster Wilhelm Stieber. The fact that there was no army of spies and Stieber was a police chief rather than a master of espionage did not matter. Through to the outbreak of war in 1914, spy mania was created and sustained by memories of France's defeat in 1871 and by a spy literature which played on national anxieties about France's vulnerability to foreign espionage.[59] The British public demonstrated a similar appetite for espionage stories and invasion scares, of which some of the most widely read were produced by William Le Queux. It was in the context of a wave of greatly exaggerated official and popular concern over the threat of foreign espionage that a British security service was established in 1909.[60]

Fictional representations of international politics as a struggle for survival between national intelligence services thus played an important role in the evolution of both French and British intelligence before the First World War. Between the two world wars, spy adventures stories, and even spy films, became a permanent fixture of Western popular culture. This trend continued through the Cold War era. Graham Greene, John Le Carré, Ian Fleming and Tom Clancy are only the most prominent of several generations of novelists who used intelligence as both medium and metaphor when interpreting the era of superpower rivalry. For most of the twentieth century, representations of intelligence in popular culture were far and away the most influential factors shaping public attitudes and perceptions. Yet with a few notable exceptions, scholars have been reluctant to reflect upon the implications of this in their analyses of the relationship between intelligence and politics. Once again, there is potentially interesting work being done in the cognate field of cultural history that could enrich the study of intelligence. Cultural historians, especially those interested in Cold War popular and political culture,

have begun to pay careful attention to the role of film and fiction in shaping both elite and popular attitudes towards international politics. The intersection between this work and the study of intelligence has not received the attention it deserves.

Fictional representations of intelligence form the basis of much public understanding. As Nigel West observes, no less an authority than former SIS Chief Sir Colin McColl considered James Bond 'the best recruiting sergeant the service ever had'[61] – perhaps the converse view of intelligence critic Philip Knightley who complained that the 'fictional glorification of spies enables the real ones to go on playing their sordid games'.[62] A more perplexing if intriguing relationship between reality and fiction is illustrated by the occasion recounted by Jeremy Black when the Soviet Politburo issued instructions to the KGB to acquire the gadgetry displayed in the latest Bond film.[63] Fiction also provides a range of ethical representations of intelligence.[64] The world of James Bond is characterized by good and evil, while the world of John le Carré is a complex of moral ambiguity, nuance and ambivalence. Fiction nevertheless illustrates specific ethical problems and dilemmas that are underexplored in the literature of intelligence studies. How far an intelligence organization is prepared to risk or sacrifice its own 'side' in pursuit of a 'higher' objective, for example, is a popular theme, as well-illustrated in le Carré's *The Spy Who Came in From the Cold*.[65]

Literary and cinematic representations also encompass various themes commonly found in conspiracy theories, not least that intelligence services are malign and all pervasive.[66] Fictional conspiracy theories frequently accord with the genuine kind in giving meaning to events and resonate with James Der Derian's analysis of Hollywood's representation of conspiracy, when he writes of it making 'sense to find in coeval events, synchronicities, even odd accidents, the intellectual evidence and psychological comfort of the hidden hand'.[67] Yet the mere fact that hidden hands fulfil psychological needs does not mean that hidden hands do not exist. One reason why there are conspiracy theories is because there are conspiracies. Indeed the history of covert action is the history of conspiracy. While it would be simplistic to suggest that the former begat the latter, covert action is nevertheless the sturdy twin of conspiracy theory.

The issue of how far fiction corresponds to reality raises questions about how we perceive and construct reality. Le Carré's novels are widely accepted as authentic depictions of the techniques and tradecraft of espionage – though his representation of the ethics of the service provoked anger from within.[68] More recently, the film *U-571* was criticized for

depicting the seizure of the German naval Enigma by American rather than by British forces. There is of course a long tradition of changing or manipulating historical 'events' for dramatic effect. But to what extent do such fictional representations actually shape popular attitudes? This is a question that awaits systematic exploration. How far fictional representations are *intended* to frame popular understandings has received rather more attention – particularly in the recent boom of studies on the cultural history of the Cold War.[69] The events of 9/11 and the 'war on terror' have given these questions a new saliency and urgency. How Hollywood will now depict intelligence services and how it will represent the American government will be issues to watch carefully.

conclusion

The publication in 1946 of the lengthy and detailed Congressional report on the Pearl Harbor attack provided the primary raw material for one of the founding texts in the intelligence studies canon. Roberta Wohlstetter's marriage of communications theory with detailed historical research in *Pearl Harbor: Warning and Decision* demonstrated the rich potential of an interdisciplinary approach to the study of intelligence and policy-making.[70] Whether or not the recently published Congressional report on the surprise attacks of 9/11 turns out to be an equally seminal text, the events of the past few years are bound to have profound implications for the study of intelligence.

Michael Herman has argued that 'Governments' and peoples' views of intelligence will be permanently affected by the events of September 11'.[71] While this is debatable, it is undeniable that intelligence occupies a more prominent place in the public sphere than ever before. Quite apart from the publication of secret intelligence on Iraq, debates about the practice of intelligence now take place on a scale and at a level that would have been inconceivable three years ago. Issues such as the relative importance of human intelligence as against 'technical assets', the importance of international intelligence collaboration and the cognitive obstacles to effective analysis and warning have all been debated. These developments will doubtless provide both challenges and opportunities to scholars interested in the study of intelligence.

Should the 2001 terror attacks in New York and Washington force us to rethink the subject we are studying? Will they change the nature and conduct of intelligence operations forever? If so, how will this affect the study of intelligence and its role in world politics? These are questions that bear further reflection in any exercise aimed at establishing a future agenda for intelligence studies. The evidence so far suggests that, while the role of intelligence in international politics has certainly evolved, and scholars will have to adjust to its evolution, the changes may not be as revolutionary as they first appeared. As in other areas of world politics, the immovable object of change confronts the irresistible force of continuity.

It is true that there was no Pearl Harbor precedent for current debates about the ethical restraints on intelligence activity, nor was there much public discussion in the 1940s of the need for transnational intelligence cooperation. These differences reflect changes that have taken place in world politics since the Second World War. International norms have evolved and now place greater limitations on the exercise of power than those that existed during and after the Second World War. Globalization, and in particular advances in information technology, have thrown up new challenges that require new solutions. But there are nonetheless remarkable parallels between the debates over Pearl Harbor and 9/11. In both instances, predictably, the overwhelming focus was on learning lessons and prescribing policies. Many of the themes here are very similar: the inability to conduct effective espionage against a racially or culturally 'alien' adversary; the failure to organize and coordinate inter-service intelligence collection and analysis; the lack of resources for both gathering, translating and analysing intelligence; and, finally, the failure of political leaders to understand the value and limitations of intelligence. The surprise attack on United States territory in December 1941 killed over 2000 people and precipitated America's entry into war in Europe and Asia. Pearl Harbor wrought a fundamental transformation in America's role in world politics, and indeed in world politics itself. The surprise attack on United States territory on 11 September 2001 killed a similar number of people (though they were not military personnel and included many hundreds of non-Americans). It too precipitated American wars in Afghanistan and Iraq. How far it has transformed world politics will remain open to debate. Whatever the case, the need to continue to study the theory and practice of intelligence in international relations is now established beyond any doubt.

notes

*   This chapter draws upon our 'Journeys in Shadows' in our edited volume *Understanding Intelligence in the Twenty-First Century: Journeys in Shadows* (London: Routledge, 2004), pp. 1–28, which was part of a research project funded jointly by the British Academy and the University of Wales, Aberystwyth, to whom we express our gratitude and indebtedness. We would

also like to thank our colleague, Jonathan Colman, for his valuable help with this chapter.

1. Sherman Kent, *Strategic Intelligence for American World Policy* (Princeton, NJ: Princeton University Press, 1949).

2. Christopher Andrew and David Dilks (eds), *The Missing Dimension: Governments and Intelligence Communities in the Twentieth Century* (Urbana: University of Illinois Press, 1984).

3. Christopher Andrew, 'Intelligence in the Cold War: Lessons and Learning', in Harold Shukman (ed.), *Agents for Change: Intelligence Services in the 21st Century* (London: St Ermin's Press, 2000), pp. 1–2; Christopher Andrew, 'Intelligence, International Relations and "Undertheorisation"', in L. V. Scott and P. Jackson (eds), *Understanding Intelligence in the Twenty-First Century: Journeys in Shadows* (London: Routledge, 2004), pp. 29–41 (also published as a theme issue, *Intelligence and National Security*, 19 (2) (2004)). For recent research on signals intelligence, see Matthew Aid and Cees Wiebes (eds), 'Secrets of Signals Intelligence during the Cold War and Beyond', theme issue, *Intelligence and National Security*, 16 (1) (2001).

4. James Der Derian, *Antidiplomacy: Spies, Terror, Speed and War* (Oxford: Blackwell, 1992), p. 19; see also Michael Fry and Miles Hochstein, 'Epistemic Communities: Intelligence Studies and International Relations', in Wesley K. Wark (ed.), *Espionage: Past, Present, Future?* (London: Frank Cass, 1994), pp. 14–28 (also published as a theme issue, *Intelligence and National Security*, 8 (3) (1993)).

5. David Kahn, 'An Historical Theory of Intelligence', *Intelligence and National Security*, 16 (3) (2002) 79. For a thoughtful comparative analysis of the concept of intelligence in different national contexts, see Philip H. J. Davies, 'Ideas of Intelligence: Divergent National Concepts and Institutions', *Harvard International Review*, 24 (3) (2002) 62–6. For an earlier valuable collection of essays dealing with these issues, see Kenneth G. Robertson (ed.), *British and American Approaches to Intelligence* (London: Macmillan, 1987).

6. Examples include Richard Thurlow, *The Secret State: British Internal Security in the Twentieth Century* (Oxford: Blackwell, 1994); Amy Knight, *Beria: Stalin's First Lieutenant* (Princeton, NJ: Princeton University Press, 1993); Robert Gellately, *The Gestapo and German Society: Enforcing Racial Policy 1933–1945* (Oxford: Oxford University Press, 1990).

7. Michael Herman, *Intelligence Power in Peace and War* (Cambridge: Cambridge University Press, 1996).

8. John Ferris, 'Intelligence', in Robert Boyce and Joseph Maiolo (eds), *The Origins of World War Two: The Debate Continues* (London: Palgrave, 2003), p. 308.

9. Kent, *Strategic Intelligence*, p. ix.

10. A useful recent discussion of the nature of open-source intelligence (OSINT) is Mark Lowenthal, *Intelligence: From Secrets to Policy* (New York: CQ Press, 2003), esp. pp. 79–82.

11. For a discussion, see Lowenthal, *Intelligence*, pp. 54–86; William E. Odom, *Fixing Intelligence for a More Secure America* (New Haven: Yale University Press, 2003), pp. 66–74.

12. The best discussion of these technical issues remains Herman, *Intelligence Power*, pp. 61–81.

13. Michael Herman, 'Diplomacy and Intelligence', *Diplomacy and Statecraft*, 9 (2) (1998) 1–2.
14. For an excellent discussion of the evolution of the concept of collective and 'all-source' analysis, see Herman, *Intelligence Power*, esp. pp. 100–12.
15. Elizabeth Anderson, 'The Security Dilemma and Covert Action: The Truman Years', *International Journal of Intelligence and CounterIntelligence*, 11 (4) (1998–99) 403.
16. Sun Tzu, *The Art of War*, ed. by S. B. Griffith (Oxford: Oxford University Press, 1971), pp. 144–5.
17. Much of the information in the preceding paragraph is drawn from the first chapter of David Kahn, *The Codebreakers: The History of Secret Writing*, rev. edn (New York: Scribner, 1996). This study, first published in 1967, remains the classic and indispensable source for the history of signals intelligence. See also the many important historical articles on this subject in the journal *Cryptologia*, including, for a discussion of Arabic code-breaking, Ibrahim A. Al-Kadi, 'The Origins of Cryptology: The Arab Contributions', *Cryptologia*, 16 (2) (1992) 97–126.
18. Martin Van Creveld, *Command in War* (Cambridge, MA: Harvard University Press, 1985), pp. 19–34.
19. M. S. Anderson, *The Rise of Modern Diplomacy 1450–1919* (London: Longman, 1993), pp. 1–20; Gordon Craig and Alexander George, *Force and Statecraft: Diplomatic Problems of our Time*, 3rd edn (New York: Oxford University Press, 1995), pp. 10–14.
20. Charles Howard Carter, 'The Ambassadors of Early Modern Europe: Patterns of Diplomatic Representation', in C. H. Carter (ed.), *From the Renaissance to the Counter-Reformation: Essays in Honour of Garrett Mattingly* (London: Cape, 1966), pp. 269–95.
21. Herman, *Intelligence Power*, pp. 10–11; André Catthiew, 'La Cryptologie', in P. Lacoste (ed.), *Le Renseignement à la Française* (Paris: Economica, 1998), pp. 287–8.
22. On the organization and functioning of the Napoleonic command and intelligence systems, see Hermann Giehrl, *Der Feldherr Napoleon als Organizator: Betrachtungen über seine Verkehrsund Nachrichtenmittel, seine Arbeits und Befehlsweise* (Berlin: Ernst Siegfried Mittler und Sohn, 1911), esp. pp. 55–7 for material on the activity of the Cabinet Noir. See also Jay Luvaas, 'Napoleon's Use of Intelligence', *Intelligence and National Security*, 3 (3) (1988) 40–54; and Van Creveld, *Command in War*, pp. 65–74.
23. See Gordon Craig, 'Military Diplomats in the Prussian and German Service: the Attachés, 1816–1914', *Political Science Quarterly*, 64 (1) (1949) 65–94; Maureen O'Connor, 'Sanctioned Spying: The Development of the Military Attaché in the Nineteenth Century', in Peter Jackson and Jennifer Siegel (eds), *Intelligence and Statecraft: The Uses and Limits of Intelligence in International Society since 1870* (Westport, CT: Greenwood Press, forthcoming); Philip Towle, 'Introduction', in Philip Towle (ed.), *Estimating Foreign Military Power* (London: Croom Helm, 1982), pp. 26–9; and especially Alfred Vagts, *The Military Attaché* (Princeton, NJ: Princeton University Press, 1967).
24. Van Creveld, *Command in War*, pp. 111–14; Holger Herwig, 'Imperial Germany', in Ernest R. May (ed.), *Knowing One's Enemies: Intelligence Assessment before the Two World Wars* (Princeton, NJ: Princeton University Press, 1984),

pp. 63–71. The Prussian system charged estimates of foreign military power to two 'Quartermasters General' that would eventually evolve into *Fremde Heere West* and *Fremde Heere Ost* ('Foreign Armies West' and 'Foreign Armies East' respectively).

25. For excellent discussions of these issues, see Dennis Showalter, 'Intelligence on the Eve of Transformation', in Walter T. Hitchcock (ed.), *The Intelligence Revolution: A Historical Perspective* (Washington, DC: US Air Force Academy, 1991), pp. 15–34; and the essays in May, *Knowing One's Enemies*.

26. John Ferris, 'The Road to Bletchley Park: The British Experience with Signals Intelligence, 1892–1945', *Intelligence and National Security*, 17 (1) (2002) 65.

27. On Nazi Germany, see Michael Geyer, 'National Socialist Germany: The Politics of Information', in May, *Knowing One's Enemies*, pp. 310–46; Gellately, *Gestapo and German Society*; Eric Johnson, *Nazi Terror: The Gestapo, Jews and Ordinary Germans* (New York: Basic Books, 1999). On intelligence and Soviet state control see, in addition to the ever-increasing literature on Stalinist Terror, Amy Knight, *The KGB: Police and Politics in the Soviet Union* (London: Unwin Hyman, 1988); Christopher Andrew and Oleg Gordievsky, *KGB: The Inside Story* (London: Hodder and Stoughton, 1990).

28. Richard Aldrich, *Intelligence and the War Against Japan: Britain, America and the Politics of Secret Service* (Cambridge: Cambridge University Press, 2000), pp. 377–8.

29. Aldrich, *Intelligence and the War Against Japan*, pp. 375–9. The literature on intelligence and the Second World War is far too vast even to attempt to summarize here.

30. Richard Aldrich, *The Hidden Hand: Britain, America and Cold War Secret Intelligence* (London: John Murray, 2001), p. 642 (emphasis in original).

31. Michael Herman, *Intelligence Services in the Information Age* (London: Frank Cass, 2001), pp. 159, 161.

32. On these issues see, among many others, Gregory Treverton, *Reshaping National Intelligence for an Age of Information* (Cambridge: Cambridge University Press, 2001); Bruce Berkowitz, *The New Face of War* (New York: Free Press, 2003); Bruce Berkowitz (with Allan Goodman), *Best Truth: Intelligence in the Information Age* (New Haven: Yale University Press, 2000). On the evolution of communications intelligence during the Cold War, see James Bamford, *Body of Secrets* (London: Arrow Books, 2002).

33. For a recent example of the possibilities of this approach, see the uniformly excellent essays in R. Betts and T. Mahnken (eds), *Paradoxes of Strategic Intelligence: Essays in Honor of Michael Handel* (London: Frank Cass, 2003). Other classics include Michael I. Handel, *The Diplomacy of Surprise* (Cambridge, MA: Center for International Affairs, Harvard University, 1980); Michael I. Handel, 'Intelligence and Military Operations', in Michael I. Handel (ed.), *Intelligence and Military Operations* (London: Frank Cass, 1990), pp. 1–95; Richard Betts, 'Analysis, War and Decision: Why Intelligence Failures are Inevitable', *World Politics*, 31 (1) (1978) 961–88; Robert Jervis, 'Intelligence and Foreign Policy', *International Security*, 2 (3) (1986–87) 141–61.

34. On the imperial dimension, see Martin Thomas, 'French Intelligence Gathering in the Syrian Mandate, 1920–1940', *Middle Eastern Studies*, 38 (1) (2002) 1–32; Martin Thomas, *Intelligence and Empire: Security Services and Colonial Control in North Africa and the Middle East, 1919–1940* (Berkeley: University of California

Press, forthcoming); Richard J. Popplewell, *Intelligence and Imperial Defence: British Intelligence and the Defence of the Indian Empire, 1904–1924* (London: Frank Cass, 1995).

35. Andrew, 'Intelligence, International Relations and "Undertheorisation"', p. 34.

36. See, in particular, Aleksandr Fursenko and Timothy Naftali, *'One Hell of a Gamble': Khrushchev, Castro, Kennedy and the Cuban Missile Crisis 1958–1964* (London: John Murray, 1997); Andrew and Gordievsky, *KGB*; Benjamin B. Fischer, *A Cold War Conundrum: The 1983 Soviet War Scare* (Washington, DC: Central Intelligence Agency, Center for the Study of Intelligence, 1997).

37. Aldrich, *Hidden Hand*, p. 6. On this important methodological issue, see also Aldrich, *Intelligence and the War Against Japan*, pp. 385–7; P. Jackson, 'The Politics of Secret Service in War, Cold War and Imperial Retreat', *Contemporary British History*, 14 (4) (2003) 423–31.

38. See Sheila Kerr, 'KGB Sources on the Cambridge Network of Soviet Agents: True or False', *Intelligence and National Security*, 11 (3) (1996) 561–85; Sheila Kerr, 'Oleg Tsarev's Synthetic KGB Gems', *International Journal of Intelligence and CounterIntelligence*, 14 (1) (2001) 89–116; Nigel West, 'No Dust on KGB Jewels', *International Journal of Intelligence and CounterIntelligence*, 14 (4) (2001–02) 589–92.

39. See, for example, Mark Urban, *UK Eyes Alpha: The Inside Story of British Intelligence* (London: Faber and Faber, 1996); Michael Smith, *New Cloak, Old Dagger: How Britain's Spies Came in From the Cold* (London: Victor Gollancz, 1996). The pre-eminent figure in combining recently released archival material with the fruits of personal disclosure and oral testimony is undoubtedly Peter Hennessy: see his *The Secret State: Whitehall and the Cold War* (London: Allen Lane, 2002).

40. Carl von Clausewitz, *On War*, ed. by Anatol Rapoport (New York: Penguin, 1968), p. 162. For analysis of Clausewitz on intelligence, see John Ferris and Michael I. Handel, 'Clausewitz, Intelligence, Uncertainty and the Art of Command in Military Operations', *Intelligence and National Security*, 10 (1) (1995) 1–58.

41. Machiavelli, *The Prince, Selections from the Discourses and Other Writings*, ed. by John Plamenatz (London: Fontana/Collins, 1975), pp. 252–71.

42. Hobbes, *De Cive,* cited in Toni Erskine, '"As Rays of Light to the Human Soul"? Moral Agents and Intelligence Gathering', in Scott and Jackson, *Understanding Intelligence*, p. 195.

43. Fry and Hochstein, 'Epistemic Communities', p. 14.

44. For a good example of the possibilities offered by such approaches, see the important recent study by Amy Zegart, *Flawed by Design: The Evolution of the CIA, JCS, and NSC* (Palo Alto: Stanford University Press, 1999).

45. Andrew Rathmell, 'Towards Postmodern Intelligence', *Intelligence and National Security*, 17 (3) (2002) 87–104. See also the work of James Der Derian – for example, *Antidiplomacy* – who has written extensively on aspects of intelligence from a postmodern perspective.

46. John Ferris, 'Netcentric Warfare: C4ISR and Information Operations: Towards a Revolution in Military Intelligence', in Scott and Jackson (eds), *Understanding Intelligence*, pp. 54–77.

47. During the inter-war period, for example, more than 85 per cent of the information gathered and analysed by French intelligence came from open sources: see Peter Jackson, *France and the Nazi Menace: Intelligence and Policymaking, 1933–1939* (Oxford: Oxford University Press, 2000), pp. 11–44.
48. Thomas, 'French Intelligence Gathering'; Martin Thomas, 'Bedouin Tribes and the Imperial Intelligence Services in Syria, Iraq and Transjordan in the 1920s', *Journal of Contemporary History*, 38 (4) (2003) 539–61. These issues are also the central theme of Thomas' forthcoming *Intelligence and Empire*.
49. For constructivist approaches to IR, see, for example, Peter J. Katzenstein (ed.), *The Culture of National Security: Norms and Identity in World Politics* (New York: Columbia University Press, 1996); Alexander Wendt, *Social Theory of International Politics* (Cambridge: Cambridge University Press, 1999).
50. Hennessy, *Secret State*, p. xiii. See also Lawrence Freedman, 'Powerful Intelligence', *Intelligence and National Security*, 12 (2) (1997) 198–202.
51. Percy Cradock, *Know Your Enemy: How the Joint Intelligence Committee Saw the World* (London: John Murray, 2002).
52. See William Wallace, 'Truth and Power, Monks and Technocrats: Theory and Practice in International Relations', *Review of International Studies*, 22 (3) (1996) 301–21; Ken Booth, 'A Reply to Wallace', *Review of International Studies*, 23 (3) (1997) 371–7; Steve Smith, 'Power and Truth: A Reply to William Wallace', *Review of International Studies*, 23 (4) (1997) 507–16.
53. We are grateful to Stephen Twigge for this information.
54. For scrutiny of the relationship between US academia and US intelligence, see Robin Winks, *Cloak and Gown: Scholars in the Secret War* (New York: William Morrow and Company, 1987).
55. Wolfgang Krieger, 'German Intelligence History: A Field in Search of Scholars', in Scott and Jackson, *Understanding Intelligence*, pp. 42–53.
56. Cradock, *Know Your Enemy*, p. 4.
57. Sara-Jane Corkem, 'History, Historians and the Naming of Foreign Policy: A Post-Modern Reflection on American Strategic Thinking during the Truman Administration', *Intelligence and National Security*, 16 (3) (2001) 146–63. For an important contribution to this area, see John Prados, *Presidents' Secret Wars: CIA and Pentagon Covert Operations From World War II Through the Persian Gulf*, rev. edn (Chicago: Ivan R. Dee, 1996).
58. Aldrich, *Hidden Hand*; Stephen Dorril, *MI6: Fifty Years of Special Operations* (London: Fourth Estate, 2000); Mark Curtis, *Web of Deceit: Britain's Real Role in the World* (London: Vintage, 2003).
59. See Michael Miller, *Shanghai on the Metro: Spies, Intrigue and the French Between the Wars* (Berkeley: University of California Press, 1994), pp. 21–36.
60. On this question, see Christopher Andrew, *Secret Service: The Making of the British Intelligence Community* (London: Sceptre, 1985), pp. 67–137; Nicholas P. Hiley, 'The Failure of British Espionage Against Germany, 1907–1914', *Historical Journal*, 26 (2) (1983) 866–81.
61. Nigel West, 'Fiction, Faction and Intelligence', in Scott and Jackson, *Understanding Intelligence*, pp. 122–34.
62. Philip Knightley, 'Spy Lies', *Saturday Night* (September 1988), 72, quoted in Wesley K. Wark, 'Introduction: Fictions of History', in Wesley K. Wark (ed.), *Spy Fiction, Spy Films and Real Intelligence* (London: Frank Cass, 1991), p. 9.

63. Jeremy Black, 'The Geopolitics of James Bond', in Scott and Jackson, *Understanding Intelligence*, pp. 135–46.
64. J. J. Macintosh, 'Ethics and Spy Fiction', *Intelligence and National Security*, 5 (4) (1990) 161–84.
65. John le Carré, *The Spy Who Came in From the Cold* (London: Victor Gollancz, 1963). For discussion of these themes, see Jeffrey Richelson, 'The IPCRESS File: the Great Game in Film and Fiction, 1953–2002', *International Journal of Intelligence and CounterIntelligence*, 16 (3) (2003) 462–98.
66. Witness, for example, the films *Three Days of the Condor* (1975), and *The Bourne Identity* (2002).
67. James Der Derian, 'The CIA, Hollywood, and Sovereign Conspiracies', *Queen's Quarterly*, 10 (2) (1993) 343.
68. For the views of Sir Dick White, former Chief of SIS and Director General of MI5, on le Carré, see Tom Bower, *The Perfect English Spy: Sir Dick White and the Secret War, 1935–1990* (London: Heinemann, 1995), p. 275.
69. See, for example, Frances Stonor Saunders, *Who Paid the Piper? The CIA and the Cultural Cold War* (London: Granta, 1999); Scott Lucas, *Freedom's War: The US Crusade Against the Soviet Union, 1945–1956* (Manchester: Manchester University Press, 1999); and Giles Scott-Smith and Hans Krabbendam (eds), 'The Cultural Cold War in Western Europe 1945–1960', theme issue, *Intelligence and National Security*, 18 (2) (2003).
70. *Hearings Before the Joint Committee on the Investigation of the Pearl Harbor Attack, 79th Congress*, 39 vols (Washington, DC: United States Government Printing Office, 1946); Roberta Wohlstetter, *Pearl Harbor: Warning and Decision* (Palo Alto: Stanford University Press, 1962).
71. Herman, *Intelligence Services*, p. 228.

7
propaganda, communications and public opinion

susan l. carruthers

Propaganda, many of its most prolific historians insist, is a timeless mode of human communication. Whether embossed on coins, embedded in triumphalist architecture, emblazoned on banners, embroidered on uniforms, etched on tablets of stone, or echoing through vast auditoria, propaganda – as persuasive communication that seeks to manipulate cognition through symbolic systems – has always been with us. It is 'an activity that dates back to the time when man first picked up a club in anger', announces Philip Taylor in his study of war propaganda from 'the ancient world to the nuclear age', *Munitions of the Mind*. Or, as other historians point out, it is an activity that dates from the time that humans first attempted to extract compliance with words rather than clubs.[1] If that is so, then we might conclude that its systematic scholarly study began belatedly, largely in the shadow of the twentieth century's two total wars. Yet within international history, after a flurry of exploratory and expository activity in the 1970s and 1980s, Propaganda as a sub-field now shows certain signs of decline, or dispersal at the very least.[2] 'Whatever happened to propaganda?', communications scholar, Michael J. Sproule, enquired in 1989. His question remains as pertinent today as it was then.[3]

On the surface, the propaganda paradigm's eclipse appears to constitute a paradox more perversely perplexing than most. As many popular titles on the 'persuasive arts' remind us, we live in an 'Age of Propaganda', conscious of being stuck in an endlessly gyrating 'Spin Cycle'.[4] The word itself remains firmly lodged in our everyday vocabularies, shaded with negative connotations accrued over a century that spawned countless sinister synonyms: brainwashing, thought control, mind-management.

By mid century, it was not uncommon for Cold War era social scientists to announce annihilation of the autonomous self as a more real and present danger than nuclear armageddon – with 'menticide' billed by some Americans as the twentieth century's most devastating weapon of mass destruction. So why, 50 years later, with public culture saturated by Orwellianisms (perhaps more profoundly than ever), has propaganda become so unfashionable an analytic category for historians and social scientists?[5] Have we become so inured to the corruption of 'ideal speech' that we no longer think its examination as a historical phenomenon worthy of attention? Or is it that at least some historians have become sceptical as to whether propaganda – as a bounded and specific form of 'tainted' communication – can be, or *ought* to be, disentangled from the wider webs of meaning spun by humans in their complex processes of social interaction? Is 'propaganda' too broad or too narrow a lens through which to view communicative behaviour? Might it, perhaps, be both?

This chapter begins with an account of propaganda's emergence as a distinct object of scholarly (and not always quite so scholarly) enquiry in the early twentieth century. Although the term 'propaganda' derives from the seventeenth century (when the Pope tasked a commission of cardinals with propagation of the Catholic faith), the phenomenon first received sustained scholarly attention in the immediate aftermath of the First World War, when communications studies emerged as a new interdisciplinary field – straddling political science, sociology and psychology – in the United States. The study of propaganda as a branch of international history was, however, a development largely confined to the last quarter of the twentieth century. This scholarship took, and continues to take, a variety of forms: from sweeping surveys of propaganda as a particular genus of human behaviour to organizational histories of specialized agencies, and micro-studies of the production and reception of single exemplary propaganda texts. The first half of the chapter concludes with a survey of how this field of international history has developed, assessing the themes and cases to which it has been particularly attentive.

Many Propaganda pioneers have issued bold claims on behalf of this new specialization's innovative dynamism: its capacity as a 'missing dimension' to add depth and perspective to a field all too often flattened into two-dimensionality in its preoccupation with the diplomatic and military contours of international encounters. In prioritizing questions of 'perception', this framing offers a way for 'the public' to be inserted into international historians' hitherto underpopulated narratives.[6] Methodologically, a concentration on propaganda also necessitates that the historian draw on other cognate, but commonly neglected, disciplines: psychology, sociology and communications. Propaganda, it is announced, offers an obvious pathway into transdisciplinarity for international history. But how convincingly are these assertions exemplified in the practice of Propaganda history?

The second part of the chapter subjects these positive claims to critical scrutiny, asking what remains missing, or might be actively obscured, in choosing to elevate propaganda to a position of analytic primacy. In so doing, I suggest why Propaganda has not – at least in my charting of its trajectory – risen as far or as fast as its boosters predicted: why, indeed, its star appears to be waning. This enquiry requires us to consider more systematically the way in which studies of propaganda are commonly framed and executed: what processes or mentalities they illuminate; over how wide or narrow a terrain they shed light; and with how powerful or dimly flickering a wattage.

In the main, Propaganda historians have tended to share a common set of (usually implicit) epistemological assumptions. As this brand of unreflective empiricism has found its commonsensical ground shaken by various 'turns' in the humanities and social sciences, so has a certain – hitherto predominant – approach come to appear less satisfactory, at least to some advocates of the 'new international history'. These discontents are explored by a discussion of how historians working in certain empiricist, Marxian and postmodern traditions have, in quite distinct ways, found problematic either the epistemological assumptions bound up in most historians' conceptions of what propaganda is, or the methodological approaches commonly espoused in explicating its effects – if not both.

the birth of communications

As many disciplinary genealogies have noted, the distinct field of communications studies first came into being at a moment of profound political crisis, domestic and international, in the inter-war United States.[7] Its coming of age as a fully-fledged discipline followed the Second World War, as a massive state investment sought to reorient wartime intellectual production to Cold War ends. Of course, no scholarly knowledge is delivered into the world innocent. As early as 1918, Thorstein Veblen remarked on the modern university as 'a business house dealing in merchantable knowledge'.[8] But it is also true that the development of certain academic disciplines has been more heavily monitored and managed by the state and its interested agencies than others. Of the latter, communications studies was born of 'artificial insemination' to an uncommon degree. Scholarship spawned by this process was intended to equip the 'donors' with serviceable guidelines for the most efficacious and invisible ways in which behaviour might be modified in the interests of ruling elites.

What particular circumstances galvanized this investment in applied social engineering? First, at the broadest level of generality, the emergence of mass media (newspapers, then cinema and radio) during the nineteenth and early twentieth centuries animated concern among elites that a new phenomenon – an agglomerated 'mass society' and its nuclei, 'mass man' – required urgent understanding. In both Europe and North America, news and entertainment media spread rapidly in the years immediately before and after the First World War. War facilitated their widespread social penetration while also generating political pressures that led to the expanded participation of working men, and increasingly also of women, in the electoral politics of many industrialized states. The dawn of the media age thus coincided with, and apparently contributed to, the extension of participatory democracy. Several historians duly suggest that the age of propaganda *proper* begins in the twentieth century, as this cluster of modernizing developments prompted elites to take hitherto nebulous 'public opinion' seriously for the first time. Writing on the eve of the Second World War, the renowned historian of international relations, E. H. Carr, heavily underscored this notion of a decisive break:

> The problem of power over opinion in its modern mass form has been created by developments in economic and military technique – by the substitution of mass-production industries for individual craftsmanship and of the conscript citizen army for the volunteer professional force. Contemporary politics are vitally dependent on the opinion of large masses of more or less politically conscious people … . The problem is one which no modern government ignores.[9]

There is much that could be debated over how 'the public' impresses itself on the consciousness of the powerful, and the extent to which mass media, conscription, and the universal franchise brought 'ordinary people' into elites' purview in ways they had never before figured. Arguably, this 'transformation of visibility' (in John Thompson's phrase) occurred some centuries earlier as the print revolution brought monarchs into the public eye, and masses into monarchical calculation.[10] Nevertheless, it is hard to dispute that ruling classes did take twentieth-century 'massification' very seriously indeed – often demonstrating a deeply anti-democratic mistrust of the public under the influence of media that were conceived, however contradictorily, as both stupefying atomized and incapable electors while also arousing masses into impassioned, irrational frenzies.[11] To many elite observers, the development of mass media carried profound political consequences, just as sites of mass entertainment seemed replete with injurious social ramifications.

Much prominent early research in the US laboured to correlate habits of cinema-going with the rising incidence of juvenile delinquency, though it proved hard to quantify movies' deleterious influence.[12] It appeared rather easier, however, to uncover calculated and wilful attempts to manipulate opinion: in other words, to analyse *propaganda*. A second, more specific, context for communications studies' emergence lies in the highly-charged debate that raged during the 1920s and 1930s over US participation in the Great War, and the role that British propaganda allegedly played in effecting it. With isolationists insisting that duplicitous Britons had duped a guileless nation into entering a war quite against the United States' best interests, studies that sought to uncover the stratagems of British propaganda intervened in a heavily politicized debate – whether they aspired to polemicism or not.[13] The years following the First World War thus spawned an enduring genre of propaganda analysis: the exposure of 'official' attempts to manipulate and deceive. Arthur Ponsonby's *Falsehood in Wartime* (1928) found a ready readership on both sides of the Atlantic, and was followed by a spate of similar treatises.[14]

As new cataclysms in Europe and East Asia loomed, so isolationists' search to unmask interventionist propaganda quickened, with Hollywood's 'foreign-born' moguls a favourite target for Congressional investigators of 'un-American activities'.[15] But the more scholarly study of propaganda also derived impetus from growing awareness that the European dictatorships – especially Nazi Germany, fascist Italy and Stalin's USSR – were using mass communication in ways, and to degrees, hitherto unknown. Their injection of state ideology into every facet of public life – from the monumental style favoured in architecture to the content of movies and other ostensibly harmless entertainments – suggested to many distant observers that Hitler, Mussolini and Stalin must have marshalled public opinion into unquestioning unanimity. But more than bludgeoning citizens into passive conformity, the Nazis' and fascists' grandiose orchestrations of mass participation appeared to have enraptured their populations into enthusiastic assent for whatever expansionist projects their leaders planned. In short, the emergence of states in which propaganda was ardently espoused and openly announced – in which politics had become spectacularized, and where fascism 'fascinated' – constituted a third compelling reason for communication studies' consolidation at a particular historic juncture.[16] So too did the fact that both the USSR and Germany were exporting their propaganda efforts across state borders using powerful radio transmitters. International broadcasting threw non-interventionist norms of state sovereignty into turmoil, as border controls that monitored the physical flow of persons and products across national boundaries could scarcely halt radio transmissions in their tracks. Nor was this internationalization of propaganda activity confined to radio broadcasts. As E. H. Carr put it in *The Twenty Years' Crisis*, 'Since the end of the Middle Ages, no political organisation had claimed to be the repository of universal truth or the missionary of a universal gospel' – until the Soviet Union established the Comintern and attempted to proselytize for revolution on a global basis.[17]

Early communications scholars certainly did not lack material to study or motives for studying it with a certain degree of urgency. As several subsequent chroniclers of the discipline's origins have shown, two divergent approaches soon marked the study of communication and propaganda in the United States. The schism revolved around divergent prescriptions for democracy's efficient functioning in the age of 'mass opinion'. It pitted those who believed that authority should be vested in elite technocrats (with superior facility for discerning 'the facts', and formulating policy on this solid foundation) against progressives who advocated the need for an informed public (better versed in detecting propaganda and hence capable of reaching well-informed judgements). The first camp clustered around the new discipline's most significant shapers, Walter Lippmann and Harold Lasswell. Where the former attracted enduring attention for his discussion of the 'pseudo-environments' in which alienated modern subjects dwell in isolation from one another and from reality, the latter pioneered the academic study of propaganda in 1927 with *Propaganda Technique in the World War*, asserting that 'government management of opinion' had become an 'unescapable corollary of large-scale modern war'.[18] Furthermore, in his opinion (together with the founder of modern public relations and nephew of Sigmund Freud, Edward Bernays) this 'management' was as necessary in peacetime as in war. Rather than fixating on the socially injurious, 'disintegrative' properties of mass media, the democracies would be well-advised to ponder how the dictatorships forged enviable cohesion on the 'new hammer and anvil of social solidarity' – propaganda.[19]

Such elitism was challenged, however, by progressives who rejected Lasswell's insistence on public unfitness for meaningful participation in democratic processes. If the electorate was 'incompetent', the answer lay not in delegating authority upwards but in eradicating ordinary citizens' suggestibility by teaching them to distinguish carefully substantiated arguments from tendentious appeals. Mass society's democratic deficit could be arrested by a 'direct attack upon gullibility itself'.[20] This consciousness-raising orientation informed the establishment, in 1937, of the Institute for Propaganda Analysis (IPA) at Columbia University's Teachers College. Until the Second World War's proliferation of 'opinion management' agencies made the investigation of manipulative appeals within the US politically unacceptable, its newsletter exposed the calculated appeals of everything from the pro-fascist Father Coughlin's radio broadcasts to the public relations ploys of the Ford motor company.[21]

defining propaganda

But whether urging the state to remedy 'the defective organization of public opinion' (in Lippmann's phrase) or, alternatively, encouraging individuals to adopt a more sceptical stance towards mushrooming sources of printed and broadcast information, how did these early scholars conceive of propaganda?[22] Certainly, the two broad epistemic communities espoused different valuations of propaganda in their split over whether the modern state ought to practice it more effectively or whether citizens needed to deconstruct it more astutely. But how prominently did the value attached to propaganda colour definitions of the process that went by that name? How far was there a shared consensus over what exactly propaganda was?[23]

The inter-war years generated numerous definitional attempts to capture propaganda's essence, from which a number of recurrent themes emerge and persist. Perhaps the most prominent was an insistence that propaganda should not – as a particular form of persuasive communication – be regarded as intrinsically dubious or immoral, nor should its content be synonymized with deliberate deception and lies. Lasswell was certainly adamant (in an idiosyncratic analogy) that propaganda was 'no more moral or immoral than a pump handle'.[24] But did progressives associated with the IPA agree that propaganda was in itself 'amoral'? Those grouped under this humanist umbrella held rather different opinions, while harbouring doubts that manipulative appeals would diminish in an age of intensified consumer capitalism and the concomitant growth of advertising. Departing from the neutralism of Lasswell, some built into their preferred definition a value-laden component that distinguished propaganda by the ends to which it was directed. Leonard Doob (a member of the IPA's advisory board), for instance, characterized it as 'the attempt to affect the personalities and to control the behavior of individuals toward ends *considered unscientific or of doubtful value* in a society at a particular time'. For Doob, its decisive characteristic was control 'through suggestion', 'regardless of whether or not the propagandist intends to exercise the control'.[25] His perplexing evocation of an unwitting 'suggester' is, however, abandoned in most definitions, which take propaganda to be an intrinsically interested, and hence knowing, form of communication, designed to elicit certain results congenial to the propagandist – whether it succeeds or not; whether the desired ends are 'unscientific' or otherwise; and whether the propagandist would regard their endeavours as 'propaganda' or understand their catalytic efforts in loftier terms.[26]

For some analysts, propaganda may additionally (or alternatively) be identified by the modes of address and techniques it typically deploys. If behaviour modification spans a broad spectrum of activity, propaganda must be differentiated from direct physical coercion at one end and from education at the other. In Lasswell's view, propaganda functions through the mobilization of 'significant symbols ... stories, rumors, pictures, and other forms of social communication'. It is, in short, 'the technique of influencing human action by the manipulation of representations'.[27] Taking a more pejorative tack, others – including Bertrand Russell – were minded to insist that the specific nature of this 'manipulation' was a visceral appeal to 'irrational causes of belief'.[28] From the early 1930s onwards, such definitions often found reinforcement in Adolf Hitler's enunciation of basic principles in *Mein Kampf*. Hitler's insistence that propaganda be calibrated to the meagre intelligence of the masses, and hence limited to a few points and slogans endlessly reiterated, seemed entirely consonant with his demagogic practice as Führer, as ample newsreel footage and Leni Riefenstahl's documentary, *Triumph of the Will*, vividly attested.

With this proliferation of definitional activity in the 1920s and 1930s, one could plausibly contend that by 1939 key developments in both propaganda (as a practice of social control and statecraft) and Propaganda (the field of study) had already been made. Although methodological fashions have changed over the last 60 years, there has arguably been rather little conceptual innovation among students of propaganda since then, though debate swings back and forth as to whether commercial advertising, public relations and political marketing merit inclusion under the same banner – with many historians tending to bracket these latter enterprises off as distinct, if related, phenomena.[29]

communications at war

If propaganda gave its more adept exponents a helping hand during the Great War, in the Second World War it formed the 'fourth arm' of the war effort, interlinked (not always amicably) with intelligence and both conventional and unconventional applications of military force.[30] Wartime in the United States inaugurated the mobilization, or voluntary enlistment, of many pioneers of the academic study of propaganda for active service in the 'psychological' wing of the war effort. Their tasks were many and varied. Some concentrated on work with journalists, opinion-formers and the Hollywood studios aimed at ensuring, and measuring, cohesiveness on the home front. Progressives like Doob, alongside 'managerialists' such as Lasswell, and other key figures from the discipline of communications (like Wilbur Schramm, Paul Lazarsfeld, Hadley Cantril, George Gallup, and various members of the Frankfurt School) either worked directly in, or were contracted to undertake studies for, the Office of War Information (OWI).[31] Others, working in branches of the military and intelligence apparatus, pioneered techniques of 'psychological warfare', a term that first entered English-language usage in 1941 as a loose translation of the Nazi term *Weltanschauungskrieg* ('world-view warfare').[32] This branch of applied communications studies calculated means by which enemy civilians and service personnel alike might be confused, terrorized and demoralized to the point of losing the will to continue supporting their state's war effort. Optimally, defeatism would translate into surrender to the Allies by enemy personnel, and acts of anti-regime defiance or sabotage on the part of civilians.

Another significant area of work lay in developing the still nascent field of public opinion research. Several scholars undertook studies to gauge the effectiveness of America's own wartime propaganda efforts, especially those directed at US citizens whose responses could be readily monitored in controlled experimentation – most particularly GIs who formed captive audiences for 'motivational' films. Their reactions both to propaganda and to military institutionalization were minutely scrutinized.[33] But while the American soldier became an object of intense scrutiny so too did the psyche of 'the enemy' – with the state summoning a vast array of expert opinion to help deconstruct the mindset of Germans and Japanese alike. Content analysis of enemy broadcasts was undertaken to better appreciate Nazi propaganda technique, but also to provide insight into how German opinion had been conditioned under Goebbels' intensive direction, and hence how it might be 'reconstructed' once the war was over. With enemies duly defeated and their territories under Allied occupation, it is no surprise that communications scholars played significant roles in the effort to recondition militarized and authoritarian 'national characters' along more liberal, pluralistic and tolerant lines: a central objective of the twin processes of denazification and 're-education'.[34]

As this ongoing engagement in shaping the 'psychological' dimensions of postwar occupation policy implies, many knowledge producers were not simply demobilized at war's end. Rather, like workers in other strategically significant manufacturing industries, scholars' expertise was claimed by the state in pursuit of hastily readjusted geopolitical objectives. Some were duly routed into the work of transforming enemies into allies, while others took their places on the frontline of a new total war that almost immediately substituted one 'totalitarian' enemy for another. Since this was a cold war – fought (as contemporary argot had it) for the 'hearts and minds of men' within and across state boundaries – psychological strategies formed the defining *modus operandi* of this decades-long struggle for ideological allegiance. Communications studies was thus thoroughly embedded in the US national security state as it solidified in the late 1940s and 1950s: six of its most important university centres being, in one scholar's estimation, 'de facto adjuncts of government psychological warfare programs'.

If the sheer volume of funding that came from the state is striking, so too is the entrenchment of a particular kind of quantitative, positivist approach to communications research during this period. Following a model already prominent in interwar and wartime research, 'communication' was construed essentially as top-down, unilinear manipulation. Given their orientation towards the production of immediately serviceable knowledge, scholars continued to seek perfection over techniques for measuring direct 'effects', eager to improve the means by which human behaviour could be patterned by crafting better appeals or by superior manipulation of the environment within which individuals received and processed messages.[35] The overwhelming Cold War imperative lay in understanding how 'totalitarians' apparently elicited absolute control over opinion, as exemplified in Stalin's show trials, and the new phenomenon of 'thought reform' (soon popularly recast as 'brainwashing') in communist China.

Knowing the Cold War enemy – in order that Washington might sharpen its own appeals to Eastern bloc and Chinese citizens – guided communications research in particular channels. Over the Cold War's long duration, scholars were instrumental in calculating how best to reach citizens cloistered behind the Iron Curtain via radio broadcasting, balloons, leaflets, and a variety of psychological stratagems that ran the gamut from attempts to rollback revolution in one or other Soviet satellite to ever-more fanciful machinations to bring about Castro's demise, or, at the very least, the depilation of his luxuriant beard.[36] Contra the claims of some cold warriors and Propaganda historians who insist that persuasion was infinitely to be preferred over fighting – that 'changing minds' saved lives – it is necessary to recall that East–West competition was also pursued in devastatingly *material* form in many locations in the South over four decades. Far from obviating the need for guns and bombs, psychological warfare was in fact a core component of – and conceived by its practitioners as indivisible from – military strategy. 'Psyops' were certainly integral to the two most destructive 'hot wars' of the era, in Korea and Vietnam, while 'psychological' considerations contributed to the varieties of violence wrought by the broader US postwar project of forestalling, or reversing, revolution in the developing world through the twin tracks of 'modernization' and 'counter-insurgency'.[37]

history discovers propaganda

Communications emerged as a scholarly field in the US in ways not wholly replicated elsewhere – though clearly America was not the sole country in which opinion, and opinion control, was exhaustively studied during the first half of the twentieth century. The states from which Lasswell and others thought the US had most to learn – Germany, in particular – also undertook pioneering work in attitude manipulation and measurement, two subjects rather dear to the hearts of the Third Reich leadership, even if the results of opinion research failed always to gratify.[38] Likewise in the USSR, where propaganda was woven unabashedly into the fabric of Communist Party activity and state management over information and culture, psychologists and scholars from other cognitive and behavioural fields also laboured to fathom the mysteries of human communication.[39] Of these, none achieved greater prominence in the West than Ivan Pavlov, whose celebrated canine experimentation on the conditioned reflex was much studied in early Cold War America. As anxieties over 'brainwashing' mounted during the Korean War (with several thousand US POWs incarcerated by 'Red China', and allegedly subjected to a battery of terrifying and terrifyingly effective mind control techniques), CIA-financed studies strove to deduce not only whether communist psychology could indeed produce perfectly roboticized humans but also how the US might replicate a 'Manchurian candidate' of its own.[40]

What remains striking about the disciplinary trajectory of communications studies within the US is both the density and intricacy of the feedback loop whereby Propaganda scholars were (and in some cases remain) also propaganda's most prominent practitioners – simultaneously in the service of the state while announcing the non-ideological, value-free, scientific status of their findings. The 'founding fathers' of communications constantly crossed back and forth across a very tenuous (or wholly notional) line demarcating the world of the academy from that of government service. In studying propaganda, scholars were equipping themselves to become more adept propagandists. In turn, their contributions to wartime and Cold War praxis have formed much of the stuff upon which historical scholarship in Propaganda has dwelt. If early postwar accounts of official propaganda (many produced by its scholar/practitioners) tended to obfuscate the unusually symbiotic nature of theory and practice in this field, more recent genealogical work has exposed the US state's instrumental investment in shaping communications scholarship in particularly self-interested ways – as a 'science of coercion'.[41]

European and North American historians of propaganda have, then, commonly grounded their studies on the conceptual foundation laid by communications studies' academic analysts/agents, whether using these tools to appraise those same individuals' activities as propagandists, or to assess the initiatives of other states and actors. Canonical works of the post-1945 period constitute, to a striking degree, the product of wartime practitioners: Daniel Lerner's *Sykewar: Psychological Warfare against Germany* (first published 1949; revised second edition published as *Psychological Warfare against Nazi Germany: The Sykewar Campaign, D-Day to VE-Day*, 1971), William Daugherty and Morris Janowitz's *Psychological Warfare Casebook* (1958), and Lasswell, Lerner and Speier's three-volume series, *Propaganda and Communication in World History* (1979–80).[42] From the United Kingdom, several prominent participants in Second World War psyops also remain widely cited, including Michael Balfour, Richard Crossman and Lindley Fraser.[43] Meanwhile, German émigré Siegfried Kracauer produced in *From Caligari to Hitler: A Psychological History of German Film* (1947) both a precursor to later studies of Nazi propaganda and a foundational text for the application of psychoanalytic theory to film studies.[44]

Given this inseparable overlapping of identities – communications scholars as both observers and participants, their texts both secondary and primary sources for pursuant Propaganda historians – it is no wonder that the field of Propaganda bears a decidedly involuted character. Several related particularities also require attention. Whether deriving from a different academic discipline or none, most writing on propaganda is not produced by either self-professed or professionally recognized historians, let alone by members of that small coterie of international historians. The frisson occasioned by demolishing big lies and unmasking hidden manipulators makes Propaganda analysis attractive to non-academic commentators – of widely varying degrees of seriousness and substance. Some, as indicated by titles like *The Rape of the Masses*, clearly trade not only in sensationalism but in a 'feminizing' of the ostensible gullibility of 'the masses'.[45] However, journalistic accounts may provide important reflections on the media's contribution to mass mobilization or mystification. Indeed, one could construct an alternative lineage of Propaganda studies in Britain derived from economist and journalist J. A. Hobson's *The Psychology of Jingoism* (1901) – an undeservedly overlooked volume, detailing the role of the popular press and music hall in animating Britons' 'spectatorial passion' for the Boer War.[46]

If this heterogeneity makes the field of Propaganda wildly uneven, it is also striking how few studies treat communicative processes as complex transnational phenomena. Most, whether by historians or others, confine themselves to the practice of propaganda within one particular polity, and it bears noting that E. H. Carr insisted in *The Twenty Years' Crisis* that 'since power cannot be internationalised, there can be no such thing in politics as international opinion, and international propaganda is as much a contradiction in terms as an international army'.[47] In an age of global media corporations and multilateral forces, many might dispute this assertion in both claims. But nevertheless, students of Propaganda have been remarkably bound by the state as their unit of analysis. Predictably, overwhelming attention has been devoted to those in which 'thought work' has been undertaken most unabashedly (often to ends considered by its chroniclers to be dubious if not 'unscientific', in Doob's parlance). Of these, Nazi Germany and the USSR incontestably constitute the privileged loci of Propaganda history, with the People's Republic of China (since its birth in 1949) lagging some way behind. Similarly, not all media have proven equally magnetic to Propaganda historians, with film proving a good deal more mesmerizing than less alluring channels of persuasion.

Of course, not all Propaganda history concentrates on single states or isolated media. Given a marked preoccupation with war and its precursors, some scholars necessarily consider propaganda as an activity directed across national borders, although even studies temporally confined to wartime often treat states as discrete – more or less self-contained – units, in which propaganda is of interest as the means through which national identity and particular political and/or racial ideologies are articulated and inculcated. Exceptions to this single-case generalization include historians such as Richard Taylor, who has undertaken comparative analysis twinning Nazi Germany and the Soviet Union. Appearing in the same year as the first edition of Taylor's *Film Propaganda: Soviet Russia and Nazi Germany*, Michael Balfour's *Propaganda in War* (1979) essayed an unusual, and productive, comparison of Goebbels' Reichsministerium für Volksaufklärung und Propaganda and Britain's Ministry of Information, both of which believed they were appropriating their antagonist's innovations.[48] Additionally, a number of works (including postwar studies produced by its practitioners) have analysed Allied 'psywar' efforts as a conflict-ridden whole.[49]

Wholly consonant with the typical preoccupations of international history, the fascination with propaganda 'in war and crisis' (the title of a Lerner-edited collection from 1951) can be traced back to professional historians' earliest attempts to rise above charges that they were too frequently the uncritical proponents of propaganda 'myths' about recent events themselves, something for which the president of the American Historical Association took his peers to task in his 1921 banquet address.[50] By the 1930s, US history journals were beginning to publish critical dissections of earlier eras' propaganda, on such topics as the British government's machinations over the Oregon purchase, the Cuban junta's manoeuvrings during the Spanish-American-Cuban War of 1898, pacifist propaganda and the treaty of Guadaloupe Hidalgo (by no less a figure than Merle Curti), and French press propaganda during the Franco-Prussian War.[51] Significant monographs, such as Philip Davidson's classic *Propaganda and the American Revolution*, also appeared during this pre-Second World War period.[52]

Within the historical profession, Propaganda's most intense flowering occurred from the late 1960s through the 1980s, ironically (perhaps) at the precise moment that the paradigm had lost its purchase over communications studies, if not its appeal to the sociological imagination of scholars such as Jacques Ellul, whose *Propaganda: The Formation of Men's Attitudes* became the most influential philosophic treatise on a subject that – until the late 1990s – attracted a dwindling number of theorizations.[53] But where theorists refused to tread, historians rushed in. Areas of dense specialization have, at risk of oversimplification, followed something of a chronological progression from the First World War to the Second World War, followed by the Cold War.

The First World War, already amply surveyed during the inter-war years, received major treatments from Cate Haste, Philip Taylor and Michael Saunders, and Nicholas Reeves during the 1970s and 1980s.[54] No conflict, however, has been more exhaustively analysed than the Second World War – with a flurry of works, particularly on psychological warfare and 'morale', appearing during and immediately after the war, but with voluminous exploration of Nazi propaganda beginning in the 1960s and 1970s when the scholarly work of Bramsted, Baird and Zeman was supplemented by publication of extracts from Goebbels' copious diaries and conferences.[55] The 1970s and the 1980s saw not only further activity in this field but also landmark studies of British broadcasting and the Ministry of Information, and several treatments on the fertile symbiosis of Hollywood and the OWI, on British wartime cinema, and on the role of film in Soviet society.[56]

With new intensity and enhanced archival access since the demise of the USSR, much of the most recent historical work in the field focuses on uncovering clandestine dimensions of Cold War propaganda. Several authors have tackled the covert role of the CIA in sponsoring a distinctive brand of 'Cold War liberalism' in Western intellectual and cultural life.[57] Others assess the broader politico-military dynamics, and diplomatic reverberations, of US attempts to perforate the Iron Curtain.[58] Although the Cold War itself generated many studies of Soviet propaganda and 'disinformation' that functioned as contributions to the superpowers' ideological war of positions, since the Soviet Union's collapse, historians have tended to concentrate on Western salvoes against the USSR and its satellites. Whether due to a paucity of archival materials or the unevenness of terrain whose high-ground was undoubtedly occupied by Washington (with Soviet moves tending towards the defensive, exemplified by Moscow's greater budgetary commitment to radio jamming than to 'active measures'), few studies have yet elaborated Soviet Cold War cultural offensives, or constructed a multi-sided account of the superpowers' dynamic interaction in the global struggle to promote particular 'ways of life'.[59]

But clearly if there have been significant clusterings of publication in particular areas, historians have not marched inexorably away from earlier conflicts towards later ones. Much new work adds ever more intricate cross-hatching to this triptych of world wars and cold war, detailing hitherto under studied protagonists (particularly the defeated powers of both world wars) and neglected media, particularly radio.[60] At present, a steady flow of periodical literature explores propaganda in the classical and early modern eras (particularly its religious manifestations), and in later centuries and settings other than those of the twentieth century's major cataclysms.[61] Additionally, the 'smaller' and 'unconventional' wars of the twentieth century have received growing attention from Propaganda historians.[62]

Since the 1980s, propaganda and empire – in both its militarized and mercantilist forms – has emerged as a significant new site of enquiry, in tandem with the reinvigoration of imperial history more broadly. With inquiry into colonialism given an extreme makeover by postcolonial theorists, imperial history has somewhat burnished its dusty, metropole-fixated image, although the encounter between theory and history has not always resulted in productive cross-fertilization.[63] Certain unreconstructed imperial historians evince profound unease over the abstruse theorizations of postcolonial scholarship, fretting over literary critics' reification of cultural artefacts (the novel, in particular), at the expense of archival deposits left by those who actually administered empire. As these historians see it, Edward Said and fellow textualists fail to elaborate the real nexus between culture and power. Postcolonial theorists may thus assert that colonialism required an imagination of racialized difference, without demonstrating to these empirically-oriented historians' satisfaction how Orientalist constructions directly informed day-to-day imperial governance. But perhaps it is a measure of how far postcolonial theory has demanded a hearing, even among resolutely sceptical historians, that John MacKenzie (pioneer of the study of propaganda and empire in Britain), who failed to acknowledge Said at all in *Propaganda and Empire* (1984), subsequently devoted a whole volume to a critique, albeit hostile, in his *Orientalism: History, Theory and the Arts* (1995). Meanwhile, some international historians have engaged more positively with postcolonial scholarship in studies of imperial propaganda, or colonial constructions of self and other differently defined.[64]

That those interested in exploring issues of identity formation and cross-cultural interactions do not invariably do so under the banner of Propaganda returns us to a point ventured at the outset: that propaganda's insufficiency as a lens through which to appreciate either macro structures and/or micro processes that shape human subjectivity appears better recognized now than two decades ago. So while international history has become more attentive to cultural and communicative processes across time and space, and, accordingly, to more sophisticated theorizations of power, Propaganda has scarcely added weight to this tilt in the field's centre of gravity. Indeed, as a sub-field, it has been somewhat left adrift by this shift, the nature of which is indicated by a cursory survey of some titles dealing with phenomena that might alternatively have been organized around a conceptualization of 'propaganda': *Marketing Marianne; Imperial Persuaders; Promoting the Colonial Idea; Cold War Orientalism; Imagining Vietnam and America*.[65] Of course, one could argue that this list merely attests the substitution of one synonym for another: that a preference for 'persuasion', 'promoting' or 'marketing' over 'propaganda' can be over-interpreted. But as talk of a 'new international history' suggests, there is surely something more profound at work than simple lexical substitution: rather, reconceptualization of a sub-discipline more attentive to the wider terrain within which meanings, identities and subjectivities are constructed, transmitted and negotiated. Historians intrigued by such phenomena seem increasingly dissatisfied with propaganda as a clarifying optic.

doing and undoing propaganda history

What, then, does doing Propaganda history entail? And what limitations with this approach have occasioned its (at least partial) undoing? Many criticisms levelled at international history – never more forcefully than by its most self-reflective practitioners – apply with particular force to Propaganda scholarship.[66] The weightiest such criticism is undoubtedly the field's state-centrism, and an accompanying tendency to privilege war as the most significant moment of collision between states often conceived as billiard balls whose 'insides' have precious little bearing on their trajectories. Obviously not all international history wears this statist straightjacket. Studies of transnational social movements and cultural processes have begun to erode the primacy of diplomacy, and its continuation by military means, as the central object of attention.[67] But despite slow eddying currents within the discipline of history that have encouraged revisionings from the bottom-up, and a reframing of cross-border phenomena as transnational rather than inter-state, Propaganda historians generally do still focus on the machinations of states – as the monopolistic entities best placed to channel sentiment and manipulate behaviour in significant ways. That the few synoptic histories of propaganda, such as Taylor's *Munitions of the Mind*, take the phenomenon to be synonymous with wartime behaviour also tells its own story.

Propaganda history may thus appear elitist in its continuing fixation with the 'communication-as-domination' model early espoused by the Lasswellian branch of communications studies. To the extent that the power elites tirelessly studied tend to be male, this sub-field also often presents a blithely masculinist history, oblivious to the occlusions that flow from overlooking gender as a core analytic category – with the exception of works focusing on propagandistic appeals specifically addressed to women as war-workers, consumers or vessels of national fertility.[68] But Rosie the Riveter and Leni Riefensthal aside, Propaganda historians have exhibited an especial fascination with Europe's 'great dictators' and communications studies' 'founding fathers'. If international history favours 'chaps and maps' (in Zara Steiner's memorable phrase), then Propaganda history's particular fixation might be labeled 'chaps with megaphones'.[69]

As these criticisms imply, international history has also drawn charges of under-theorization. In the Propaganda sub-field, many scholars have been remarkably unreflective about their central conceptual device, devoting scant attention to specifying the precise object of study. Most content themselves with a few paragraphs, or at most a couple of pages, that deal with definitional issues, often asserting a case for scholars to understand propaganda as a neutral term for a self-serving activity, à la Lasswell. But these brief excursuses do not necessarily resolve the larger question of what exactly the historian is concerned to elucidate under the rubric of propaganda: in other words, what contribution – other than unearthing instances of hitherto hidden, or inadequately understood, state manipulation – the study of propaganda might make to a more sophisticated appreciation of historical processes and complex interactions. In philosopher Stanley Cunningham's judgement, 'case studies and history, especially when unallied to theorizing, do not come very close to telling us what propaganda is'.[70] As the following sections suggest, Propaganda poses both epistemological and methodological problems for historians (and others) from at least three distinct positions.

empiricism and communication 'effects'

Viewed from different critical perspectives, Propaganda history may appear either too empiricist or insufficiently so. For some international historians, inclining toward the 'cultural turn' but mindful of disciplinary gatekeepers' repeated injunctions that they duly serve up generous portions of 'beef', Propaganda appears to offer a way of delivering the goods that other culturalists cannot.[71] In other words, propaganda-centred studies claim immunity from generalized charges that cultural approaches, lacking mechanisms to demonstrate how culture shapes specific attitudinal or behavioural outcomes, fail to trade in the only convertible currency of international relations scholarship: namely, power. In a recent article on *Mission to Moscow* – one of the most discussed Hollywood films of the

Second World War, whose laudatory portrait of Stalin made it 'exhibit A' in the House Un-American Activities Committee's postwar search for un-American agents in the movie industry – Todd Bennett makes this precise claim on behalf of Propaganda history, insisting that his empirically-grounded study of the movie's troubled production and reception can illuminate 'elusive linkages between culture and power'.[72]

Clearly, it is easier to offer 'hard evidence' that might satisfy empiricist qualms over the insubstantiality of cultural approaches if the field of vision is constricted to one discrete cultural artefact – especially one emerging from a richly documented interaction between the realms of statecraft, wartime 'information management' and Hollywood, and whose reception by distinct audiences can be at least impressionistically gleaned, if not necessarily quantified. However, even this careful micro-approach might not completely lay to rest the problems that a stringent empiricism has with propaganda as an essentially unverifiable domain of activity, in which neither the intent of propagandists nor the efficacy of their efforts can ever be satisfactorily adduced, leaving the significance of propaganda as a practice, and its merit as an object of historical enquiry, profoundly in doubt.

From this point of view, too many studies of propaganda simply assume the salience of what they study: reading effects on opinion-formation from the volume of propagandistic activity rather than from any convincing evidence that efforts to manipulate opinion duly succeeded in forging consensus or moulding behaviour in determinative ways.[73] To establish a causal chain between propagandistic efforts and the (re-)orientation of public opinion is a fraught enterprise. To determine the precise relationship between individual attitudes and social behaviour presents a yet harder challenge. At stake is the vexed relationship between ideational and material forces that has long been a core concern of social scientists and humanists alike: namely, whether one attributes some independence to 'ideas' as sources of individual or collective action, or rather stresses the conditioning role of group dynamics, class relations, gender constructs, environmental factors, and an array of constraining and enabling circumstances and structures that shape human activity. To those accentuating the salience of social relations and the webs of power from which they emerge, then, a propaganda-centred approach is likely to fall short as it attempts to disentangle discrete communication 'inputs' from the densely textured fabric of social life.

Many Propaganda historians, however, do attempt to hypothesize direct 'effects', encountering substantial (but rarely acknowledged) methodological problems along the way. Pioneering communications studies scholars, who favoured the Lasswellian model of communication as 'who says what to whom with what effect', broke the equation down into its constituent parts. Their positivist commitments enabled them to proceed on the basis that the 'who' and the 'whom', the 'what' and 'what effect', were all known (or discoverable) variables. Hence these social scientists strove to measure attitude change in individuals exposed to discrete 'messages' supplied by the researcher himself. But clearly historians – even those content to regard the 'what' of any particular communication as a stable quantity – cannot hope to replicate this kind of controlled experiment through historical enquiry. Nor, if propaganda is considered to be (as Lindley Fraser insisted) the art of 'inducing others to behave in a way in which *they would not behave in its absence*', can the historian operationalize this definition without getting mired in counterfactual speculation of the kind that many find deeply problematic.[74] Some have done exactly that, however. Robert Herzstein, for example, presented propaganda as *The War that Hitler Won*, by contending that Goebbels' consummate orchestration of a parallel world of myth and fantasy encouraged Germans to fight on tenaciously even when defeat should have been (and perhaps was) visibly etched on the wall. Without the distraction, consolation or false counsel of propaganda, Herzstein suggests, Germans would hardly have offered such concerted opposition to encircling Allied forces.[75]

Herzstein's approach illustrates a number of problems that beset Propaganda history more broadly. At an evidentiary level, his assertion might be challenged by public opinion data (gathered by the SS) that attest a good deal more disobedience, defeatism and despair than his account allows for. Ian Kershaw's *The Hitler Myth* points to the steady crumbling of popular support for Hitler after 1942, in part occasioned by the fact of military defeat (which could scarcely be disguised, despite Goebbels' best efforts to conceal news of irreparable losses on the Eastern front), and in part by the Nazi leadership's retreat into unreality, which underscored their distance from, and apparent disregard for, the mounting privations of 'ordinary Germans'.[76] Herzstein's counterintuitive thesis of a military campaign spectacularly lost alongside a psychological war unexpectedly won, thus begs two questions: first, whether Germans did indeed fight on with the kind of irrational stubbornness he implies; and, second (if he is right on the first point), how far Germans' failure to lapse into defeatism when defeat was inevitable was directly conditioned by propaganda? Herzstein assumes that behaviour which conforms to propagandists' desired outcomes can be chalked up as a propaganda victory. But this assumption returns us to the problematic broached earlier: how propaganda operates in conjunction with (or friction against) other material structures and ideological forces in shaping action.

Many students of propaganda have asserted, contra Fraser, that it can only succeed in reinforcing existing attitudes, stereotypes and behavioural patterns. The propagandist seeks less to 'implant' ideas than to 'canalize an already existing stream', Aldous Huxley proposed in 1936. 'In a land where there is no water, he digs in vain.'[77] The historian's task, then, is to offer an account of the broader stream into which propaganda flows as a tributary. For some scholars, returning again to the case of Nazi Germany, propaganda has very little to do with why 'ordinary Germans' lent themselves not only to the war effort in general but to the genocidal work of extermination in particular. For historians such as Christopher Browning, social structures, peer pressure and group dynamics account for unexceptional men's participation in exceptional brutality. For others, such as Omer Bartov, racial ideology looms large as genocide's central enabling factor – with Nazi propaganda cultivating but not implanting a conviction in Aryan supremacy that was defined in lethal opposition to Jewish and Slavic subhumanity. For both Bartov and Browning, propaganda plays only a limited role in accounting for attitudes and actions.[78] The same is true of many other scholars, working in different settings, who have wrestled with how institutions, ideology, power relations and culture structure the realm of social action.

propaganda and ideology

Within Marxian traditions of historiography, Propaganda has found only limited acceptance. This is scarcely surprising given the unspoken liberal assumptions that inform so much Propaganda history. Historians' fascination with Nazi Germany and the USSR appears to lend at least tacit support to Hannah Arendt's claim that propaganda marks a defining characteristic of totalitarian societies alone: necessitated by ideologies that seek to immure citizens in a parallel world built on falsehoods which propaganda then strives to make unfalsifiable by eliminating independent thought, just as the total state seals its borders against foreign, potentially dissonant, influences.[79] In the eyes of left critics, historians' privileging of propaganda as a property of totalitarian states serves to buttress a particular liberal self-image – structured around the myth of untrammelled free will enjoyed by self-determining subjects in democratic polities.[80] In reality, human agency is always constrained by individuals' location within particular relations of dominance: hence

Marx's dictum that 'men make their own history, but they do not make it just as they please'.[81]

From a left perspective, Propaganda historians' recent turn towards the US national security state as prime mover in postwar propaganda has redirected attention to America without jettisoning the same normative liberal assumptions: that propaganda, a *sine qua non* of authoritarian states, represents a lamentable aberration for democratic polities, and hence demands attention as a breach of contract between state and citizens. That such a frisson could be occasioned by Frances Stonor Saunders' *Who Paid the Piper?* is explicable only because so many reviewers shared its author's liberal insistence that state interference in intellectual and cultural life – the CIA's 'paying of pipers', in this case – is not meant to occur in democratic states.[82] Why, though, should these tired 'revelations' have caused any surprise? Dominant elites constantly attempt to secure a privileged hearing (if not an outright monopoly) for ideas most congenial to maintaining the status quo. And they necessarily do so – in 'free societies' – in ways that obfuscate their interference in the much-vaunted (yet entirely rigged) 'free market of ideas'.

From a left perspective, then, Arendt was quite right in announcing a dynamic relationship between propaganda and ideology, but wrong in asserting that totalitarians enjoy exclusive ownership of both. In states of all political complexions, propaganda – as 'discourse in the service of ideology' – diffuses into broader processes through which particular ideas achieve primacy and instantiate themselves as 'common sense'.[83] The great weakness of most Propaganda scholarship lies in its failure to account for the ways in which ideology invariably structures the social realm – continuously, often 'invisibly', such that a dominant value system comes to appear so natural as to vaporize into the very air we breathe. Propaganda analysis tends to examine only readily identifiable processes of calculated 'manipulation'. But heavy-handed opinion engineering is epiphenomenal to the less easily grasped ways in which ideology constrains the realm of imaginable possibilities. Ultimately, it is ideology – not ephemeral propaganda campaigns which often do too poor a job of masking their own partiality to be very effective – that sustains relations of domination, operating at a level beyond the cognition of ideologues and ideologized alike, since those two categories overlap.[84]

Ideology critique thus tends to abandon the insistence on intention to distort or deceive that marks so many approaches to propaganda analysis. Those actors and agents who do most to sustain hegemony (a concept associated with Antonio Gramsci) may often not recognize themselves as defenders of a particular set of social relations, while nevertheless naturalizing inequity as simply the 'way things are'.[85] The Disney corporation, for example, might well not regard its comic books and filmstrips as legitimating US neo-colonialism in South America. In all probability, Donald Duck and his anthropomorphized friends were not deliberately invented as vehicles for demeaning stereotypes of Latino/a 'Otherness' that would perpetuate the South's psychological subordination to the North, while rendering structural asymmetries seemingly timeless and inevitable. And yet that, according to Ariel Dorfman and Armand Mattelart, is precisely how Disney cartoons operate – as vehicles of 'cultural imperialism', all the more devastatingly effective for their ostensible apolitical harmlessness.[86]

Viewed in this light, then, most Propaganda historians pose back-to-front questions. Rather than fixating on top-down state manipulation of media (especially in wartime), a more searching critique would enquire why – often in the absence of overt intrusions – news media and the culture industry nevertheless restrain 'acceptable' discourse within extremely narrow parameters. Exploring the intersection of ideology and professional routines in this work of boundary-maintenance forms the approach taken by Daniel Hallin in The 'Uncensored' War.[87] Others have elaborated the world-view of Western news media whose aetiolated conception of newsworthiness, and restricted spectrum of opinion across which 'balance' is sought, owes little to propaganda as conventionally defined. Rather, the ideo-scape constructed by powerful media organizations might better be construed as flowing from, and securing, an 'occidental cosmology', in Johan Galtung and Richard Vincent's phrase.[88] These expanded enquiries shift analysis away from the narrow purview of Propaganda.

postmodernity and propaganda

Ideology critique of this kind, however, also has its critics. And if ideology appears an outmoded category, then how much more so its most clunky vehicle, propaganda? According to Terry Eagleton, we live in an age of 'epistemological scepticism which would hold that the very act of identifying a form of consciousness as ideological entails some untenable notion of absolute truth'.[89] To the extent that postmodernists and poststructuralists (as primus inter pares among epistemological sceptics) conform to Eagleton's sketch, 'post-' approaches surely would reject as unworkable classical Marxist notions of 'false consciousness' that equate ideology with the mystification of class oppression necessary to sustain relations of dominance. Starting from a position that all communication is interested, and value-free speech an empty shibboleth, notions of ideology as systematically distorted communication are voided of utility. Either everything or nothing would then be 'propaganda'. The former option is pursued in some recent works such as Alex Edelman's *Total Propaganda,* which announces that all communication – including (and perhaps especially) disquisitions on propaganda – is and are propaganda. The sum of these cacophonous propagandas is 'totalprop'.[90] But given the conceptual cul-de-sac into which such analysis quickly leads, many postmodern critics abandon the term – since most definitions of propaganda presume an impossible condition of innocent speech 'from nowhere' – rather than extend it over all discourse.

From this perspective, definitions of propaganda as the calculated skewing of 'truth', along with the associated mode of analysis that proceeds by exposing untruths peddled by powerful corporate or state interests that serve to keep 'reality' hidden, pose particular epistemological problems. Yet this *modus operandi* is one of the commonest forms of Propaganda critique. For example, the most widely-read left critic of US foreign policy on both sides of the Atlantic, Noam Chomsky, together with Edward Herman, advances a 'propaganda model' to explain – via a five-layered process of filtration – the systematic distortion required to 'manufacture consent' for an unjust order within the US, and for the advantageous asymmetries which it perpetuates (with no little military force) beyond its own borders.[91] Postmodernist scholars might concur, partially, with Chomsky and Herman's assertion that the media 'function to amuse, entertain, and inform, and to inculcate individuals with the values, beliefs, and codes of behavior that will integrate them into the institutional structures of the larger society', but not without serious caveats.[92]

First, Chomsky and Herman's model suggests the possibility of lofty neutral ground from which to arbitrate the distortedness or correctness of information communicated by the media. In other words, it requires a belief that 'messages' can be categorically determined either 'truthful' or not. Second, since this approach implies that meaning is fixed and static – simply *there* – within media texts, it denies receivers any role in negotiating meaning, forestalling the possibility that audiences might read texts in discrepant ways, or resist dominant value-systems. Surely not everyone is thoroughly integrated into 'institutional structures'? But to the extent that human subjects are enmeshed – with whatever degrees of friction and resistance – into a social order's disciplined material and mental regimes, then the processes that effect this integration are both larger and yet more infinitesimal than the blunt stultification effected by the mainstream media.[93] In accounting for this disciplining of subjectivities, postmodern approaches might well favour culture over ideology as the 'flexible invisible cage' that 'offers to the individual a horizon of latent possibilities', in Carlo Ginzburg's language.[94] Or they might mobilize the more Foucauldian notion of 'bio-power', which loosely approximates Jacques Ellul's conception of 'sociological propaganda' as 'a progressive adaptation to a certain order of things, a certain concept of human relations, which unconsciously molds individuals and makes them conform to society'.[95]

So does this mean that the postmodern project and Propaganda are utterly incommensurable? The answer is surely yes. Up to a point. Several recent histories of cross-cultural encounters, whose authors read archival documents and cultural texts through a lens sharpened by postmodern theory, do not frame their enquiry in terms of propaganda. Under this heading we might include Mary Renda's *Taking Haiti: Military Occupation and the Culture of US Imperialism* and Uta Poiger's *Jazz, Rock, and Rebels: Cold War Politics and American Culture in a Divided Germany*, both of which explore – in very different settings – the reception of Americans, and of US militarized paternalism, consumer products and cultural values (and, in Renda's case, the reciprocal negotiation of 'Haiti' in US self-fashioning).[96] But while scholars concerned with mapping cultural transactions may incline away from propaganda altogether, historians who remain drawn to sites of obvious state intrusion into the realm of cultural production could profitably enrich their analyses through a more sustained engagement with postmodern philosophy. Literary and cultural theory can provide tools to deconstruct both the aesthetic and ideological strategies of propaganda texts, while simultaneously encouraging historians to invest audiences with greater agency than they generally have. Cultural artefacts, in other words, ought not to be flattened and read as though they were simply diplomatic documents – more engagingly packaged. If historians are sometimes guilty of reading films 'as if they were written scripts rather than complex audiovisual artefacts', then it is also true that they are apt to read films (or other texts) as transparent reflections of ideology, and, further, to assume the smooth transmission of state-sanctioned ideas from the simple fact of their having been intensively cultivated. But if meaning is made by audiences – not simply 'found' where ideologues implant it – then deconstructive approaches have much to offer Propaganda history. All too often, as Eric Rentschler suggests, in historians' hands, 'Propaganda does not show or suggest; it speaks. Sometimes it whispers; usually it shrieks.'[97] Paradoxically, the effect of historians' concentration on intentions, messages and surfaces has long been to invest propaganda

– particularly as practised by the 'total state' – with greater potency than even its most calculating exponents dared expect.

conclusion: the death of propaganda?

If the holy grail of historical endeavour is an understanding of the 'secret springs of social action', few nowadays would be likely to insist, along with Lasswell, that ultimate revelation lies in illuminating 'the mechanism of propaganda'.[98] This is not to say, however, that propaganda has no place in the study of international history. Indisputably, there remains a lot of it about. The current 'war on terror' daily reprises tropes of Cold War demonology, while revivifying US 'public diplomacy' agencies and outlets that languished for much of the 1990s. Where Washington deployed Radio Freedom and Radio Liberty in the bid to reach and 'detach' Eastern bloc listeners during the Cold War, today's battle for the hearts and minds of Middle Eastern Muslims brings us Al-Hurra ('The Free One'), a new US-sponsored satellite TV station, whose tagline runs: 'You think, you aspire, you choose, you express, you are free, Al-Hurra, just the way you are.' Unsurprisingly, Arab viewers voice scepticism over the platitudinous bromides of a station so clearly unfree in its allegiances and agenda. Conscious that 'weapons of mass deception' may have been trained on them prior to the assault on Iraq in March 2003, North American and European audiences meanwhile are turning to treatises that offer a twenty-first-century reanimation of the tradition of propaganda critique first espoused by the IPA in the 1930s.

So long as privileged interest groups enjoy access to, or monopolies over, channels of opinion-formation, and attempt to use their advantage to replace contestation with unchallenged consent, then there surely remains a place for propaganda in historical analysis and contemporary commentary alike. But as this chapter suggests, exposing *Lies And the Lying Liars Who Tell Them* (to borrow from the title of one unbridled recent polemic) forms only part – and perhaps a rather small part – of the work required to understand how certain ideas establish themselves as unchallengeable common sense, and with what consequences.[99] Integrating propaganda into more nuanced, theoretically-informed investigations of ideology, culture and power is unlikely to produce best-selling exposés, but it will certainly enrich a field in sore need of nutrients.

notes

1. Philip M. Taylor, *Munitions of the Mind: War Propaganda from the Ancient World to the Nuclear Age* (Wellingborough: Patrick Stephens, 1990), p. 11;

Gladys Thum and Marcella Thum, *Persuasion and Propaganda in War and Peace* (Evanston, IL: McDougal, Littell, 1974), p. 3.

2. For the sake of clarity, I capitalize Propaganda to denote the disciplinary field, differentiating it from the concept and material practice (propaganda, in the lower case).

3. J. Michael Sproule, 'Social Responses to Twentieth-Century Propaganda', in Ted J. Smith (ed.), *Propaganda: A Pluralistic Perspective* (New York: Praeger, 1989), p. 5. Communications scholars, including Sproule himself in *Propaganda and Democracy: The American Experience of Media and Mass Persuasion* (Cambridge: Cambridge University Press, 1997), have seen some recent signs of rejuvenation; but such claims remain confined to new treatments from within the field of communications studies and rhetoric.

4. Anthony Pratkanis and Elliot Aronson, *Age of Propaganda: The Everyday Use and Abuse of Persuasion* (New York: W. H. Freeman, 1992); Howard Kurtz, *Spin Cycle: Inside the Clinton Propaganda Machine* (London: Pan, 1998).

5. Brett Gary suggests that the answer lies (at least in part) in the pejorative connotations attaching to the term: *The Nervous Liberals: Propaganda Anxieties from World War I to the Cold War* (New York: Columbia University Press, 1999), p. 8. James Shanahan, remarking on the rarity of critical perspectives on propaganda within communications, muses whether 'the fall of the Berlin Wall, the decline of communism and the end of Reaganism ... deprived us of our best practitioners of the blacker arts of communication': 'The End of Propaganda?', in James Shanahan (ed.), *Propaganda Without Propagandists? Six Case Studies in US Propaganda* (Cresskill, NJ: Hampton Press, 2001), p. 1.

6. Philip M. Taylor, *British Propaganda in the Twentieth Century: Selling Democracy* (Edinburgh: Edinburgh University Press, 1999), p. ix.

7. For accounts of this disciplinary history, see Gary, *Nervous Liberals*; Sproule, *Propaganda and Democracy*; J. Michael Sproule, 'Propaganda Studies in American Social Science: The Rise and Fall of A Critical Paradigm', *Quarterly Journal of Speech*, 73 (1) (1987) 60–78; Christopher Simpson, *Science of Coercion: Communication Research and Psychological Warfare, 1945–1960* (New York: Oxford University Press, 1994); Daniel J. Czitrom, *Media and the American Mind from Morse to McLuhan* (Chapel Hill: University of North Carolina Press, 1982); Wilbur Schramm, *The Beginnings of Communication Study in America: A Personal Memoir* (London: Sage, 1997); Stuart Ewen, *PR! A Social History of Spin* (New York: Basic Books, 1996).

8. Thorstein Veblen, cited in Patrick Brantlinger, *Crusoe's Footsteps: Cultural Studies in Britain and America* (New York: Routledge, 1990), p. 4.

9. E. H. Carr, *The Twenty Years' Crisis, 1919–1939* (London: Macmillan, 1939), p. 169.

10. John Thompson, *The Media and Modernity: A Social Theory of the Media* (Cambridge: Polity, 1995), pp. 119–48. See also the treatment of public opinion by a leading propaganda scholar (and wartime practitioner), Hans Speier, 'The Rise of Public Opinion', in H. D. Lasswell, D. Lerner and H. Speier (eds), *Propaganda and Communication in World History*, 3 vols (Honolulu: University Press of Hawaii, 1979–80), *Vol. 2: Emergence of Public Opinion in the West*, pp. 147–67.

11. Patrick Brantlinger, *Bread and Circuses: Theories of Mass Culture as Social Decay* (Ithaca: Cornell University Press, 1983).

12. The most influential of these, conducted during 1929–33, were the Payne Fund studies, discussed by Garth Jowett and Victoria O'Donnell, *Propaganda and Persuasion*, 2nd edn (London: Sage, 1992), pp. 93–4.

13. On this debate and its legacy, including attempts to outlaw foreign agents of influence in inter-war America, see Nicholas J. Cull, *Selling War: The British Propaganda Campaign Against American 'Neutrality' in World War II* (New York: Oxford University Press, 1995).

14. Arthur Ponsonby, *Falsehood in Wartime* (London: George Allen and Unwin, 1928); James Read, *Atrocity Propaganda, 1914–1919* (New Haven: Yale University Press, 1941). For a first-hand account by a German propagandist in the US, see George Viereck, *Spreading Germs of Hate* (London: Duckworth, 1931).

15. Thomas Doherty, *Projections of War: Hollywood, American Culture and World War II* (New York: Columbia University Press, 1993).

16. Typical of this genre is Alexander J. Mackenzie, *Propaganda Boom* (London: J. Gifford, 1938). The classic statement on 'Fascinating Fascism' is Susan Sontag's 1975 essay, reprinted in *Under the Sign of Saturn* (New York: Vintage, 1981), pp. 71–105.

17. Carr, *Twenty Years' Crisis*, p. 175.

18. Walter Lippmann, *The Phantom Public* (London: Macmillan, 1925); Harold Lasswell, *Propaganda Technique in the World War* (New York: Knopf, 1927), quote at p. 15.

19. Lasswell, *Propaganda Technique*, p. 221; on Bernays, see Ewen, *PR!*

20. W. W. Biddle, cited by Sproule, 'Social Responses', p. 11.

21. For a sample of its output, see IPA, 'How to Detect Propaganda', in Robert Jackall (ed.), *Propaganda* (London: Macmillan, 1995), pp. 217–24. See also Sproule, 'Propaganda Studies', 72–3.

22. Walter Lippmann, cited by Simpson, *Science of Coercion*, p. 17.

23. A useful short survey of propaganda definitions over the course of the twentieth-century is offered by David Welch, 'Propaganda, Definitions of', in Nicholas J. Cull, David Culbert and David Welch (eds), *Propaganda and Mass Persuasion: A Historical Encyclopedia, 1500 to the Present* (Santa Barbara: ABC-CLIO, 2003), pp. 317–23.

24. Lasswell, *Propaganda Technique*, pp. 222–3.

25. Leonard Doob, cited by Welch, 'Propaganda, Definitions of', p. 318 (emphasis added).

26. On whether one can 'suggest' unwittingly, see Richard Taylor, *Film Propaganda: Soviet Russia and Nazi Germany*, 2nd edn (London: Tauris, 1998), p. 8; Welch, 'Propaganda, Definitions of', p. 318.

27. Harold Lasswell, cited by Welch, 'Propaganda, Definitions of', p. 319.

28. Bertrand Russell, cited by Welch, 'Propaganda, Definitions of', p. 319.

29. On the lack of definitional innovation in the latter part of the twentieth century, see Stanley B. Cunningham, *The Idea of Propaganda: A Reconstruction* (Westport: Praeger, 2002).

30. Charles Cruickshank, *The Fourth Arm: Psychological Warfare 1938–1945* (London: Davis-Poynter, 1977).

31. Simpson, *Science of Coercion*, p. 26; Gary, *Nervous Liberals*.
32. The Army's Psychological Warfare Division had on its wartime payroll many who would most significantly shape the postwar academic fields of sociology and communications, including Morris Janowitz, Daniel Lerner and Edward Shils. Meanwhile, the forerunner of the Central Intelligence Agency (CIA), the Office of Strategic Services (OSS), enlisted the contributions of Alex Inkeles and Herbert Marcuse: see Simpson, *Science of Coercion*.
33. GIs' responses to Frank Capra's *Why We Fight* series of motivational films were analysed in C. I. Hovland, A. A. Lumsdaine and F. D. Sheffield, *Experiments on Mass Communication* (Princeton, NJ: Princeton University Press, 1949). Little direct attitudinal change of the kind desired could be detected. On the army and the role of the 'primary group', see Samuel Stouffer *et al.*, *The American Soldier*, 2 vols (Princeton, NJ: Princeton University Press, 1949).
34. Hans Speier, *Social Order and the Risks of War: Papers in Political Psychology* (Cambridge, MA: MIT Press, 1952); Nicholas Pronay and Keith Wilson (eds), *The Political Re-education of Germany and her Allies after World War II* (London: Croom Helm, 1985).
35. Simpson, *Science of Coercion*, p. 4.
36. Scott Lucas, *Freedom's War: The US Crusade against the Soviet Union, 1945–1956* (Manchester: Manchester University Press, 1999).
37. Simpson, *Science of Coercion*; Christopher Simpson (ed.), *Universities and Empire: Money and Politics in the Social Sciences during the Cold War* (New York: New Press, 1998); Michael Latham, *Modernization as Ideology: American Social Science and 'Nation Building' in the Kennedy Era* (Chapel Hill: University of North Carolina Press, 2000).
38. On the evolution of communications research in 1930s Germany, see Ladislas Farago, *German Psychological Warfare* (New York: Putnam and Sons, 1942); on the Nazi SS collection of public opinion reports, evidencing a good deal of dissident opinion, see Ian Kershaw, *The Hitler Myth: Image and Reality* (Oxford: Clarendon, 1987).
39. David Wedgwood Benn, *Persuasion and Soviet Politics* (Oxford: Blackwell, 1989).
40. John D. Marks, *The Search for the 'Manchurian Candidate': The CIA and Mind Control* (New York: Times Books, 1979); Susan L. Carruthers, '*The Manchurian Candidate* (1962) and the Cold War Brainwashing Scare', *Historical Journal of Film, Radio and Television*, 18 (1) (1998) 75–94.
41. See Simpson, *Science of Coercion*; Gary, *Nervous Liberals*.
42. Daniel Lerner, *Psychological Warfare against Nazi Germany: The Sykewar Campaign, D-Day to VE-Day*, 2nd edn (Cambridge, MA: MIT Press, 1971); William Daugherty, in collaboration with Morris Janowitz, (ed.), *A Psychological Warfare Casebook* (Baltimore: Johns Hopkins University Press, 1958); Lasswell *et al.*, *Propaganda and Communication in World History*. For an exhaustive bibliography, see Simpson, *Science of Coercion*.
43. See Michael Balfour, *Propaganda in War, 1939–1945* (London: Routledge and Kegan Paul, 1979); Richard Crossman's autobiographical contributions in Lerner, *Psychological Warfare*, pp. 78–80, 323–46; Lindley Fraser, *Propaganda* (Oxford: Oxford University Press, 1957).

44. Siegfried Kracauer, *From Caligari to Hitler: A Psychological History of German Film* (Princeton, NJ: Princeton University Press, 1947).

45. Serge Chakotin, *The Rape of the Masses: The Psychology of Totalitarian Political Propaganda* (London: Routledge, 1940).

46. John A. Hobson, *The Psychology of Jingoism* (London: G. Richards, 1901), quote at p. 12.

47. Carr, *Twenty Years' Crisis*, p. 176.

48. Richard Taylor, *Film Propaganda: Soviet Russia and Nazi Germany* (London: Croom Helm, 1979); Balfour, *Propaganda in War.*

49. Paul Linebarger, *Psychological Warfare*, 2nd edn (Washington, DC: Combat Forces Press, 1954); Cruickshank, *Fourth Arm*; Lerner, *Psychological Warfare.*

50. Daniel Lerner (ed.), *Propaganda in War and Crisis* (New York: G. W. Stewart, 1951); F. H. Hodder, 'Propaganda as a Source of American History', *Mississippi Valley Historical Review*, 9 (1) (1922) 3–18.

51. On this history, see Sproule, 'Propaganda Studies', 65, 76; and R. H. Lutz, 'Studies of World War Propaganda, 1914–33', *Journal of Modern History*, 5 (4) (1933) 496–516, for an overview of inter-war production; Merle Curti's contribution was 'Pacifist Propaganda and the Treaty of Guadaloupe Hidalgo', *American Historical Review*, 33 (3) (1928) 596–8.

52. Philip Davidson, *Propaganda and the American Revolution, 1763–1783* (Chapel Hill: University of North Carolina Press, 1941).

53. On the demise of the 'propaganda paradigm' in communications studies, see Nicholas Burnett, 'Ideology and Propaganda: Toward an Integrative Approach', in Smith, *Propaganda*, p. 131; Jacques Ellul, *Propaganda: The Formation of Men's Attitudes* (New York: Knopf, 1965).

54. Cate Haste, *Keep the Home Fires Burning: Propaganda in the First World War* (London: Allen Lane, 1977); M. L. Sanders and P. M. Taylor, *British Propaganda during the First World War, 1914–1918* (London: Macmillan, 1982); Nicholas Reeves, *Official British Film Propaganda during the First World War* (London: Croom Helm, 1986).

55. E. Bramsted, *Goebbels and National Socialist Propaganda, 1925–1945* (London: Cresset Press, 1965); Z. A. B. Zeman, *Nazi Propaganda* (Oxford: Oxford University Press, 1973); Jay Baird, *The Mythical World of Nazi War Propaganda, 1939–1945* (Minneapolis: University of Minnesota Press, 1974); Willi Boelcke (ed.), *The Secret Conferences of Dr Goebbels, October 1939-March 1943* (London: Weidenfeld and Nicolson, 1970); Hugh Trevor-Roper (ed.), *The Goebbels Diaries: The Last Days* (London: Secker and Warburg, 1978).

56. From a vast literature, see, for example, Ian McLaine, *Ministry of Morale: Home Front Morale and the Ministry of Information in World War II* (London: Allen and Unwin, 1979); Allan M. Winkler, *The Politics of Propaganda: the Office of War Information, 1942–1945* (New Haven: Yale University Press, 1978); Clayton R. Koppes and Gregory D. Black, *Hollywood Goes to War: How Politics, Profits, and Propaganda Shaped World War II Movies* (London: Tauris, 1988); Philip M. Taylor (ed.), *Britain and the Cinema during the Second World War* (London: Macmillan, 1988); Peter Kenez, *Cinema and Soviet Society, 1917–1953* (Cambridge: Cambridge University Press, 1992). Publications on all these areas continue to appear.

57. Frances Stonor Saunders, *Who Paid the Piper? The CIA and the Cultural Cold War* (London: Granta, 1999); Giles Scott-Smith, *The Politics of Apolitical Culture: The Congress for Cultural Freedom, the CIA and Post-War American Hegemony* (London: Routledge, 2002); Volker Berghahn, *America and the Intellectual Cold Wars in Europe* (Princeton, NJ: Princeton University Press, 2001).

58. Lucas, *Freedom's War*; Walter L. Hixson, *Parting the Curtain: Propaganda, Culture and the Cold War, 1945–1961* (New York: St Martin's, 1997).

59. David Caute, *The Dancer Defects: The Struggle for Cultural Supremacy during the Cold War* (Oxford: Oxford University Press, 2003); note, also, the promise inherent in Nigel Gould-Davies, 'The Logic of Soviet Cultural Diplomacy', *Diplomatic History*, 27 (2) (2003) 193–214.

60. Germany's propaganda in the First World War is the subject of a recent treatment by David Welch, *Germany, Propaganda and Total War, 1914–1918: The Sins of Omission* (New Brunswick: Rutgers University Press, 2000); on Japan, see Abe Mark Nornes and Fukushima Yukio (eds), *The Japan/America Film Wars: World War II Propaganda and its Cultural Contexts* (Langhorne, PA: Harwood, 1994); on radio, see, for example, Martin Doherty, *Nazi Wireless Propaganda: Lord Haw-Haw and British Public Opinion in the Second World War* (Edinburgh: Edinburgh University Press, 2000); H. J. P. Bergmeier and R. E. Lotz, *Hitler's Airwaves: The Inside Story of Nazi Radio Broadcasting and Propaganda Swing* (New Haven: Yale University Press, 1997).

61. For a recent collection of essays, ranging widely in both temporal and thematic coverage, see Bertrand Taithe and Tim Thornton (eds), *Propaganda: Political Rhetoric and Identity, 1300–2000* (Stroud: Sutton, 1999).

62. The broader interdisciplinary literature on 'war and the media' is too voluminous to survey here, but for a useful bibliographic overview see Daniel Hallin, 'The Media and War', in J. Corner, P. Schlesinger and R. Silverstone (eds), *International Media Research: A Critical Survey* (London: Routledge, 1997), pp. 206–31; for a synoptic account, see Susan L. Carruthers, *The Media at War: Communication and Conflict in the Twentieth Century* (London: Palgrave, 2000).

63. David Fieldhouse, 'Can Humpty-Dumpty be Put Together Again? Imperial History in the 1980s', *Journal of Imperial and Commonwealth History*, 12 (2) (1984) 9–23; Dane Kennedy, 'Imperial History and Post-Colonial Theory', *Journal of Imperial and Commonwealth History*, 24 (3) (1996) 345–63.

64. John MacKenzie, *Propaganda and Empire: The Manipulation of British Public Opinion, 1880–1960* (Manchester: Manchester University Press, 1984); John MacKenzie, *Orientalism: History, Theory and the Arts* (Manchester: Manchester University Press, 1995). For a more appreciative discussion of Said, see Matthew Connelly, 'Taking Off the Cold War Lens: Visions of North–South Conflict during the Algerian War for Independence', *American Historical Review*, 105 (3) (2000) 739–69.

65. Robert J. Young, *Marketing Marianne: French Propaganda in America, 1900–1940* (New Brunswick: Rutgers University Press, 2004); Anandi Ramamurthy, *Imperial Persuaders: Images of Africa and Asia in British Advertising* (Manchester: Manchester University Press, 2003); Tony Chafer and Amanda Sackur (eds), *Promoting the Colonial Idea: Propaganda and Visions of Empire in France* (New York: Palgrave, 2002); Christina Klein, *Cold War Orientalism: Asia in the*

Middlebrow Imagination, 1945–1961 (Berkeley: University of California Press, 2003); Mark Bradley, *Imagining Vietnam and America: The Making of Postcolonial Vietnam, 1919–1950* (Chapel Hill: University of North Carolina Press, 2000).

66. *Diplomatic History* has been the major site of this disciplinary introspection (although not, in its substantive content, always as receptive to as sustained an engagement with 'theory' as the latter's advocates might have wished).

67. Attention to international organization and transnational movements has been most prominently championed by Akira Iriye, at greatest length in his *Cultural Internationalism and World Order* (Baltimore: Johns Hopkins University Press, 1997).

68. Leila J. Rupp, *Mobilizing Women for War: German and American Propaganda, 1939–1945* (Princeton, NJ; Princeton University Press, 1978); Jo Fox, *Filming Women in the Third Reich* (Oxford: Berg, 2000); Claudia Koonz, *Mothers in the Fatherland: Women, the Family, and Nazi Politics* (New York: St Martin's, 1987).

69. Zara Steiner, 'On Writing International History: Chaps, Maps and Much More', *International Affairs*, 73 (3) (1997) 531–46.

70. Cunningham, *The Idea of Propaganda*, p. 79.

71. Robert Buzzanco, 'Where's the Beef? Culture without Power in the Study of US Foreign Relations', *Diplomatic History*, 24 (4) (2000) 623–32.

72. Todd Bennett, 'Culture, Power and *Mission to Moscow:* Film and Soviet-American Relations during World War II', *Journal of American History*, 88 (2) (2001), 489–518.

73. Tony Shaw's recent work on British cinema and the Cold War, for example, might be critiqued in this vein for announcing a consensus in the UK that is never actually demonstrated: *British Cinema and the Cold War: The State, Propaganda and Consensus* (London: Tauris, 2001).

74. Fraser, *Propaganda*, p. 1 (emphasis added).

75. Robert Herzstein, *The War that Hitler Won: The Most Infamous Propaganda Campaign in History* (London: Hamish Hamilton, 1979).

76. Kershaw, *Hitler Myth*, pp. 169–225.

77. Aldous Huxley, 'Notes on Propaganda', *Harper's*, 174 (December 1936) 32–41 (quotation at 39).

78. Christopher Browning, *Ordinary Men: Reserve Police Battalion 101 and the Final Solution in Poland* (New York: HarperCollins, 1992); Omer Bartov, *Hitler's Army: Soldiers, Nazis and War in the Third Reich* (New York: Oxford University Press, 1991).

79. Hannah Arendt, *The Origins of Totalitarianism* (New York: Harcourt Brace, 1951), esp. pp. 341–65.

80. Michael Halberstam, *Totalitarianism and the Modern Conception of Politics* (New Haven: Yale University Press, 1999).

81. Karl Marx and Friedrich Engels, 'The Eighteenth Brumaire of Louis Bonaparte', in Karl Marx and Friedrich Engels, *Selected Works in One Volume* (London: Lawrence and Wishart, 1968), p. 96.

82. See, for example, Josef Joffe, 'America's Secret Weapon', *New York Times*, 23 April 2000, Section 7, p. 15. Joffe fiercely criticizes Saunders for her 'strident anti-anti-Communism that refuses to accord the Western cause the moral

worth it deserves', arguing that the clandestine activities detailed were eminently justified by circumstances; yet he agrees with the basic point that they 'defie[d] the very core of the liberal-democratic faith'.

83. The phrase is Nicholas Burnett's, 'Ideology and Propaganda', p. 127. Of course, this definition of propaganda is open to the objection that *all* discourse is surely ideological, and if that is so then both propaganda and ideology cease to be very meaningful categories. For a discussion of how 'ideology' can be rescued from this kind of emptying, see Terry Eagleton, *Ideology: An Introduction* (London: Verso, 1991).

84. Nick Stevenson, *Understanding Media Cultures: Social Theory and Mass Communication* (London: Sage, 1995), pp. 9–46.

85. David Forgacs (ed.), *The Gramsci Reader: Selected Writings, 1916–1935* (New York: New York University Press, 2000), pp. 189–221.

86. Ariel Dorfman and Armand Mattelart, *How to Read Donald Duck: Imperialist Ideology in the Disney Comic* (New York: International General, 1975). For a hostile diplomatic historian's critique of theories of cultural imperialism, see Jessica Gienow-Hecht, 'Shame on US? Academics, Cultural Transfer and the Cold War – a Critical Review', *Diplomatic History*, 24 (3) (2000) 465–94.

87. Daniel Hallin, *The 'Uncensored' War: the Media and Vietnam* (New York: Oxford University Press, 1989).

88. Johan Galtung and Richard C. Vincent, *Global Glasnost: Toward a New World Information and Communication Order?* (Cresskill, NJ: Hampton Press, 1992), esp. pp. 13–17. See also the account of 'structural propaganda' advanced in Mark Alleyne, *News Revolution: Political and Economic Decisions about Global Information* (London: Macmillan, 1997), pp. 39–43.

89. Eagleton, *Ideology*, p. xii.

90. Alex Edelstein, *Total Propaganda: From Mass Culture to Popular Culture* (Mahwah, NJ: Lawrence Erlbaum, 1997).

91. Edward Herman and Noam Chomsky, *Manufacturing Consent: The Political Economy of the Mass Media*, 2nd edn (New York: Pantheon, 2002).

92. Herman and Chomsky, *Manufacturing Consent*, p. 1.

93. For a rebuttal of the various assaults on the 'propaganda model', see Edward Herman, 'The Propaganda Model: a Retrospective', *Journalism Studies*, 1 (1) (2000) 101–12.

94. Carlo Ginzburg, *The Cheese and the Worms* (New York: Penguin, 1983), pp. xx–xxi.

95. Ellul, *Propaganda*, p. 4; Paul Rabinow (ed.), *The Foucault Reader* (London: Penguin, 1986), pp. 257–89. It is worth stressing that culture and ideology are in no way mutually exclusive categories. Indeed, the British school of cultural studies – deeply influenced by the Marxist historiography of E. P. Thompson, Christopher Hill, *et al.* – was always attentive to matters of culture and 'consciousness'. On the parallel evolution of cultural studies in the UK and US, see Brantlinger, *Crusoe's Footsteps*. For a sophisticated account of culture as a category for international history, see Anders Stephanson, 'Considerations on Culture and Theory', *Diplomatic History*, 18 (1) (1994) 107–19.

96. Mary Renda, *Taking Haiti: Military Occupation and the Culture of US Imperialism, 1915–1940* (Chapel Hill: University of North Carolina Press, 2001); Uta Poiger,

Jazz, Rock, and Rebels: Cold War Politics and American Culture in a Divided Germany (Berkeley: University of California Press, 2000); Heide Fehrenbach and Uta Poiger (eds), *Transactions, Transgressions, Transformations: American Culture in Western Europe and Japan* (New York: Berghahn, 2000).

97. Eric Rentschler, *The Ministry of Illusion: Nazi Cinema and its Afterlife* (Cambridge, MA: Harvard University Press, 1996), p. 11. See also, for a similar rejection of heavy-handed Propaganda analysis of film, Linda Schulte-Sasse, *Entertaining the Third Reich: Illusions of Wholeness in Nazi Cinema* (Durham: Duke University Press, 1996).

98. Lasswell, *Propaganda Technique*, pp. 222–3.

99. Al Franken, *Lies (And the Lying Liars Who Tell Them): A Fair and Balanced Look at the Right* (New York: Penguin, 2003). See also Joe Conason, *Big Lies: The Right-Wing Propaganda Machine and How it Distorts the Truth* (New York: St Martin's, 2003); David Corn, *The Lies of George W Bush: Mastering the Politics of Deception* (New York: Crown, 2003).

8

non-governmental organizations and non-state actors

jeremi suri

The field of modern international history has traditionally focused upon the study of states. Research on the origins of various wars and the expansion of European empires has, quite naturally, led scholars to examine the archival records of prime ministers, presidents, foreign ministers and other high-ranking state officials in considerable depth. This state-centred work is valuable and it will surely remain at the heart of the field. States, however, are not the only influential and important actors on the international stage. Non-governmental organizations (NGOs) and non-state actors (NSAs), the subjects of this chapter, have also received, and will continue to receive, considerable scholarly attention.

NGOs and NSAs are frequently depicted as offering oppositional alternatives to state power.[1] This is not necessarily the case. NGOs are institutionalized groupings of people and resources, often from multiple societies, operating outside the direct authority of any particular government or collection of governments. Individuals, not nations, are generally the constituent elements of an NGO. They organize around a wide array of issues – from human rights activism to sports enthusiasm, from the spread of scientific knowledge to business profit-seeking. NGOs (such as Amnesty International and the US-China Business Council) are distinguished from inter-governmental organizations (including the United Nations (UN), the World Trade Organization, and many others) that are comprised of states and reflect the wishes of collected opinion among state leaders. NGOs can oppose state policies, but they can also (and often do) work cooperatively with states. They are, in this sense, international institutions working in parallel with the prime ministers, presidents and foreign ministers who dominate national newspaper headlines.[2]

NSAs are less organized and often less multinational than NGOs. They are, as Thomas Friedman has put it, 'Super-empowered individuals' or small groups that operate with little state control.[3] NSAs rarely challenge states explicitly, but they use their resources to affect policies, perceptions and behaviour across societies. NSAs derive their influence from some combination of independent wealth, public prestige, popular following and private connections. Like NGOs they can pursue a wide range of aims and interests.

As entities operating in parallel with states, NGOs and NSAs share many of the complex motivations that observers have long recognized in national governments. NGOs and NSAs can pursue high-minded idealistic goals and they can also advocate realist programmes that serve the interests of their specific organizations. They can operate democratically by consensus or they can autocratically reflect the whims of a select few. Most significantly, they can pursue peace and stability, or they can embrace goals that include violence and brutality. This latter point requires some elaboration because it runs against the common assumption that NGOs and NSAs, by definition, contribute to international peace.[4] One must keep in mind that the world of NGOs is populated not only by do-gooders, but also by extremists, zealots and even terrorists. Peter Bergen, among others, has made the alarming point that Al-Qaeda is a very effective NGO, utilizing a global range of resources and interests to evade state controls. By extension, one might also conclude that Osama bin Laden is an NSA, by virtue of his wealth and public appeal in some communities.[5]

Most scholars who write about NGOs and NSAs believe in the overall virtues of these organizations in protecting human rights, advancing environmental awareness, promoting economic justice and advocating various other liberal-minded concerns. This is, of course, a fair judgement. Nonetheless, one must not assume that NGOs and NSAs *necessarily* serve these worthy purposes. Quite the contrary, NGOs and NSAs are malleable entities that sometimes contribute to the elements of warfare so common in international relations. Once again, this is evidence for the proposition that NGOs and NSAs act in parallel with, and not as alternatives to, the system of relations between states.

international society

What, in practice, does it mean to say that NGOs and NSAs act in parallel with the system of intra-state relations? This question has motivated scholars to reconceptualize what we mean when we speak of the modern 'international system'. States remain the central actors, but they no longer serve as the exclusive agents of change. Power now appears much more fluid, diffusing beyond prime ministers, presidents and foreign ministers to include activists, intellectuals, and businesspeople. Change also depends less narrowly on the global balance of military and economic might. Ideas, images, and cultural assumptions now deserve serious consideration in conjunction with the traditional, and still crucial, assessments of material capabilities.

The 'international system', in this reconceptualized scheme, is really an 'international society'. This latter term draws theoretical grounding and inspiration from the work of the Australian scholar, Hedley Bull. Writing in 1977, Bull recognized that while the realm of international relations was anarchical because it lacked an overarching authority structure, it was also orderly because of common understandings that guided daily intercourse among states and peoples.[6] Drawing a cogent analogy with domestic society, Bull pointed to the unlegislated but still widely recognized standards of behaviour for interpersonal interactions that make the peaceful functioning of everyday life possible. These standards evolve over time, and they are disseminated by the intermediary non-state institutions (including social clubs, activist groups, leisure organizations and religious institutions) that many associate with the term 'civil society'.[7] Force and wealth are prominent parts of local life, but they are not predominant. We live in societies, rather than anarchies or tyrannies, because of the rich complexity of the relations that order everyday behaviour.

International society reflects many of the same qualities found in domestic society, according to Bull. The very idea of the 'nation', and the assumption of self-determination for a people that it carries, is a common understanding that guides international interactions in the contemporary world. Of course, this was not always the case. Ideas about the nation became global with the spread of largely European concepts and images in the eighteenth and nineteenth centuries.[8] Similarly, the language of democracy and human rights reflects a constellation of ideas and images that spread to influence international behaviour during the twentieth century.[9] Common understandings have crucially shaped the structure and application of material capabilities in the international system.

For those who reject assumptions about the nation, democracy, and human rights, alternative common understandings have evolved to order opposition. 'International communism' in the twentieth century and 'radical Islamism' in the early twenty-first century provide social networks for organized activism at the international level. These visions have forged bonds between individuals from various corners of the globe, and they have transformed the basic ways in which peoples interact with one another. International communism and radical Islamism have benefited from extensive state support, but they are, fundamentally, manifestations of a pluralist international society that defies state dominance.

International society has functioned with extraordinary richness in the nineteenth and twentieth centuries because intermediary institutions, particularly NGOs and NSAs, have played a widespread role in building common understandings – sometimes for better, sometimes for worse – across states. NGOs and NSAs enrich international relations largely through epistemic and cultural means. They reframe the accepted applications of state power. They influence how individuals define their allegiances. Most significantly, they socialize citizens to think of themselves as more than just members of a state. Identification with an international human rights community, for example, need not run against one's national patriotism. It does, however, encourage individuals to demand more from government policies. Evocations of the 'national interest' have remained persuasive in the contemporary international system, but they have also become less sufficient for the satisfaction of citizens who see themselves as part of an international society.

NGOs and NSAs have contributed to what Hedley Bull and Adam Watson identify as the expansion of international society in the nineteenth and twentieth centuries.[10] A set of European and American assumptions about how states and peoples should interact with one another extended to other continents through both the imperialist arms of various empires and the growth of NGOs and NSAs that included missionary societies, banking trusts and scientific consortia. The spread of European-style law, medicine and education during the nineteenth and early twentieth centuries was a particularly clear manifestation of the parallel role NGOs played with state endeavours. Governments in Britain, France and eventually Germany and the United States funded the implantation of these institutions overseas to shore up their economic and strategic interests. The individuals and organizations that actually carried out these endeavours, however, operated with a large degree of independence from the centres of state power. The lawyers, doctors and educators who found themselves in China during the late nineteenth century, for instance, sought to build a set of common understandings with local populations that would not necessarily follow state dictate.[11] International associations of professional experts grew during this period for just this purpose, with an explicit emphasis on their non-governmental qualities.

The successes of these non-governmental endeavours in expanding international society are evident in developments after the early twentieth century. Local elites drew on the common understandings and non-governmental institutions that Europeans exported to assert their independence as nations. The Congress Party in India, for example, was populated by Indians who had been professionally trained and now belonged to various international professional associations. Local activists were able to turn international society against its state sponsors because government leaders in London, Paris, Berlin and Washington could not control the flow of ideas and images in NGOs. Professional associations, in particular, gave men like Mahatma Gandhi and Jawaharlal Nehru the skills, prestige and world-wide networks to mobilize common understandings for their purposes.

Activists like Gandhi and Nehru also transformed the substance of these common understandings. Recipients of an exported European framework for international society, they operated through non-governmental channels to revise the ideas and images that circulated across the globe. They often began by challenging racial, class and economic discrimination within their professional associations and other international organizations. This then gave them a firm foundation for a broader public articulation of demands for ideological change. By the middle of the twentieth century, activists in former colonial territories had shattered assumptions about the legitimacy of imperialism and racism by drawing, at least in part, on the non-governmental networks and common understandings that imperialism first offered to them. The assumptions underpinning international society evolved, as Bull predicted, due to the opportunities that its expansion provided for the work of NGOs and NSAs populated, in part, by non-Europeans.[12]

The history of NGOs and NSAs is a history of international society that touches on crucial developments in diplomacy, imperialism and ultimately decolonization. Conceptually, attention to NGOs and NSAs has widened the webs of agency and causality in scholarly analyses of international relations. Empirically, the study of NGOs and NSAs has added a more diverse cast of characters to explanations of global change.

the origins of modern ngos and nsas

In many ways, the history of NGOs and NSAs long precedes the nineteenth and twentieth centuries. Since at least the period of the Roman Empire, mercenaries, merchant associations, and banking enterprises have operated across wide territorial terrain with little government regulation.

Christianity, of course, began as a transnational non-governmental movement within the Roman Empire: Jesus Christ was a particularly influential NSA. As in the contemporary international system, premodern NGOs and NSAs served a variety of idealistic, commercial and violent purposes. Christian martyrs, wealthy merchants, and seafaring pirates all harnessed the resources of various societies to operate in parallel with officially constituted governments.

Recognition of this lineage is important for understanding the origins of modern NGOs and NSAs. They are ancient forms of association that the modern world inherited and transformed in ways that reflect crucial changes in the nature of international relations. In particular, many observers fail to recognize that the growth of secular state power in the aftermath of the French Revolution spurred the growth of NGOs and NSAs. With the disappearance of the many 'free cities', sacred territories and open spaces that had played crucial roles as buffers between powerful governments, new institutions were needed to mediate between contending and expanding states. Following this functionalist logic, organizations formed, often with the encouragement of states, to fill the void in international society. Many began as inter-governmental organizations, such as the Central Commission for the Navigation of the Rhine, created among the government representatives at the Congress of Vienna in 1815 to assure free navigation along the strategic waterway linking France, the Netherlands and the German states of Baden, Bavaria, Hesse, Nassau and Prussia. As Paul Schroeder has shown, the Congress system created in the decades after the Napoleonic Wars emphasized inter-governmental cooperation in Europe through a variety of mechanisms, including summitry, arbitration and an emerging body of international law.[13]

Inter-governmental cooperation in an era of state expansion also centred on technical matters – sanitation, postal delivery, cable communications, seafaring standards, and many other concerns where common understandings benefited all of the most powerful European governments. The Superior Council on Health, for instance, (founded in 1838) brought European governments and the Ottoman Empire together for the purpose of preventing the spread of communicable diseases across state boundaries.[14] In later years, similar inter-governmental bodies came into existence for technical cooperation on numerous issues that were at least tacitly recognized as transnational concerns. Paul Kennedy has aptly referred to institutions regulating technical cooperation, especially in naval affairs, as the 'invisibles' of power in the nineteenth century, which built upon international consensus rather than the exertions of unilateral state authority. Kennedy shows that British merchants and government leaders made very effective use of inter-governmental endeavours to bolster international stability and the strength of their empire during this period.[15]

The flowering of intergovernmental cooperation in the nineteenth century legitimized and encouraged the activities of NGOs and NSAs. This was most true around these technical issues where, by the second half of the nineteenth century, NGOs were often more active than inter-governmental groups. The most famous example is provided by the formation of the International Red Cross. This was a private endeavour, initially begun by the Swiss doctor Jean Henri Dunant. His call for a global body that would offer impartial health services to victims of war and natural disaster received widespread non-governmental support from individuals in various states. The First Geneva Convention signed by twelve nations (not including the United States) in 1864 offered protection to medical facilities and personnel aiding the wounded in war; it also recognized the Red Cross as a neutral group. The non-governmental nature of the Red Cross ensured that it would gain wide access to war victims throughout the next century and a half, despite the political prejudices of combatants. The Red Cross has also become a trusted evaluator of attacks on civilians because of its independence from state controls.[16]

NGOs and NSAs operating in technical fields provided the kind of impartial knowledge and assistance that could not possibly come from states competing against one another in the international system. This impartial knowledge was vital for the formation of agreed standards of behaviour in war and peace. In this sense, the common understandings that Hedley Bull identified as at the core of international society gained support through NGOs and NSAs (as well as inter-governmental organizations) for utilitarian reasons. States learned that they were all better off with non-governmental organizations functioning in technical areas.

The growth of cosmopolitanism among a wider group of educated citizens also made the formation and management of NGOs and NSAs possible in the second half of the nineteenth century. With the expansion of European states, particularly in Asia and Africa, more men and women than ever before possessed knowledge of cultures other than their own. International awareness came from first-hand experience overseas and, more often, from information circulated through the scholarly and public press. The emerging cosmopolitanism of the late nineteenth century encompassed the growth of basic skills necessary for NGOs and NSAs to operate: familiarity with foreign languages; understanding of foreign points of view; and, perhaps most importantly, recognition of issues that interested influential people across societies.[17]

The growth of cosmopolitanism was not a development exclusive to Europe. The experience of foreign contact for non-Europeans created a foundation for non-governmental endeavours across a truly global landscape. Already in the early nineteenth century non-European governments, like the Ottoman Sultanate, participated in inter-governmental organizations like the Superior Council on Health. By the middle of the century, however, the growing connections between Europeans and non-Europeans made it possible for citizens in different parts of the globe to come together in the pursuit of their chosen ends.

Higher education offers the best example of this cosmopolitanism in action. In place of the eighteenth century 'Grand Tour' – whereby wealthy European aristocrats paraded through the classical ruins of Greece, Rome and elsewhere to develop their credentials as members of a cultured elite – the mid nineteenth century witnessed the development of institutions for serious global study, with transnational student bodies. China, Japan and India – three societies with a very small European presence in prior centuries – became the sites for heavy investment in new educational institutions, including medical schools, military academies and universities. These institutions combined Western pedagogy with local support among native groups intent on modernizing their societies. Governments contributed to education but the schools, like the famous Yale-in-China academy, were overseen by individuals and organizations operating with little state regulation. (The same can be said for foreign companies operating in China, Japan, India and other societies at the time.)

In Europe and the United States preparations to sponsor new educational institutions overseas were matched with the beginnings of a foreign student presence in places like Oxford, Paris, Berlin and Boston. The foreign student population remained small until the twentieth century, but it comprised a group of mostly young men who served as conduits for new debates about social and political change. Chinese students who travelled to Europe, the United States and Japan, for example, played a crucial role in bringing ideas about democracy, liberal-capitalism and Marxism to their homeland. Operating as *de facto* NSAs, intellectuals like Liang Qichao and Li Dazhao established circles of informal study and political organization around themselves when they returned to China from periods of study abroad. Foreign study made non-governmental organization for reform, and even revolution, possible. Transnational revolutionary movements, especially communism, acted as NGOs bringing foreign ideas and organizational structures to countries like China.[18]

International education in the middle of the nineteenth century encouraged elite young men and women from both Western and non-Western countries to cooperate as they had never done before. This cooperation took many forms, from the formation of Red Cross chapters around the world to the spread of communist parties outside of Europe. International education made non-governmental communication and organization possible on a nearly global scale. It provided the prerequisite for what I will call the first golden age of NGOs and NSAs.

the first golden age of ngos and nsas

The years between 1880 and 1914 marked this first golden age of NGOs and NSAs. During this period their international presence grew exponentially, as their numbers increased from approximately five in 1850 to about 330 at the outbreak of the First World War.[19] They also became more global, extending their reach in ever-larger numbers to Asia, Latin America and Africa. Most significantly, NGOs and NSAs became prominent influences on government policies and public opinion. Observers began to speak of something called 'world opinion', reflecting the allegedly homogenizing influence of NGOs and NSAs on citizen perceptions around the globe.[20]

NGOs and NSAs benefited from the same trends that contributed to the growth of international business during this period. Improved transportation and communications technologies, including the railroad and the telegraph, made it possible for individuals to share information across great distances with unprecedented speed and safety. Activists in different societies could become better acquainted with one another, helping to form organizational cultures that allowed NGOs to function. Instead of relying on a small list of core principles, non-governmental groups could collaborate with more consistency over the details of their programmes. Members of NGOs could now feel 'close' to their distant colleagues.

The increased speed of communications was a particularly important contributor to NGO and NSA growth. Individuals residing in different countries could now coordinate their daily activities, update one another on immediate developments, and efficiently disseminate messages to a large public audience. Newspapers, drawing on telegraphed reports, were particularly valuable for publicity.[21] Better dissemination made NGOs and NSAs more effective at propagating their positions; better coordination allowed NGOs and NSAs to adjust them to the foreign policy agendas of the most powerful states.

International peace activists were the most successful failures of this period. The outbreak of the Great War in 1914 proved that they never managed to outlaw armed conflict, but their ideas had undermined many of the traditional assumptions about military force. During the second half of the nineteenth century, a growing cohort of prominent aristocrats and intellectuals from Europe and other continents assembled for nearly annual 'Universal Peace Congresses', designed to outline alternatives to war among states. In 1892 the International Peace Bureau (IPB) was founded by Peace Congress participants to coordinate various anti-war efforts in different countries. The IPB's offices in Berne, Switzerland, worked to disseminate proposals for disarmament and international cooperation. The IPB also organized various attempts to lobby government figures, including Tsar Nicholas II of Russia.[22]

The creation of the Nobel Foundation in 1900 and the award of the first annual Nobel Peace Prize in 1901 contributed considerable money and prestige to NGO peace efforts. Alfred Nobel, the Swedish engineer and chemist who invented dynamite, had amassed a personal fortune that allowed him to act as an NSA on behalf of international peace activism. On his death he endowed what would become the most coveted award in this field, often given to NGOs and their leaders. In 1901 Jean Henri Dunant (the founder of the Red Cross) and Frédéric Passy (the founder of the first French peace society) shared the Nobel Peace Prize. In 1902 Élie Ducommun and Charles Albert Gobat, both Secretaries-General of the IPB, received the award. This was an extraordinary case where an NSA authored a mechanism for enriching and empowering NGOs. The award of the Nobel Peace Prize became a widely publicized event, drawing the attention of citizens across the globe to international disarmament and humanitarian assistance efforts.[23]

NGO and NSA peace activism between 1880 and 1914 provided an internationalist counter-balance to the forces of nationalism and imperialism that also grew in strength during this period. Akira Iriye has pointed out that, if anything, heightened rivalries between states drove individuals from various parts of the world to push ever harder for cooperative alternatives. Scientists, lawyers, academics, doctors and others reached out to one another across societies. They participated in a proliferation of international congresses and associations designed to exchange knowledge and create a culture of mutual assistance, rather than competition. Most significantly, internationalists acting through the new webs of NGOs and NSAs created many avenues for permanent interaction among diverse peoples, which operated with consistency despite fluctuating rivalries among states. Iriye points to the international interactions of the late nineteenth century as a source of cultural internationalism that bridged geographic, ethnic, and linguistic barriers. A single international 'civilization' began to come into existence, including not only Europeans, but also citizens of the United States, Japan, India and other parts of Asia, Latin America and Africa.[24]

Scholars have been wary of using the term 'civilization' in recent years, for fear of the assumptions about Western superiority that are often attached to it. Iriye's extensive work on NGOs and NSAs, however, illustrates that the common understandings emerging in international society during the late nineteenth century reflected Western influence, but not complete domination. Japan, in particular, played an increasingly prominent role in the work of NGOs and NSAs engaged in peace advocacy, civilian assistance and knowledge sharing. Western concepts and prejudices (including racism) did indeed continue to exert disproportionate influence on the operations of international organizations through the second half of the twentieth century. Nonetheless, NGOs and NSAs offered a more open and democratic environment for non-European peoples than the traditional instruments of diplomacy.[25]

Similarly, groups often excluded from political representation also asserted their membership in a common international civilization through the use of NGOs and NSAs. The most enduring example of this phenomenon is the international women's movement that mobilized female social and political activists from at least four continents before the First World War. As mostly male professionals assembled in a proliferating number of international conferences, so too did women. In 1878 the first international women's congress – the Congrès International du Droit des Femmes – met in Paris. This conference gave rise to a regular series of women's assemblies and the formation of the International Council of Women (ICW) in 1888. The ICW became an umbrella organization for coordination among newly formed national non-governmental women's councils. In addition, it served as the initial foundation for a proliferation of NGOs that argued for peace, children's welfare and women's rights in the late nineteenth and early twentieth centuries. The NGOs formed soon after the creation of the ICW included the International Alliance of Women and the Women's International League for Peace and Freedom. Leila Rupp has shown that these NGOs constructed a new consciousness across societies that was both internationalist and feminist. The two reinforced one another, providing local women's activists with international legitimacy and women from distant countries with a common transnational bond. The internationalism of the women's movement in the early twentieth century also offered a basis for coalitions with other NGOs that contributed to a general shift in the common understandings of social justice within international society.[26]

If feminist NGOs made the personal political for international society, so more explicitly cultural NGOs elevated the significance of personal consumerism within it. The proliferation of 'World's Fairs' in the late nineteenth century showcased national industrial and intellectual accomplishments by appealing to a common embrace of 'progress' among the citizens of the world. International cooperation appeared to offer abundance, sophistication and prosperous living to the masses that attended the expositions in Paris, Chicago and other cities. Like the conferences among scholars and other professionals, the World's Fairs contributed to a sharing of reform ideas and the collaboration of activist organizations across societies. Nations were represented at the World's Fairs, but so were NGOs involved in peace activism, social justice and scientific exchange.[27]

The consumerist embrace of internationalism at the World's Fairs appealed to mass audiences with more leisure time and disposable income than in earlier decades. The growth of international sport is a prime example of how leisure and consumerism connected with the spread of NGOs and NSAs. Though generally under-studied by historians, athletic competition in the late nineteenth and early twentieth centuries contributed to the growth of international society through events and organizations free from direct state control. The revival in 1896 of the Ancient Greek Olympic ideal of peaceful sporting competition was at the centre of this development. The International Olympic Committee (IOC), established in Lausanne two years earlier, saw global athletics as an alternative to state-driven warfare. The IOC sought to include as many societies as possible, on an equal footing, in the games. While athletes were identified by their state of origin, national governments did not arbitrate the events. The leadership of the IOC was comprised of a cross-section of individuals who answered not to their countries but to international Olympic ideals. The IOC was an NGO that helped organize the spread of mass sporting competition in a way that appealed to an increasingly international, rather than a local or national, audience.[28]

Many scholars have pointed to the role mass sports played in the formation of national identities and the spread of nationalist agendas.[29] This is, no doubt, true. Government leaders, business executives and citizens frequently imbued athletic prowess with assertions of group superiority. Victory in a particular Olympic competition became a source of national pride. These assertions of nationalism, however, went hand-in-hand with a redoubled internationalism. NGOs like the IOC contributed to a proliferation of international sporting competitions that brought diverse peoples together in a peaceful and relatively egalitarian setting. NGOs contributed to broad and peaceful interaction among diverse citizens through the spectacle of shared sporting competition.

Just as internationalism and nationalism both accompanied the spread of mass sports, peace activism and war-making coexisted between 1880 and 1914. This was the first golden age for the growth and spread of NGOs and NSAs. It was also a period when their promise paled before the rising tensions between states. The very same forces that contributed to NGO and NSA growth – improved transportation and communications, industrialization, mass politics and a more global vision – also encouraged state leaders to militarize their politics.[30] Citizens grew more internationalist and nationalist at the same time, a point evidenced by the popularity of war among members of the Socialist International throughout Europe, and especially in Germany. The first golden age of NGOs and NSAs ended in the macabre trenches of the First World War, horrifying symbols of how states could now mobilize a seemingly endless supply of young men to die for king and country. Internationalist ideals seemed buried and forgotten at the Somme and Verdun.

the second golden age of ngos and nsas

Despite the horror and devastation of war, however, international society and the NGOs and NSAs that underpinned it managed to survive. The First World War was a total war in that it required the full mobilization of societies for more than four years. It also enveloped lands far from Europe, including India, China and eventually the United States. These characteristics of total war notwithstanding, the fighting did not choke off all NGO and NSA activity. Prominent peace advocates continued to travel and preach for a silencing of all guns. The International Red Cross performed yeoman's work as a respected and impartial source of aid for wounded combatants. Other NGOs, including the International Peace Bureau and the Women's International League for Peace and Freedom, continued to meet and lobby governments for an end to hostilities. In fact, the supporters of these NGOs grew in number as the senseless fighting continued on the battlefields.

At the end of the war, President Woodrow Wilson's rhetoric of international cooperation and his orphaned child, the League of Nations, ignited a desperate surge of activity among advocates of inter-governmental and non-governmental authority.[31] The 1920s and 1930s were not, as some assume, a period of naive idealism. Men and women who had witnessed the horror of the First World War understood the limits of international cooperation. Wilson, as John Milton Cooper has shown, was one of many realists who looked to international organizations as mechanisms not for replacing states, but instead for helping them to avoid self-defeating warfare. Wilson's League of Nations was an inter-governmental body designed to foster 'collective security'. Its creation inspired and legitimized a proliferation of NGOs and NSAs seeking the same end.[32]

Despite its rejection of the Versailles Treaty and the League of Nations, the United States took a leading role in the creation and support of NGOs and NSAs during the inter-war years. Common assumptions to the contrary, historians have concluded that this was not a period of American 'isolation'.[33] American businesses, philanthropic organizations, educational institutions and activists' groups became more international in their conceptualization and practice than ever before. The newly formed Social Science Research Council and the American Council of Learned Societies, for example, made international research a newly lucrative and prestigious part of scholarly work in the United States. Many of the future American scholars of Europe and other foreign areas would benefit from the internationalization sponsored by these NGOs.[34] The International Chamber of Commerce, formed in 1920, served as an important NGO for growing American businesses seeking new markets and partners abroad.[35] As Emily Rosenberg has shown, American international non-governmental expansion during the 1920s and 1930s served a broad coalition of economic and cultural interests in the United States.[36]

The expanded American presence in NGOs and NSAs during the inter-war years coincided with similar trends in Europe, as well as Asia and Latin America. Between 1914 and 1939 the number of international NGOs across the globe grew from about 330 to approximately 730.[37] While few of these organizations were officially recognized by the League of Nations, many of them collaborated with this and other inter-governmental bodies created in the aftermath of the Paris Peace Conference and subsequent disarmament meetings among the most heavily armed states.[38] Inter-governmental bodies frequently dealt with technical matters, including telegraph and telephone communications across state boundaries, shipping regulations and new rules for the commercial use of airspace. NGOs and NSAs shared knowledge and lobbied for enforcement of standards. In this sense, they became integral parts of a more complex, technically sophisticated and interdependent international system.

One must note that NGOs and NSAs did not escape the political controversies of the period. Their growing presence, in fact, made them attractive targets for state manipulation. Emily Rosenberg elucidates this point when she highlights the efforts of American leaders, particularly Secretary of Commerce and later President Herbert Hoover, to press NGOs into service as the chosen instruments of the White House. American financial advisers and philanthropists, according to Rosenberg, used their monetary and knowledge resources to restructure the economies of Latin American and Asian societies along lines that benefited exporters in the United States. Many of these 'financial missionaries' were officially independent from government and associated with NGOs committed to international assistance. Their policies, however, encouraged the kinds of market formation, resource extraction and private property protection that disempowered local citizens. Those who preached economic and social reform on behalf of NGOs and NSAs were sincere, but in many cases their assumptions were disproportionately beneficial to the United States. Herbert Hoover recognized this fact, and he encouraged the work of NGOs for this reason.[39]

Other states similarly manipulated NGOs and NSAs for their own purposes. The 1936 Olympics in Berlin offer a notorious instance of when fascists hijacked an idealistic enterprise. Adolf Hitler used the presence of the Olympics in his capital to showcase Nazi racial ideas and the alleged physical superiority of the Aryan race. The African-American track star Jesse Owens famously defied Hitler's aims by winning four gold medals, but his accomplishments paled in comparison with the public spectacle of Nazi salutes, fascist propaganda and open hostility to 'inferior' peoples. Despite the IOC's internationalist aims, Hitler made the Olympics a legitimizing enterprise for his racist and nationalist policies.

As the first golden age of NGOs and NSAs witnessed the dualistic development of internationalism and nationalism, the second golden age saw the frequent and self-conscious manipulation of NGOs and NSAs by state leaders. These organizations were now more pervasive than ever before. If the First World War discredited many of the traditional methods through which states forcefully pursued their interests, NGOs and NSAs offered a more acceptable means for practising *realpolitik*. This was certainly not the aim of many who joined NGOs and NSAs for sincere internationalist reasons, but states possessed formidable sources of leverage that proved difficult to resist. After all, territory in the international system remained the monopoly of states. NGOs and NSAs needed jurisdictional rights that only government leaders could grant. Money also flowed in state-denominated, and therefore state-controlled, currencies. As NGOs and NSAs grew in prominence they were, in fact, more vulnerable to indirect state controls.

The Great Depression of the 1930s also contributed to the vulnerability of international organizations. Like most other institutions, they now faced a scarcity of resources. At the same time, financially strapped states turned to NGOs and NSAs because they served important social and political goals without draining government coffers. Most significantly, the global privations of the Great Depression turned many citizens away from the ideals of internationalism. Local and national concerns dominated popular thinking by the middle of the 1930s. Public intolerance and a popular revolt against cosmopolitanism contributed to what many recognized as a backward lurch to world war. Once again, NGOs and NSAs failed to halt state-driven destruction. If anything, NGOs and NSAs were co-opted and subsumed by nationalist militarism.

ngos, nsas and the cold war

On 1 January 1942, only weeks after the United States formally entered the Second World War in Europe and Asia, 26 countries – including Great Britain, the Soviet Union and the US – signed the 'Declaration of the United Nations'. This was a broad pledge for inter-governmental cooperation in pursuit of 'complete victory' against Germany, Japan and Italy.[40] In August 1944, representatives from the US, Britain, the Soviet Union and China met in Washington, DC, at the Dumbarton Oaks mansion, to transform the United Nations into a permanent international body that would combine the cooperative institutions of the League of Nations with a more pragmatic awareness of the utility and limits of international force. Less than a year later, on 26 June 1945, 50 nations signed the official charter of the UN in San Francisco, creating the largest and most prominent body for global inter-governmental cooperation in human history.[41]

The UN gave NGOs and NSAs an unprecedented institutional home. In addition to the 50 nations represented at the San Francisco meeting in June 1945, there were also approximately 250 NGOs in attendance. These non-governmental groups established a close working relationship with the national delegations, particularly the US representatives, and they convinced the signatories of the UN Charter to give them an official role in the new international body. Article 71 of the Charter gave the Economic and Social Council of the United Nations authority to 'make suitable arrangements for consultation with non-governmental organizations'. Christy Jo Snider has explained that the US government favoured the entry of NGOs and NSAs into the UN architecture because it saw no real alternative. These groups had grown in number, influence and range during the inter-war years. Government leaders recognized that they could only legitimize the UN's universal claims and control the activities of NGOs and NSAs if the new body included more than just states. In addition, NGOs and NSAs offered vital resources for reconstruction after the devastation wrought by the Second World War. They helped to define social and economic challenges, they offered creative solutions, and they assisted with the implementation of policies. Through the UN, NGOs and NSAs provided useful services both to international society and to states.[42]

Emboldened by their new international standing, the number of NGOs and NSAs grew astronomically during the decades after the Second World War. Between 1939 and 1980 the number of international NGOs multiplied from approximately 730 to almost 6000.[43] The historical literature on this period, however, provides little evidence that the proliferation of NGOs and NSAs at first made much of a tangible difference to policy or everyday life. Contrary to the periods before and after the First World War, NGOs and NSAs were straight-jacketed after 1945 in a Cold War world that emphasized bipolarity, nationalism and state-centred power. Akira Iriye and Lawrence Wittner have described the energetic endeavours undertaken by non-governmental groups to transcend Cold War politics, but these international reform impulses amounted to very little at a time when the largest states mobilized vast resources to assure their dominance across regions. Even the UN was deadlocked by the animosities and Security Council vetoes of the United States and the Soviet Union.[44]

NGOs and NSAs became effective at influencing international change in the 1960s. This was their breakout decade in the Cold War. Public discontent with the stalemated strategic relationship between the United States and the Soviet Union led many citizens in the US, Europe, Latin America and Asia to turn to NGOs and NSAs in the search for new ideas and alternatives to Cold War institutions.[45] The rapid retreat of European empires in Africa and Asia also encouraged individuals, particularly intellectuals and activists, to leverage NGOs and NSAs for new cooperative connections across continents. Non-governmental groups interested in 'development' and 'modernization' proliferated during this period, including the Society for International Development (SID), originally founded in 1957. SID quickly evolved from being simply an international association of diverse professionals interested in development to function as an agenda-setter for economic assistance programmes across the globe. By the middle of the 1960s, SID had chapters on five continents, connecting prominent international thinkers with local activists.[46] Established NGOs and NSAs, like the Ford Foundation and Save the Children, also devoted extensive resources to developmental endeavors during this period.[47]

In the last decade, scholars have extensively criticized the developmental programs pursued during the latter decades of the Cold War. In particular, they have pointed to the mix of condescension, economic self-interest and narrow-mindedness that drove many well-intentioned figures to advocate destructive policies.[48] James Scott has condemned the 'high modernism' of international developmental programmes for repressing the wisdom and pragmatism of local knowledge.[49] NGOs and NSAs in this field surely fell prey to many of these shortcomings, but they also embraced a wider spectrum of social and economic points of view than the state-driven institutions, like the World Bank (officially the International Bank for Reconstruction and Development) and the United Nations Development Programme.[50] Akira Iriye has argued that less rigid programmes for global development did at least achieve an airing, if not overwhelming policy support, within NGOs and NSAs.[51] Harold Jacobson makes the case that while the outcomes of developmental efforts might have been mixed, international activism on behalf of this end gave claims of basic human equality across societies more legitimacy. After the early 1960s it became more difficult to justify policies that presumed the inferiority of foreign peoples.[52] In this sense, the expanded work of NGOs and NSAs made equality a common understanding in international society.

Common understandings of human rights also emerged from the work of NGOs and NSAs, beginning most vigorously after the 1960s. The upheavals of the period undermined the validity of Cold War arguments that justified domestic privations in the name of 'national security'. In every major society – capitalist and communist alike – citizens demanded more attention to the individual freedoms promised, but frequently not delivered, by ruling regimes. These internal pressures reached a violent crescendo with the 'global disruption' of 1968.[53] In the following years, the energies of domestic activists poured into NGOs and NSAs seeking to mobilize international opinion in defence of human rights. This was an attempt to use international society as a bulwark against national repression, particularly in the Soviet Union and Soviet-dominated Eastern Europe.

Founded in 1961, Amnesty International became the leading public exponent of human rights during this period, marshalling world-wide attention for the plight of dissidents and threatened groups. Amnesty International and other NGOs monitored the plight of suffering individuals and kept their stories alive in the international media. Government leaders like Richard Nixon and Leonid Brezhnev found that they could no longer avoid the issue of human rights in their policy-making endeavours. This became evident when Soviet and American negotiators reluctantly added human rights to their agenda, bowing to public pressure.[54]

Arguably the most successful NGOs of the Cold War era were the Helsinki Watch Groups and Charter 77, all of which were founded in the Soviet Union and Eastern Europe following the conclusion of the Conference on Security and Cooperation in Europe in 1975. The 35 states, including the United States and the Soviet Union, that signed the Helsinki Final Act at the end of the conference pledged to protect basic human rights within their societies. Almost immediately, dissidents in Soviet-dominated states formed the Helsinki Watch Groups and Charter 77 to expose the communist violations of this agreement. They not only embarrassed their regimes but also created pressures for foreign intervention and reprisal. Western 'hard-liners', affiliated with NGOs like the Council on Foreign Relations, the International Institute for Strategic Studies, and the Committee on the Present Danger, used the reports from these groups to justify an arms buildup, trade embargoes, and other measures that undermined Soviet security.[55]

Helsinki Watch Groups, Charter 77 and other human rights NGOs did not only create pressures for change in the communist world, they also offered avenues for reform. A number of scholars have pointed to the East–West associations and new ideas for cooperative politics that emerged through the efforts of scientists, disarmament activists and human rights advocates operating in the aftermath of the Helsinki conference. Common understandings about collective security, social market economies and technology transfer emerged from many of these endeavours to emphasize interdependence, rather than Cold War competition. These ideas filtered through to government leaders, particularly Soviet General Secretary Mikhail Gorbachev and his coterie of relatively young advisers, anxious to infuse their own society with some refreshing 'new thinking'. NGOs and NSAs did not single-handedly end the Cold War, but they offered a promising path to international reform that delegitimized many of the Cold War assumptions about capitalist–communist conflict. Human rights NGOs, in particular, constructed new common understandings among citizens and leaders across Cold War divides.[56]

beyond the cold war

The history of NGOs and NSAs after 1991 remains to be written. The end of the Cold War was a triumph for NGOs, NSAs and international society against the pressures of capitalist–communist division. New communications technologies, particularly the internet, contributed to a continued growth in the number of non-governmental entities. NGOs and NSAs also became more emboldened to challenge state governments, including that of the United States, on issues of social justice and political rights. Environmental NGOs, like Greenpeace (founded in 1971), became especially prominent in condemning the ecological damage inflicted by states, businesses and other 'traditional' international actors.[57]

The terrorist attacks of 9/11 showed, however, that NGOs and NSAs could also work with incredible effectiveness to deploy violence across the globe. Osama bin Laden and his Al-Qaeda network use the very same institutional and communicative tools that allow peaceful NGOs and NSAs to function. Terrorism and human rights activism are both parts of the non-governmental sector of international society in the twenty-first century. The contemporary 'war on terror' creates a cloud of uncertainty over whether NGOs and NSAs will in future be most salient for continued activities in parallel with state governments or for being permanently at war with them, as nations are threatened by international forces they cannot control. The future of NGOs and NSAs thus depends on the future of international society, on whether new common understandings can emerge there and on what those understandings might be.

notes

1. See, for example, Lawrence Wittner's magisterial history of anti-nuclear activism, *The Struggle Against the Bomb*, 3 vols (Stanford: Stanford University Press, 1993–2003).
2. The literature on NGOs generally excludes businesses and religious institutions from its coverage, an arbitrary move that reflects the idealistic and secular biases of scholars working in the field. The following analysis will be more inclusive, since this allows for a fuller understanding of NGOs' historical interaction with the other prominent features of the international system. One of the early seminal studies of international NGOs also encompassed both businesses and religious institutions: see Lyman Cromwell White, *International Non-Governmental Organizations: Their Purposes, Methods, and Accomplishments* (New Brunswick: Rutgers University Press, 1951).
3. Thomas L. Friedman, *The Lexus and the Olive Tree*, rev. edn (London: HarperCollins, 2000), esp. pp. 14–15.
4. For the most eloquent, thorough and scholarly articulation of this position, see Akira Iriye, *Global Community: The Role of International Organizations in*

the Making of the Contemporary World (Berkeley: University of California Press, 2002).

5. Peter L. Bergen, *Holy War, Inc.: Inside the Secret World of Osama bin Laden* (New York: Free Press, 2001).

6. Hedley Bull, *The Anarchical Society: A Study of Order in World Politics*, 2nd edn (New York: Columbia University Press, 1995), esp. pp. 3–50. The first edition of this classic text appeared in 1977.

7. For a classic and widely influential description of civil society, see Jürgen Habermas, *The Structural Transformation of the Public Sphere: An Inquiry into a Category of Bourgeois Society* (Cambridge, MA: MIT Press, 1989).

8. Adam Watson, 'European International Society and its Expansion', in Hedley Bull and Adam Watson (eds), *The Expansion of International Society* (Oxford: Clarendon, 1984), pp. 13–32.

9. Mary Ann Glendon, *A World Made New: Eleanor Roosevelt and the Universal Declaration of Human Rights* (New York: Random House, 2001).

10. Hedley Bull and Adam Watson, 'Introduction', in Bull and Watson, *Expansion of International Society*, pp. 1–9. See also John Boli and George Thomas (eds), *Constructing World Culture: International Nongovernmental Organizations since 1875* (Stanford: Stanford University Press, 1999).

11. Michael H. Hunt, *The Making of a Special Relationship: The United States and China to 1914* (New York: Columbia University Press, 1983); Eileen P. Scully, *Bargaining with the State from Afar: American Citizenship in Treaty Port China, 1844–1942* (New York: Columbia University Press, 2001).

12. Hedley Bull, 'The Emergence of a Universal International Society' and 'The Revolt Against the West', in Bull and Watson, *Expansion of International Society*, pp. 117–26 and 217–28 respectively.

13. Paul Schroeder, *The Transformation of European Politics, 1763–1848* (Oxford: Clarendon, 1994).

14. Iriye, *Global Community*, p. 11.

15. Paul Kennedy, *The Rise and Fall of British Naval Mastery,* rev. edn (London: Macmillan, 1983), esp. pp. 149–237 on the nineteenth century.

16. For further details on the history and activities of the International Committee of the Red Cross, see http://www.icrc.org (accessed 17 June 2004).

17. The evidence for increased understanding of foreign cultures during the mid nineteenth century does not mean that Europeans were free of prejudice. Edward Said has pointed to a set of condescending 'Orientalist' views that played a prominent role in European discourse about the non-Western world in the nineteenth and twentieth centuries. Although Said's analysis is persuasive, it only captures part of the story since 'Orientalism' did not preclude cultural understanding in many areas, nor were 'Orientalist' views embraced by all Europeans at the time: see Edward W. Said, *Orientalism* (New York: Pantheon, 1978). For an analysis of understandings among Western and non-Western elites, see David Cannadine, *Ornamentalism: How the British saw their Empire* (London: Allen Lane, 2001).

18. Maurice Meisner, *Li Ta-chao and the Origins of Chinese Marxism* (Cambridge, MA: Harvard University Press, 1967); Marilyn Levine, *The Found Generation: Chinese Communists in Europe during the Twenties* (Seattle: University of Washington Press, 1993).

19. Harold K. Jacobson, *Networks of Interdependence: International Organizations and the Global Political System*, 2nd edn (New York: Knopf, 1984), p. 10.

20. The best analysis of how people interpreted the concept of 'world opinion' is Frank Ninkovich, *Modernity and Power: A History of the Domino Theory in the Twentieth Century* (Chicago: University of Chicago Press, 1994).

21. This was a period when newspaper readership in major urban areas grew enormously: see, for example, Peter Fritzsche, *Reading Berlin, 1900* (Cambridge, MA: Harvard University Press, 1996).

22. The IPB has remained in existence through the twenty-first century. Its offices have moved from Berne to the home of many NGOs, Geneva. For further information, see http://www.ipb.org (accessed 17 June 2004).

23. The Nobel Foundation in Stockholm, Sweden, oversees the Nobel endowment and the various annual prizes. According to the terms of Alfred Nobel's will, a committee of Norwegians (assisted by the Norwegian Nobel Institute), awards the Nobel Peace Prize. For further details on the history of the Nobel Foundation, see http://www.nobel.se (accessed 17 June 2004), and on the Norwegian Nobel Institute, see http://www.nobel.no (accessed 17 June 2004).

24. Akira Iriye, *Cultural Internationalism and World Order* (Baltimore: Johns Hopkins University Press, 1997), pp. 13–50.

25. Iriye, *Cultural Internationalism*, pp. 36–49; Iriye, *Global Community*, p. 13.

26. Leila J. Rupp, *Worlds of Women: The Making of an International Women's Movement* (Princeton, NJ: Princeton University Press, 1997), pp. 13–48, 130–55; Leila J. Rupp, 'Constructing Internationalism: The Case of Transnational Women's Organizations, 1888–1945', *American Historical Review*, 99 (5) (1994) 1571–600. See also Estelle B. Freedman, *No Turning Back: The History of Feminism and the Future of Women* (New York: Ballantine, 2002).

27. Daniel T. Rodgers, *Atlantic Crossings: Social Politics in a Progressive Age* (Cambridge, MA: Harvard University Press, 1998); Alan Dawley, *Changing the World: American Progressives in War and Revolution* (Princeton, NJ: Princeton University Press, 2003); James T. Kloppenberg, *Uncertain Victory: Social Democracy and Progressivism in European and American Thought, 1870–1920* (New York: Oxford University Press, 1986).

28. For further information on the history of the IOC, see http://www.olympic.org. See also Barbara Keys, 'The Internationalization of Sport, 1890–1939', in Frank Ninkovich and Liping Bu (eds), *The Cultural Turn: Essays in the History of US Foreign Relations* (Chicago: Imprint, 2001), pp. 201–20; Iriye, *Global Community*, p. 16.

29. Eric Hobsbawm and Terence Ranger (eds), *The Invention of Tradition* (Cambridge: Cambridge University Press, 1983); Barbara Keys, 'Spreading Peace, Democracy, and Coca Cola®: Sport and American Cultural Expansion in the 1930s', *Diplomatic History*, 28 (2) (2004) 165–96.

30. See Paul Kennedy, *The Rise and Fall of the Great Powers: Economic Change and Military Conflict from 1500 to 2000* (New York: Random House, 1987), pp. 194–274.

31. On Woodrow Wilson's internationalist vision and its lasting influence, see Thomas J. Knock, *To End All Wars: Woodrow Wilson and the Quest for a New World Order* (New York: Oxford University Press, 1992).

32. John Milton Cooper Jr, *Breaking the Heart of the World: Woodrow Wilson and the Fight for the League of Nations* (New York: Cambridge University Press, 2001).

33. For seminal work on American internationalism during the inter-war years, see Emily Rosenberg, *Spreading the American Dream: American Economic and Cultural Expansion, 1890–1945* (New York: Hill and Wang, 1982); Frank Costigliola, *Awkward Dominion: American Political, Economic, and Cultural Relations with Europe, 1919–1933* (Ithaca: Cornell University Press, 1984); Melvyn P. Leffler, *The Elusive Quest: America's Pursuit of European Stability and French Security, 1919–1933* (Chapel Hill: University of North Carolina Press, 1979).

34. Akira Iriye, 'A Century of NGOs', *Diplomatic History*, 23 (3) (1999) 425. For further details on the activities of these organizations, see http://www.ssrc. org and http://www.acls.org respectively (accessed 17 June 2004).

35. White, *International Non-Governmental Organizations*, pp. 19–32.

36. Rosenberg, *Spreading the American Dream*.

37. Jacobson, *Networks of Interdependence*, p. 10.

38. Bill Seary, 'The Early History: From the Congress of Vienna to the San Francisco Conference', in Peter Willetts (ed.), *'The Conscience of the World': The Influence of Non-Governmental Organisations in the UN System* (London: Hurst, 1996), pp. 22–4.

39. Rosenberg, *Spreading the American Dream*; Emily Rosenberg, *Financial Missionaries to the World: The Politics and Culture of Dollar Diplomacy, 1900–1930* (Cambridge, MA: Harvard University Press, 1999).

40. For the text of the Declaration of the United Nations, 1 January 1942, see http://www.yale.edu/lawweb/avalon/decade/decade03.htm (accessed 17 June 2004).

41. For the text of the United Nations Charter and a short history of the organization, see http://www.un.org (accessed 17 June 2004); Evan Luard, *A History of the United Nations*, 2 vols (New York: St Martin's, 1982); Townsend Hoopes and Douglas Brinkley, *FDR and the Creation of the UN* (New Haven: Yale University Press, 1997).

42. Christy Jo Snider, 'The Influence of Transnational Peace Groups on US Foreign Policy Decision-Makers during the 1930s: Incorporating NGOs into the UN', *Diplomatic History*, 27 (3) (2003) 377–404.

43. Jacobson, *Networks of Interdependence*, p. 10.

44. Iriye, *Global Community*, pp. 37–95; Wittner, *The Struggle Against the Bomb*, vol. 1.

45. See Jeremi Suri, *Power and Protest: Global Revolution and the Rise of Détente* (Cambridge, MA: Harvard University Press, 2003), pp. 7–130.

46. For further details on the SID, see http://www.sidint.org (accessed 18 June 2004).

47. Iriye, *Global Community*, pp. 79–82.

48. See Nick Cullather, 'Miracles of Modernization: The Green Revolution and the Apotheosis of Technology', *Diplomatic History*, 28 (2) (2004) 227–54; David C. Engerman, Nils Gilman, Mark H. Haefele and Michael E. Latham (eds), *Staging Growth: Modernization, Development, and the Global Cold War* (Amherst: University of Massachusetts Press, 2003); Suri, *Power and Protest*, pp. 131–63.

49. James C. Scott, *Seeing Like a State: How Certain Schemes to Improve the Human Condition Have Failed* (New Haven: Yale University Press, 1998).
50. On inter-governmental approaches to development, especially through the UN, see Evan Luard, *International Agencies: The Emerging Framework of Interdependence* (London: Macmillan, 1977), pp. 240–63.
51. Iriye, *Global Community*, pp. 81–2.
52. Jacobson, *Networks of Interdependence*, pp. 310–63.
53. Suri, *Power and Protest*, pp. 164–212.
54. For further details on Amnesty, see http://www.amnesty.org (accessed 18 June 2004); Helena Cook, 'Amnesty International at the United Nations', in Willetts, *'The Conscience of the World'*, pp. 181–213.
55. See Daniel C. Thomas, *The Helsinki Effect: International Norms, Human Rights, and the Demise of Communism* (Princeton, NJ: Princeton University Press, 2001).
56. See Matthew Evangelista, *Unarmed Forces: The Transnational Movement to End the Cold War* (Ithaca: Cornell University Press, 1999); Richard Ned Lebow and Thomas Risse-Kappen (eds), *International Relations Theory and the End of the Cold War* (New York: Columbia University Press, 1995); Wittner, *The Struggle Against the Bomb*, vol. 3; Jeremi Suri, 'Explaining the End of the Cold War: A New Historical Consensus?', *Journal of Cold War Studies*, 4 (4) (2002) 60–92; Thomas Risse-Kappen (ed.), *Bringing Transnational Relations Back In: Non-State Actors, Domestic Structures, and International Institutions* (New York: Cambridge University Press, 1995).
57. For further details on Greenpeace, see http://www.greenpeace.org (accessed 18 June 2004).

9

the imperial and the postcolonial

mark philip bradley

'Words do not seem to convey the same meaning to Annamites and French', wrote the Vietnamese philosopher Tran Duc Thao in a 1946 essay on the eve of the outbreak of the French war to reclaim its colony in Indochina, 'and discussions usually end with accusations of bad faith'. Thao was referring less to the contemporary movement toward war than the larger perceptual disjuncture that divided French and Vietnamese apprehensions of the colonial encounter. For the French, he argued, Vietnam occupied a peripheral 'horizon of the imperial community'. But what was marginal for the French, Thao suggested, defined the centre for the Vietnamese:

> Vietnam as it would have been without colonialism is not for him a 'mere hypothesis,' but a project actually lived, the project even of his existence, that which defines even his existence as an Annamite. This world of possibilities forms the background on which appear perceived realities and which provide them with their meaning. Erupting into this world, colonialism's contribution reveals its negativity immediately.[1]

Like the divergent understandings of the French and Vietnamese that are the subject of Thao's phenomenological musings, there is a deep and sometimes seemingly unbridgeable schism in the writing of the history of the imperial and postcolonial worlds. On one side are historians of the metropole, whose work largely focuses on high diplomacy and great power politics to make sense of the Euro-American conquest of non-Western peoples and the rise and fall of empire as a central feature of the international system from the mid nineteenth to late twentieth centuries. Here the operative tools of analysis are European and American actors (and less frequently Russia and the Soviet Union, the Ottoman Turks and Japan), and the global and domestic dimensions of power and economics. At the same time, historians of the non-Western world take as their focus indigenous actors, exploring the imperial encounter, the rise of anti-colonialism and the coming of postcolonial independence. Operating in a largely cultural register, these works seek not only to accord agency to non-Western states and peoples but also to recover the complicated political, social and ideational interplay between colony and metropole in the making of the modern world.

One might initially assume a complementarity between these two kinds of history, with the possible result, in perhaps too optimistically Hegelian synthetic terms, being a more capacious historical narrative that brings the colonizers and the colonized into the same frame to illuminate the complex processes of imperialism and decolonization. As one reviewer wrote of the recent multi-volume *Oxford History of the British Empire*, 'It should be now ... a golden rule that imperial history is as much about subjects as about rulers.'[2] In recent years, some historians have indeed begun to bring these dual concerns into productive interplay. And yet in many ways the two approaches to imperialism and postcolonialism remain in a state of fundamental tension, if not outright hostility, over questions of method and interpretative approach. Walking the borders between them is therefore still a central challenge for international historians.

A chapter of this kind cannot pretend to present a comprehensive narrative of the immense and varied historiography of imperialism and postcolonialism; nor can it consider the full geographical sweep of the imperial project throughout the globe. Rather it focuses on a narrower range of exemplary works that illuminate critical, if often competing, historical efforts to uncover Euro-American and non-Western apprehensions of the imperial and postcolonial moments. It concludes with a discussion of more recent studies that mark a nascent interpretative effort to transcend existing accounts of the imperial and postcolonial worlds and which contain the potential for recasting our understanding of the place of the imperial in the international history of the nineteenth and twentieth centuries.

empire and the great powers

It is fair to say without too much exaggeration that the focus of imperial studies for most of the last 100 years has been on the perceptions and policies of the Euro-American powers and the ways in which state power politics and the global economy animated the nature of the new imperialism after 1870. This dauntingly vast and rich literature resists easy summary. To capture a sense of its possibilities and its limits, I foreground a consideration of critical debates over causality and a sense of their historiographical manifestations in the study of American empire, the 'scramble for Africa' and the nature of decolonization from the perspective of imperial powers.

Between 1870 and 1914, most of the world outside Europe and the Americas came under the informal or formal imperial rule of Britain, France, Germany, Italy, the Netherlands, Belgium, the United States and Japan. As Eric Hobsbawn notes in his *Age of Empire*, 'one-quarter of the globe's land surface was distributed or redistributed as colonies among a half-dozen states' with Africa and the Asia-Pacific region almost 'entirely divided up' among the imperial powers.[3] Much of the vigorous scholarly debate on the new imperialism of the nineteenth and twentieth centuries has been preoccupied with identifying and explaining its causes. The literature on European and American imperialism has tended to focus on the rival merits of economic and political theories of causality. For proponents of economics, the expansion of global industrial capitalism that sought to open and control overseas markets best explains the rise of imperialism. The Industrial Revolution in Europe, they argue, stimulated the emergence of the imperial system and the integration of colonial markets into the world economy in a manner that facilitated the export of colonial wealth and resources to the industrial metropole and tended to hinder the development of industrial capitalism in the colonial periphery. Scholars who favour explanations for the new imperialism centring on state power politics concentrate rather on the decisions of metropolitan political leaders and great power rivalries in the international system, as well as growing instability on the borders of the European empires in Asia and Africa.[4]

The main lines of these debates first emerged at the very height of the new imperial moment with publication of J. A. Hobson's *Imperialism* in 1902, which had a profound impact on subsequent discussions of the rise and meaning of imperialism. Hobson saw the central issue as a problem of what to do with the economic surplus generated by global capitalism. Domestic markets, Hobson argued, were increasingly unable to consume their own manufacturing output and their capital surplus. The perception that underconsumption and the absence of industrial opportunities posed a serious threat to continuing economic growth at home prompted states and firms to turn to overseas markets. Euro-American states, Hobson argued, sought colonies to which their own national companies would have exclusive or privileged access and which would provide a safe and productive haven for their export capital. Hobson, a strong liberal critic of imperialism, argued that the costs of colonial wars and of the administration necessary for the operation of the imperial order ultimately prevented the implementation of necessary social welfare projects at home.[5] Hobson's critique deeply influenced Lenin's more radical *Imperialism, the Highest Stage of Capitalism* (first published in 1916), which also stressed the global ubiquity of finance capitalism and its competitive export to underdeveloped colonial territories, though for Lenin the inevitable future failure of the imperial system would mean the desirable self-destruction of capitalism and the ultimate rise of socialist modes of production.[6]

Economic explanations for the rise and nature of imperialism persisted in the period of decolonization after the Second World War, most notably in the form of dependency and world-systems theories. Most closely associated with Andre Gunder Frank and work in Latin American studies, dependency theory saw underdevelopment in the non-Western world as the outcome of an imperial capitalist structure and as central to its continued development. For dependency theorists, imperialism was structured hierarchically with a metropolitan Euro-American core and a number of satellite non-Western peripheries that provided raw materials, cheap labour and potential markets for products produced in the core. Critical to this system, dependency theorists argued, was the presence of a willing collaborative elite in the periphery who accepted their own exploitation from the centre in return for a limited portion of the economic surplus otherwise transferred to the West and the military, political and economic support the core provided to maintain their power. In world-systems theory, pioneered by Immanuel Wallerstein, the notion of a developed core and underdeveloped periphery remained central. But Wallerstein introduced a third conceptual category of the semi-periphery and a metahistorical frame that placed the origins of the new imperialism in the emergence of Portuguese and Spanish mercantile capitalism in the fifteenth century. The industrial and finance capitalism that underlay Euro-American imperialism after 1870, Wallerstein contended, was yet another manifestation of a broader imperial system of unequal power and wealth.[7]

The nature of the internecine debates between and among proponents of Hobsonian, Marxist, dependency and world-systems approaches to imperialism, and what sometimes seemed to be their endlessly elaborated articulations, need not concern us. But they did influence the historiography of the new imperialism, prompting both approbation and sharp critique from historians working in the field. The influence of Hobson has been especially important for one critical strand of the historiography on the origins of American imperialism. Walter LaFeber's *The New Empire* and William Appleman Williams' *The Roots of the Modern American Empire*, key works emerging from the American New Left in the 1960s, stressed the significance of the search for new markets in the emergence of the United States as an imperial power in the late nineteenth century.[8] For some historians of British colonialism, however, these economic arguments have been less persuasive. David K. Fieldhouse's 1973 work *Economics and Empire* drew on sustained statistical evidence to refute claims for the necessity of overseas investment and trade as essential to the survival of capitalism and the rise of imperial order. He suggested that the metropole's trade with its own colonies was relatively insignificant and that there was no direct correlation between overseas investment possibilities and territorial expansion. Although Fieldhouse acknowledged that economic factors were a part of the imperial project, he argued that they were not a sufficient or complete explanation for its emergence and development.[9] From a quite different perspective, Niall Ferguson's recent contribution to the debate has made a case for the economic successes of British empire, while at the same time insisting that those domestic economic benefits did not necessarily lead to the ultimate impoverishment of British and other colonial territories.[10]

For many historians of Euro-American imperialism, economic explanations for its rise and nature are far less compelling than those that focus on international politics and state power. These works, their generalized conception of the balance of power and *realpolitik* notwithstanding, are considerably less theoretically driven than most economic accounts of imperialism. Analyses that privilege state and global power politics in the study of the late-nineteenth-century 'scramble for Africa' aptly illustrate this approach and its methods. Focusing on the relationship between imperialism and tensions and strains in European balance of power politics before the First World War, the power politics argument is most closely associated with classic works such as William L. Langer's *The Diplomacy of Imperialism* (1935), A. J. P. Taylor's *Germany's First Bid for Colonies* (1938) and the early writings of David Fieldhouse. As Fieldhouse argued in 1961, the new imperialism in Africa was 'the extension into the periphery of the political struggle in Europe. At the centre the balance was so nicely adjusted that no major change in the status or territory of any side was possible. Colonies became a means out of this impasse.' Similarly, Taylor contended German colonies in Africa were the almost unintended by-product of Bismarck's wish to build an entente with France against Britain to protect German security at home.[11]

In their seminal 1961 work *Africa and the Victorians*, Ronald Robinson and John Gallagher shifted the focus of great power concerns from Europe to Africa, and specifically to anxieties about how burgeoning Egyptian and South African nationalism might jeopardize wider imperial interests there. European state rivalries, they argued, prompted an escalating series of annexations of African territory by Britain and France (and eventually Germany, Belgium and Italy) in an effort to deny each other colonial possessions. In this sense Africa provided the great powers with an arena for working out rivalries that had little to do with Africa itself, but which were nonetheless stimulated by fears of the potential geopolitical implications of events on that continent.[12] If these political and state-based interests have dominated historical interpretations of the scramble, intriguingly Hobson's interpretation of the broader economic processes of imperialism has re-emerged in recent work by P. J. Cain and A. G. Hopkins, which views the partition of Africa in terms of 'gentlemanly capitalism'. In their *British Imperialism: Innovation and Expansion*, Cain and Hopkins argue that the British occupation of Egypt and South Africa was less the product of the strategic imperatives posited by Robinson and Gallagher than of concerns with public finance, British investment and the role of gold in the value of the pound.[13]

Much of the literature on decolonization from the perspective of the metropole also takes state political interests and the workings of the international system as its starting point. One important manifestation of this approach is the historiography on decolonization in the British case, where accounts of state politics and radical shifts in power, wealth and legitimacy at the international level have been central to narratives of the end of empire. In his *European Decolonization*, R. F. Holland argued that in Britain, and in Europe more generally, the emergence of social democracy, a high consumption society and the new strategic threat from the Soviet Union eroded the will to sustain empire. John Darwin's *Britain and Decolonisation: The Retreat from Empire in the Post-War World* looked more fully at the international level to suggest that British efforts directed at preserving its empire were undermined by the greater power of the United States and the Soviet Union. But if geopolitical necessity prompted Great Britain to retreat from formal imperial control, Darwin argued, the British were not necessarily willing to detach themselves altogether from the bonds of empire, with the British Commonwealth coming to serve what he terms an imperialism of informal influence. Nicholas Tarling's *Britain, Southeast Asia and the Korean War* has more recently portrayed a Britain similarly keen on using what it hoped was the salutary model of its efforts to manage the decolonization process, and a variety of special relationships with the United States, India and the Commonwealth, to maintain British interests in Southeast Asia in the postcolonial period. The efforts detailed by Darwin and Tarling were, however, not always successful, particularly given the strains in Anglo-American relations in the early Cold War period, as Wm. Roger Louis suggested in his *British Empire in the Middle East, 1945 – 1951*.[14] Interpretations based on economic factors have played a muted role in this literature. In fact, David Fieldhouse's *Merchant Capital and Economic Decolonization* and Nicholas White's *Business, Government, and the End of Empire* conclude from consideration of the African and Malay cases that British officials had an almost complete disregard for the commercial interests of expatriate business.[15]

The focus on Europe and America in these diverse works and the prevalence of analyses that concentrate on global economic forces and great power politics in the international system clearly illuminate key dimensions of the imperial order. But these approaches both largely ignored the other side of the colonial equation – that of the colonized – and also failed to attend sufficiently to the ways in which socio-cultural forces may have shaped imperialism at home and abroad. A partial nod to the significance of the ruled was made through the notion of 'informal empire', initially introduced in Robinson and Gallagher's 1953 essay 'The Imperialism of Free Trade' and later further elaborated by Robinson and a number of other scholars, in which native collaborating elites become more fully developed actors in the rise and fall of the new imperialism.[16] Yet even in this work the conceptual focus remained on the ways in which the agency of elite collaborators served the concerns of the metropole. When a more fundamental shift in perspective did come it would do so from scholars working outside a Euro-American framework. These alternative formulations of the nature and operation of the new imperialism would not be enthusiastically (or at times graciously) received by many of the leading practitioners of geopolitical and economic approaches to imperial order.

the colonial and postcolonial turn

The appearance of Edward Said's *Orientalism* in 1978 and the simultaneous emergence of Subaltern Studies marked a seminal break in the study of empire, shifting the terrain of the field and stimulating innovative efforts to explore the colonial and postcolonial worlds from the perspectives of the colonized.[17] Said's influential if controversial work argued that European imperial powers deployed supposed essentialist differences between an immutable Orient and a dynamic West as tools to reinforce European political and cultural mastery. Orientalism, Said claimed, provided a stable, durable and authoritative vocabulary through which European colonial officials, abetted by scholars and writers, rendered the Oriental backward, degenerate and inferior and thus offered up the Orient as a locale that required Western attention and reconstruction. For Said, whose work emphasized literary and political texts and borrowed from Foucaultian notions of power and 'governmentality', cultural production simultaneously reflected and shaped manifestations of imperial power and control. In a subsequent work, *Culture and Imperialism* (1993), Said turned his attention to the interstices between ruler and subject, analysing the ways in which the imperial project profoundly shaped lives in the metropole and at the same time was transformed by colonized intellectuals in their efforts to articulate languages of liberation.[18]

Along with Said, the emergence of Subaltern Studies in South Asian historiography aimed at retrieving the lived experience of colonized subalterns, those its proponents argued were subordinated on account of class, caste, gender, race, language and culture by both indigenous elites and Western imperialism. A collective project in spirit and organization, its overarching concerns were shaped by the work of Ranajit Guha. In influential essays such as 'The Prose of Counter-Insurgency' and books including *Elementary Aspects of Peasant Insurgency in Colonial India*, Guha argued that existing accounts of popular colonial insurgency written by imperial officials and nationalist elites ignored and elided the agency and subjectivity of the subaltern insurgent. In the absence of writings by subalterns themselves, Guha sought to recover the peasant world – its myths, cults, ideologies and bonds of community, which were often at odds with dominant notions of nation and class – by reading colonial records and existing historiographical representations of subaltern experiences against the grain.[19] Like Said, subaltern historians drew upon Foucault and other structuralist and poststructuralist writers like Saussure, Lévi-Strauss and Barthes to inform their often textually-based studies. Along with their focus on the lived experience of subaltern peoples, South Asian historians such as Partha Chatterjee, Shahid Amin and Gyan Prakash working in this mode have directed attention to the ways in which colonial officials and indigenous elites sought to silence subaltern voices and the political work such silences could do for the project of colonialism and elite nationalism. For example, Amin's *Event, Metaphor, Memory*, which explored the outbreak of peasant violence in 1922 that led Gandhi to suspend the non-cooperation campaign against British rule, demonstrated the ways in which the event was first criminalized in colonial juridical discourse and later nationalized by elite nationalists, initially through amnesia and later by selective memory and reappropriation.[20]

Together the work of Said and Subaltern Studies opened up a new realm of scholarship on the colonial experience, attentive to issues of language and culture along with a focus on the overlapping and intertwined relationship between the colonial and colonized worlds. Renewed attention to the study of translation in an effort to more carefully unpack the nuances of the colonial encounter has been one critical avenue of study. Two central works in this vein are Vicente L. Rafael's *Contracting Colonialism*, a study of Christian conversion in the Spanish Philippines, and Lydia Liu's *Translingual Practice*, an examination of what she terms 'translated modernity' in China. Rafael argued that conversion required translation of Christian texts into native languages, a process which set the limits and possibilities of the Spanish imperial conversion project itself. In a close reading of Tagalog texts, one both historically grounded and theoretically informed by poststructuralist critics such as Barthes and Derrida, Rafael focused on the transfer of meaning and intention between the colonizer and colonized. He argued that translation not only revealed Spanish ideas about the representation of power but also, in the vernacularization of conversion in Tagalog culture, a sense of alternative indigenous responses to Spanish rule and authority.

If Rafael was concerned with translation as a project forced upon a local population by a colonial power, Liu's study of modernity in China sought to move beyond interpretations of the Chinese encounter with the West in the early twentieth century in which the Chinese had been rendered as passive recipients of novel Western political and cultural terms. Liu suggested that modernist meanings and modes of representation about the individual and the nation, which often entered Chinese through a Japanese as well as a Western idiom in multiple processes of translational circulation, are best viewed as constituting a 'guest' language which was sometimes usurped, and at other times transformed, in what became a Chinese discourse of modernity. More recently in her edited volume *Tokens of Exchange*, Liu has explored the ways in which these translingual practices shaped the articulation and legitimation of new approaches to international law in nineteenth-century China.[21]

Along with a concentration on language, important work in anthropology and literary studies has looked at the complexities of hegemonic colonial projects that drew the colonized into and under subtle forms of imperial domination. Jean and John Comaroff's *Of Revelation and Revolution: Christianity, Colonialism, and Consciousness in South Africa*, a study of the encounter between British missionaries and the Southern Tswana peoples of the South African frontier, explored the ways in which new relations between individuals, the circulation of commodities, and the colonial labour market began to govern the quotidian rhythms of both Tswana and missionary life. Gauri Viswanathan's *Masks of Conquest: Literary Study and British Rule in India* demonstrated how imperial projects of education, even when appropriated by colonial subjects, enmeshed them in a constellation of beliefs that signaled the superiority of the West.[22]

Perhaps the most far-reaching effort to rethink the terms of the imperial encounter along cultural lines is Dipesh Chakrabarty's *Provincializing Europe*. Chakrabarty calls for removing Europe from the centre of historical study and instead viewing it, and the imperial project that was central to European experience, as coeval and deeply intertwined with the colonized world. Importantly, Chakrabarty specifically rejects efforts to dismiss altogether notions of modernity, liberal values, science, reason and grand narrative. Rather, he argues, 'European thought is at once both indispensable and inadequate in helping us to think through the experiences of political modernity, and provincializing Europe becomes the task of exploring how this thought – which is now everybody's heritage and which affects us all – may be renewed from and for the margins.' In this task, Chakrabarty draws on Marx in an effort to demystify secular ideologies present in both Western and Indian thought, and on Heiddeger to uncover what he calls the diversity of life-worlds in which humanism and 'the world of gods and spirits' are simultaneously present and shape modernity in the colonial and colonized worlds.[23]

The cultural and linguistic turns clearly inform these approaches to the imperial encounter that have become increasingly dominant in efforts to recover non-Western experiences of colonial rule and its aftermath; those turns have also had considerable further impact in broadening the subject and scope of what we consider to be the history of imperialism. In part the cultural approach has prompted an imaginative re-examination of the tools and purposes of imperial policy. Paul Rabinow's *French Modern* considered the ways in which French colonies, whose inhabitants were often equated with destitute populations in the metropole, consciously served as laboratories for social reform at home. Gwendolyn Wright's *The Politics of Design in French Colonial Urbanism* and Timothy Mitchell's *Colonizing Egypt* reflected a similar approach in their consideration of architecture and urban planning in French Indochina and

Morocco and British Egypt. Deeply influenced by Saidian analysis, Thomas R. Metcalf's *An Imperial Vision: Indian Architecture and Britain's Raj* argued that 'the choice of architectural style, the arrangement of space within a building, and the decision to erect a particular structure all testified...to a vision of empire' that reinforced colonial dominance and superiority. Increased scrutiny of colonial social policy was also shaped by emphases on the intersection of culture and power. For instance, David Arnold's *Colonizing the Body*, a study of state medicine and epidemic disease in British India, explored the ways in which colonial health policy worked to maintain imperial authority rather than serving the welfare of colonial subjects.[24]

Other scholars have focused on the interpenetration of the socio-cultural dimensions of empire at home and in the colonies. Anne McClintock's *Imperial Leather* made clear the racial, gendered and class dimensions of Victorian imperial politics, issues previously ignored in the writing of the history of British and other national imperialisms. In similar ways, Robert Rydell's *All the World's a Fair* and P. A. Morton's *Hybrid Modernities* explored the racialized cultural politics of colonial exhibitions and fairs in the United States and France. Antoinette Burton's *At the Heart of the Empire* and Ann Laura Stoler's *Race and the Education of Desire* emphasized the continuing invention of gendered and racial categories of difference and their role in effecting imperial domination. In his *Imperial Encounters*, a study of religion and modernity in India and Britain, Peter van der Veer argued that the colonial encounter mutually constituted the articulation of both the religious and secular spheres, and their blurring, in Britain and India. Kristin Hoganson's *Fighting for American Manhood: How Gender Politics Provoked the Spanish-American and Philippine-American Wars*, Mary A. Renda's *Taking Haiti: Military Occupation and the Culture of US Imperialism, 1915 – 1940* and Laura Briggs', *Reproducing Empire: Race, Sex, Science, and US Imperialism in Puerto Rico,* along with several important collections of essays – including Amy Kaplan and Donald E. Pease's *Cultures of United States Imperialism,* Julian Go and Anne L. Foster's *The American Colonial State in the Philippines* and Gilbert M. Joseph *et al.*'s *Close Encounters of Empire: Writing the Cultural History of US-Latin American Relations* – illustrate the range and depth of this culturally inflected work for the study of American imperialism.[25]

Scholarship in the relatively new field of what might be termed diasporas of empire can also trace its genealogies to the cultural turn in imperial studies. This work transcends the national boundaries of most of the existing work in the field, analysing the experiences of peoples displaced, sometimes by choice, other times by force, as a result of imperial rule. Of particular importance is the rise of work on the African diaspora, marked by the appearance of Paul Gilroy's *The Black Atlantic* in 1993. In its wake, an outpouring of studies have considered the historical construction of African diasporic identity, the contributions of black migrant and colonial intellectuals to rethinking the modern West, and the ways in which migration, culture, communications and global capital have continually reinvented a sense of Africa and its diaspora.[26] Asian diasporic communities, again shaped by the imperial experience, have also received recent scholarly attention. Ji-Yeon Yuh's *Beyond the Shadow of Camptown* draws on sustained oral histories and contextualizes the lives of Korean military brides in the United States within the experiences of Japanese and American colonialism in Korea and the legacies of military prostitution. Sandhya Shukla's *India Abroad* traces the development of Indian communities in England and the United States from Indian independence in 1947 to the present, through an examination of the creation of diasporic newspapers, literature, film, fashion and entrepreneurial enclaves. In these works and others like them, imperialism serves as a critical motor that ultimately provokes a transnational recasting of race, ethnicity, economic and cultural production and politics in the diaspora.[27]

Approaches to imperialism by Said, the Subaltern group, and those influenced by it are not without their critics. Scholars more sympathetic to the larger aims of the cultural turn have offered cautionary and often trenchant critiques. For some, culture too frequently simply supplants power and economics as an independent explanatory variable. Without rejecting the salience of culture, these critics question how studies of the cultural construction of empire can reduce the roots of expansionism to a single cause or account for the multidimensional political, economic, social and cultural nature of the imperial and postcolonial experience. Others are uncomfortable with the binaries of ruler and subject central to much of the cultural approach, arguing that they prove too limiting to allow for the full analysis of the complexities that informed quite varying structures of colonial rule and that they ignore the often very real limitations on imperial power in practice.[28]

Among historians of great power imperialism, however, cultural approaches, and their attention to historicizing the nature of imperialism from the perspective of the colonized, have too often been greeted with outright hostility and ultimately a kind of disdainful dismissal. As one leading scholar of British imperialism recently argued, the problem of rendering the colonized historiographically visible 'is not to be solved by dubious means of "representing" the "voiceless", still less by the vacuous sentimentalism of much "post-modernist" writing, whose intellectual rigour and use of evidence would hardly satisfy an early modern astrologer'.[29] Others, like Niall Ferguson in his oddly celebratory *Empire*, see little value in the study of the colonized at all and instead reinscribe past claims for empire as a largely progressive force in human history. With almost no reference to the lived experience of empire in the colonies, Ferguson argues that the British Empire 'undeniably pioneered free trade, free capital movements and, with the abolition of slavery, free labour. It invested immense sums in developing a global network of modern communication. It spread and enforced the rule of law over vast areas ... [and] maintained a global peace unmatched before or since.'[30]

crossing borders

The way forward in studies of empire and postcolonialism lies not with such inexplicably wrong-headed, and often aggressively defensive, claims. A more promising approach – one that thoughtfully addresses the more measured critiques of cultural studies of imperialism – examines the interpenetration of the global, the national and the local for subjects and rulers in the political, economic, social and cultural construction of the imperial world. Tellingly, while this new work does not ignore the high diplomacy of the great powers, it often takes as its point of departure what is usually considered the periphery of Euro-American empire.[31] Perhaps the most important of these works is Louise Young's *Japan's Total Empire*, a study of Japanese imperialism in Manchuria whose analytical framework offers a salutary model for future work in the field.

For Young, the existing historiography on Japanese empire, like that of empire studies more broadly, has been too focused on top-down analyses of the agency of the state in the political, economic and cultural realms. 'It took more than ministers and generals,' she argues, 'to make empire.' And yet she suggests that the 'millions of people' who were involved in its construction through such organizations as chambers of commerce, political parties, business groups and labour unions are virtually absent in the existing scholarly literature. At the same time, Young argues, the political, economic and cultural dimensions of empire, in terms of both state and society, were far from autonomous spheres:

In an age of unified markets, globalized mass communications, and the exposure of the individual to multiple systems of meaning, it is impossible to look at the economic without considering the political, to study the cultural without thinking about the social, to discuss the national without reference to the international. Therefore we need to look at the ways in which economics, politics, culture and society work together as a unit and the ways in which national systems are integrated into international systems.

In crafting her narrative and analysis of Japanese empire in Manchuria, Young does not ignore more traditional approaches to the international context of imperial order. Indeed she roots her exploration of Japanese expansion in the 1930s in northeast China in a 'complex geometry of imperialism' marked by great power rivalry in which Japanese empire builders acted and reacted within a shifting global political and economic system. After carefully articulating this critical international frame, she turns to the place of Japanese state and society in the domestic processes of mobilization for the military, economic and migratory components of the imperial project in Manchuria. Her examination of the forces shaping the new Japanese military imperialism of the 1930s concentrates on the growth of domestic institutions of mass culture and politics. Young's approach to the economic methods of imperial expansion highlights the roles of middle-class business and intellectual elites. Finally, her analysis of the growth of Japanese colonization in Manchuria rests on the interplay of state experiments with social management and popular national social movements aimed at resolving the social crisis industrial capitalism produced in rural Japan. In the end, Young produces a sweeping and supple work with profound implications for the study of the new imperialism in a variety of national contexts.

Young's approach to, and methodology for studying, Japanese imperialism rests on a concept of 'total empire'. She argues:

> total empire was made on the home front. It entailed the mass and multidimensional mobilization of domestic society: cultural, military, political, and economic. The multidimensionality of total empire relates to the question of causality as well. Manchukuo emerged from multiple, overlapping, and mutually reinforcing causes; it was an empire propelled by economic forces as well as strategic imperatives, by political processes and cultural determinants, by domestic social forces as well as international pressures. In themselves, none of these variables explains or determines imperialism; rather their synergy or concatenation is what gave total imperialism its peculiar force.

In employing the conceptual framework of total empire, Young does not suggest that all formal colonies or informal spheres of influence within the new imperialism were analogous to the Japanese case. And yet her focus on the interpenetration of multiple top-down and bottom-up forces in Japanese state and society to explain the rise of Japanese empire in Manchuria suggestively proposes a model for rethinking the new imperialism, one that transcends many of the conceptual rigidities that have characterized previous scholarship that was more narrowly focused on the political, economic or cultural dimensions of Euro-American imperialism.[32]

In its largest sense, Young's study of Japanese empire also seeks to reveal the relationship between forces of modernity – and their complex political, economic and socio-cultural manifestations in Japan – and the transnational processes of imperialism. This concern with modernity as a way of approaching the place of the global and the local in the making of the imperial and postcolonial worlds also informs my work on the encounter between Vietnamese revolutionaries and the United States during the period of the consolidation and decline of French empire in Indochina. In *Imagining Vietnam and America*, I argue Vietnamese and American perceptions of one another and their imaginings of Vietnam's postcolonial future drew on a shared vocabulary mediated through external sources and then reproduced and transformed in a variety of Vietnamese and American idioms. The perceptions of the United States and articulations of postcolonial Vietnam by Vietnamese revolutionaries were shaped by modernist currents of thought that entered Vietnam through the works of reformers and radicals in China and Japan and through the experiences of French colonial rule. The ensemble of assumptions through which Americans apprehended the Vietnamese, initially posed in social Darwinian, neo-Lamarckian or Orientalist terms and later through modernization theory, were a part of the culturally hierarchical discourse that infused the theory and practice of Western imperialism. In the mutually constitutive processes that shaped the making of both Vietnamese and American visions of postcolonial Vietnam, these transnationally circulating languages of modernism and imperialism were susceptible at different points to appropriation, usurpation and transformation. I draw on this analysis to locate the relationship between Vietnam and the United States in the global discourses of colonialism, race, modernism and postcolonial state-making that at once were profoundly implicated in, and for the Vietnamese ultimately transcended, the dynamics of imperial order.[33]

Among the most suggestive of the new works on the fall of empire, the nature of the postcolonial moment, and the place of the transnational in it, is Matthew Connelly's *A Diplomatic Revolution* which examines the Algerian struggle for independence from France. Like Young, Connelly approaches his subject from multiple perspectives, assessing the perceptions and policies of France and the great powers as well as those of the Algerian Front de Libération Nationale. His attention to the domestic and international dimensions of political, economic and socio-cultural fragmentation and integration in the Algerian conflict also closely parallels key aspects of Young's notion of total empire, albeit that his empire is one in decline. But Connelly goes further to suggest that the processes of decolonization were made up of novel transnational forces – among them population growth, environmental scarcities, international institutions, new media and the conscious agency of colonized peoples seeking to promote radical systemic change – that severely weakened imperial order and gave shape to the postcolonial world. The Algerian war for independence, Connelly argues, 'affords a privileged perspective on the wider processes of decolonization' in which states and peoples were both shaped by these novel transnational forces and employed them to construct their own postcolonial futures.[34]

In part what unites these works, and contributes to their interpretative novelty, is a facility with languages beyond English, French and German, as well as a primary source base that draws as fully on non-Western texts as those from the West and which both looks to and beyond the archives of the state. Ultimately, however, their significance lies in a willingness to reconsider, to reformulate and to begin to transcend our existing apprehensions of imperial worlds and their aftermath. Taken together, they constitute an approach to the history and historiography of the imperial and the postcolonial that promises to bridge not only the conceptual chasms that have divided historians of the new imperialism, but also the perceptual disjunctures articulated by Tran Duc Thao that separated the lived experiences of the colonizers and the colonized.

notes

1. Tran Duc Thao, 'Sur l'Indochine', *Les temps modernes,* 1 (5) (February 1946) 878, 881; translation from Shawn Frederick McHale, *Print and Power: Confucianism, Communism, and Buddhism in the Making of Modern Vietnam* (Honolulu: University of Hawaii Press, 2004), p. 174.
2. D. A. Low, 'Rule Britannia: Subjects and Empire', *Modern Asian Studies* 36 (2) (2002) 494.
3. Eric Hobsbawm, *The Age of Empire, 1875 – 1914* (New York: Pantheon, 1987), pp. 57–8.
4. Among the synthetic accounts of these debates which inform the following discussion are Wolfgang J. Mommsen, *Theories of Imperialism,* trans. by P. S. Falla (New York: Random House, 1980); Roger Owen and Bob Sutcliffe (eds),

Studies in the Theory of Imperialism (London: Longman, 1972); Giovanni Arrighi, *The Geometry of Imperialism*, trans. by Patrick Camiller (London: Verso, 1978). For a sustained introduction to the historiography on the British and French dimensions of the new imperialism shaped by aspects of these approaches, see Wm. Roger Louis *et al.* (eds), *The Oxford History of the British Empire. Vol. 3: The Nineteenth Century*, and *Vol. 4: The Twentieth Century* (Oxford: Oxford University Press, 1998); Jean Meyer (ed.), *Histoire de la France coloniale*, 2 vols (Paris: Colin, 1990–91).

5. J. A. Hobson, *Imperialism* (London: James Nisbet, 1902).

6. V. I. Lenin, *Imperialism, the Highest Stage of Capitalism*, 3rd edn (London: Communist Party of Great Britain, 1927).

7. See, for example, Andre Gunder Frank, *Dependent Accumulation and Underdevelopment* (London: Macmillan, 1978); and Immanuel Wallerstein, *The Modern World-System*, 3 vols (New York: Academic, 1974–89).

8. Walter LaFeber, *The New Empire: An Interpretation of American Expansion, 1860–1898* (Ithaca: Cornell University Press, 1963); William Appleman Williams, *The Roots of the Modern American Empire* (New York: Random House, 1969).

9. David K. Fieldhouse, *Economics and Empire, 1830–1914* (Ithaca: Cornell University Press, 1973).

10. Niall Ferguson, *Empire: The Rise and Demise of the British World Order and the Lessons for Global Power* (New York: Basic Books, 2003).

11. William L. Langer, *The Diplomacy of Imperialism, 1890–1902*, 2 vols (New York: Knopf, 1935); A. J. P. Taylor, *Germany's First Bid for Colonies, 1884–1885* (London: Macmillan, 1938); David Fieldhouse, 'Imperialism: An Historiographical Revision', *Economic History Review*, 2nd ser. 14 (2) (1961) 205.

12. Ronald Robinson and John Gallagher, *Africa and the Victorians: The Official Mind of Imperialism* (London: Macmillan, 1961).

13. P. J. Cain and A. G. Hopkins, *British Imperialism: Innovation and Expansion, 1688–1914* (London: Longman, 1993).

14. R. F. Holland, *European Decolonization, 1918–1981* (London: Macmillan, 1985); John Darwin, *Britain and Decolonisation: The Retreat from Empire in the Post-War World* (London: Macmillan, 1988); Nicholas Tarling, *Britain, Southeast Asia and the Korean War* (Singapore: Singapore University Press, 2005); Wm. Roger Louis, *The British Empire in the Middle East, 1945–1951* (Oxford: Clarendon, 1984). See also Prosser Gifford and Wm. Roger Louis (eds), *Decolonization and African Independence: The Transfers of Power, 1960–1980* (New Haven: Yale University Press, 1988).

15. David Fieldhouse, *Merchant Capital and Economic Decolonization: The United Africa Company, 1929–1987* (New York: Oxford University Press, 1994); Nicholas White, *Business, Government, and the End of Empire: Malaya, 1942–1957* (New York: Oxford University Press, 1996).

16. John Gallagher and Ronald Robinson, 'The Imperialism of Free Trade', *Economic History Review*, 2nd ser. 6 (1) (1953) 1–15; Ronald Robinson, 'Non-European Foundations of European Imperialism: Sketch for a Theory of Collaboration', in Owen and Sutcliffe, *Studies in the Theory of Imperialism*, pp. 117–42; D. A. Low, *Lion Rampant: Essays in the Study of British Imperialism* (London: Cass, 1973); Gwyn Prins, *The Hidden Hippopotamus: Reappraisal in African History: The Early Colonial Experience in Western Zambia* (Cambridge: Cambridge University

Press, 1980); Burton Stein, *Thomas Munro: The Origins of the Colonial State and his Vision of Empire* (New York: Oxford University Press, 1989).

17. For a useful discussion of colonial studies before the rise of Said and Subaltern Studies, see Frederick Cooper, 'Decolonizing Situations: The Rise, Fall, and Rise of Colonial Studies, 1951–2001', *French Politics, Culture and Society*, 20 (2) (2002) 47–76.

18. Edward Said, *Orientalism* (New York: Pantheon, 1978); Edward Said, *Culture and Imperialism* (New York: Knopf, 1993).

19. Ranajit Guha, 'The Prose of Counter-Insurgency', in Ranajit Guha (ed.), *Subaltern Studies: Writings on South Asian History and Society, Vol. 2* (Delhi: Oxford University Press, 1983), pp. 1–42; Ranajit Guha, *Elementary Aspects of Peasant Insurgency in Colonial India* (Delhi: Oxford University Press, 1983); Ranajit Guha, *Dominance without Hegemony: History and Power in Colonial India* (Cambridge, MA: Harvard University Press, 1997).

20. Partha Chatterjee, *Nationalist Thought and the Colonial World: A Derivative Discourse* (London: Zed Books, 1986); Partha Chatterjee, *The Nation and its Fragments: Colonial and Postcolonial Histories* (Princeton, NJ: Princeton University Press, 1993); Shahid Amin, *Event, Metaphor, Memory: Chauri Chaura, 1922–1992* (Berkeley: University of California Press, 1995); Gyan Prakash, *Bonded Histories: Genealogies of Labor Servitude in Colonial India* (Cambridge: Cambridge University Press, 1990); Gyan Prakash (ed.), *After Colonialism: Imperial Histories and Postcolonial Displacements* (Princeton, NJ: Princeton University Press, 1995). For a detailed analysis and critique of the influence of Subaltern scholarship on the study of imperial history, one which informs my discussion here, see the contributions by Gyan Prakash, Florencia Mallon and Frederick Cooper in 'AHR Forum: Subaltern Studies as Postcolonial Criticism', *American Historical Review*, 99 (5) (1994) 1475–545.

21. Vicente L. Rafael, *Contracting Colonialism: Translation and Christian Conversion in Tagalog Society under Early Spanish Rule* (Ithaca: Cornell University Press, 1988); Lydia Liu, *Translingual Practice: Literature, National Culture, and Translated Modernity – China, 1900–1937* (Stanford: Stanford University Press, 1995); Lydia Liu (ed.), *Tokens of Exchange: The Problem of Translation in Global Circulations* (Durham: Duke University Press, 1999).

22. Jean Comaroff and John Comaroff, *Of Revelation and Revolution. Vol. 1: Christianity, Colonialism, and Consciousness in South Africa* (Chicago: Chicago University Press, 1991); Gauri Viswanathan, *Masks of Conquest: Literary Study and British Rule in India* (New York: Columbia University Press, 1989).

23. Dipesh Chakrabarty, *Provincializing Europe: Postcolonial Thought and Historical Difference* (Princeton, NJ: Princeton University Press, 2000), quotes at pp. 6, 16.

24. Paul Rabinow, *French Modern: Norms and Forms of the Social Environment* (Cambridge, MA: MIT Press, 1989); Gwendolyn Wright, *The Politics of Design in French Colonial Urbanism* (Chicago: Chicago University Press, 1991); Timothy Mitchell, *Colonising Egypt* (New York: Cambridge University Press, 1988); Thomas R. Metcalf, *An Imperial Vision: Indian Architecture and Britain's Raj* (Berkeley: University of California Press, 1989), quote at p. 2; David Arnold, *Colonizing the Body: State Medicine and Epidemic Disease in Nineteenth-Century India* (Berkeley: University of California Press, 1993).

25. Anne McClintock, *Imperial Leather: Race, Gender, and Sexuality in the Colonial Contest* (New York: Routledge, 1995); Robert Rydell, *All the World's a Fair: Visions of Empire at American International Expositions, 1876–1916* (Chicago: University of Chicago Press, 1984); Patricia A. Morton, *Hybrid Modernities: Architecture and Representation at the 1931 Colonial Exposition, Paris* (Cambridge, MA: MIT Press, 2000); Antoinette Burton, *At the Heart of the Empire: Indians and the Colonial Encounter in Late-Victorian Britain* (Berkeley: University of California Press, 1998); Ann Laura Stoler, *Race and the Education of Desire: Foucault's History of Sexuality and the Colonial Order of Things* (Durham: Duke University Press, 1995); Peter van der Veer, *Imperial Encounters: Religion and Modernity in India and Britain* (Princeton, NJ: Princeton University Press, 2001); Kristin Hoganson, *Fighting for American Manhood: How Gender Politics Provoked the Spanish-American and Philippine-American Wars* (New Haven: Yale University Press, 1998); Mary A. Renda, *Taking Haiti: Military Occupation and the Culture of US Imperialism, 1915–1940* (Chapel Hill: University of North Carolina Press, 2001); Laura Briggs, *Reproducing Empire: Race, Sex, Science, and US Imperialism in Puerto Rico* (Berkeley: University of California Press, 2002); Amy Kaplan and Donald E. Pease (eds), *Cultures of United States Imperialism* (Durham: Duke University Press, 1993); Julian Go and Anne L. Foster (eds), *The American Colonial State in the Philippines: Global Perspectives* (Durham: Duke University Press, 2003); Gilbert M. Joseph *et al.* (eds), *Close Encounters of Empire: Writing the Cultural History of US-Latin American Relations* (Durham: Duke University Press, 1998).

26. Paul Gilroy, *The Black Atlantic: Modernity and Double Consciousness* (Cambridge, MA: Harvard University Press, 1993). For an important assessment of African diaspora studies, see Tiffany Ruby Patterson and Robin D. G. Kelley, 'Unfinished Migrations: Reflections on the African Diaspora and the Making of the Modern World', *African Studies Review*, 43 (1) (2000) 11–45.

27. Ji-Yeon Yuh, *Beyond the Shadow of Camptown: Korean Military Brides in America* (New York: New York University Press, 2002); Sandhya Shukla, *India Abroad: Diasporic Cultures of Postwar America and England* (Princeton, NJ: Princeton University Press, 2002); Kandice Chuh and Karen Shimakawa (eds), *Orientations: Mapping Studies in the Asian Diaspora* (Durham: Duke University Press, 2001); Aihwa Ong and Donald Nonini (eds), *Ungrounded Empires: The Cultural Politics of Modern Chinese Transnationalism* (New York: Routledge, 1997).

28. See, for example, the critiques that emerge in Dagmar Engels and Shula Marks (eds), *Contesting Colonial Hegemony: State and Society in Africa and India* (London: British Academic Press, 1994); Homi K. Bhabha, 'Of Mimicry and Man: The Ambivalence of Colonial Discourse', in Frederick Cooper and Ann Laura Stoler (eds), *Tensions of Empire: Colonial Cultures in a Bourgeois World* (Berkeley: University of California Press, 1997), pp. 152–60; John D. Kelly and Martha Kaplan, *Represented Communities: Fiji and World Decolonization* (Chicago: University of Chicago Press, 2001).

29. John Darwin, 'Decolonization and the End of Empire', in Wm. Roger Louis *et al.* (eds), *The Oxford History of the British Empire. Vol. 5: Historiography* (Oxford: Oxford University Press, 1999), p. 556.

30. Ferguson, *Empire*, p. xxi.

31. Along with the works discussed in more detail here, suggestive studies that re-examine empire from perspectives beyond Euro-American high

imperialism include: Karen Barkey and Mark von Hagen (eds), *After Empire: Multiethnic Societies and Nation-Building: The Soviet Union and the Russian, Ottoman, and Habsburg Empires* (Boulder: Westview Press, 1997); Daniel R. Brower and Edward J. Lazzerini (eds), *Russia's Orient: Imperial Borderlands and Peoples: 1700–1917* (Bloomington: Indiana University Press, 1997); Jane Burbank and David L. Ransel (eds), *Imperial Russia: New Histories for the Empire* (Bloomington: Indiana University Press, 1998); Stefan Tanaka, *Japan's Orient: Rendering Pasts into History* (Berkeley: University of California Press, 1993); Peter Duus, *The Abacus and the Sword: The Japanese Penetration of Korea, 1895–1910* (Berkeley: University of California Press, 1995); Prasenjit Duara, *Sovereignty and Authenticity: Manchukuo and the East Asian Modern* (Lanham: Rowman and Littlefield, 2003); and Fatma Müge Göçek, *Rise of the Bourgeoisie, Demise of Empire: Ottoman Westernization and Social Change* (New York: Oxford University Press, 1996). For a suggestive critical overview, see Mark von Hagen, 'Empires, Borderlands, and Diasporas: Eurasia as Anti-Paradigm for the Post-Soviet Era', *American Historical Review*, 109 (2) (2004) 445–68.

32. Louise Young, *Japan's Total Empire: Manchuria and the Culture of Wartime Imperialism* (Berkeley: University of California Press, 1998), quotes at pp. 10, 13.

33. Mark Philip Bradley, *Imagining Vietnam and America: The Making of Postcolonial Vietnam, 1919–1950* (Chapel Hill: University of North Carolina Press, 2000).

34. Matthew Connelly, *A Diplomatic Revolution: Algeria's Fight for Independence and the Origins of the Post-Cold War Era* (New York: Oxford University Press, 2002), quote at p. 13.

10
culture

andrew j. rotter

Writing about culture and international history is an act of condensation, for both culture and history are enormously shaggy and complicated concepts. One thinks of the comedian Woody Allen, who claimed to have read *War and Peace* in twenty minutes: 'it involves Russia', he concluded. In Sophia Coppola's 2003 movie *Lost in Translation*, Bill Murray plays an actor named Bob Harris, in Japan to film a series of advertisements promoting Suntory whiskey, who is treated to several minutes of elaborate instruction in Japanese, which he does not speak. When the instruction ends, Harris asks a translator what he has been told. 'Just act natural', says the translator. It is an old joke, but a good one.

For the international or foreign relations historian, the problem with culture begins with definition, with rendering culture a thing sufficiently condensed that it is useful for interpreting relations between people and nations in the past. The task is made frustrating not least because anthropologists, who as far as one can tell exist largely because culture exists and because they discovered and described it, have grown increasingly disillusioned with the idea of culture, frequently substituting for it, in the postmodern age, the word 'discourse'. What the anthropologists may wish to put aside, historians, along with political scientists, economists and literary critics, have more and more employed as central to their work. While they have not reached agreement on the definition of culture, many seem content to take the view of Clifford Geertz, that culture is constituted of 'webs of significance' spun by human beings. What the web metaphor lacks in precision and parsimony it more than makes up for in vividness of image and conceptual flexibility. Webs have structure, strength and suppleness. They present form without hierarchy. The filaments of webs can be discerned individually but give strength to the whole by their connections to other filaments. And they are, after all, good enough for Geertz, and for his intellectual forebear Max Weber.[1]

Foreign relations historians have discerned in the webs of culture a variety of filaments, which they equate with analytical categories useful for studying their subjects; it is as if the web is positioned between the author and her subject, with each of its threads providing a particular insight into the Opium War, the construction of canals or dams in other people's countries, and the Soviet launch of Sputnik, to suggest a few possible examples. The most assertive practitioners of cultural analysis see as threads in the web race and gender, for although these analytical categories are often used independently they are nevertheless products of human activity, constructs of human beings, inflected by history and symbolism and the senses – in short, things culturally determined. Other threads in the cultural web include religious beliefs, ideas about class and caste, concepts of time and space, even gestures, customs, folkways, songs, poems, rituals and games. Culturalists ask: 'What, if anything, do these threads in the web of significance tell us about observed phenomena, about the Opium War and Sputnik, about relations between people and nations?'

language, identity, values

Like housework or an unbidden weekend guest, the culture concept in international history tends to expand to fill every available space. Three big ideas in particular have come to be associated with the cultural approach. The first of these is *language*. Traditional diplomatic history (as it was called) showed occasional interest in parsing the language of diplomats, in ways that corresponded to lexicons established by diplomats themselves: 'frank discussions' between national representatives meant, for example, that the representatives sharply disagreed. Cultural international history takes a more broadly theoretical view of language, both as it is expressed in words and by the body. Culture itself has been described as 'software' or 'syntax'.[2] The elements of spoken or written language – its metaphors, tropes, and word choices – reveal much about the assumptions and emotions of its speakers and writers; so too with body language, the postures, gestures or facial expressions that indicate the attitude of one participant in a conversation toward another. As Frank Costigliola notes, 'By shaping the patterns of perception through which people categorize and make sense out of events, tropes direct attention to certain aspects of those events while making other aspects appear less relevant or visible.' Language can 'freeze' perceptions of others, hardening generalizations into stereotypes and eliminating from consideration evidence that might undo them.[3]

Language is both a cause and effect of culture – a fact as frustrating as it is true. Language and culture are thus intimately related. Costigliola shows, for example, that George Kennan's language in his famous Long Telegram, written in early 1946 and catechized by the Harry S. Truman administration soon after that, represented the Soviet government as a rapist exercising (in Kennan's words) 'insistent, unceasing pressure for penetration and command' over the West, and as a mental patient, ill with 'a psychosis which permeates and determines [the] behavior of [the] entire Soviet ruling caste'.[4] Loy Henderson, the US Ambassador to India in the late 1940s and early 1950s, once described India's Prime Minister Jawaharlal Nehru as 'vain, sensitive, emotional, and complicated', four adjectives invariably gendered feminine in the United States.[5] In Kennan's language the Soviet leadership was cast as menacing in the most culturally provocative fashion, as aggressors determined to violate others' bodies sexually and emotionally; sexual predators and the mentally unbalanced equally require confinement. If Nehru, who was regarded by Americans as the personification of India, was as difficult and flighty and effeminate as Henderson implied, it would be hard for US policy-makers to achieve a serious meeting of the minds with him.

The second idea associated with culturalist international history is *identity*, or the *perception* of self and other. Identity is an idea at least as fashionable as culture, and the concepts are frequently and properly linked. Identity, according to Peter J. Katzenstein, is 'a shorthand label for varying constructions of nation- and statehood'. These constructions, in turn, are shaped by norms, laws, rules, and conventions, all culturally determined, that constitute international and domestic environments. How a state sees itself affects the ways in which it relates to other states, how it defines national security and how it comes to understand its interests and objectives. Because it is socially constructed, identity is never static, and as it shifts it changes the state's relationships, definitions and understandings.[6]

Identity is perception projected large. Selves, individually or collectively, tend to discover their identities with reference to their perceptions of others. This is not necessarily an alienating process – as David M. Kennedy suggests, while the creation of others 'may be essential to the definition of identity ... it need not take the form of outright, hostile, aggressive *enmity* in order to do its cultural work'. It need not do so, but of course it can: during the Second World War, white Americans, at least, defined themselves in opposition to the Japanese enemy they despised. On Guadalcanal in 1942, a Marine told correspondent John Hersey: 'I wish we were fighting against Germans. They are human beings, like us ... . But the Japanese are like animals.'[7] People project onto others undesirable characteristics they suspect exist in themselves, but which they are unwilling or unable to abide or control. Resisting or controlling the other is thus a substitute for resisting or controlling one's own bad impulses. So, for example, atrocities committed by US soldiers against the Japanese during the Pacific War were explained by Americans as a reflection of atrocious behaviour by the Japanese against them, or as the only way to subdue vicious animals. Responding to the concerns of Samuel Cavert, the general secretary of the Federal Council of the Churches of Christ in America, two days after the dropping of an atomic bomb on Nagasaki, President Truman wrote that 'when you have to deal with a beast you have to treat him as a beast'. Beasts deserve beastly behaviour. Atrocious others, harbouring the worst secret features of projected selves, require the sort of discipline that selves resist.[8]

Finally, culture is associated with a nation's *values*. This concept, popular with International Relations (IR) specialists, is entangled with identity, for values say much about how a people see themselves in normative or moral terms. Like identity, values are contingent on culture, and they in turn condition a nation's foreign policies. Let us return to the example of using nuclear weapons. One day after defiantly explaining to Samuel Cavert why the United States had dropped atomic bombs, Truman read a first-hand report of the destruction of Hiroshima, which estimated that no less than 100 000 people had been killed in the city, and viewed graphic reconnaissance photographs taken of the devastation. Appalled, he ordered that no more atomic bombs be used without his express permission; he said, according to Commerce Secretary Henry Wallace, that 'the thought of wiping out another 100 000 people was too horrible'.[9] Thereafter developed what Richard Price and Nina Tannenwald termed a 'taboo' preventing the further use of nuclear weapons by the United States. A convenient but constructive amnesia set in: US policy-makers came to believe, as Price and Tannenwald put it, that the use of nuclear weapons was 'contrary to Americans' perceptions of themselves'. When asked why the United States had not gone nuclear during the 1991 Persian Gulf War, a State Department official replied, 'We just don't do things like that.'[10]

the rise of culturalist international history

Culturalist international history may be the 'next big thing', to paraphrase Michael J. Hogan.[11] But the absence of cultural interpretation from international history is a relatively recent phenomenon. Certainly Thomas

Bailey, one of the architects of the modern practice of US diplomatic history, used culture-based images of Americans and others to explain why governments acted as they did toward other governments. The problem was that Bailey's characterizations of others – Chinese workers were 'docile and industrious', while the Japanese took 'a hara-kiri gamble' at Pearl Harbor – were often caricatures or stereotypes, what a later generation of historians would criticize as 'essentialist' or even racist.[12] (The same label could be applied to the policy-driven anthropology of the Second World War, including Ruth Benedict's *The Chrysanthemum and the Sword*.[13]) But even before the essentialist charge began to stick, the Cold War seemed to overwhelm any previously meaningful peculiarities of nations based on culture.[14] What did it matter if Belgians and Congolese had culturally-shaped misunderstandings of each other, since their relationship was dominated by the US-Soviet rivalry? Or so it was assumed.

What the Cold War obscured by its presence was uncovered by its absence. International relations specialists were surprised when the Cold War ended and the Soviet Empire unravelled in the late 1980s and early 1990s. Existing theories, especially realism, had failed to predict events. 'Realism may be the royal theory of international relations', writes Frank Ninkovich, 'but, like royalty, it is prone to hemophilia and suffers from severe bleeding whenever it is scratched. And the conceptual wounds inflicted over time have been many' – especially since 1991.[15] The retreat of Soviet power also exposed, in the Balkans and among the former Soviet states, sharp ethnic and cultural differences that had previously been suppressed. As much as the world welcomed the emergence of freedom in lands previously tethered to Moscow, the process inspired conflict in Yugoslavia, Chechnya and Azerbaijan, among other places. However one balanced the scale between liberation on the one hand and the advent of violence on the other, that culture had become meaningful again was undeniable. And what was meaningful on the ground was meaningful as a way of understanding the world as well. The trick now was to avoid essentialism.

There were changes occurring simultaneously in the realm of ideas. In the 1980s, postmodernism emerged as a strident, and fashionable, critique of modernism and indeed all post-Enlightenment ways of seeing and knowing. Modernism held that truth was an objective reality, more and more knowable by increasingly enlightened men and women whose explorations of history were governed by the logic of experimental science. The watchwords of modernity included 'rationality', 'pragmatism', 'efficiency', and 'functionalism'. In historiographical terms its volume was capacious, admitting the French Annales school (which pursued a 'total history' involving, at bottom, climate and geography), the Marxists (with their emphasis on economics and class and what was known by the 1970s as 'history from below'), and the American modernization theorists (whose scientific view of history led to quantitative studies of matters such as slavery, the structure of the family and the structure of slave families).[16]

Postmodernism – sometimes called 'poststructuralism', sometimes not – sought to destabilize modernity's assumptions about the self and the self's quest for truth, on which rested all forms of Enlightenment-inspired history. The attack was led (though not in tandem) by the French philosophers Michel Foucault and Jacques Derrida, whose thinking was influenced in turn by Friedrich Nietzsche, Martin Heidegger and linguist Ferdinand de Saussure. Postmodernists declared that the self – the 'subject', in postmodern parlance – is a constructed thing, that truth is a chimera, science a catspaw of power, and language a conundrum that distances human beings from anything like 'reality'. As a trio of historians has put it, 'Foucault and Derrida made Western Man into a modern-day Gulliver, tied down with ideological ropes and incapable of transcendence because he can never get beyond the veil of language to the reality "out there".'[17]

The practice of history was not immune to the assault of the postmodernists. Most historians, to be sure, rejected as nihilistic the claim that there was no graspable truth, no standard by which human conduct in the past could be understood and judged. But many historians looked again at the reliability of their analytical categories, re-examined their use of language and tempered their claims to intellectual authority. Most of all, postmodernism triggered among historians greater interest in culture, both as a method and a subject of enquiry. If there was a tangible 'reality' to be found in history, it likely lay in the deepest recesses of human experience, in customs, religious practices and webs of significance. Culture as realm and method seemed less fraudulently logical than economics, politics or even society, and at the same time more respectful of language, idiosyncrasy, irrationality and passion – all areas of interest for postmodernists. Most important, in the view of Clifford Geertz, culture did not try to be about 'power, something to which social events, behaviors, institutions, or processes can be causally attributed'; instead, 'it is a context, something within which they can be intelligibly – that is, thickly – described'. To historians troubled by the complications in the cause-effect relationship introduced by Foucault and Derrida, cultural history offered an escape hatch. One might 'decode meaning' in history rather than try to hack through a thicket of language in futile pursuit of causes and effects, of realities, of truths.[18]

One particular twist in the cultural turn in history deserves mention, and that is postcolonial or Subaltern Studies. The late Edward Said was the intellectual and ideological father of the school, and his 1978 book *Orientalism* its founding text. The subaltern historians were much interested in power, especially the deployment of it by the Western empires. (Most of the early studies in the field concerned India, and many were written by Indians.) Like Said, the subaltern historians acknowledged debts to Marx and to the Marxist writer Antonio Gramsci. But in their interest in education, literature and discourse generally, the subaltern scholars resembled more closely the postmodern critics, who were cited heavily in their footnotes. More than anything else, the subalterns insisted that the voices of the less powerful participants in the imperial relationship must be heard. While empire, in their view, was undeniably cruel and oppressive, it also entailed a dialogue between sub- and superalterns, a negotiation of power by local people who found imaginative ways to resist outsider control, and in so doing forged political identities that frequently flowered into nationalism. It is in their ascription of agency to others, in their demand that the evidently weaker participants in international relationships must nevertheless receive their due, that Said and the postcolonialists made their greatest contribution – and here is where we return to the impact of culture on international history.[19]

Historians of the international system, of diplomacy as it was called in the United States, were not the first in the discipline to make the cultural turn. Their response to postmodernism and its offspring Subaltern Studies ranged from polite interest to open hostility, with most mired in indifference somewhere in the middle. The only early enthusiast for cultural diplomatic history was Akira Iriye, though Iriye's work, while pathbreaking and imaginative, did not engage much with culture as method or theory – on which more presently. Michael H. Hunt included a long chapter on race in his superb *Ideology and US Foreign Policy* (1987), in which 'ideology' seemed tantalizingly close in substance to Geertz's version of culture; Hunt quoted Geertz with approval. In *War Without Mercy: Race and Power in the Pacific War* (1986), John W. Dower showed that Japanese and American racial stereotypes of each other intensified the brutality of their combat in the Pacific between 1942 and 1945. Inspired in part by the feminist scholar Joan W. Scott, Emily S. Rosenberg brought gender to the study of international history; as 'powerful rhetorical devices', she argued, gendered images '*exemplified*' the presumed naturalness of the hierarchical arrangements inherent in empire. In June 1990, the *Journal of American History* published a 'Round Table' called 'Explaining the History of American Foreign Relations', which included essays by Iriye, Hunt and Rosenberg, among others; *Diplomatic History* followed in the fall of 1990 with a 'symposium' on 'Writing the History of US Foreign Relations', in which Rosenberg was once more represented. The book *Explaining the History of American Foreign Relations*, edited by Michael J. Hogan and Thomas G. Paterson, came out in 1991, and included versions of the Iriye and Hunt essays from the *Journal of American History* and a version of the Rosenberg essay from *Diplomatic History*.[20]

Here was a promising start. And scholars of international history followed with work that derived from these pioneering efforts and expanded them in scope. In Iriye's culturalist idiom came work on cultural relations that might or might not involve the state. One could study cultural contact at World's Fairs, for example, or in European attitudes toward Americans and their products, or in tourism, or in non-governmental organizations (NGOs).[21] Inspired by Hunt and others, historians have increasingly discerned in imperial and Cold War history the influence of race thinking and the impact of race relations at home on a nation's policies abroad.[22] Gender, together with its concomitants paternalism and masculinity, has found much favour especially as a way of examining relations between nations or peoples of unequal power.[23] Postmodernism and the turn toward culture encouraged some broadly theoretical work that frequently encompassed race and gender, or tried to do so. The postcolonial twist found its way into the field of international history by stealth: while few works acknowledged debts to Said and other postcolonialists, a good number of them drew implicitly on his call for a 'contrapuntal' analysis of relations between people – one, that is, that included the voices of subalterns in dialogue with more powerful interlocutors.[24]

debating the cultural turn

The rise of culturalist international history, and its incursions into the field's important journals and anthologies, attracted resistance from critics. The attacks took a variety of forms. First, and this derived from anthropologists' disillusionment with culture, the point was made that all human beings who observe others through webs of significance are equally enmeshed in their own. It is a conceit particularly of Western anthropology to posit that Americans, Britons and the French, for instance, are sufficiently free of culture as to be able the see the cultures of others with an unbiased and unblinkered eye. No one can cleanly place a web between him- or herself and his or her subject, for he or she is as much entangled in his or her own cultural assumptions as anyone he or she is hoping to observe and understand. The sight lines are blocked by his or her own prejudices, deep ways of thinking and feeling about gender relations, the existence of an all-powerful God, or the design of the cosmos. Thus captive, he or she can only reduce, and even essentialize, the experiences of others.[25]

Tied to this is an unease felt not only by anthropologists but by others who use culture to explain human behaviour. Webs are stretchy things, in theory unlimited in size or number of filaments. The culture concept thus lacks distinctiveness and parsimony. Culture seems to be, or to include, nearly everything: race and gender, yes, but also table manners, styles of dance, themes in painting and film, even ideas about time and space and the movements of celestial bodies. What *is not* culture, or what is there in human behaviour that cannot be explained by it? Lucian Pye, one of the pioneers in the use of 'political culture' to understand international relations, has decried the deployment of culture as 'the explanation of the last resort', and a circular one at that: 'The Chinese act that way because they are Chinese', is how Pye caricatures some of the offspring of his own work.[26]

A third objection, advanced especially by diplomatic historians who tend to ply a fairly traditional trade, is that the very amorphousness of culture obscures agency in the matter of deciding who, exactly, did what, and when, and for what reason. For example, the British and French governments decided, in 1956, to send troops into Suez. One can readily discern strategic and perhaps economic reasons for this decision, but where is the place of culture in it? If culture can be found somewhere at the margins of decision-making – if, for instance, the British and French believed that Egyptian President Gamal Abdel Nasser was incompetent to manage the Suez Canal because he was (in racial terms) immature and (in gendered ones) emotional – that does not tell us much about why the Europeans chose to act, and at the time and in the manner that they did. Culture is in any case likely to be contingent on more important and tangible things. So during the Pacific War, Americans called the Japanese 'sneaks', 'automatons', 'exploiters' and 'brutes', while the Chinese were rendered 'clever', 'loyal', 'hardworking' and 'scrappy'. By 1950, five years into the US occupation of Japan and a year after the victory of communism in China, these descriptors were mostly reversed. Perceptions thus failed to determine anything, but were themselves the product of policy shifts undertaken by states for logical, if imprudent, reasons.[27]

Practitioners of culturalist international history have to some extent brought this kind of criticism on themselves. Emphasizing context over cause and effect, they have seemed to abandon concerns over historical agency; too often in their writing, culturalists revert vaguely to a thing's 'constructedness', or a 'discourse', without apparently caring who constructed the thing or how the discourse made something actually happen. In her insightful book *Taking Haiti*, Mary Renda claims that a 'paternalist discourse succeeded in conscripting many Americans into the logic of empire'.[28] That sentence leaves too many degrees of separation between the 'discourse' and either its makers or its subjects. And while culturalists use interesting nouns, they have a problem with verbs. Favourites include 'illuminate' (or 'shed light on' or 'open a window on'), 'shape', 'affect', 'influence' and 'inflect'. These are not powerful words, like 'cause', 'make' or 'determine'. Culturalist verbs sound by comparison indirect and subtle, lacking the force and colour preferred by policy-makers and general audiences alike.

This literal difficulty with verbiage brings us to the most discomfiting criticism made of culturalism: that it seems uninterested in explaining power. International relations are about power, and a focus on perceptions, or gender, or ideas about religion, omits consideration of it. Power can be measured, while the influence of ideas on relations between nations cannot. Robert Buzzanco, for example, disagrees with Iriye's claim that 'power and economy are concepts as elusive as culture'. Instead, Buzzanco insists, 'investment and trade figures, military aid amounts, the location of bases, or troop deployments can be measured empirically with much more facility than the impact of a play that opened in 1824 in New York' – the reference is to William T. Moncrieff's *Cataract of the Ganges*, to which I referred in an article on gender and relations between the US and India.[29] While culture might describe some of the features of a diplomatic relationship, it cannot account for economic rivalry, for military threat and coercion, for markets and money, or for the fact that the Soviet dictator Josef Stalin understood only one kind of language: 'The Pope? How many divisions has *he* got?'[30] There was nothing discursive or 'inflected' in that.

These criticisms have prompted some defensiveness on the part of those interested in culture as a category of analysis. Thus, for example, in her study of the role of culture in French military thinking and training prior to the Second World War, Elizabeth Kier concedes, 'some may think it foolish to argue that the conditions in the international system do not determine doctrinal development by influencing the decisions made by civilian policymakers'.[31] That the criticism of culture has been sharpest from those on the political left, with which many culturalists affiliate themselves, has proved particularly wounding.

The responses to critics' objections have usually been implicit, contained in the culturalists' work. Let us tease them out. In the first place, it is of course true that culture engulfs both the author and his or her subject, that webs can occlude as much as they reveal. That, culturalists suggest, is precisely the point: even those who pretend that they are doing the rigorous and logical work of analysing diplomacy with reference only to strategy or economics or some other allegedly quantifiable thing are in fact enmeshed in a web of significance that they refuse to acknowledge. Those who make decisions are creatures of culture, not just policy wonks who shed their images of others like raincoats at the office door. That is equally true of historians. They use language in particular ways; they have identities that (nothing for it) shape their perceptions of others; they have values that inevitably creep into their analyses. These realities present two choices: either pretend that one is not constrained by language, identity and values – pretend, in other words, that one can make clear judgements about allegedly straightforward matters such as power – or acknowledge that one bears the trappings of one's own culture, which is not a raincoat but part of what one is, whether one is writing or being written about. All of us are creatures of culture. That makes things complicated, but far less so than if we claim implicitly that we are somehow innocent of culture.

Logical parsimony is something to aspire to in historical explanation, and a circular argument – Pye's caricature that 'the Chinese act that way because they are Chinese' – is no argument at all. But parsimony must not come at the expense of subtlety, or a recognition of a subject's complexity. History abhors parsimony because most human beings do. People do not act as they do on complex matters for single, obvious reasons. We cannot, of course, merely toss the culture concept, undifferentiated and uncondensed, in the direction of any serious historical question that arises. The solution, for diplomatic historians, is Pye's (and others') term 'political culture' which consists, according to Sidney Verba, 'of the system of empirical beliefs, expressive symbols, and values which defines the situation in which political action takes place'. Culture is thus bounded by the political arena and connected to the expression of power. Political culture is the coming together of institutions and the people who inhabit them – its source, according to Pye, is both the 'collective history of a political system' and the 'life histories of the individuals who currently make up the system' – the joining of the popular and the elite, the public and the private. The culture concept is both confounding and enlightening because it disrupts the binary categories by which we classify the world. Selves versus others? The boundaries are seldom as fixed as that division implies.[32]

The charge that culturalist international history obscures agency is frequently telling, as I have noted. Its adherents too often use the word 'discourse' loosely and uncritically, delight in thick description to the exclusion of showing why something happened as it did, and play at the margins of events rather than plumbing their cores for meaning. Combine this with the final criticism of the cultural agnostics – that practitioners of culturalism are uninterested in power and thus neglect the most important subject of international history – and there emerges the harshest indictment of culturalism that has yet been made.

the culture of power

One response, advanced by Akira Iriye and by some IR 'constructivists', is that both culturalists and their critics have been too much absorbed in the idea that the state is the locus of power. There exists a thing called 'soft power', as Joseph Nye has described it, which concerns suasion, influence and cultural hegemony even in the absence of state-over-state domination.[33] The state might get involved in the projection of soft power, or it might leave the task to institutions and individuals outside itself. Wendy Wall has shown, for example, that in 1948 Italian Americans, stirred to action by 'Italian-language newspapers and radio stations, the Catholic Church, fraternal organizations, and community leaders', undertook a campaign to write letters to their families back in Italy, extolling the 'American way of life' and warning against voting for the communists in upcoming elections.[34] During the Cold War, families of American military officers based in Japan and Germany took it upon themselves to show their hosts a gentler side of American power than that represented by the military itself; officers' wives might join Japanese women for flower-arranging classes, then invite them over to drink lemonade and admire their modern kitchen appliances.[35] Iriye himself has sought recently to shift the focus, or exclusive focus, off the state and onto important NGOs, including Amnesty International and the World Wildlife Fund.[36] In these ways, international historians have discovered culture by doing a virtual end run around the state.

There is another way to meet the criticism that culturalists are too much concerned with context and not enough with power, and that is to say that culture and power are not distinct entities but inhere in each other. One cannot, that is, speak of culture *and* power, but must recognize instead the culture *of* power. This argument suggests, in the first place, that 'soft' or cultural power is meaningful power. Consider Christina Klein's analysis of the Richard Rodgers and Oscar Hammerstein musical *The King and I*, which opened on Broadway in 1951 and was made into a movie in 1956. The play was based on two fictionalized memoirs by the Englishwoman Anna Leonowens, who spent five years in the 1860s as a teacher in the royal court of Siam. Hammerstein's libretto renders Anna an American, one determined to end the authoritarianism of the Siamese king and to get his subjects thinking for themselves. This is a story, writes Klein, 'of how a Western woman promotes the modernization and democratization of a small Southeast Asian nation'. Conquest and colonialism are out of fashion, and in any case do not work as well as Anna's exercise of 'the power of love and tools of culture': the Siamese (or Thais) are more successfully persuaded than coerced.

The King and I made millions of Americans who saw the play or movie imagine that Thai children were endearing and ready to be taught a new geography, in which Thailand was not the centre of the universe. In a play-within-the-play performance of a version of Harriet Beecher Stowe's *Uncle Tom's Cabin* ('The Small House of Uncle Thomas'), Siamese actors demonstrate that they are sufficiently civilized so as not to require control by imperialists, in this case British, and are at the same time impatient with the oppressive practices of their king – the Burmese concubine Tuptim uses the performance to demand her liberation from the king's service in order to join her lover. The message, ultimately, is that Thailand must enter the modern age, politically and economically, and on terms set by the West. This was 'sentimental modernization', designed to replace imperialism with managed self rule and to turn rising Asian nationalism away from an alluring but deadly embrace with communism. *The King and I* was a story that echoed and reinforced a postwar Western narrative of liberalization and modernization of allegedly backward Asian societies. 'Rodgers and Hammerstein's Anna,' Klein concludes, 'like M[assachusetts] I[nstitute of]T[echnology]'s Walt Rostow, was only the latest in a long line of Europeans and Americans who claimed to be modernizing the East by educating it in the ways of the West.'[37] Here, then, was soft power, a cultural text that gave Americans a set of images and assumptions about Thais that indicated how they might best be treated.

Many cultural international historians would go further. Not only (they would say) is it possible to locate culture outside the state, in the realm of soft power, but to find culture and power bound together at the centre of the state, what it is and what it does. Ronald L. Jepperson, Alexander Wendt and Peter J. Katzenstein put this bluntly: 'It makes little sense', they write, 'to separate power and culture as distinct phenomena or causes: material power and coercion often derive their causal power from culture'. These three, who are political scientists, construct an elaborate social-science model to measure the impact of culture on foreign policy, but it amounts basically to this: state actors operate in domestic and international environments that are constructed of norms, identities and values, all of which are rooted in culture. Every decision officials make is necessarily affected by these forces, and by webs of significance that enmesh them. Perceptions of national security, for example, are not positivist givens but shift according to understandings of national identity; recall, for example, Richard Price and Nina Tannenwald's argument that nations that see themselves as civilized, and for which civilization is an important value, can talk themselves out of using certain uncivilized weapons. And note Thomas U. Berger's claim that the cultures of anti-militarism that emerged in Germany and Japan after the Second World War have largely prevented those countries from developing more assertive national defence policies.[38]

Culture *is* power. How selves imagine others, how they speak and write about them, how they represent them in editorial cartoons, tour books, poems and plays, affect the policies they adopt toward them. If one nation or people sees another nation or people as racially distinct and inferior to themselves, it will treat those other people dismissively, cruelly, or with contempt, and that will damage relations between the two peoples. If a nation or people believes the religious practices of another nation or people incline those others toward fanaticism, it may refuse to take the others seriously (for how can fanatics negotiate reasonably?), or seek to control those others in order to keep their fanaticism from spreading. If a nation or people believes that it is more manly and therefore wiser or tougher or more logical than another nation or people, it will behave toward the others paternalistically, hoping to curb their allegedly feminine emotions. Or if a nation's leaders use metaphors to define their relations with others – Winston Churchill's 'Iron Curtain', for example, or Harry Truman's references to diplomacy as 'poker playing', or Dwight Eisenhower's 'dominoes' – they subconsciously but quite vividly condition their diplomacy. An Iron Curtain is unyielding. Poker is best played by bluffers and risk takers. Dominoes are inanimate objects, governed not by the rules of human societies but by the laws of physics.

Much of this sounds reasonable, if not unexceptionable. Yet the stridency of opposition to the culturalist approach to the field of international history suggests that there is some deep animus at work here. Many of the sharpest critics of culturalism – Melvyn Leffler, Robert Buzzanco and Bruce Kuklick, for example – see themselves as defending a leftist or liberal interpretation of diplomatic history, one emphasizing strategic or economic concerns over such analysands as gender, religion and emotion, which are more difficult to measure. In fact, the admission to the realm of analysis of these and other cultural filaments is quite compatible with a leftist critique of power, as long as the academic left can admit to its ranks not only what remains of Marxism in the West but also feminism and secular humanism, for example. (It may be that foreign relations revisionists feel uncomfortable with the cultural turn because they sense themselves outflanked on the left, to their considerable anxiety.) But there *is* a culturalist bogey on the right: the 'Clash of Civilizations' school associated with Samuel Huntington, Lawrence E. Harrison and their colleagues at the Cultural Values and Human Progress project at Harvard University.[39]

One cannot say for sure, but it may be that leftist critics of culturalism in the field of international history believe that the Geertzian culturalists and the 'Clash of Civilizations' writers are making the same argument in much the same way. Both groups proclaim the importance of culture and cite some of the same sources. But the differences between them are more important. First, the culturalists tend to be historians or IR constructivists sympathetic to historical methodology. They research the past and dig deep into archives, so their work is empirically grounded. The Huntingtonians make sweeping comparative judgements about how societies should develop; their work is more prescriptive than descriptive. The culturalists are relativists, insisting, perhaps to a fault, that cultures different from each other cannot be hierarchically ranked on an axis of progress. The 'Clash' school takes as its baseline for judgement what it calls 'Western Civilization', and it readily evaluates others according to Western values and practices. While culturalists describe culture as fluid, shifting, without boundary and negotiable, the Huntingtonians imply that culture holds still: indeed, it functions as a straitjacket, susceptible to release only by forceful outside intervention. And if the foreign relations culturalists might be accused of explaining everything in terms of culture – the parsimony problem – Huntington, Harrison and others tend to reduce culture to its essential (and essentialized) elements; in Huntington's case, religion. Culturalism derives from postmodernism and postcolonial studies. The Huntingtonians dismiss or reject these intellectual movements, embracing instead the premises of national character studies from an earlier era.

The acid test of culturalism is, of course, whether it explains anything about how and why nations and people act toward others as they do. One can proclaim that the opera *Aida* is a discourse, and show that it reveals something of Giuseppe Verdi's vision of Egypt circa 1900.[40] But that is not international history, at least not by itself. And the work of Iriye and others, important as it is, does not (by its own admission) confront state power, which remains the chief locus of interest for most historians in the field. In the remainder of this chapter, let me offer three case studies of state-to-state relations in which culture, broadly defined, has been of significance. I will avoid cases in which gender and race have played the most prominent roles: the first out of deference to the chapter on gender that appears elsewhere in this book; the second because it has gained autonomy as an analysand in the field. The first case study, which concerns US relations with Israel and is largely based on the work of Michael N. Barnett, concerns the matter of identity. The second, a glimpse at American relations with India in 1951, has to do with the collision of values in the relationship. The third case study is an attempt to make sense of the George W. Bush administration's decision to go to war with and occupy Iraq from 2002 through 2004, and in particular the role played by language and emotion in propelling the conflict forward and giving it its increasingly gruesome shape. Any conclusions in this third case study must necessarily be provisional and preliminary.

case study: the united states, israel and national identity

Barnett begins as most culturalists do, assuming that another form of explanation – in this case, realism – is preferred by analysts of the United States-Israel alliance, then suggesting that such an explanation has weaknesses and must be at least supplemented by an understanding of identity. In particular, he argues that strategic and US domestic political factors inadequately explain the alliance, given the presence of abundant oil supplies beneath the soil of Israel's Arab neighbours and the need for Jewish voters in the United States to persuade those actually in power (rarely Jews) that a high level of support for Israel is 'consistent with the beliefs and values of most Americans'. 'The oft-heard mantras – "the only democracy in the Middle East," and "shares values and principles" – signify something substantial and causal and gives [*sic*] meaning and substance to the term *special relationship*.' Israel's identity, Barnett argues, is made up of four 'strands' – religion, nationalism, the Holocaust and liberal democracy. Israel is first of all a Jewish state, an identity that associates it with Western civilization through the postwar fabrication of 'Judeo-Christianity', and at the same time positions it at some remove from the secular West; Jewish law, however contested, remains the guiding force of Israeli society. Israeli nationalism is Zionism, the movement by which the Jewish state was founded and the rationale by which it demands its unique position in the world. The lesson of the Holocaust for many Jews, and surely most Israelis, is that a distinctively Jewish state is essential if Judaism is to survive. The Zionists were right, Israelis say: in the absence of a safe haven for Jews, one well-prepared to defend itself against all enemies, Jews are vulnerable to extermination. It follows that Israelis expect their enemies to desire their annihilation. Their Arab neighbours, they say, have not disappointed them. The fourth strand, liberal democracy, has, more than any of the first three, endeared Israel to the West, though (as Barnett points out) the Israeli government's treatment of the nation's Arab minority and its behaviour in Arab territories occupied since the 1967 war have cast doubt on its democratic status.[41]

While the US–Israel relationship has had its ups and downs, the United States has overall been a steadfast supporter of Israel. This is because Americans have generally accepted at face value Israeli professions of their identity and have seen their own self-definition inscribed in it. Like Israelis, most Americans call themselves religious, and Americans' Christianity – or, at bottom, their monotheism – inclined them to discern right and wrong, good and evil, in the configuration of the Cold War and the conflict in the Middle East. As Secretary of State John Foster Dulles said in 1953, 'Our American history, like Hebrew history, is also rich in the story of men who through faith, wrought mightily.'[42] The Zionist quest for return to the promised land, biblically sanctioned, seemed to echo the seventeenth-century Puritan dream of founding 'God's American Israel', a mission that most Americans still strove to perfect in the middle of the twentieth century. Surely part of the reason for Harry Truman's support for the state of Israel in 1948 was his revulsion toward the Holocaust, and the way in which the United States' failure to act against it, whether justified or not, threatened Americans' self perception as a righteous people who must not countenance genocide. Indeed, after hearing a report that stateless Holocaust survivors were being held in miserable camps in Europe after 1945, Truman insisted that the British allow 100 000 Jewish refugees to enter Palestine immediately.[43]

Americans were impressed with the way Israelis fought, apparently as underdogs, against the Arab armies that menaced them, as if determined to cast off the stigma of meek acquiescence to the Nazis. These Jews were tough and masculine, youthful and determined Davids battling the brutish Arab Goliath. (Tough Jews populated novels and films during the 1950s and 1960s, including Leon Uris' book *Exodus* (1958), the 1960 film version of the book, and the 1959 movie *Ben Hur*, in which the Jewish title character, played by Charlton Heston, proves himself tougher than any of his Roman adversaries.) And Americans also admired Israel's democracy, which, they flattered themselves, found its fullest expression in their own country. Following a visit to Israel in 1951, Senator John F. Kennedy called the place 'the bright light now shining in the Middle East', and Kennedy's presidential policies toward the region as a whole were strongly favourable to the Israeli position.[44]

The common identity forged between Israel and the United States was not enough to overcome every problem that emerged in the relationship. When the Israelis refused to negotiate territory with the Arab states, the Eisenhower administration criticized them, and Eisenhower himself was livid over Israeli participation in the attack on Suez in 1956. In his effort to remasculinize the Jewish people after the Holocaust, David was entitled to a slingshot, but the Israeli construction of a nuclear reactor drew President Kennedy's ire. During the 1990s, officials in the Clinton administration showed more sympathy for the Palestinians than had any previous adminstration, proving willing at least to nudge the Israelis toward a settlement. Still, it is a measure of the strength of their mutual identity that Americans and Israelis have nonetheless remained staunch allies, especially given that US strategic and economic interests would be better served by alignment with the oil-rich Arab states. Realism would suggest that the United States should long ago have pressured Israel to make meaningful concessions to its neighbours, under threat that the United States would leave Israel to its fate if the Jewish state failed to act. It is identity, and thus a cultural approach to the Israel–US alliance, that explains its resilience.

There is another identity involved in US policy toward the Middle East, namely that of the Arabs. Syrians, Egyptians, Lebanese, Jordanians and others do not, of course, actually share a single identity. But Americans, in an act of cultural condensation and condescension, have lumped these nationalities together under a set of stereotypes that denigrate Arabs and set them apart from the Westerners doing the lumping. Arabs, most Americans concluded, were racially inferior to them, and at best quaint reminders of the foolish and volatile people whose image had been fashioned through the mythology of *Arabian Nights* and the wide-eyed exoticism of *National Geographic* magazine. Truman goggled after he met Abdullah Suleiman, the Saudi Finance Minister, in 1947: Suleiman was, reported the president, 'a real old Biblical Arab with chin whiskers, a white gown, gold braid, and everything'. The State Department's

Robert McClintock labelled Arabs 'fanatical and overwrought'; 'as for the emotion of the Arabs,' he wrote, 'I do not care a dried camel's hump'. The CIA in 1949 thought Arabs 'skillful mainly at avoiding hard work' and inclined to 'astonishing acts of treachery and dishonesty'. To Dulles, Arab nationalists were 'pathological', 'naive' and 'wily', while Ambassador to Libya Henry Villard concluded that Libyan leaders 'show[ed] little change from [the] barbary pirate tradition' during negotiations over a US air base in 1954.[45]

In these ways has identity conditioned the relationship between the United States and the nations of the Middle East. Barnett is at pains to remind us that 'material forces', including 'strategic logic', nonetheless remain important sources of motivation for actors in the international system. He also points out that identity is never fixed, since it is socially constructed and social circumstances change. It is this perception that offers the barest glimmer of hope for US–Israel relations and the Middle East generally: Israeli Jews who see their religion as foundation for their nationalism, who wish never to repeat the Holocaust, and who believe themselves to be, like Americans, liberal democrats, may decide that a greater Israel that includes vast Jewish settlements, especially in the West Bank, will ultimately jeopardize all these things.[46]

case study:
the united states, india and contested values

Like identity, values are rooted in culture, and they play an important role in the foreign policy a nation pursues. If identity is what peoples and nations imagine themselves to be, values express the principles on which they hope to act. To illustrate the role of values in international relations, let us turn to an episode in US–India relations: a decision by the Truman administration, protracted by Congress over the first six months of 1951, to provide a loan of wheat to famine-stricken India. The episode reveals something significant about the values of both sides, and about the ability of culture to complicate what would seem to be the most straightforward of transactions.

Here is what happened. In 1950, drought struck the agricultural zones of India, first south, then north. It was followed by torrential rains in the wheat-growing areas of northeast India that washed out those crops that had managed to take hold. In December, India's Prime Minister, Jawaharlal Nehru, ordered Vijayalakshmi Pandit, India's Ambassador to the United States (and also Nehru's sister), to request from the US government 2 million tons of wheat to feed his hungry people. Secretary of State Dean Acheson, who received the request, resolved within a month that it should be honoured; President Truman dutifully asked Congress, on 12 February 1951, for a $190 million grant that would enable India to obtain American food.

But the measure got stuck in both houses of Congress. Legislators raised a variety of objections to the bill. Some demanded that India pay for its wheat, at least in part, through sales to the United States of strategically important minerals that the Indians were said to be hoarding, among them manganese, beryl and monazite. Other law-makers objected to helping a nation they accused of consorting with communist states, refusing to back the United States fully in the Korean War – 'India has proved to us that it is not our friend in the Korean struggle', said a Republican Congressman. 'We are going to look like a bunch of stupid jackasses if we pick that nation and give them a gift of $190,000,000' – and flirting with socialism at home. And a few members of Congress otherwise sympathetic to the Indian plight nevertheless felt that aid should be given not as a grant but as a loan; requiring the Indians to pay for food might compel them to behave more responsibly in the future. The administration did not agree with these conditions but felt the need to compromise, at least on the strategic materials issue. Nehru, who witnessed the Congressional debate with mounting exasperation, let it be known that he would prefer a loan to a grant if it meant that other stipulations attached to the bill were eased and the matter quickly resolved. With these concessions the bill passed Congress in early June, and the President signed it into law.

The fight had been hard, but the forces of generosity had won. India would get its wheat. US officials hoped that the passage of the bill would make Indians grateful, and inclined toward greater sympathy for US foreign policy generally. Because the result of the legislative process was good, policy-makers expected that Nehru would reconsider his suspicions of the materialistic Americans.

But Nehru would not reconsider. While the outcome of the process was favourable, he and his country had been insulted by things said in Washington during the debate. The Americans had confirmed their crassness. Nehru had been manipulated throughout the months of waiting by US officials, asked to make humiliating concessions, chastised for his non-aligned foreign policy, and threatened with conditions, like that involving minerals, that had nothing to do with feeding his hungry people. In March 1951, in the midst of the Wheat Bill debate, Nehru met with the American writer Edgar Mowrer in New Delhi. Mowrer reported on the conversation. 'Nehru appeared bent forward and glum.

Expression: underlip protruding, chewing on something like gum and obviously expecting to accomplish an unpleasant duty.' When Mowrer broached the subject of the Wheat Bill, and noted that India had not been fully supportive of the United States at the United Nations, Nehru flew into a rage. 'The way in which you are handling our request for grain is insulting and outrageous', he stormed. 'I can tell you that if we go through centuries of poverty and if millions of our people die of hunger we shall never submit to outside pressure.' Even after the bill passed, Nehru failed to express gratitude, to the irritation of the US Ambassador, Loy Henderson. (Decades later, the memory of Nehru's seeming rudeness still rankled with Henderson.)

At play in this strategically and economically inexplicable series of events were the values of Americans and Indians, deeply held and in this case competing. The American value involved here was generosity. Americans see themselves as a magnanimous, giving people, willing to share their good fortune with others. While acts of generosity, undertaken by groups or individuals, are undeniably abundant in the American past, it is also true that giving comes with strings attached. Americans presume that recipients of their largesse will not use it in ways that subvert what Americans see as the freedoms of others, whether to suppress free speech or to foment anti-democratic (or anti-capitalist) protest – and never mind that these two conditions might contradict each other. Americans also insist that generosity be a reward for hard work, not a substitute for it. And Americans expect reciprocity for their generous acts – at minimum, gratitude for an act of kindness. Gratitude confers necessary status on the donor for giving. The donor has given something valuable. The recipient must repay at least part of his or her debt with the coin of gratitude. Generosity is thus an American value that carries with it other cherished values.

The Indian counterpart to generosity is the Sanskrit word *dana*, which translates as 'magnanimous giving'. *Dana* suggests that any powerful or wealthy superior has an obligation to give to those less powerful or wealthy. The superior is by definition a donor, socially expected to be generous. No possible recipient should have to ask a donor to give, but if asked the donor should give without hesitation. A superior who refuses to give, who gives only grudgingly, who gives for personal benefit, or who attaches conditions to the gift, has violated the obligations of the donor and may be spurned by the recipient. Above all, the obligation incurred most emphatically by the *dana* subordinate is that he or she *not* express gratitude for a gift. To do so would so skew power in the relationship in favour of the donor that it would humiliate the recipient. Donors must not expect thanks for doing what *dana* requires them to do.

This different understanding of generosity, this difference in values between Americans and Indians, helps to explain the hurt feelings on both sides resulting from the Wheat Bill of 1951. The Americans believed themselves to be acting with generosity; the conditions finally attached to the bill were (they thought) either trivial or reasonable, given American assumptions about the need to protect freedom, encourage hard work and receive gratitude for their selflessness. The Indians, on the other hand, thought they were being humiliated by a set of expectations that they had had no hand in shaping. Worst of all, as far as they were concerned, were the American depictions of them as beggars, even if they were executed by commentators and law-makers sympathetic to the Indian case. Beggars symbolized humiliation to Indians, for they were outcastes in India's social hierarchy. The representation of India as a beggar, even for a magnanimous purpose, dismayed Indians because of what it seemed to say about the status of their country. 'You give us a great deal of aid', the Indian intellectual N. K. Bose once told the American sociologist Nathan Glazer. 'It makes us feel like beggars. How does it make you feel?' Glazer's response went unrecorded.

Thus did different values – or rather, different versions of the same value – sour US–India relations in 1951. There were other instances of American-Indian disagreement on the basis of values. Christian monotheism, for example, was incompatible with a polytheistic Hindu ethic that implicitly rejected a single version of the truth, even during the Cold War. The American insistence on toughness in world affairs, an institutional machismo that pervaded US foreign policy, encountered a more subtle and nuanced posture in India, whose male leaders did not embrace the affect of Western masculinity. Not all values clashed, of course – both India and the United States were committed to democracy, for instance – and for strategic and economic reasons the two nations often found reason to agree in spite of their different ways of looking at things. The lesson is merely that values are shaped by culture, and that values matter in international relations.[47]

case study:
language and emotion in the iraq war, 2002–04

We come now to the role of language and emotion in foreign policy-making, and to a case that is as problematic as it is urgent: the decision by the George W. Bush administration to go to war in Iraq. This example is better suited to analysis by IR specialists or media pundits than by historians, who crave both a full documentary record and the perspective provided by chronological distance. And yet the Iraq War has unfolded in a remarkably public way, uncovering material sufficient for at least preliminary judgement, especially where the emphasis is on the manner in which the administration has represented the war to the public. Besides, the Iraq War is too important to be left to the superficial analysis of television's talking heads.

The assumption here is that language both constitutes and is constituted by the circumstances it endeavours to describe and explain. Those who choose words, who fashion images and metaphors, are hoping to make observed happenstance understandable, to themselves and to their readers and listeners, in certain ways. Like culture, language condenses 'realities' into manageable bits; it makes it possible to get the mind around 'realities', but it necessarily excludes parts of those 'realities' so as to make them comprehensible. Language is of course a strategy too, a way of representing or structuring 'realities' so as to persuade others that its user's version of the truth should also be theirs. Words and phrases are chosen for their emotional impact. Frank Costigliola offers as an example of this President Kennedy's publicly announced blockade of Cuba during the missile crisis of October 1962. While Kennedy spoke of the United States' 'patience and restraint', he indicted the Soviets for their 'clandestine, reckless, and provocative threat to world peace'. The American response would be a 'quarantine' of Cuba – a noun that suggested the need to isolate a disease. The President used passive voice ('further action will be justified') to warn the Soviets of consequences should the blockade be violated. This had the effect, notes Constigliola, of preventing anyone 'thinking that the US might also be taking offensive steps' to resolve the impasse. Metaphor – what Costigliola terms 'perhaps the most important figure of speech in Western languages' – shapes the way that its user and its audience think about the world. If, for example, communism or terrorism is represented as a disease, the mind goes instantly to the kind of threat a disease suggests: insidious because unseen, contagious and potentially deadly, but at the same time manageable if its possible victims can be protected and the disease itself not just contained but eradicated.[48]

President Bush and his speechwriters have used language to rouse emotions and garner support for the war in Iraq. In his State of the Union Address in January 2002, Bush famously declared the existence of an 'Axis of Evil': Iran, North Korea and Iraq.[49] The phrase had vivid connotations. The word 'axis' is most closely associated with the

German-Italian-Japanese Axis of the Second World War. If not always well-coordinated, this trio was nevertheless ideologically compatible and bent on aggression, jointly or separately, against other states. A moment's thought reveals that Bush's 'Axis of Evil' was not a common enterprise, nor were its nations demonstrably planning aggression against outsiders anytime soon. The use of the word 'axis' was designed to suppress the differences between 1941 and 2002. 'Evil', of course, is a word with deep emotional resonance. To be evil is to be irredeemably heinous, so steeped in existential nastiness as to reside outside the boundaries of civilization. The word forms a natural binary with the word 'good', meaning that the two concepts represented by the words necessarily exclude each other. Americans, and those like them, embody what is pure and right and just, Bush implied. Those in the 'Axis of Evil' exist beyond the pale of reason, are the embodiment of the maculate, the wrong and the unjust. The only logical course was Armageddon: a fight to the finish between the forces of good and the forces of evil.

In the months of run-up to the war in Iraq, Bush was asked frequently why he thought so many Muslims in particular opposed US policy as it was developing toward the Middle East, and why some engaged in terrorism. Bush replied, 'because they hate our freedom'. This struck some as an odd explanation for why young men would forfeit their lives, though Bush may have been thinking of the resentment many of the world's poor and powerless felt toward the rich and powerful United States. Again, though, the phrase appealed to the emotions of those in the West who heard it uttered. Others did not 'dislike' or 'mistrust' or even 'envy' our freedom – they hated it, and thus felt for it the strongest possible revulsion. What 'they' hated was something we possessed. It was ours versus theirs, us versus them. Finally, the word 'freedom' is in essence what Americans cherish most about their nation, and what most believe makes their nation unique. No value is held more fundamental to the American spirit than freedom. Thus nothing is deemed more precious or more vulnerable. Bush could not have chosen a more sensitive way to inspire in Americans a feeling that some in the Middle East, including Iraq, wanted to destroy what Americans value most.

War is highly susceptible to summary by metaphor. Always a complicated and dirty business, war must be made sufficiently simple and palatable to gain the support of a population asked to make sacrifices in its name. Metaphor can also be used to convey danger in concrete terms, better than by reference to some far off and abstract threat. During the early years of the Vietnam War, for example, American Presidents referred to the 'domino theory', which represented the belief that if one Southeast Asian nation – in this case, South Vietnam – fell to communism, the other nations in the region would in turn topple like upright dominoes, mechanically and inevitably. (The domino theory has re-emerged, ironically, during the Iraq War: US policy-makers hope that the establishment of democracy in Iraq will initiate a move toward democracy throughout the Muslim Middle East; this time, the dominoes are to tumble favourably for the Western democracies.)[50]

Two other metaphors, or a metaphor and slightly different figure of speech, have characterized war talk since 9/11, with reference not only to Iraq but to the 'war against terrorism'. The metaphor is 'connect the dots'. The phrase refers to an exercise in which someone, usually a child, draws lines between consecutively numbered dots on a page. If the exercise is done successfully, an inchoate sprinkling of points is transformed into a picture of something; from disjointed clues comes an image, recognizable and whole. Since 9/11, many American commentators have lamented that those in the intelligence community failed to 'connect the dots', bits of evidence that if seen as a linked whole would have revealed the terrorists' plan of attack. The metaphor has been used more recently to regret similar intelligence failures to predict the stubbornness of resistance to the US occupation of Iraq, and to encourage more foresight on the part of those planning the transition to sovereignty for Iraqis: planners must 'connect the dots' between ongoing security concerns and the demand by Iraqis for political autonomy. Despite the catastrophic failures by policy-makers to see the whole picture prior to 9/11 and prior to the invasion of Iraq in 2003, the 'dots' metaphor is in the end an optimistic one. It implies that the clues already exist on the page. All that is necessary is to draw the lines between them, as millions of children have successfully done. Terrorist attacks are preventable. The solution to the Iraq problem is within reach.

The somewhat different figure of speech – it carries the feature of analogy as a metaphor does, but is more precisely a slang synecdoche – is the term 'bad guys', used by the US military to describe its enemies in Iraq. There is a clear reference in this term to America's nineteenth-century western frontier, and especially to Hollywood's version of it. In that mythical world there were only good guys and bad guys, which keeps moral confusion to a minimum. In the early twenty-first century, 'bad guys' are the people who live in the 'Axis of Evil' countries, among others. The number of bad guys in a western film or television show was finite; if you killed them all before they got you, the good guys won. 'Bad guys' is therefore a term that is meant to give comfort to Americans and others concerned about Iraq: identify the bad guys, get rid of them, and the troubles will be over. Of course, the situation is not that simple. 'When will we learn that we're not going to end the mess in Iraq by getting bad guys?' wondered Paul Krugman in the *New York Times*. 'There are always new bad guys to take their place.'[51] Atrocities committed by US soldiers in Iraq, including those inside Abu Ghraib prison reported in spring 2004, doubtless create more bad guys – better translated here as those who are, for one reason or another, fed up with the American occupation of their country.

Finally, and related to the earlier discussion of values, there is one feeling, one emotional condition, to which all the parties to the Iraq War refer again and again. It is 'humiliation', and it has had a role in how and why the war is fought. President Bush has said that there were three main reasons to go to war with Saddam Hussein's Iraq: to destroy, and prevent further production of, weapons of mass destruction (WMD); to fight Islamic terrorism, in which Bush claimed Saddam's regime was implicated; and to rid Iraq of dictatorship and create there a democracy that might serve as an example to other autocratically-run nations in the region. (At the time of writing, no WMD have been found, the war seems to have bred more terrorists than it has destroyed, and there is no indication that anything resembling democracy will emerge in Iraq soon, much less in Iraq's neighbours.) There was surely another reason why Bush went to war in Iraq: he was frustrated, even humiliated, by the United States' inability to capture the Al-Qaeda leader, Osama bin Laden. The Americans dismantled the Taliban government in Afghanistan. The problem with the new terrorism, however, is its statelessness; even deprived of sanctuary in Afghanistan, Al-Qaeda and related organizations have remained dangerously uncontrolled. If the US military is fairly good at getting rid of adversary regimes, it is less good at fashioning new ones, and not very good at all at combating stateless terrorism. On a psychological level, Bush needed terrorism to materialize in a state, in this case Iraq, which could then be taken down by conventional military means. The President most likely convinced himself that there was a link between Al-Qaeda and Saddam Hussein's regime, since evidence to the contrary was simply incompatible with the United States' urgent need to redress the terrible attacks against it on 9/11. The humiliation born of failure to capture bin Laden would dissipate by displacement, with Saddam, a far easier target, standing in for the elusive Al-Qaeda leader.

It is partly fear of humiliation that keeps the United States in Iraq. While historical analogies are never perfect, the spectre of the Vietnam

War haunts the Bush administration. In 1965, John McNaughton, the Assistant Secretary of Defense for international security affairs, worked out the reasons for sending US troops to South Vietnam (SVN). It broke down as follows:

70% – To avoid a humiliating US defeat (to our reputation as a guarantor).
20% – To keep SVN (and the adjacent) territory from Chinese hands.
10% – To permit the people of SVN to enjoy a better, freer way of life.[52]

(Richard Nixon would later insist that the United States must not behave in Southeast Asia like 'a pitiful, helpless giant'.)[53] The same credibility issue remains in place for the Bush administration. Having committed to pre-emptive war over the objections of many of its allies, the administration believes, as McNaughton believed in 1965, that the nation's reputation is on the line. To leave Iraq to its instability and insecurity would be unworthy of a great power. If the United States departed and Iraq fell into chaos, the administration believes that American credibility would suffer a humiliating blow from which it might not recover.

Humiliation has a different meaning for Iraqis, one that is multilayered. No doubt there was humiliation in having been 'liberated' by an outside power. There was humiliation as well in day-to-day encounters with Americans once Baghdad fell, inspired by American behaviour that was to its perpetrators helpful but to many Iraqis paternalistic and insulting. Most prominently, the disclosures of atrocities by American soldiers at Abu Ghraib gives clear indication that humiliation was both the point and the result of the abuse. An investigative report by General Antonio Taguba, undertaken early in 2004, noted that US military intelligence had instructed the Military Police 'to deprive some prisoners of clothing to humiliate them'.[54] A prisoner named Hayder Sabbar Abd, one of those shown in lurid photographs made public in May 2004, told the *New York Times* that he and other Abu Ghraib inmates were beaten, stripped naked, forced to straddle each others' backs and to simulate oral sex. 'It was humiliating', said Abd. He could not return permanently to his home; he would be too ashamed, he said.[55]

To note that humiliation has been an emotion felt by those on both sides of the Iraq War is to suggest both the problems and possibilities of a broadly cultural approach to international history. Humiliation is part of the context of the war, though it alone cannot explain why and how the war was fought. It is hard to measure, other than anecdotally. Because it exists on both sides, it is not logically parsimonious; it does not much advance our understanding of the conflict to say that everyone involved in it felt humiliated at some point. At the same time, if we know that the Bush administration felt humiliated by its inability to catch bin Laden, feared the humiliation of appearing weak, and believed that its credibility and honour would be jeopardized if it failed to 'stay the course' in Iraq, and if we also know that Iraqis felt humiliated because of their treatment by Americans, then we understand something of why the United States went to war, why the United States is reluctant to abandon its virtual unilateralism in the war, and why many Iraqis seem not to think they have been liberated from Saddam Hussein so much as delivered from one humiliating station to another, and therefore why many of them, terrorists or 'bad guys' or not, continue to fight.

culturalism and the master narrative of international history

If historians are ill suited to analysing the present, they are probably even less well-advised to engage in predicting the future. Still, it is worth closing with a thought about the future of culturalist international history. The field has known great paradigms, or 'master narratives', in the past. For a time it was governed by the 'American exceptionalism' thesis, which held that the United States, largely untroubled by foreign enemies and free of the imperialism that tainted the otherwise-civilized states of Western Europe, had risen to world power because of its beneficent institutions and had extended to others 'the blessings of liberty', in the phrase of historian Samuel Flagg Bemis. Here was a master narrative to embrace: it confirmed American rectitude, glorified the American past and justified the Cold War as a necessary exercise of US power. But not all embraced it. Foreign relations revisionism, spearheaded by William Appleman Williams, sought to puncture the hubris of the 'exceptionalist' paradigm with the argument, derived from Charles Beard, that the United States had always pursued territorial expansion and overseas markets, usually at the expense of other people and in ways that were recognizably imperialistic. Revisionism was perhaps a much less palatable master narrative, at least for many Americans, but it nevertheless gained considerable standing with a new generation of international historians dubious about Bemis's triumphalism, especially in the light of the Vietnam War.[56]

By the 1980s, it was clear that neither of these narratives held sway any more, though the 'exceptionalist' thesis remained durable in some school textbooks and with much of the American public. The best the field could do was anoint a 'post-revisionism', which in synthesizing elements of the two leading narratives lost any claim to being a master narrative itself. It was followed by culturalism, in its multivalent splendour of forms. Even less than post-revisionism is culturalism suited for status as a master narrative in American foreign relations history. It has many iterations, it sprawls ambitiously and inconveniently across the globe rather than confining itself to the United States alone, and it is by nature subversive of hierarchy, such as a master narrative would seem to demand. Is it then time to suspend, at least, the very notion of a master narrative in international history? Probably. Yet in a world where multiple iteration corresponds to the emergence of peoples and nations insistent on making themselves heard, where corporations, NGOs, technology and terrorism operate beyond the reach of states, and where the rediscovery of culture as a force in global affairs has invited greater consideration of its sources and consequences, it is not difficult to grasp the wide appeal and expansive potential of this approach that focuses squarely on human beings in their cultural settings, where history is made every day.

notes

1. Clifford Geertz, *The Interpretation of Cultures* (New York: Basic Books, 1973), p. 5; Alan Barnard and Jonathan Spencer, 'Culture', in Alan Barnard and Jonathan Spencer (eds), *Encyclopedia of Social and Cultural Anthropology* (London: Routledge, 1996), pp. 136–42; Volker Depkat, 'Cultural Approaches to International Relations: A Challenge?', in Jessica Gienow-Hecht and Frank Schumacher (eds), *Culture and International History* (New York: Berghahn, 2003), p. 179.
2. Raymond Cohen, 'Conflict Resolution across Cultures: Bridging the Gap', in Dominique Jacquin-Bendal, Andrew Oros and Marco Verweij (eds), *Culture in World Politics* (New York: St Martin's, 1998), pp. 116–17.
3. Frank Costigliola, 'The Nuclear Family: Tropes of Gender and Pathology in the Western Alliance', *Diplomatic History*, 21 (2) (1997) 163–83 (quote at 164). See also Frank Costigliola, '"Unceasing Pressure for Penetration": Gender, Pathology, and Emotion in George Kennan's Formation of the Cold War', *Journal of American History*, 83 (4) (1997) 1309–39.
4. Costigliola, '"Unceasing Pressure for Penetration"', 1310.
5. Loy Henderson to Dean Acheson, 18 June 1949, Loy Henderson Papers, Box 8, Manuscript Division, Library of Congress, Washington, DC.
6. Peter J. Katzenstein, 'Introduction: Alternative Perspectives on National Security', and Ronald L. Jepperson, Alexander Wendt and Peter J. Katzenstein, 'Norms, Identity, and Culture in National Security', in Peter J. Katzenstein (ed.), *The Culture of National Security: Norms and Identity in World Politics* (New York: Columbia University Press, 1996), pp. 1–32 and 33–75 respectively (quote at p. 6).

7. David M. Kennedy, 'Culture Wars: The Sources and Uses of Enmity in American History', in Ragnhild Fiebig-von Hase and Ursula Lehmkuhl (eds), *Enemy Images in American History* (Providence: Berghahn, 1997), pp. 339–56 (quotes at pp. 345, 354).

8. Harry S. Truman to Samuel McCrea Cavert, 11 August 1945, in Dennis Merrill (ed.), *Documentary History of the Truman Administration. Volume 1: The Decision to Drop the Atomic Bomb on Japan* (Bethesda: University Publications of America, 1995), p. 213. See also Andrew J. Rotter, *Comrades at Odds: The United States and India, 1947–1964* (Ithaca: Cornell University Press, 2000), pp. xxiii–xxv.

9. J. Samuel Walker, *Prompt and Utter Destruction: Truman and the Use of Atomic Weapons Against Japan* (Chapel Hill: University of North Carolina Press, 1997), p. 86.

10. Richard Price and Nina Tannenwald, 'Norms and Deterrence: The Nuclear and Chemical Weapons Taboos', in Katzenstein, *Culture of National Security*, pp. 114–52 (quotes at pp. 119–21, 139).

11. Michael J. Hogan, 'The "Next Big Thing": The Future of Diplomatic History in a Global Age', *Diplomatic History*, 28 (1) (2004) 1–21.

12. Thomas A. Bailey, *A Diplomatic History of the American People*, 10th edn (Englewood Cliffs, NJ: Prentice-Hall, 1980), pp. 393, 739.

13. Ruth Benedict, *The Chrysanthemum and the Sword: Patterns of Japanese Culture* (Boston: Houghton-Mifflin, 1946).

14. Valerie M. Hudson, 'Culture and Foreign Policy: Developing a Research Agenda', in Valerie M. Hudson (ed.), *Culture and Foreign Policy* (Boulder, CO: Lynne Rienner, 1997), p. 1.

15. Frank A. Ninkovich, 'Introduction: The Cultural Turn', in Frank A. Ninkovich and Liping Bu (eds), *The Cultural Turn: Essays in the History of US Foreign Relations* (Chicago: Imprint, 2001), p. 1. See also Katzenstein, 'Introduction: Alternative Perspectives on National Security', pp. 2–3.

16. Joyce Appleby, Lynn Hunt and Margaret Jacob, *Telling the Truth About History* (New York: Norton, 1994), pp. 76–90.

17. Appleby *et al.*, *Telling the Truth*, p. 208.

18. Appleby *et al.*, *Telling the Truth*, pp. 217–23 (citing Clifford Geertz at p. 219).

19. Edward Said, *Orientalism* (New York: Pantheon, 1978); Leela Gandhi, *Postcolonial Theory: A Critical Introduction* (New York: Columbia University Press, 1998); 'Roundtable: Empires and Intimacies: Lessons from (Post) Colonial Studies', *Journal of American History*, 88 (3) (2001) 829–97; Partha Chatterjee, *The Partha Chatterjee Omnibus* (Delhi: Oxford University Press, 1999); Gauri Viswanathan, *Masks of Conquest: Literary Study and British Rule in India* (New York: Columbia University Press, 1989); Gyan Prakash (ed.), *After Colonialism: Imperial Histories and Postcolonial Displacements* (Princeton, NJ: Princeton University Press, 1995).

20. Akira Iriye, 'Culture and Power: International Relations as Intercultural Relations', *Diplomatic History*, 3 (2) (1979) 115–28; Akira Iriye, *Power and Culture: The Japanese-American War, 1941–1945* (Cambridge, MA: Harvard University Press, 1981); Michael H. Hunt, *Ideology and US Foreign Policy* (New Haven: Yale University Press, 1987); John W. Dower, *War Without Mercy: Race and Power in the Pacific War* (New York: Pantheon, 1986); 'A Round Table: Explaining the History of American Foreign Relations', *Journal of American*

History, 77 (1) (1990) 93–180; 'Writing the History of US Foreign Relations: A Symposium', *Diplomatic History*, 14 (4) (1990) 553–605; Michael J. Hogan and Thomas G. Paterson (eds), *Explaining the History of American Foreign Relations* (New York: Cambridge University Press, 1991). The quotations from Emily S. Rosenberg are taken from her essay 'Walking the Borders', reprinted in Hogan and Paterson, *Explaining the History*, p. 33 (emphasis in original). A second edition of *Explaining* was published by Cambridge University Press in 2004 and contains, in addition to updated essays by Iriye, Hunt and Rosenberg, new chapters relevant to culture by Frank Costigliola, Jessica Gienow-Hecht and Kristin Hoganson.

21. See, for example, Robert Rydell, *All the World's a Fair: Visions of Empire at American International Expositions, 1876–1916* (Chicago: University of Chicago Press, 1984); Richard Pells, *Not Like Us: How Europeans Have Loved, Hated, and Transformed American Culture Since World War II* (New York: Basic Books, 1997); Rob Kroes, 'American Empire and Cultural Imperialism: A View from the Receiving End', in Thomas Bender (ed.), *Rethinking American History in a Global Age* (Berkeley: University of California Press, 2002), pp. 295–313; Dennis Merrill, 'Negotiating Cold War Paradise: US Tourism, Economic Planning, and Cultural Modernity in Twentieth-Century Puerto Rico', *Diplomatic History*, 25 (2) (2001) 179–214; John Boli and George M. Thomas (eds), *Constructing World Culture: International Nongovernmental Organizations since 1875* (Stanford: Stanford University Press, 1999).

22. See, for example, Neil Parsons, *King Khama, Emperor Joe, and the Great White Queen: Victorian Britain through African Eyes* (Chicago: University of Chicago Press, 1998); Kathleen Paul, *Whitewashing Britain: Race and Citizenship in the Postwar Era* (Ithaca: Cornell University Press, 1997); Gerald Horne, 'Race to Insight: The United States and the World, White Supremacy and Foreign Affairs', in Hogan and Paterson, *Explaining the History*, 2nd edn, pp. 323–35; Penny Von Eschen, *Race Against Empire: Black Americans and Anticolonialism, 1937–1957* (Ithaca: Cornell University Press, 1997); Mary Dudziak, *Cold War Civil Rights: Race and the Image of American Democracy* (Princeton, NJ: Princeton University Press, 2001); Thomas Borstelmann, *The Cold War and the Color Line: American Race Relations in the Global Arena* (Cambridge, MA: Harvard University Press, 2001).

23. See, for example, Kristin Hoganson, 'What's Gender Got to Do with It? Gender History as Foreign Relations History', in Hogan and Paterson, *Explaining the History*, 2nd edn, pp. 304–22; Kristin Hoganson, *Fighting for American Manhood: How Gender Politics Provoked the Spanish-American and Philippine-American Wars* (New Haven: Yale University Press, 1998); Robert Dean, *Imperial Brotherhood: Gender and the Meaning of Cold War Foreign Policy* (Amherst: University of Massachusetts Press, 2001); Mary A. Renda, *Taking Haiti: Military Occupation and the Culture of US Imperialism, 1915–1940* (Chapel Hill: University of North Carolina Press, 2001); Petra Goedde, *GIs and Germans: Culture, Gender, and Foreign Relations, 1945–1949* (New Haven: Yale University Press, 2003).

24. See, for example, the essays in Amy Kaplan and Donald E. Pease (eds), *Cultures of United States Imperialism* (Durham: Duke University Press, 1993); and Christian G. Appy (ed.), *Cold War Constructions: The Political Culture of United States Imperialism, 1945–1966* (Amherst: University of Massachusetts Press, 2000). See also Rotter, *Comrades at Odds*; Andrew J. Rotter, 'Saidism without

Said: *Orientalism* and US Diplomatic History', *American Historical Review*, 105 (4) (2000) 1205–17; Mark Philip Bradley, *Imagining Vietnam and America: The Making of Postcolonial Vietnam, 1919–1950* (Chapel Hill: University of North Carolina Press, 2000); Matthew Connelly, *A Diplomatic Revolution: Algeria's Fight for Independence and the Origins of the Post-Cold War Era* (New York: Oxford University Press, 2002).

25. James Clifford, *The Predicament of Culture: Twentieth-Century Ethnography, Literature, and Art* (Cambridge, MA: Harvard University Press, 1988); Ninkovich, 'Introduction', p. 7.

26. Lucian Pye, quoted in Hudson, 'Culture and Foreign Policy', p. 2.

27. Criticism of culturalism often begins with Bryan D. Palmer, *Descent into Discourse: The Reification of Language and the Writing of Social History* (Philadelphia: Temple University Press, 1990). See also Melvyn Leffler, 'New Approaches, Old Interpretations, Prospective Reconfigurations', *Diplomatic History*, 19 (2) (1995) 173–96; Bruce Kuklick, 'Confessions of an Intransigent Revisionist about Cultural Studies', *Diplomatic History*, 18 (1) (1994) 121–4; Robert Buzzanco, 'Where's the Beef? Culture without Power in the Study of US Foreign Relations', *Diplomatic History*, 24 (4) (2000) 623–32.

28. Renda, *Taking Haiti*, p. 21.

29. Buzzanco, 'Where's the Beef?', 627; Andrew J. Rotter, 'Gender Relations, Foreign Relations: The United States and South Asia, 1947–1964', *Journal of American History*, 81 (2) (1994) 518–42.

30. Quote from Josef Stalin, in conversation with Pierre Laval in 1935, in Winston S. Churchill, *The Second World War: Vol. 1: The Gathering Storm*, rev. edn. (London: Penguin, 1985), p. 121.

31. Elizabeth Kier, 'Culture and French Military Doctrine Before World War II', in Katzenstein, *Culture of National Security*, p. 200.

32. Lucian Pye, 'Introduction: Political Culture and Political Development', in Lucian Pye and Sidney Verba (eds), *Political Culture and Political Development* (Princeton, NJ: Princeton University Press, 1965), pp. 7–8; Sidney Verba, 'Comparative Political Culture', in Pye and Verba, *Political Culture*, p. 513.

33. Joseph S. Nye Jr, *The Paradox of American Power: Why the World's Only Superpower Can't Go it Alone* (New York: Oxford University Press, 2002), pp. 8–12.

34. Wendy L. Wall, 'America's "Best Propagandists": Italian Americans and the 1948 "Letters to Italy" Campaign', in Appy, *Cold War Constructions*, p. 89.

35. Donna Alvah, '"Unofficial Ambassadors": American Military Families Overseas and Cold War Foreign Relations, 1945–1965', unpublished PhD dissertation (University of California-Davis, 2000).

36. Akira Iriye, 'Internationalizing International History', in Bender, *Rethinking American History*, pp. 47–62.

37. Christina Klein, *Cold War Orientalism: Asia in the Middlebrow Imagination, 1945–1961* (Berkeley: University of California Press, 2003), pp. 191–222.

38. Jepperson *et al.*, 'Norms, Identity, and Culture in National Security', p. 40; Price and Tannenwald, 'Norms and Deterrence'; Thomas U. Berger, 'Norms, Identity, and National Security in Germany and Japan', in Katzenstein, *Culture of National Security*, pp. 317–56.

39. Samuel P. Huntington, *The Clash of Civilizations and the Remaking of the World Order* (New York: Simon and Schuster, 1996); Lawrence E. Harrison and Samuel P. Huntington (eds), *Culture Matters: How Values Shape Human Progress* (New York: Basic Books, 2000).

40. As does Edward Said in *Culture and Imperialism* (New York: Random House, 1993), pp. 111–32.
41. Michael N. Barnett, 'Identity and Alliances in the Middle East', in Katzenstein, *Culture of National Security*, pp. 400–47 (quotes at pp. 433–4; emphasis in original).
42. John Foster Dulles, quoted in Michelle Mart, 'Tough Guys and American Cold War Policy: Images of Israel, 1948–1960', *Diplomatic History*, 20 (3) (1996) 367.
43. Douglas Little, *American Orientalism: The United States and the Middle East since 1945* (Chapel Hill: University of North Carolina Press, 2002), p. 80.
44. Little, *American Orientalism*, p. 95. See also Melani McAlister, *Epic Encounters: Culture, Media, and US Interests in the Middle East, 1945–2000* (Berkeley: University of California Press, 2001).
45. Little, *American Orientalism*, pp. 25–8.
46. Barnett, 'Identity and Alliances', pp. 443–7.
47. This case study is drawn from Rotter, *Comrades at Odds*, pp. 249–80, where full references to all quotations may be found. Note that different understandings of gratitude have troubled other countries' relations too: see O. Mannoni, *Prospero and Caliban: The Psychology of Colonization*, 2nd edn (New York: Praeger, 1964); Louis A. Perez Jr, 'Incurring a Debt of Gratitude: 1898 and the Moral Sources of United States Hegemony in Cuba', *American Historical Review*, 104 (2) (1999) 356–98.
48. Frank Costigliola, 'Reading for Meaning: Theory, Language, and Metaphor', in Hogan and Paterson *Explaining the History*, 2nd edn, pp. 279–303 (quotes at pp. 281, 292).
49. President George W. Bush, State of the Union Address, 29 January 2002; available at: http://www.whitehouse.gov/news/releases/2002/01/20020129 –11.html (accessed 6 September 2004).
50. A variant of the 'domino theory', first used by Dean Acheson at the time of the origins of the Truman Doctrine in 1947, is the 'bad apple' analogy. In Iraq, it has been used to suggest that *only* a few 'bad apples' perpetrated atrocities against Iraqi prisoners at Abu Ghraib prison; remove the 'bad apples' and the rest of the barrel retains its integrity.
51. Paul Krugman, 'Snares and Delusions', *New York Times*, 13 April 2004, p. A25.
52. John McNaughton, quoted in Neil Sheehan, *A Bright Shining Lie: John Paul Vann and America in Vietnam* (New York: Random House, 1988), p. 535.
53. Richard Nixon, quoted in Robert J. McMahon, *The Limits of Empire: The United States and Southeast Asia Since World War II* (New York: Columbia University Press, 1999), p. 160.
54. Thom Shanker and Dexter Filkins, 'Army Punishes 7 with Reprimands for Prison Abuse', *New York Times*, 4 May 2004, pp. A1, A6.
55. Ian Fisher, 'Iraqi Recounts Hours of Abuse by US Troops', *New York Times*, 5 May 2004, pp. A1, A18.
56. Frank Costigliola and Thomas G. Paterson, 'Defining and Doing the History of United States Foreign Relations: A Primer', in Hogan and Paterson, *Explaining the History*, 2nd edn, pp. 10–34; Robert J. McMahon, 'Toward a Pluralist Vision: The Study of American Foreign Relations as International History and National History', in Hogan and Paterson, *Explaining the History*, 2nd edn, pp. 35–50.

11
gender

glenda sluga

In 1988 the American historian Joan Wallach Scott published a path-breaking collection of essays entitled *Gender and the Politics of History*, which discussed gender as a category of historical analysis. Almost two decades later, Scott's volume still stands as perhaps the most useful English-language resource for comprehending the relevance of gender in the study of international history. Scott defined gender as 'the social organization of sexual difference', 'knowledge about sexual difference' and 'the knowledge that establishes meanings for bodily differences'. On these definitions, using gender as a category of historical analysis entailed a fundamental shift of perspective on the nature of historical research: 'The story,' she claimed, 'is no longer about the things that have happened to women and men and how they have reacted to them; instead it is about how the subjective and collective meanings of women and men as categories of identity have been constructed.'

Scott was differentiating the gender approach to history from women's history, which had been a significant component in the social history that had dominated historiography since the 1970s. Drawing largely on Marxist theories of society, that history had sought to recover 'hidden histories' of the disempowered and the disenfranchised, and to make them as important as the history of the intellectual and political elites that had hitherto populated the discipline. Gender history was also interested in the experiences of women but it adopted a different perspective, inspired by poststructuralist thinking. Instead of focusing on what individuals or groups did, it focused on discourses and language, and analysed the ways in which conceptions and representations of gender – specifically sexual difference – shaped the world in which those individuals acted and reacted, and the ways in which they thought about themselves and about others. The poststructuralist bases of the gender approach encouraged attentiveness to the ways in which meanings were established through conflictual processes, and to 'the importance of textuality, to the ways arguments are structured and presented as well as to what is literally said'. Poststructuralism also mandated the study of 'multiple rather than single causes, of rhetoric or discourse rather than ideology or consciousness'. Feminist politics, moreover, imbued this gender approach with a practical aim: 'to point out and change inequalities between women and men'.

Historians of women aiming to recover female agency in the past had also been interested in improving women's political and social status. Such scholars tended to tackle international history with an eye to the lost and silenced contribution of women to international relations, and particularly of feminists to the ideal of internationalism. By contrast, for gender historians, the pertinence of the gender framework for international history was to be found in the fact that, as Scott described, gender is 'an aspect of social organization generally' and 'the meanings of sexual difference are invoked and contested as part of many kinds of struggles for power'. Because 'knowledge is a way of ordering the world' and 'inseparable from social organization', the study of the construction of knowledge about and meanings of sexual difference involved the study of 'institutions and structures, everyday practices as well as specialized rituals, all of which constitute social relationships'. Moreover, institutional structures were 'premised on sexual divisions of labor' and 'references to the body often legitimize[d] the forms institutions take'.[1]

Although Scott called in 1988 for the application of gender analyses to the study of 'High Politics', such approaches have only recently been adopted by international historians to significant effect, and their relevance, like that of women's history, is still widely contested. The concerns of this chapter are to explain this relatively slow incorporation of gender into the mainstream study of international history, to chart its changing features and to assess the potential impact of gender analyses on the nature of international history itself. As I will argue, international history has, to a significant extent, pursued a somewhat errant track when it comes to gender studies. While the form of gender analysis outlined by Scott has become an important feature of current gender approaches in international history, substantial 'recovery' work in fact still needs to be done in the realm of the women's history of international relations, albeit within a gender framework that allows for a reconceptualization of power in the international arena.

the women's history of international relations

International history has long involved the story of the rise of international organizations linked to pacifism and political idealism, such as the International Court of Justice, the League of Nations and the United Nations (UN). Indeed, the emergence of a modern, truly international sphere of political engagement – a crucial precondition for the very concept of international relations – is marked by that organizational history. The so-called 'women's history of international relations' has also long engaged with these same themes, and particularly the emergence of internationalism and its links to feminism in the late nineteenth century in Europe and North America. Through the twentieth century this field gradually expanded to encompass the broader study of women in global politics, a topic that was generally completely sidelined in mainstream international history.[2]

The long-standing tradition of 'feminist' international relations history was consolidated in the 1970s, as a consequence of the growing influence of social history and women's history. It now sat at the interstices of histories of feminism on the one hand, and the conventional state-based historical study of international relations on the other.[3] It included studies of missionaries, nurses and peace movements and of 'Women in International Development'. It still tended to be written as part of the story of 'first wave' feminism, and told of the coming to consciousness of international sisterhood through the creation of international organizations made up of women, or devoted to the 'woman question', such as the International Council of Women and the Women's International League for Peace and Freedom, each of which were also involved in promoting the League of Nations and other internationalist causes, including the modern study of International Relations (IR). More recently some accounts of this history have also tackled the intersections of gender and race in these processes. Thus Leila Rupp's *Worlds of Women: The Making of an International Women's Movement* laid out the extent of women's engagement in international affairs and how that engagement defined the nature of 'the international', as well as the complex relationship between national and international motivations among these women, their relative Eurocentrism and the race prejudices that shaped and inhibited their thinking on universal sisterhood.[4]

To the extent that the women's historians of international relations aimed to affirm the significant place of women in international history, they had yet to make the case that the kind of agency women exerted in their own international organizations should be central to the concerns of international historians. (This was perhaps less because they were unable to, than because this was not their prime purpose or real interest.) However, another thin strand of women's history was also being developed which was engaged with giving women a place in mainstream international history, with its preoccupations with the machinations of diplomacy, foreign policy, and elite actors. In 1992, Edward Crapol could justly write in the preface to the second edition of his edited work on *Women and American Foreign Policy: Lobbyists, Critics, and Insiders* (first published in 1987) that the collection remained the only volume on women and foreign policy available. Crapol described his aim as being to recover the role of women in American foreign policy, and to move away from the assumption that women had no place in the traditional study of international relations. He acknowledged that the idea of recovery involved some reconsideration of the kinds of contributions that could be made to foreign policy, and the kinds of power that could be exercised. Hence the women in his volume exercised power as 'lobbyists' or 'critics' and only more rarely as 'insiders'. They were not operating from the centre of foreign-policy-making, but they nonetheless attempted to assert their influence from the sidelines, whether as an Eleanor Roosevelt or a Jane Fonda.[5]

Crapol's edited volume was significant for illuminating the contribution to American foreign policy of a number of women whose distinctive efforts and aims were otherwise lost to history. Yet although it accepted that historically women's influence on international relations may have occurred in unconventional forms (as pacifist lobbyists, or as the wives of state leaders, or as famous movie stars) it was also very much of the 'add women and stir' variety of history that was the subject of increasing criticism from feminist historians. For example, Scott's enjoinder to use gender as a category of analysis in 'High Politics' stipulated that a gender approach demanded more than the addition of women to existing historical narratives, since '[n]ew facts might document the existence of women in the past, but they did not necessarily change the importance (or lack of it) attributed to women's activities'.[6] Moreover, in 1990, another American historian, Emily S. Rosenberg, pointed out that the exceptional status of the women's history of international relations reified rather than historicized sex-segregated attitudes and activities, obscuring 'the complex processes by which gender boundaries are constantly redrawn over time'.[7]

ir studies of women and gender

Scott and Rosenberg were certainly not isolated in voicing opinions such as these, since they spoke within the context of the general and accelerating

impact on the humanities and social sciences of poststructuralism, with
its emphasis on discourse as constitutive of identity and experience.
Their views also shadowed changes that were already occurring within
the discipline of International Relations (IR), in ways that were to have
important implications for international history. In 1990 Rosemary Foot
noted in the otherwise cautious journal *Diplomatic History* that

> [u]nlike other related disciplines, international relations has been
> slow to incorporate feminist ideas, a characteristic that is in some
> respects odd considering how heavily the field has borrowed from other
> disciplinary areas. ... During the last few years, however, there has been
> a growing recognition of the gender-specific consequences of a range
> of international policies and processes, a recognition that has been
> given impetus by the erosion of the tendency to compartmentalize
> the domestic and international environments as analysts have delved
> into the effects that external actions have on societies and into how
> societies themselves affect those international actions.[8]

Foot drew her examples from Cynthia Enloe's *Bananas, Beaches, and Bases:
Making Feminist Sense of International Politics* (1990) and Crapol's *Women
and American Foreign Policy*. These volumes were both feminist in that
– at least by implication – they challenged the public/private divide
that framed understanding of the difference between international and
'domestic' (as in national) politics, and between conventional notions of
masculinity and femininity – wherein the public was a male space and
the private was a female space. However they also made quite distinctive
and contrasting contributions to the study of the place of women in
international relations, in the past and in the present.

As Crapol had explained, his aim was to add women to the history of
international relations. By contrast, Enloe's book picked up on the
importance of understanding the predominance of men and masculinity
in international politics. Enloe, Professor of Government at Clark
University, argued that gender was reconcilable with 'curiosity about
arms dealers, presidents' men, and concepts such as "covert operations"'.[9]
Her own curiosity extended to exploring the social impact of international
relations, especially in the 'Third World', as well as the gender politics
of militarization and the global economy. Her approach exposed the
ways in which the field of international relations relied upon and
reinforced the separation of the public and private and the underlying
sexual dichotomy of the whole separate spheres ideology. On the basis
of this gender framework, she could dissect areas of international relations

that impacted upon women but were not conventionally regarded as part of the international relations field, because their ambit was not within the typical purview of the state. These areas included migration and employment policy, as well as the effects of foreign affairs, the military and corporations on women's everyday lives. The question was not so much (as with Crapol): what influence did women exert on international relations, that is, what power did they have or exercise; but, rather, how did international relations affect women, and how did they render them powerless?

While such studies expanded the empirical basis of gender analyses of international relations, other feminist political scientists addressed the specific problems of theory and method in IR. The early 1990s saw a feast of such feminist critiques, including V. Spike Peterson's *Gendered States*, J. Ann Tickner's *Gender in International Relations* and Christine Sylvester's *Feminist Theory and International Relations in a Postmodern Era*.[10] For all its variations, this literature shared a number of assumptions, including the view that there was no single feminist theory of international relations. There were, however, shared feminist aims, including an overarching concern with the gender inequities and iniquities involved in the sexual politics of international relations. This body of work exposed the 'gender bias in key concepts in realism and ... the profoundly gendered imagery and symbolism employed in realist texts' and more broadly within the study of IR.[11]

Feminists exposed the ways in which the state-centrism of both 'real world' international relations and academic IR was anchored in gendered discourses and ideology, particularly specific representations of masculinity. At the same time, the shared interest of these critiques in poststructuralism meant a common scepticism towards the status of women as 'subject', the idea that women were an homogeneous group, and the conception of femininity as a stable identity. These studies were sceptical, too, of the changes that the recovery of women's experience in international relations could make, because that approach was not sensitive to the ways in which the very categories 'woman' and 'man', and conventional views of respective feminine and masculine attributes, were being marked out by the field itself. Thus in a self-conscious theoretical shift from her earlier work on the 'woman question' in IR, Marysia Zalewski edited (with Jane Parpart) *The 'Man' Question in International Relations* (1998). Zalewski and Parpart argued that the collection was the result of disillusionment with the recovery approach: '[i]nspired by feminist analysis, we initially tried to highlight the absence of women in the field [of IR] as well as the power and dominance of men. However, we began to question those traditional feminist methods.'

According to Zalewski and Parpart, the aim of focusing on the 'man question' was to destabilize the field in ways which merely adding women to the conventional subject matter of IR had not made possible, and thus to 'problematize the subjectivities of men, the subject of man, and the effects of masculinities in international relations'.[12] The essays brought together in The 'Man' Question tried to unpick the gendered public/private divide that informed IR studies, and the ways in which IR contributed to the masculinization of international public affairs and spaces. Theorizing the instability of gender identities and the nature of subjectivities led to a reconsideration of just how 'man' might be the proper study of IR and of its realist paradigm. The point of focusing on men was to deconstruct their dominance of the field, and of the role that perceptions and representations of masculinity and femininity had in sustaining that dominance. The intention was to highlight how representations of gender difference influenced the nature of IR. This approach also shifted the focus of studies from the state and individual agency to society and culture more broadly.

culture and gender in international history

Insofar as the study of gender within international history has grown significantly since Scott's rueful proclamation of its relative absence, this development has been the consequence primarily not of the influence of women's history, or of the impact of trends in IR, but rather of the flourishing interest in cultural history. A key feature of this recent development in gender and international history is a focus on the 'man question'. The cultural history approach to international relations implies a rethinking of the nature of the political and the positing of an alternative view of power, which has very productively encouraged gender analyses; but this does not necessarily imply a feminist perspective on the study of gender, for within this literature women may not be a key concern, and indeed are often once more marginalized.

Although it would be difficult to fix a single view of what culture is or where it can be found (here the reader is advised to turn to Andrew Rotter's contribution in this volume), in general it can be argued that cultural history, like gender history, has its roots in poststructuralism. In an exchange published in Diplomatic History in 2000 on the controversial status of the cultural history approach to international history, Robert Dean claimed that '[t]his debate among historians of international relations mirrors the larger debate in the profession over so-called post-modernist (a much-abused epithet) approaches that analyze language and culture, gender, race, class, etc. as elements of social power and historical experience'.[13]

We can say that on both a poststructuralist and a cultural history view, politics is mediated through systems of cultural representation, and cultural representation occurs in the domain of language. Language systems constitute discourses – or ways of knowing the world. Discourses – along with narratives and practices – are microsites of power. On this view, systems of power produce historically significant effects that are not confined exclusively to state to state relations; they are, in the words of Rosenberg, 'multiple and complex, arranged simultaneously through nation-states and regional relationships; through networks of capital, communications, and technology; through constructions of sex, gender, ethnicity, race, and nationality'.[14]

Although not all the new work in the cultural history of international relations attends to gender, when gender is incorporated into the cultural history of diplomacy and international relations, the focus tends to be on masculinity. Thus American historian Kristin Hoganson's book *Fighting for American Manhood* concentrates on the late-nineteenth-century form of 'imperial manhood' which helped lead the American nation into war. This idea of masculinity was combative, emotional and aggressive; it was also based on the social Darwinist view of the irresistible nature of racial instincts and national struggle. According to Hoganson, 'gender served as a cultural motive that easily lent itself to economic, strategic, and other justifications for war'. She also describes as critical to the role that a general manhood discourse was to play in foreign policy the specific influence of an overall climate of sexual anxiety, brought on by the aspirations for the renegotiation of male and female roles incarnated in the liberal demands of feminists and others at this time.[15]

The theme of 'imperial manhood' in the American context has also been taken up by Robert Dean in a book tellingly entitled *Imperial Brotherhood: Gender and the Making of Cold War Foreign Policy*. Dean sets out to understand American military intervention in Southeast Asia during the Kennedy and Johnson years. This constitutes a relatively conventional international history question, but Dean claims his method of answering that question is radically different. He attends to a *longue durée* cultural and historical context for understanding the actions of men who made decisions to go to war in the mid twentieth century. That context is their 'imperial masculinity', a model of manhood that became popular and hegemonic in the late nineteenth century, and which Hoganson had already outlined. According to Dean, in the twentieth century this model was inculcated at elite boarding schools, through volunteer military service and in the construction of networks of patronage across generations. Men like Kennedy were socialized into a prescriptive view of the importance of manliness, a prescription which compelled them 'to defend their society against internal and external threat':

> A lifetime of immersion in masculine competition and a culture celebrating militarized manhood gave many highly educated, privileged, and powerful men the conviction that duty and the protection of both their own power and that of the nation demanded a war.

Dean also explores the specific context of the ways in which manhood ideologies became pathological in the post-Second World War period, particularly with the McCarthy era purges of homosexuals in the State Department. These purges, he argues, added the potency of sexuality and secrecy to the armoury of an imperial form of manhood in American foreign policy.[16]

The role of gender discourse as both a cultural and individual motive for going to war in Vietnam, and its relationship to late-nineteenth-century discourses of imperial masculinity employed in the United States as arguments for the Philippine-American wars, has also been taken up Fabian Hilfrich, a German historian. Hilfrich also emphasizes the importance in the context of the Vietnam war of a discourse of manliness rooted in the late nineteenth century. He argues, not unlike Dean, that 'gendered rhetoric did not merely "seep" into the speeches of the "interventionists"' but rather 'constituted an integral part of their argumentative strategies': 'the interventionists basically defined both the annexation of the Philippines and the war in Vietnam as "manly" endeavours, as the choices that a "normal" man would make'. As Hilfrich notes too, this required the deployment of stereotypes of effeminacy, and thus femininity, as constituting negative forms of political behaviour. While these gender tropes transcend the specificity of the late nineteenth and mid twentieth centuries, Hilfrich provides evidence that in both cases historically specific crises of masculinity were critical factors, and that after the 1960s the imperial manhood model was redefined to some extent in terms of rationality rather than emotion.[17]

There are other examples of the cultural history approach to gender in international history, much of it focusing on the post-Second World War period and the role of the United States. On the whole, this work illuminates the ways in which representations of sexual difference exert symbolic and discursive power in political debate, often as metaphor and as ideal. Brenda Plummer, for example, has focused on the discussion surrounding the status of so-called 'brown babies' – that is the offspring of African-American soldiers and white German women born during the American 'occupation' of Germany – as representing a microsite of postwar policy conflict involving issues of race and gender. She looks at the place of these children in the broader context of postwar decision-making: by pointing out how in 1945 American policy was to block inter-racial marriages in the zones of occupation, rendering these babies illegitimate, she shows how 'during the occupation's brief "colonial" moment', the United States 'sorted out the hierarchies of race, nationality, and gender'.[18]

The role of the United States in the Cold War is also a favoured site for gender analysis from a cultural history perspective.[19] Robert Dean describes his own work as the examination of 'the role of class and gender in domestic political battles over Cold War foreign policy and in the decision-making process itself'.[20] Frank Costigliola has examined the significance of gender in George Kennan's conceptualisation of the Cold War;[21] and I have analysed gender in my study of the role of international bodies in the resolution of the 'Trieste problem' from 1945 to 1954. A territory contested between a 'post-fascist' Italy and communist Yugoslavia, Trieste was made the jurisdiction of a British-American Allied Military Government for nearly a decade while its fate was under international consideration. In the mode of Plummer, but extending the analysis to Britain as well as America, I suggest that in the decade after the Second World War, and in the context of the Cold War ideological struggle between communism and liberal-capitalism, the British-American military government contributed to the reassertion of a gender hierarchy as definitive of its broader ideological ambitions. Indeed one can plot the unfolding Cold War in relation to the increasing relevance in international politics of normative perceptions of gender identities and roles.[22] Similarly, Laura Belmonte has shown that during the Cold War, elites in the US State Department and the United States Information Agency were concerned to project a certain view of America that revolved around a conservative view of gender, and sexually differentiated separate spheres. She asserts that '[I]mages of gender and the family proved valuable tools in explaining the American way of life to foreign audiences'. The ideals of domestic life, and representations of women as mothers, wives and homemakers, were used to discredit communism. Once again, as in other cultural history studies, these generic tropes are deemed to assume their political potency in the context of a specific 'crisis'. Belmonte argues that 'many Americans embraced domesticity as an antidote to anxieties unleashed by atomic weapons and political instability.'[23]

As these examples suggest, cultural history has helped make gender critical to rethinking the operation of power in international politics. In particular, the poststructuralist understanding of power has invited a reconsideration of agency and raised new questions about why leaders act as they do and how their cultural beliefs shape the range of their possible actions. If language as discourse makes the world as much as reflects it – shaping the priorities, preferences and meanings given to the political – its study also concentrates attention on the ways in which the 'realism' of foreign policy is created, the real in *realpolitik* made and on the place of gender in those processes. This theoretical viewpoint assumes that accrued representations of gender difference have contributed to the shaping of power relations between states and between individuals participating in international relations practices. However, this approach has also been criticized for its distance from the conventional aims of the historiography of international relations, especially as regards the problem of causation.

Some of these criticisms have been launched against the cultural history of international relations in general, but have obvious pertinence for gender approaches. In Jessica Gienow-Hecht and Frank Schumacher's edited book, *Culture and International History*, a collection that draws together European (mainly German) and American historians, Volker Depkat maintains that 'the underlying concept of culture is so broad and all-encompassing that it is no longer analytically meaningful'. He points to Dean's work as an example of the ways in which using gender as a focus for international history 'eventually explains everything and nothing', since '[t]o understand cultural constructions in such a broad fashion actually means that there is no aspect of past realities that is not gendered'.[24] In the same volume another German historian, Marc Frey, points out that even the crises of masculinity which many of these authors use to situate their gender discussions are not time-specific – gender norms are inherently unstable and always in 'crisis'. On his view, utilizing the context of crisis merely emphasizes the problem of 'the plausible connection of long-term trends, of a history interested in the *longue durée*, with more readily definable event-related interpretations.'[25]

Hoganson, a key representative of the cultural gender history approach, acknowledges in her work that 'the nebulous thing we call culture might affect the way people engage the world around them, but it appears too amorphous to readily explain specific decisions and events'. She is clear, however, about the importance of cultural history to her work as well as its limitations. As she lists the variety of conventional non-gender explanations of the reasons for American involvement in the Spanish-American and American-Philippine wars, she claims that a gender approach has a deeper understanding to offer than other explanations which stress individual agency or even economic causation. She also refines her view of culture to focus specifically on a particular understanding of political culture – 'the assumptions and practices that shaped electoral politics and foreign policy formulation' – and on 'the gender convictions' that did so much to define its contours. Echoing Scott, Hoganson sums up that 'by stipulating social roles for men and women, gender beliefs have significantly affected political affairs', including the exclusion of women from electoral politics and the legitimation of male political authority.[26] Dean defends his own work by arguing that cultural history does amplify our understanding of why, even as it throws new light on questions of agency and causality. 'How,' Dean asks, 'can diplomatic historians fully make sense of the actions of their traditional subjects, political leaders and decision-makers if they do not thoroughly explore the way statesmen made sense of their world?'[27]

There are other concerns about the influence of cultural history on gender analyses in international history. Some feminists are arguing that the new 'male question' approach to the study of both IR and international history merely reinforces the marginality of women and women's experiences in international affairs.[28] In other words, the focus on masculinity is in itself symptomatic of the manner in which in the past historians have written women out of international history by assuming that the forms and spaces of international relations that are worthy of study are masculine, if not by nature, then by result of their appropriation of them. This remains a very problematic issue, and it illustrates how the debate about gender and culture both has a number of dimensions and is far from over; yet it also promises to be the source of the kind of reflection that will renew and rejuvenate international history, even as it polarizes its practitioners.

women, men and gender in international historiography

In her 1990 review, Rosemary Foot argued that when gender has been tackled in the study of the history of international relations the result has tended to take one of two forms, either 'an attempt to recapture women's experiences in order to fill out an incomplete record of the past or – perhaps a more difficult task – the production of new perspectives and knowledge that has involved rethinking what is important in the past'.[29] As we have seen, in the decade since those remarks there has been some headway in respect to the latter more difficult task, through a focus on masculinity and the intersections of race and gender in the historical analysis of foreign affairs, international relations and diplomacy. Culturally-focused studies have shifted understanding of where power might lie and how it might work. Cultural history has interrogated not only how a broader cultural context explains actors and actions, but also how particular forms of agency in the international sphere reconstitute the gender conventions of the broader culture. It has also encouraged a focus on the gender narratives and/or systems of cultural representation that have shaped international relations and diplomacy, even if not to the exclusion of other forms of hierarchical differentiation.

Contra to Foot's claim, however, less work has been done to rectify the relatively limited and partial incorporation of women into international history. Some attention has been paid to women's exceptional involvement in international relations, particularly in the formulation of foreign policy.[30] Yet at the same time, the history of women – and of their internationalism – continues to be viewed as separate from, and a marginal site of, *real* international history and *realpolitik*. Although one of the worst mistakes an historian can make is to assume that gender is synonymous with women, it seems that in international history gender hardly ever concerns women. I want to conclude by suggesting that a great deal still needs to be done to realize the inclusion of women into mainstream international history; moreover, achieving this goal has the potential not only to fundamentally shift our views on what is important in the past but also to illuminate the role of disciplinary knowledge in silencing women and their concerns. The poststructuralist gender approach to history outlined by Scott resonates with the interests of feminist IR theory. It emphasizes the importance of understanding how social science and historical narratives have silenced women, and to what extent those narratives have retained a masculinist bias even when women have been belatedly included. This understanding requires analyses of how gender inequalities have been institutionalized, even in the corporate practices of a discipline such as history. In this particular instance, the force of this critique can be demonstrated by considering international history itself and the marginal status of the women's history of this field.

Recent work on the women's strand of international history suggests that 'adding women and stirring' can indeed constitute a radical step in the gendering of mainstream international history. In the case of the history of international peace-making in 1919, for example, a gender-conscious analysis attentive to the meanings attributed to sexual difference, and the questions of how and why women were excluded from international discussions for a new world order, reveals a transnational consensus among the representatives of liberal states that women did not automatically exercise individual rights within nations, and that the ascription of female political rights to the realm of an international 'principle' potentially jeopardized the autonomous identity and sovereignty of nations. In an earlier essay, I examined how in 1919 a large number of politically active, predominantly middle-class, liberal-minded women keen to intervene in plans for a new world order, negotiated existing discourses of sexual and national difference in order to have the 'woman question' made part of the agenda for a new democratic world order and to reconceptualize the international as a more 'feminine' sphere. I argued that by juxtaposing the 'women's history of international relations' with conventional international history sources, the history of peace-making at the end of the First World War exposes critical aspects of the gender dimension of power relations in the victor states and in the constitution of international relations at that time.

This history also attends to the gender implications of the new international sphere grounded in the ideal of national self-determination, whereby women and their causes were relegated to the national, and therefore placed outside the domain of international relations. Of particular relevance to international history, internationally-minded liberal feminists and their organizations attempted – particularly in respect to the organization of the League of Nations – to become 'insiders' in 1919, influencing international policy areas specifically relevant to women, such as health and employment, and specific foreign policy issues, including the neo-colonialism of the mandate system devised at that time. However, they were self-consciously excluded by the leaders of the victor states from formal proceedings and committees. When compelled to consider the political status of women in the new world order, key political leaders and experts involved in the peace process insisted that, except for labour legislation and the League of Nations, sexual difference was an issue of 'domestic' or national significance, linked to precedents established within nations. This shows how a gender perspective can cast crucial new light on the reconstitution of the principles and norms of international relations during the postwar peace-making – indeed, on the very definitions of 'sovereignty' and 'the international'. There may even be an important coincidence in the gradual 'feminization' of the League and its subsequent lack of international legitimacy.[31] The efforts of these women were, however, subsequently largely excluded from the international history of the momentous events surrounding the 1919 settlement.

In similar ways, a feminist-inspired gender history of the study of international relations attentive to questions of recovery can show that women were key figures in the propagation of IR as a discipline in the period prior to 1919. Many of the women engaged with delineating the field of IR studies belonged to organizations such as the Institut International de la Paix, the World Congress of International Associations, Institutions Internationales, the Workers' Educational Association, the Association for the Study of International Relations, the Union of Democratic Control, the Women's International League and the Women's Cooperative Guild. Before 1919, recommended reading on international relations included a generous smattering of texts authored by women, among them the American social scientist Jane Addams and the English writer Lucia Ames Mead on patriotism and the new internationalism. Women such as these, and others including American economist Emily Greene Balch, Louise Weiss, the French editor of *L'Europe Nouvelle*, and Helena Swanwick, the editor of the English progressive journal *Foreign Affairs*, initially contributed significantly to the growth of interest in the study of IR, and the approach they nurtured was idealist.[32] By the 1930s the idealist school had been superseded by the realists and the study of IR had hardened into a masculine and male-dominated discipline. The key institutions promoting the study of IR and international history, the Royal Institute for International Affairs in London and the Geneva-based Graduate Institute of International Studies, were created out of the efforts of the very same progressivist men who had presided at the peace of 1919 and marginalized women's efforts to influence that peace. The earlier exertions of women were thereby excised from the historical record, just as women's texts, and their preferred subject areas, were eliminated from the agenda of international studies.[33]

conclusion

Historically, there is no question that women have made explicit the issue of sexual difference implicit in international affairs, that sexual difference has been used by women as a rationalization for their participation nationally and internationally, or that European women have in the past invoked and employed national and racial hierarchies in their attempts to delineate a gender-inclusive international order. This raises questions about the role of historians in the marginalization of women from international history. The question for feminist historians is how and why did the subject of women and internationalism come to be viewed as marginal to mainstream international history, and how and why did women's role in international relations come to be seen as secondary or even irrelevant to the main concerns of this history, namely nation-building and security? Adding women to the mainstream history of international relations reminds us both of their exclusion, and of the considerable ideological work that women undertook in order to alter their situation and that men employed to make them irrelevant to the concerns of international relations. In this context gender analyses can show that women 'were there', and can highlight the ways in which representations of sexual difference and of feminism (specifically First World feminism) have been implicated in the constitution and conceptualization of international relations, as well as the different relevance for men and women of international culture and politics.

It is important to note that awareness of the gender bias in international relations is hardly the exclusive provenance of late-twentieth-century feminists. Helena Swanwick, born in Germany in 1864, and a citizen of England from the age of four, a member during the war of the politically progressive men's and women's organization the Union of Democratic Control, chair of the British Section of the Women's International League for Peace and Freedom, and later the League's Vice President in Geneva, a pioneer of the League of Nations Society, and appointed by Ramsay MacDonald to be a member of the British government delegation to the League of Nations Assembly in 1924 and in 1929, certainly understood that bias well. It was on her way home from the first of her stints at the League of Nations, acting as a substitute sub-delegate, that she reflected on this theme:

> I was to feel at Geneva the enormous pull that the majority of men in public life have over women. To receive, even for a few weeks, only such Foreign Office papers as are distributed to delegates, gave me an insight that probably thousands of men get daily and a bare dozen of women ever get. Women, outside the closed doors, have to guess, to infer, to put two and two together, to reconstruct imaginatively what men are told by obsequious secretaries and industrious officials, or hear in conference or though dispatches. ... It seemed to me that we were artificially handicapped in all ways: bodily by our clothes and customs, mentally by the denial to us of sources of information and conditions of development open to men as men. Even the trifling increase of status that I enjoyed from having held so small

a governmental position as that of Substitute Delegate had a subtle effect on my little public and also on myself. I had tasted a little of that queen-bee food which transforms the unimportant private man into the Public Person. As soon as he has become a Person, he is listened to, followed, praised and blamed perhaps. But he has influence. He becomes a little Superman.[34]

An historian should know well that the obstacles to women's participation in international relations in the early twentieth century were in many ways specific to that time, pertaining to the kinds of clothes women had to wear, the closing off of higher posts and the insistence of celibacy among women in government posts. Indeed, by contrast, in 1996 Madeleine Albright confidently described to an American Women's Foreign Policy Group how

today women are engaged in every facet of global affairs, from policymaking to dealmaking, from arms control to trade, from the courtroom of the War Crimes Tribunal to the far-flung operation of the UN High Commissioner for Refugees. Even in the UN Security Council there is, thanks to President Clinton, one skirt to balance the fourteen suits. I like to think that is just about even odds.[35]

Of course, Albright was not the first American woman to be appointed as a UN ambassador, and certainly not the first woman. Even if Albright's appointment as Secretary of State signalled a greater leap for womankind, and Condoleezza Rice's more recent elevation to that position has the hallmarks of a significant ethnic, racial and gender advance, Crapol's earlier claim that '[i]ndisputably the formulation and conduct of American diplomacy remains male-dominated and male oriented' still stands.[36] In the context of current studies of the longer-standing culture of masculinity that has influenced the nature of foreign policy, at least in America, little has changed fundamentally, and the general theme of separate spheres and gender roles remains pertinent, just as representations of women's physical and psychical selves remain relevant to the political roles they are allowed legitimately to assume.

There are still many historical questions to be asked about the significance of sexual (and other kinds of) difference to the history of international relations and diplomacy. For example, Zalewski and Parpart look at the problem of the exceptional status of women another way, arguing that '[t]he presence of female state leaders can expose both the centrality of women in international relations and the uneasiness and ambiguity surrounding issues of gender'.[37] What neither the old women's history nor the new cultural approach to gender and international history have dealt with adequately is the significance of different experiences – some local, some national – of gender conventions and expectations in the sphere of international relations. Moreover, questions remain to be asked about the dominance of American scholars and themes in these fields: the examples I have drawn from in this chapter highlight the ways in which the new cultural history of international relations is markedly American in its focus and origins.[38] Considering the ways in which cultural history approaches have attuned us both to the role of historiography in rehearsing and reifying gender norms and to the masculinity of IR studies, the 'Americanization' of the cultural gender history approach should also make us wary. For if focusing on men entrenches women's marginality to IR studies, then concentrating on the United States may reinforce the US prominence in the domain of international relations. The benefits of a gender approach thus accrue not just in terms of enhancing our understanding of the nature of international relations in the past, but also in terms of compelling us to rethink the nature of our own scholarly practices. Used as a category and tool of historical analysis, gender has profitably alerted at least some international historians to the importance of understanding the influence of the tropes, ideals and norms of sexual difference on the preferences, priorities and perspectives of both IR and the historiography of international relations.

notes

1. J. W. Scott, *Gender and the Politics of History* (New York: Columbia University Press, 1988), pp. 2–7.
2. The US-based online bibliographical resource 'Core Lists in Women's Studies' has sections devoted to international history, international politics and transnational feminism, detailing work on the international history of the women's movement, gender and international relations and global feminisms; available at: http://www.library.wisc.edu/libraries/WomensStudies/core/coremain.htm (accessed 24 June 2004).
3. See, for example, E. F. Hurwitz, 'The International Sisterhood', in R. Bridenthal and C. Koonz (eds), *Becoming Visible. Women in European History* (Boston: Houghton Mifflin, 1977), pp. 325–45; L. Costin, 'Feminism, Pacifism, Internationalism and the 1915 International Congress of Women', *Women's Studies International Forum*, 5 (3–4) (1982) 301–15; R. Sherrick, 'Toward Universal Sisterhood', *Women's Studies International Forum*, 5 (6) (1982) 655–61; N. Black, 'The Mothers' International: The Women's Co-Operative Guild and Feminist Pacifism', *Women's Studies International Forum*, 7 (6) (1984) 467–76; F. P. Bortolotti, *La donna, la pace, l'Europa* (Milan: Franco Angeli, 1985); J. Vellacott, 'A Place for Pacifism and Transnationalism in Feminist Theory:

The Early Work of the Women's International League for Peace and Freedom', *Women's History Review*, 2 (1) (1993) 23–56; D. Stienstra, *Women's Movements and International Organizations* (New York: St Martin's,1994).

4. L. J. Rupp, *Worlds of Women: The Making of an International Women's Movement* (Princeton, NJ: Princeton University Press, 1997). See also N. Berkovitch, *From Motherhood to Citizenship: Women's Rights and International Organizations* (Baltimore: Johns Hopkins University Press, 1999).

5. E. Crapol, 'Preface to the Second Edition' and 'Introduction', in E. Crapol (ed.), *Women and American Foreign Policy. Lobbyists, Critics, and Insiders*, 2nd edn (Delaware: Scholarly Resources, 1992), pp. vii–viii and ix–xv respectively.

6. Scott, *Gender and the Politics of History*, p. 3.

7. E. S. Rosenberg, 'Gender', *Journal of American History*, 77 (1) (1990) 118.

8. R. Foot, 'Where are the Women? The Gender Dimension in the Study of International Relations', *Diplomatic History*, 14 (4) (1990) 615–22, quote at 616.

9. C. Enloe, *Bananas, Beaches, and Bases: Making Feminist Sense of International Politics* (Berkeley: University of California Press, 1990), p. 11.

10. V. Spike Peterson (ed.), *Gendered States: Feminist (Re)Visions of International Relations Theory* (Boulder, CO: Lynne Rienner, 1992); J. Ann Tickner, *Gender in International Relations: Feminist Perspectives on Achieving Global Security* (New York: Columbia University Press, 1992); Christine Sylvester, *Feminist Theory and International Relations in a Postmodern Era* (Cambridge: Cambridge University Press, 1994).

11. J. Steans, *Gender and International Relations* (Oxford: Polity, 1998), p. 2.

12. M. Zalewski, 'Introduction: From the "Woman" Question to the "Man" Question in International Relations', in M. Zalewski and J. Parpart (eds), *The 'Man' Question in International Relations* (Boulder, CO: Westview Press, 1998), p. 2.

13. R. Dean, 'Tradition, Cause and Effect, and the Cultural History of International Relations', *Diplomatic History*, 24 (4) (2000) 615.

14. E. S. Rosenberg, cited in Dean, 'Tradition, Cause and Effect', 620.

15. K. L. Hoganson, *Fighting for American Manhood: How Gender Politics Provoked the Spanish-American and Philippine-American Wars* (New Haven: Yale University Press, 1998), p. 8.

16. R. Dean, *Imperial Brotherhood: Gender and the Making of Cold War Foreign Policy* (Amherst: University of Massachusetts Press, 2001), quotes at p. 241.

17. F. Hilfrich, 'Manliness and "Realism": The Use of Gendered Tropes in the Debates on the Philippine-American and on the Vietnam War', in Jessica Gienow-Hecht and Frank Schumacher (eds), *Culture and International History* (New York: Berghahn, 2003), pp. 60–78, quotes at p. 61.

18. B. G. Plummer, 'Brown Babies: Race, Gender, and Policy after World War II', in B. G. Plummer (ed.) *Window on Freedom: Race, Civil Rights, and Foreign Affairs, 1945–1988* (Chapel Hill: University of North Carolina Press, 2003), p. 85.

19. This work parallels developments in feminist IR studies. In a collection of essays on the end of the Cold War, Enloe focuses on 'the varieties of masculinity and femininity that it took to create the Cold War and the sorts of transformations in the relationships between women and men it will take to ensure that the ending processes move forward': C. Enloe, *The Morning After:*

Sexual Politics at the End of the Cold War (Berkeley: University of California Press, 1993), p. 5.

20. Dean, 'Tradition, Cause and Effect', 620 n. 8. See also R. Dean, 'Masculinity as Ideology: John F. Kennedy and the Domestic Politics of Foreign Policy', *Diplomatic History*, 22 (1) (1998) 29–62.

21. F. Costigliola, '"Unceasing Pressure for Penetration": Gender, Pathology, and Emotion in George Kennan's Formation of the Cold War', *Journal of American History*, 83 (4) (1997) 1309–39.

22. G. Sluga, *The Problem of Trieste and the Italo-Yugoslav Border: Difference, Identity, and Sovereignty in Twentieth-Century Europe* (Albany: State University of New York Press, 2001).

23. L. Belmonte, 'A Family Affair? Gender, the US Information Agency, and Cold War Ideology, 1945–1960', in Gienow-Hecht and Schumacher, *Culture and International History*, pp. 79–93, quotes at p. 80.

24. V. Depkat, 'Cultural Approaches to International Relations: A Challenge', in Gienow-Hecht and Schumacher, *Culture and International History*, p. 181.

25. M. Frey, 'Gender, Tropes, and Images: A Commentary', in Gienow-Hecht and Schumacher, *Culture and International History*, p. 217.

26. Hoganson, *Fighting for American Manhood*, pp. 1–14, quotes at pp. 2–3.

27. Dean, 'Tradition, Cause and Effect', 617.

28. Many of the essays in Zalewski and Parpart, *'Man' Question*, take up this point.

29. Foot, 'Where are the Women?', 616.

30. See Rosenberg, 'Gender', 116.

31. G. Sluga, 'Female and National Self-Determination: A Gender Re-Reading of the "Apogee of Nationalism"', *Nations and Nationalism*, 6 (4) (2000) 495–521.

32. For example, J. Addams, *Newer Ideals of Peace* (New York: Macmillan, 1907); L. A. Mead, *Patriotism and the New Internationalism* (Boston: Ginn, 1906); E. G. Balch, *Approaches to the Great Settlement* (New York: Huebsch, 1918).

33. For a more conventional outline narrative of disciplinary history, see J. Gienow-Hecht, 'Introduction: On the Division of Knowledge and the Community of Thought: Culture and International History', in Gienow-Hecht and Schumacher, *Culture and International History*, pp. 3–26.

34. H. Swanwick, *I Have Been Young* (London: Gollancz, 1935), p. 415.

35. M. Albright, quoted in T. Lippman, *Madeleine Albright and the New American Diplomacy* (Boulder, CO: Westview Press, 2000), p. 9.

36. Crapol, 'Introduction', p. xiv.

37. Zalewski, 'Introduction', p. 7.

38. Exceptions include the attempt by Gienow-Hecht and Schumacher as editors of *Culture and International History* to highlight European work, although much of this too engages with the role of America and Americans.

12
global history
akira iriye

At the outset, some clarification of terminology will be useful.
Global history approaches international history by stressing global
or transnational themes. International history, as the phrase is used
throughout this volume, usually refers to the history of international
relations. 'International', of course, means interrelations among nations,
whether diplomatic, economic or cultural. The existence of sovereign
national entities is assumed, and the nation provides the key framework
of analysis. International history studies how nations (both governments
and citizens), presumably concerned with their 'national interests',
behave toward one another. The international arena tends to be seen
as a stage for the interaction of particularly powerful countries, or the
great powers. Transnational history, in contrast, does not privilege great
powers, or any sort of power, as the definer of international order. The
world explored in the framework of transnational history is concerned
with themes and phenomena that cut across national boundaries, many
of which have little to do with power. Rather than focusing on nations
and their interests, transnational history deals with supranational and
non-national forces and topics. It is concerned less with national than
with global interests.

Just to take one example, international migration is a subject that
is an important aspect of global history but which has tended to be
neglected in the study of international history. To be sure, migration
becomes a subject of study in international relations when governments
negotiate emigration and immigration treaties or when an immigration
dispute develops into an international issue. But migration takes place
all the time, in peace as well as in war. Indeed, it is a phenomenon that
is more enduring than diplomatic crises or inter-state hostilities. That is
why migration as the movement of people across national boundaries

has been more appropriately and thoroughly explored in the context of transnational history. Even though migrants originate in a particular country, such national identity may be less important than the fact that they are part of a global demographic shift. Many of the migrants are 'sojourners', working abroad for a period of years and comprising a global labour force that is constantly in search of better opportunities, while others live in refugee camps, without a home of their own. In either case, the history of transnational migration is a key feature of modern history, and yet conventional accounts of international relations pay little attention to it. This and many similar phenomena, however, comprise central themes in the study of transnational history. Thus, in a sense, transnational history deals with subjects that lie outside the usual topics in international relations, such as diplomacy, war and the pursuit of national interests. Transnational history can make up for the deficiencies of mainstream international history by moving beyond these traditional categories and focusing on more global, and indeed more human, phenomena.

the terrain of global history

Transnational history, therefore, is global history. But the two terms have not always been used interchangeably. That is in part because global history, understood as the history of the globe, goes back to the origins of humans, whereas we cannot speak of transnational history before the birth of nations. Global history, as the term is used by some historians, is essentially the history of the world, little different from world history. (Whether world history and global history are the same is a fascinating question that has attracted the attention of some scholars, but we shall not be concerned with the issue here.) Transnational history is, in that sense, modern global history, what Bruce Mazlish has called 'new global history'.[1] The term refers to a relatively recent period in which history may be said to have become truly global. Essentially, new global history is the history of globalization, although here again historians differ as to when the series of economic, technological and other changes that comprised globalization began.[2] Some date the origins of modern globalization from the circumnavigation of the earth around 1500; others consider the mid-nineteenth-century convulsions all over the world to have been a major landmark in establishing global interconnectedness; and still others argue that a qualitatively different world came into existence only around 1970, with humankind's first trip to the moon. For our purposes, it will suffice to adopt a chronology that equates global history with transnational history; in other words, if we consider globalization as having been a unifying theme of the history of the nineteenth and twentieth centuries, then transnational history becomes essentially interchangeable with global history.

Global history, then, may be considered the history of transnational developments during the last two centuries. It is distinguished from conventional international history because it does not prioritize inter-state affairs and, in particular, its chronology is not determined by international crises and wars. International history is usually periodized in terms of such events as the Napoleonic Wars and the Congress of Vienna (1790s through 1815), the breakdown of the Vienna system (1848 through the 1850s), the age of Bismarck (1871 to 1890), the road to the Great War (1890 to 1914), the inter-war years (1919 to 1939), the Second World War, the coming of the Cold War, the high Cold War (the 1950s through the 1960s), the end of the Cold War, the post-Cold War period (since 1990), and so forth. Global history does not necessarily ignore wars, hot or cold, but its chronology does not depend on them.

To go back to the example of the history of migration, crucial landmarks here are the rapid demographic expansion taking place both in the West and in China from around 1800, and the subsequent large-scale transnational movements of people (Europeans to North America, and Indians and Chinese to Southeast Asia and the Pacific) that began in the 1850s. In terms of global history, these dates would seem to have been more significant than the rise and fall of the Vienna system of international relations, still the most widely accepted framework for understanding nineteenth-century international affairs. In the twentieth century, to be sure, the two world wars significantly affected population movements, with millions forcibly driven out of their homelands and, in the worst instances, brutally killed. At the same time, however, a truly significant phenomenon of the century was that, although over 100 million people lost their lives through war, the world population more than tripled, from something less than 2 billion to about 6 billion. The decade of the 1970s was particularly significant in this story in that the world's population increased at a higher rate (about 2.2 per cent per annum) than during any other earlier decade. Such demographic explosion had obvious implications, not least in transnational migration. Larger numbers than ever crossed borders, legally or illegally, in search of jobs, housing and security. By the end of the century, it was estimated that 2 per cent of the world's population consisted of labourers working outside their countries of origin. In such a story, therefore, dates like the 1850s and the 1970s would be of greater significance than, say, 1815 or 1914.

There is clearly a need for a new way of conceptualizing the past, with a chronology that is based less on inter-state than on transnational phenomena. Unfortunately, historians in general and specialists in international history in particular have largely neglected the task of reconceptualization. This can be seen, for instance, in the fact that there are still very few studies of migration by historians: most works in this field have been written by political scientists (such as Mark J. Miller) and anthropologists (such as Robin Cohen).[3] Among historians, Wang Gungwu has taken the lead in examining what he calls the Chinese diaspora, the migration of millions of Chinese since the mid nineteenth century.[4] There are also, to be sure, numerous monographs on European emigration to North and South America, and immigration history is a rich sub-field of US history. But this literature has not been incorporated into standard histories of international relations. A popular textbook like William Keylor's *The Twentieth-Century World* has no section on transnational migration, whether European or Asian.[5] Conversely, global history surveys often provide excellent guides to how we might reconfigure international history by incorporating the phenomenon of migration. John and William McNeill's recapitulation of world history, *The Human Web*, for instance, focuses on the theme of interactions among people, goods and ideas since time immemorial.[6] The movement of people plays a crucial role in the McNeills' account, which is presented in the framework of the development of a world community. Put in such a framework, even international history takes on new significance as a story of how nations and peoples have dealt with one another even as more and more migrants cross borders. Migrants from abroad establish connections with indigenous populations, and in that process the two may establish some sort of social order, or they may collide and become estranged. That is certainly an important theme in international history, but to examine it the traditional nation-centred narrative is of little use.

Global history, then, may have a great deal to contribute to enriching the study of international history. It will enable us to resist the temptation to deal solely with nations and their policies, girding us against the intellectual timidity that deems them alone worthy of our attention. Global history, moreover, will liberate us from what may be termed the uni-national or mono-national perspective that still prevails in the study of international relations. Instead of examining international history in terms of just one country's foreign affairs, global history will enable us to become attentive to all countries and, even more important, to many entities that are not nations.

Such non-national entities are often referred to as non-state actors, and they play crucial roles in global history. Especially pertinent are four types of non-state actors: inter-governmental organizations (IGOs), non-governmental organizations (NGOs), multinational enterprises (MNEs) and regional communities. None of them is interchangeable with sovereign states, and the world community that they together make up is quite different from the international system defined by sovereign states. International relations historians have been slow to recognize these actors, let alone produce monographic work on them, because they have been entrapped in a geopolitical definition of international relations. Global history, because it is concerned with transnational trends, presents an alternative definition of the world, one in which global interconnections, or globalization, are the principal driving force.

inter-governmental organizations

Non-state actors have done more to promote globalization than sovereign states. To study such actors, then, is to deepen our understanding of the phenomenon of globalization, which in turn should serve to enrich our study of international history. Of the four non-state actors mentioned above, IGOs, or organizations that are established by governments, have been extensively studied by political scientists, but unfortunately by very few historians.[7] The reasons are not hard to seek. Historians have been more interested in international conflict, crises and warfare than in the absence of such phenomena, and even peaceful periods in international affairs have been seen as products of geopolitical developments like the balance of power, bipolarity, or the hegemonic position of one superpower. In such constructions, international organizations hardly have any role to play. In power-centred analyses of international relations, they have been relegated to a mere footnote in the larger drama of world politics. The League of Nations is thus usually treated as an insignificant chapter in inter-war diplomatic history, a product of naive idealism that failed to stop war. The United Nations similarly hardly appears in standard accounts of post-Second World War international history except as an arena for confrontation among the nuclear powers. But international organizations concern themselves with far more than conflict and war. They have been instrumental in providing humanitarian relief, for instance, or in assisting nation-building efforts. These activities are as much a part of international affairs as inter-state tensions and warfare.

Among the few historical works that take international organizations seriously as important players in world affairs is F. S. L. Lyons'

Internationalism in Europe.[8] Published in 1963, it contains rich material on the creation and development of international organizations before 1914. The book shows that even before the League of Nations was established, there had existed a rich legacy of efforts by various governments, as well as private groups, to create international agencies, ranging from the International Committee of the Red Cross to the Universal Postal Union. Most histories of international affairs in the late nineteenth century and the early twentieth century are presented in the framework of 'the origins of the First World War', in which such developments as the rise of Germany, the arms race, and colonial rivalries provide the principal story line. Events like the founding of the Red Cross hardly fit or figure here. But if we conceptualize the world as consisting not just of the great military powers and their empires but also of transnational movements that were establishing closer connections among nations, then international organizations deserve serious scholarly attention. For the alleged 'road to war' was being paved precisely at a moment in history when forces of globalization were becoming more manifest than ever.

Among recent works that re-evaluate the roles of international organizations, Dorothy Jones' *Toward a Just World* stands out. Refusing to prioritize war as the principal theme of modern international relations, she argues that, underneath the more dramatic story of geopolitical vicissitudes, there was, in the nineteenth and the twentieth centuries, another, equally significant story, that of the efforts by nations and especially by international organizations to develop a world order based on justice. Hers is a history that puts the search for justice, not military preparedness or the balance of power, at centre stage.[9] Similarly, Peter Wilson's recent study of Leonard Woolf, whose *International Government*, published in 1916, was the first serious attempt to call attention to international organizations, adds significantly to our understanding of global history. Although dismissed as a naive idealist in the heyday of realism, Woolf had a better understanding of the sources of international conflict than the realists; he argued that the great powers, pursuing their self-interests in enlarging their empires and fortifying their defences, would never be able to prevent international relations from being always in a precarious condition unless they recognized the need to establish international organizations that united nations and people throughout the world.[10]

non-governmental organizations

While Lyons, Jones and Wilson focus primarily on IGOs, other scholars have begun to pay attention to NGOs, especially of the international variety. Here again, political scientists have been far ahead of historians and have published important case studies of international NGOs such as those, for instance, engaged in humanitarian relief, developmental assistance or environmentalist activities.[11] My own work, *Global Community*, a brief history of international organizations, especially NGOs, benefited a great deal from the lively political science literature in this field.[12] Historians have been slow to interest themselves in NGOs, but a few important studies have been published. Leila Rupp's history of international women's organizations and Elizabeth Cobbs Hoffman's examination of US private organizations that inspired the establishment of the Peace Corps and worked closely with it come to mind.[13] These studies demonstrate that underneath (or above) the level of states engaged in playing power-political games and pursuing national interests, private associations of individuals across borders have established networks of interdependence. Today there are said to exist over 40 000 international NGOs. Who is to say that they do not merit scholarly attention, or that they do not count in international relations?

Democratization, for instance, is a theme in international history, but it can never be fully understood so long as we focus solely on official policies and governmental action. Much has been written about Woodrow Wilson's vision of a world to be made safe for democracy.[14] Even as geopolitically oriented a history of international relations as Henry Kissinger's *Diplomacy* takes pains to explain the Wilsonian legacy and its implications for world affairs.[15] Nevertheless, most such works have difficulty fitting that legacy into a comprehensive history of international relations. They note the enormous difficulties the United States experienced after the Great War in spreading democracy so that the vision remained essentially an unfulfilled ideal. We would gain a better understanding of the post-1919 years, however, if we recognized that efforts at democratization were continued by the League of Nations as well as numerous international NGOs, many of which were concerned with the protection of the rights of women and children and with promoting international exchanges among various groups of people such as labourers and artisans. Democratization in the sense of arousing people's awareness of their rights and encouraging their participation in political affairs was a task that was carried forward in many parts of the world during the 1920s and even during the 1930s, but one would never know it so long as one viewed these decades in the framework of the coming of the Second World War, as most historians still do. We should note that the triumph of democratic states in the war against the Axis was not just a military victory but also a prelude to the establishment of the

United Nations, followed soon afterwards by the drafting of the Universal Declaration on Human Rights. These achievements were a culmination of the tireless efforts by private organizations as well as IGOs throughout the world that had never ceased to struggle for human rights.

The decades after the Second World War will thus look very different if we bring IGOs and NGOs into the picture. The international history of these years is definable in terms of the superpower rivalry known as the Cold War only if we focus exclusively on geopolitics. If, instead, we consider the spectacular growth in the number and influence of international organizations, we shall gain a different perspective. International affairs will become less a story of the struggle for power between the two superpowers, than a drama in which more and more players arrive on the scene and challenge the centrality of power politics. Democratization, too, will come to be understood not just as the Western allies' strategy to gain influence against the Soviet bloc nations, but also, and more fundamentally, as a continuation of the efforts made earlier to redefine world order. The development of civil society in various countries will be linked to the emergence of an international civil society, not to the victory of one side in the Cold War against the other. Here again, unfortunately, historians have not contributed much to the reconceptualization of post-1945 international relations. They have missed the steady growth of civil society in various parts of the world because they have been preoccupied with the balance sheet of the bipolar Cold War struggle. But if globalization is seen as a principal theme of recent history, it is obvious that international relations must be understood in that context, and here the Cold War paradigm offers little help. Global history, rather than international history, enables us to see the past in proper perspective.

multinational enterprises

These observations equally apply to the third category of non-state actors that have been of particular significance in the international history of the last decades of the twentieth century, namely multinational enterprises. MNEs – sometimes also called multinational corporations – are business entities that combine capital, technology and labour from more than one country in order to produce goods and services, which are then to be marketed all over the world through sales offices that are also multinational. As Mira Wilkins, one of the foremost historians of MNEs, has noted, these entities began to make their appearance in the nineteenth century when business people from Britain and other

European countries established factories and marketing agencies in various parts of the world.[16] It was, however, after the Second World War, and especially during the last decades of the twentieth century, that the number and scope of MNEs grew spectacularly. According to Bruce Mazlish, there were about 1000 such enterprises world-wide in 1970 (mostly, however, of European or US origins), whereas 30 years later the number exceeded 63 000 (of which an increasing proportion originated in Asia).[17] Some of them were extremely wealthy, in fact richer than all but a handful of the world's nations if we compute their wealth in terms of gross national product.

By definition, an MNE is a combination of the resources of a number of countries. It is not identifiable with any one of them in particular. The fact, therefore, that so many of them have come to exist, and that they are wealthier than three-quarters of the 200 nations existing in the world today, should force us to reconsider the nature of international relations. World affairs have become increasingly affected by the workings of MNEs, which by definition are oriented toward profit-making by looking for the most efficient uses of capital and labour. Such considerations are fundamentally at odds with geopolitical calculations. Whether the introduction of MNEs onto the scene makes international relations more stable or less stable is an empirical question that should engage the attention of historians, but thus far few of them appear to have shown even an awareness of the problem. A good start has been made by Emily Rosenberg, whose *Financial Missionaries to the World* studies US financiers and economic advisors abroad in the first half of the twentieth century. As the title indicates, Rosenberg postulates that, far more than government officials, bankers and financial experts established connections between the United States and other countries in the hope that a more interdependent world order would be constructed.[18] To be sure such a world would be fashioned in the interests of the United States, but even so, this is to operate with a definition of foreign policy that does not prioritize power politics.

International economic relations have been examined expertly by economists. International relations historians have made use of their work, but many of them still retain conventional frameworks of analysis. For instance, Paul Kennedy's justly acclaimed *The Rise and Fall of the Great Powers*, a superb study of the subject, assumes that the world is an arena where nations vie with one another for power (including economic wealth).[19] Powers, or nations, are the primary, if not the only, units of analysis. Few historians have put business enterprises at centre stage in international relations. Andre Frank's *Re-Orient* is a notable exception.

This book offers a panoramic view of world economic history in which patterns of international trade shifted dramatically around 1800, with Western countries for the first time emerging as the major players, replacing Arab, Indian and Chinese merchants.[20] Such a thesis has important implications for the study of international history, enabling us to see, for instance, that the so-called Vienna system that emerged in Europe in 1815 was just one part of a world order that was becoming commercially interconnected. Globalization again would serve as the overarching theme, of which the growth of international trade was an economic expression and the Vienna system a political one. Britain's and other Western nations' 'informal empires' that were prying open the traditional markets of Asia and establishing beachheads in the newly independent countries of Latin America fit into such a picture.[21]

An intriguing question arises in this connection. Precisely at the moment when, in the last decades of the nineteenth century, 'informal imperialism' was giving way to more formal imperialism, globalizing forces were also becoming intensified, interconnecting areas of the world more closely than ever before. What was the relationship between globalization and formal imperialism? This is a fascinating problem that awaits rigorous historical analysis. Globalization is a major topic in global history, and imperialism in international history, so that to understand their relationship is to figure out a way to bring these two histories closer together. Hitherto the tendency has been to bring global history into the framework of international history and to argue that globalization was made possible through a system of international governance that was provided by the empires, especially the British Empire. Niall Ferguson, among recent writers, has made an explicit connection between globalization and imperialism in noting that the nineteenth-century British Empire established and sustained an international order that enabled world-wide trade and investment activities.[22] Absent imperialism, he seems to be arguing, commercial globalization could not have proceeded as smoothly as it did. The assumption is that the international order is fundamentally a political construction and that without it, no economic and other transactions can be promoted.

One might well raise objections to such an interpretation. Did not the empires hinder, rather than promote, the movement of goods, capital and people across borders? Did not the imperial powers eventually collide against each other so calamitously as to almost put an end to globalization? Even if the British Empire may be said to have been a benign hegemon providing law and order so as to facilitate transnational trade and investment activities, did not its example lead other nations to emulate it and to build up their own empires, most of which were far more exclusionary? After all, was there not something unusual, 'un-global' even, about a system of governance in which one European ruled over 99 Africans, Asians and Pacific islanders? Was not such a system destined to collapse, and if so, how could imperialism be said to have been a *sine qua non* of globalization? Actually, imperialism was destined to be a rather transient phenomenon, and globalization has proven to be a far more resilient and enduring theme in modern history. Rather than putting globalization in the context of international history, therefore, we should seek to understand imperialism in the framework of global history, as but a passing and not a very helpful phase in the more enduring story of interdependence and interpenetration across regions and oceans.

regional communities

Regional communities, the fourth and last category of non-state actors to be considered, have been better studied by historians than IGOs, NGOs or MNEs. Excellent monographs have been published on the making of the European Community (later the European Union).[23] The more we come to know the story, the stronger the impression grows that this was the truly catalytic phenomenon of the postwar era. Even in conventional international relations terms, it was a remarkable development that for the first time in modern history France and Germany, and later on other European countries, forswore war by establishing a transnational union. Clearly, these nations recognized that the only way to prevent another catastrophic disaster was to create a pan-European community, something like a United States of Europe. The idea for such a union had long existed, but that had not prevented devastating wars. Now, however, in the wake of the Second World War, something happened to reverse the course and to unite rather than divide nations. Since this occurred in Europe where the modern nation first emerged, the new development signalled nothing less than a revolution in international relations. The Treaty of Rome, signed in 1957 by France, Germany and four other countries to establish the European Economic Community, within a few years led to the establishment of the European Community and then to the European Union whose membership has grown to 25 nations by 2004. There is a long list of countries that are waiting to be admitted, and, unless some unforeseeable developments occur, it is likely that Turkey, and possibly some other Middle Eastern countries, will also become members. That will truly be a momentous development, turning the European Union into something even more geographically and culturally inclusive.

That much can be comprehended within the framework of conventional international history. But we can go a step further and put the story of European integration in the context of global history. That will mean, above all, to recognize regional integration as a major theme in recent history, an important feature of global interconnectedness, or globalization. If we do so, then the Cold War will cease to be the key story of the post-1945 world. If, instead, the growth of global interconnectedness is seen as the overriding and enduring development, the Cold War, which divided rather than integrated the world, would have to be seen as having been something of an aberration. If the world, coming out of the turmoil of the 1930s and the war years, was to resume its path of globalization, the Cold War clearly was not the way to promote such a development. On the contrary, it impeded the process of reconnecting various parts of the globe politically and economically. Of course, the United States and its allies were intent upon providing economic assistance to war-devastated Europe and eventually to all parts of the world as a way to prevent these regions from falling into the Soviet sphere of influence. The Marshall Plan and various developmental assistance programs undoubtedly contributed to the economic growth of European, Asian and other countries, which together brought about a spectacular increase in international trade and investment activities. The point here, however, is to note that even in the absence of the US–USSR geopolitical rivalry, such a development would have taken place. The Bretton Woods programmes for postwar international economic recovery and growth had been promulgated before the onset of the Cold War, and they might have functioned even better in its absence. In any event, it is clear that European integration did not owe its inspiration to the Cold War.

We lack comparable historical studies of other regional structures, such as the Association of Southeast Asian Nations or the South American economic community, Mercosur (Mercado Común del Sur). They, too, tend to be understood in the context of the geopolitical drama, but such an approach is erroneous. That they were driven by their own momentum can be seen in the continuing evolution of such entities through the last decades of the twentieth century and into the twenty-first. A global history of regional communities needs to be written, and when it is, they will be shown to have played just as important roles as IGOs, NGOs and MNEs in transforming the world.

internationalism

The growth of non-state actors demonstrates the existence of what may be called transnational consciousness, an awareness that there are interests, concerns, and aspirations that transcend national boundaries. Such consciousness has been of pivotal importance in enabling non-state actors to function as well as they have. Transnationalism, or internationalism to use a more conventional word, is essentially a faith in the power of ideas and interests that are not confined to national boundaries but that are shared widely across regions and oceans. This faith has been a driving force behind transnational movements, concerned with issues ranging from human rights to environmental protection.

Such movements usually do not figure in conventional accounts of international history. To the extent that historians of international relations do take note of them, they have tended to focus on peace-related activities. Particularly notable have been studies of international movements to 'ban the bomb' – specifically, to control and ultimately prohibit the testing, manufacturing and use of nuclear weapons – by scholars such as Lawrence Wittner and Matthew Evangelista.[24] Their work shows that no narrative of post-1945 international history is complete unless it pays due attention to the unceasing efforts of private individuals and groups on behalf of nuclear arms control. These agents shared the belief that there were interests and causes that transcended the particularistic concerns of specific states. Their partial success, for instance in inducing the nuclear powers to agree to stop atmospheric testing and to restrict the proliferation of weapons of mass destruction, shows that considerations of national interest did not entirely foreclose a willingness to listen to transnational voices of conscience.

Similarly, historians have chronicled in detail the efforts by various organizations before the two world wars on behalf of international peace. A notable recent tendency has been to point to the initiatives taken in this direction by certain social groups, such as women and ethnic minorities. In the United States, for instance, Harriet Alonso's *Peace as a Women's Issue* establishes a connection between women's and peace movements, while Thomas Borstelmann's *The Cold War and the Color Line* links Cold War geopolitics to race relations and points to Martin Luther King and other civil rights activists' leadership in calling for a warless, peaceful international order.[25] All these contributions enrich our understanding of international history by providing what may be called a social history of international relations. It is not surprising then that some social and cultural historians have become interested in international relations and have begun to produce provocative studies of the relationship between domestic and external affairs. A recent example is Helen Laville's monograph on American women during the Cold War, which shows that many of them became ardent internationalists immediately after the end of the Second World War, and yet ultimately nonetheless became enfolded and co-opted into the Cold War drama, seeking to influence foreign opinion against Soviet communism.[26] Despite this, the story should not be dismissed as a just a minor episode in the history of the Cold War; rather, it illuminates the fact that the tension between nationalism and internationalism is a perpetual phenomenon in international history.

That tension may be even more clearly seen in the story of what I have termed 'cultural internationalism'.[27] This refers to efforts by cultural leaders – artists, intellectuals, educators and others – to establish transnational connections in the belief, as Romain Rolland and other European writers asserted in their famous 'declaration on intellectual freedom' in 1919, that 'people' took precedence over states, and that intellectuals would now pledge only to serve the former irrespective of their national identities.[28] Such cultural internationalism had existed before 1914, but it grew much stronger in the wake of the unprecedented catastrophe of the Great War in Europe. Equally impressive is the fact that this sort of internationalism came to be shared by cultural leaders outside of Europe: in North and South America, the Middle East and Asia. Their efforts found an institutional expression in the League of Nations' committee on intellectual cooperation that continued its activities until the very eve of the war that came in 1939. Although the committee was an official League body in which various governments were represented, the United States and other countries that did not join the world organization established their own national committees on intellectual cooperation and worked closely with their counterparts elsewhere. They did not cease their efforts even during the Second World War, and the League committee's work was continued after the war by the United Nations Educational, Scientific and Cultural Organization (UNESCO). Here again, private individuals and groups worked closely with official representatives to carry out innumerable projects (such as a series of conferences on dialogue among civilizations, as will be noted below), all of which were sustained by and promoted the vision of an interdependent world community in which people across national boundaries shared and pursued common objectives.

Of course, the vision was not always translated into reality, and cultural leaders were frequently caught in a dilemma between internationalist aspirations and their respective national identities and loyalties. A recent study by Gabrielle Metzler chronicles this dilemma as she describes German physicists' ideas and attitudes from the late nineteenth century to the early post-Second World War years. She shows that German scientists were acutely conscious after the founding of the Reich in 1871 of their nation's need to catch up with the more advanced countries of Europe and saw their primary obligation as the development and strengthening of the nation. Although they were convinced of the universalism of scientific research, they saw no conflict between it and their commitment to 'German physics'. This was true, according to Metzler, even during the 1920s, otherwise a promising decade for cultural internationalism, and it was only after the disastrous years of Nazi rule and the Second World War that German physicists came to embrace wholeheartedly the idea as well as the practice of transnational science.[29] Such a study fits with others that have examined the relationship between science and foreign policy or, more broadly, between scholarship and politics. Works by Volker Berghahn and Ron Robin, for instance, have done much to elucidate the nuanced ways in which US social scientists, literary figures and others became caught up in the Cold War dilemma: they struggled to find universalistic meaning even in their activities on behalf of the government in solidifying the Western alliance against the Soviet bloc.[30] The story, however, was far more than one of intellectuals collaborating with the state. If that were all, it would not merit more than a footnote in the historiography of the Cold War. On the contrary, the very dilemma reveals the persistence of an internationalist consciousness that would never entirely dissipate and that from time to time would come to affect official relations among states.

environmentalism

Toward the end of the twentieth century, internationalism came to embrace much more than movements for peace, disarmament or intellectual cooperation. Starting around 1970, such non-geopolitical issues as environmental degradation and human rights abuses came to draw the attention of nations, non-state actors and individuals alike. These were non-geopolitical issues in the sense that they were not confined to specific nations but were seen as global phenomena to which only transnational responses were believed to be workable. It did not matter if environmental disasters occurred in China or in the United States, or if human rights violations were committed in Soviet bloc nations or among US allies, they were considered to be human problems to be dealt with by the collaborative action of concerned men and women everywhere. Not surprisingly, in the 1970s some, in and out of government, began talking of 'human security', indicating that security was no longer (if it ever was) just a matter of safeguarding a nation's boundaries against an attack by another or of maintaining a military balance of power. Rather, there would be no national security without clean air and water, without ensuring the survival of animals and plants and without citizens living without fear. Such a broad definition of security clearly demanded reconceptualization of the nature of international relations, and yet the historiographical literature has lagged far behind this thinking.

Most of the scholarly literature on these non-geopolitical themes has been the work of non-historians. On the environment, numerous monographs have been published by political scientists and sociologists, but very few by historians.[31] One important exception is John McNeill's *Something New under the Sun*, a thorough analysis of environmental degradation and the efforts to cope with it, from the beginning of the twentieth to the twenty-first century. The book presents a panoramic view of air and water pollution, desertification and deforestation, as well as the near or total extinction of certain fish, birds, animals and plants over the decades. McNeill notes that, starting from the early 1970s, international efforts began to be made to stem the tide and to save the ecological system of the planet.[32] This is a theme that is also stressed by Lynton Keith Caldwell whose *International Environmental Policy* documents efforts by the United Nations and NGOs to cope with problems of natural preservation and conservation.[33] Although written as environmental history, these books make a significant contribution to international history as well. Unfortunately, few international historians have made full use of them to produce less geopolitically oriented work. Their focus on individual nations' foreign policies makes it virtually impossible to deal with transnational issues like environmentalism in the framework of global strategy and action. It is true that individual nations often do undertake separate projects in order to protect the environment, but eventually they come to the realization that polluted skies, endangered species and the like know no national boundaries and threaten all countries alike. Historians will need to take cognizance of such a development and incorporate international efforts at protecting the environment into international history.

human rights

On human rights, similarly, the majority of the standard reference works and scholarly monographs have been produced by non-historians. Examples would include Jack Donnelly's *International Human Rights* and Louis Menand III's essay on the same topic.[34] Among historians, Paul Gordon Lauren has published a path-blazing history of human rights, but more work is needed to integrate the theme into the history of international relations.[35] To do so would amount not only to globalizing but also to humanizing international history: the history of human rights is essentially a history of humankind, and in that sense it clearly precedes the emergence of nations. But human rights do not exist in a separate sphere from nations or from international affairs. This can perhaps best be seen in the history of slavery, which is both very much a story of human rights, and yet also an important chapter in the history of modern international relations. Not only the transatlantic slave trade or the activities by British naval vessels to stop and search ships traversing the Atlantic after the slave trade was prohibited in the early nineteenth century, but also the emergence of an anti-slavery movement on both sides of the ocean are important episodes in international history by any definition, and show that its traditional subject matter need not be that far removed from transnational concerns.[36] Besides slavery, so many instances of human degradation and depravity have existed: the Holocaust and various other ethnic massacres, atrocities committed in wartime against civilians and prisoners of war, as well as apartheid and numerous other practices of racial discrimination. While some of these events have been mentioned as part of the histories of the two world wars and other conflicts, they have not been treated as integral parts of international history. But human rights violations occur in peace as well as in war, and because international history is concerned with peacetime relations as well as with conflict, it is imperative that historians try to integrate the story of human rights into their interpretations of international relations.

Two examples will illustrate the importance of adding the human rights dimension to international history. One concerns the physical and mental illnesses that have afflicted men, women and children throughout history. Excellent histories of diseases exist: William McNeill's *Plagues and Peoples* is just one example among many.[37] And yet such histories have not been fully incorporated into international history, which is clearly wrong. It is well-known, for instance, that more people died of influenza in the immediate aftermath of the Great War than in the conflict itself, and yet the pandemic and the war have tended to be treated as two separate episodes, not simultaneous occurrences. The process of globalization has made it much easier for germs and viruses to spread to distant parts of the world, and contagious diseases, of which Acquired Immune Deficiency Syndrome (AIDS) and Severe Acute Respiratory Syndrome (SARS) are two of the most serious recent examples, have ignored all national boundaries. This is a transnational phenomenon, and it is very much part of international history in that nations try, sometimes individually but most frequently through cooperation, to contain such diseases. International organizations, both governmental and private, have also devoted themselves to the task. A history of international relations at the end of the twentieth century and the beginning of the twenty-first will be woefully inadequate if it does not take such activities into account.

A particularly interesting subject is the treatment of the physically and mentally disabled. Literary works dealing with war – from Leo Tolstoy's *War and Peace* to Sebastian Faulks' *Birdsong*[38] – are filled with characters who have lost their limbs, their eyes and even their minds through the experience of fighting, and yet most histories of warfare, and especially surveys of international relations, pay only scant attention to them, if any at all. This is to miss the vitally human element of the story. But physical and mental health is not, of course, a matter of concern only in wartime. Michael Burleigh has described in shocking detail how the Nazi regime carried out a plan to segregate the mentally handicapped with a view to eliminating them.[39] This is obviously an important, if rather neglected, aspect of Nazi history, but it has important implications for the study of international relations, since how a regime deals with its disabled population, especially its mental patients, says a great deal about its attitude toward 'the other', those who do not 'fit'. Given that, thanks to humanitarian efforts by governments and non-state actors, the disabled are on the whole better treated today in most parts of the world than ever before, should this not count as an important theme in international history? When disabled people and mental patients, as well as victims of wartime bombing and atrocities, organize themselves across national boundaries to arouse the conscience of humankind, this surely must be considered just as significant a phenomenon as the movement for peace or for environmental protection.

The second example of human rights violations that has increasingly become a key issue in international affairs is terrorism. While there is nothing new about acts of terrorism that have affected the course of international relations – the Sarajevo incident in 1914 is the most famous but by no means the only example – there has been something particularly ominous about terrorism since the 1970s, precisely because its spread has coincided with such other phenomena in global history as the growth of IGOs, NGOs, MNEs and transnational movements for human rights and environmental protection.

The literature on international terrorism is fast growing, although most of it has been the work of non-historians. A few historians, nevertheless, have contributed to the discussion, especially in the wake of the 9/11 attacks on US targets, in order to make sense of those horrendous occurrences.[40] Most of the existing work tends to put international terrorist acts in the context of the ending of the Cold War. It is argued that as the geopolitical system defined by bipolar confrontation gave way to the emergence of the United States as the sole superpower, wars among the major powers of the world have become less and less likely. At the same time, clashes continued to occur between neighbouring states, as did civil strife within some countries, several of which were so torn by internal division as to become 'failed states'. In such a situation, it has been argued, international terrorism has emerged as another challenge to international order, in particular the United States and the globalizing world with which it is identified. Whatever new order may be said to have begun to emerge in the wake of the Cold War, according to this view, terrorists would make sure that it did not become solidified. They would rather keep the globe in conditions of uncertainty and fear and, therefore, weaken the power of the United States and other countries to impose their will on the rest of the world.

While there is much to be said for such a perspective, it would be wrong to attribute the growing menace of terrorism solely to the ending of the Cold War, for we must go back at least to the 1970s to locate the origins of the current phase of this phenomenon. It was in that decade that terrorism became a feature of international affairs. Starting with the Palestinian extremist attacks on Israeli athletes at the 1972 Munich Olympics, the decade ended with Iranian students' seizure of the US Embassy in Teheran. Lest these examples should give the impression that terror was a weapon utilized only by fanatical Muslims, we should recall that there was also state terrorism in Cambodia practised by the Pol Pot regime and anti-state terrorism perpetrated by extremist groups in such countries as Peru, Nicaragua and Sri Lanka. These acts were in sharp contrast to the rising concern with human rights everywhere, and the two were connected in contradictory ways. In some instances, terrorism was a way of protesting against human rights abuses (as in Iran under the Shah whose regime was overthrown in 1979), but in other cases, such as the Munich episode, terrorism arguably simply violated individual human rights. Either way, it is to be noted that a decade that was notable for the internationalization of human rights (as well as environmentalism and other phenomena) also saw the internationalization of terrorism. Both were aspects of a globalization that was accelerating its tempo. Terrorists, even though the majority of them were ideologically opposed to economic and cultural globalization, did not hesitate to make use of such technology as the cassette tape, the jet airplane and the fax machine, which were bringing all parts of the world into closer and closer communication. Perpetrators of terrorism not only utilized these tools in planning and carrying out their attacks, but they also made sure that their acts and their ideology would be broadcast world-wide. Terrorism thus sank into the consciousness of billions of people, perhaps for the first time in history, so that it would come to be seen as a feature of contemporary life.

What is needed, then, is a historical perspective that will take note of international terrorism as a major theme, not as some sort of an aberration, in recent history. Geopolitically-oriented conceptual frameworks will not do, preoccupied as they necessarily are with the vicissitudes of the Cold War. Rather than periodizing recent international history in terms of détente, the 'new' Cold War of the late 1970s and the early 1980s, the ending of the Cold War and the post-Cold War era, we need to comprehend all developments since the 1970s as important component elements of the contemporary globalizing world. These themes are not mutually consistent or congruous. Besides disease and terrorism, one might think of the global trafficking in drugs and illegal migrants as negative products of globalization. But they are all aspects of contemporary history. Recent global history, then, would not define itself in terms of geopolitical developments but of the simultaneous development of human rights and terrorism, environmentalism and drug-trafficking, IGOs and failed states, NGOs and religious fanaticism, regional communities and national egoisms, or MNEs and the gaps between rich and poor societies. These polarities are as significant as that of war and peace, the usual categorization in conventional international history.

the future of global history

Given such simultaneous developments and contradictory themes, is there a storyline, some sort of teleology, in global history? Where is it tending? It is the historian's task to suggest an answer, or at least to provide some framework for considering whether history is taking humankind to a more promising future or condemning it to a repetition of past tragedies.

The recent vogue for writings on the 'American empire' is not very helpful in this regard, as it perpetuates the traditional, purely geopolitical formulation of international history.[41] The United States as the sole superpower, as the hegemon or as the world empire – these are terms taken straight out of conventional international relations history. They are thus irrelevant to the realities of contemporary world affairs that are created less by geopolitics than by globalization. Whether or not the United States will be able to establish a new global order is much less susceptible to analysis within the framework of international history than within that of global history. For no matter how powerful militarily and economically the United States might be, the challenges it faces are qualitatively different from those of the past and consist of such issues as human rights, environmentalism, terrorism, NGOs, MNEs and the like. Whether the United States will be a successful world leader depends less on how it manages to maintain a global balance of power than on how it deals with these realities.

One of the most effective ways for the United States, or for other countries, to play a constructive role in the global age would be to help promote dialogue among cultures and civilizations. Samuel Huntington's *The Clash of Civilizations*, published in 1996, was perhaps the most important recent contribution to the study of international history precisely because the author argued that civilizations, not nations, were likely to be the major players in future world affairs.[42] But he came to an unjustifiable conclusion in predicting that civilizations were bound to collide. For whether civilizations were to clash or to accommodate one another was an open question, the answer to which would depend on the degree of efforts made to promote dialogue between them. Huntington assumed that no such dialogue was possible since civilizations were by definition mutually exclusive. In propagating such fatalistic determinism, he ignored one of the major developments in modern global history: serious attempts at establishing communication and dialogue among civilizations, which were made throughout the twentieth century but became particularly extensive and systematic after the Second World War.

For it may be argued that one of the most important yet little-noticed developments in international relations after 1945 was precisely this dialogue among cultures and civilizations that was promoted throughout the world. This reflected the fact that, in the wake of the catastrophic war, communication and engagement among people with their different cultural traditions and historical identities was considered, by victors and vanquished alike, the priority goal that must be promoted by the world community if it were to prevent another calamity. UNESCO was founded with such a mission. Although, as noted above, the League of Nations had undertaken a serious initiative in this direction, it was UNESCO that self-consciously and ardently undertook the task. Starting in the 1950s, when it sponsored a ten-year project to promote dialogue between Eastern and Western civilizations, all the way to the twenty-first century, UNESCO has devoted itself to bringing different cultures and civilizations together. These endeavours were assisted by numerous individuals and organizations, and collectively they challenged the Cold War-dominated view of international affairs.

Why such a preoccupation with inter-civilizational dialogue? Fundamentally, it was because UNESCO and its sponsors all over the world recognized that even more crucial than interstate affairs were the relations among people, and people were products of divergent civilizations. Their identities and loyalties did not always, or even primarily, lie with the countries in which they happened to live, but with their ways of life, with their mentalities. World peace, therefore, must be founded upon communication and understanding among cultures and civilizations. It is a remarkable fact that in 2001, the year that we tend to remember through the terrorist attacks on the United States, UNESCO and the United Nations held a series of conferences on promoting inter-civilizational dialogue. At an international symposium on 'dialogue among civilizations in a changing world' held in Rabat, Morocco, in July of that year, Koichiro Matsuura, director general of UNESCO, reiterated what that organization had been stressing time and again, namely that 'civilizations are constantly dialoguing not only with others but with themselves. That is why it may be said that every civilization is profoundly intercultural, and why it is therefore unthinkable to attempt to rank civilizations or set them in opposition to one another.' Realization of this fact was, therefore, 'the key element in the construction of a culture of peace'.[43] Throughout 2001 many similar symposia were held on dialogue among civilizations. UNESCO, moreover, sponsored many other conferences on education, bio-ethics, renewable energy technologies and the like that addressed truly transnational issues. Toward the end of the year 2001, the organization joined the Islamic Educational, Scientific and Cultural Organization to convene a conference of cultural ministers from Islamic countries. Matsuura noted on that occasion that, although in the wake of the 9/11 terrorist acts the idea of an inevitable clash of civilization had once again become popular, 'UNESCO was the first United Nations body ... to categorically reject this pernicious vision of how cultures and civilizations interact.'[44] The international history of the first year of the new millennium must surely include such a reassertion of faith in inter-civilizational dialogue, along with horrendous acts of terrorism.

Global history, to conclude, is an approach that looks at transnational themes in order to broaden our understanding of international relations as well as national developments. History will look rather different when we focus on global rather than national or international themes. If historians are not to be content with regurgitating conventional wisdom or accepting traditional chronologies without criticism but wish to try to make an original contribution to understanding the past, they will find global history an excellent guide. By engaging in research and writing under the inspiration of the fresh perspectives that it offers, they will in fact be becoming part of global history.

notes

1. Bruce Mazlish initiated a course at Massachusetts Institute of Technology called 'New Global History' in the late 1990s. He and I together taught the same course at Harvard University in 2001 and 2002.
2. Bruce Mazlish, 'An Introduction to Global History', in Bruce Mazlish and Ralph Buultjens (eds), *Conceptualizing Global History* (Boulder, CO: Westview Press, 1993), pp. 1–24.
3. Stephen Castles and Mark J. Miller, *The Age of Migration: International Population Movements in the Modern World*, 2nd edn (London: Macmillan, 1998); Robin Cohen, *Global Diasporas: An Introduction* (London: UCL Press, 1997).
4. Wang Gungwu, 'Migration and Its Enemies', in Mazlish and Buultjens, *Conceptualizing Global History*, pp. 131–51.
5. William Keylor, *The Twentieth-Century World: An International History*, 4th edn (New York: Oxford University Press, 2001).
6. J. R. McNeill and William H. McNeill, *The Human Web: A Bird's-Eye View of World History* (New York: Norton, 2003).
7. Among the pioneering works by political scientists, particularly notable is Harold K. Jacobson, *Networks of Interdependence: International Organizations and the Global Political System*, 2nd edn (New York: Knopf, 1984).
8. F. S. L. Lyons, *Internationalism in Europe, 1815–1914* (Leiden: A. W. Sythoff, 1963).
9. Dorothy V. Jones, *Toward a Just World: The Critical Years in the Search for International Justice* (Chicago: University of Chicago Press, 2002).
10. Peter Wilson, *The International Theory of Leonard Woolf* (New York: Palgrave, 2003).
11. Among the most significant recent works are Margaret Keck and Kathryn Sikkink, *Activists Beyond Borders: Advocacy Networks in International Politics* (Ithaca: Cornell University Press, 1998); John Boli and George Thomas (eds), *Constructing World Culture: International Nongovernmental Organizations since 1875* (Stanford: Stanford University Press, 1999); Sarah E. Mendelson and John K. Glenn (eds), *The Power and Limits of NGOs: A Critical Look at Building Democracy in Eastern Europe and Russia* (New York: Columbia University Press, 2002).
12. Akira Iriye, *Global Community: The Role of International Organizations in the Making of the Contemporary World* (Berkeley: University of California Press, 2002).
13. Leila J. Rupp, *Worlds of Women: The Making of an International Women's Movement* (Princeton, NJ: Princeton University Press, 1997); Elizabeth Cobbs

Hoffman, *All You Need is Love: The Peace Corps and the Spirit of the 1960s* (Cambridge, MA: Harvard University Press, 1998).

14. See, among others, Frank Ninkovich, *The Wilsonian Century: US Foreign Policy since 1900* (Chicago: University of Chicago Press, 1999); Tony Smith, *America's Mission: The United States and the Worldwide Struggle for Democracy in the Twentieth Century* (Princeton, NJ: Princeton University Press, 1994).

15. Henry Kissinger, *Diplomacy* (New York: Simon and Schuster, 1994).

16. Mira Wilkins, 'The Historical Development of Multinational Enterprises to 1930: Discontinuities and Continuities', unpublished conference paper (1999).

17. Bruce Mazlish, 'New Global History: A Framing Perspective', unpublished conference paper (2003).

18. Emily Rosenberg, *Financial Missionaries to the World: The Politics and Culture of Dollar Diplomacy, 1900–1930* (Cambridge, MA: Harvard University Press, 1999).

19. Paul Kennedy, *The Rise and Fall of the Great Powers: Economic Change and Military Conflict from 1500 to 2000* (New York: Random House, 1987).

20. Andre Frank, *Re-Orient: Global Economy in the Asian Age* (Berkeley: University of California Press, 1998).

21. For 'informal empire' and 'the imperialism of free trade', the best known and pioneering work is Ronald Robinson and John Gallagher, *Africa and the Victorians: The Official Mind of Imperialism* (London: Macmillan, 1961).

22. Niall Ferguson, *Empire: How Britain Made the Modern World* (London: Allen Lane, 2003).

23. See, for instance, William I. Hitchcock, *The Struggle for Europe: The Turbulent History of a Divided Continent, 1945–2002* (New York: Doubleday, 2003).

24. Lawrence Wittner, *The Struggle Against the Bomb. Volume 1: One World or None: A History of the World Nuclear Disarmament Movement through 1953* (Stanford: Stanford University Press, 1993); Matthew Evangelista, *Unarmed Forces: The Transnational Movement to End the Cold War* (Ithaca: Cornell University Press, 1999).

25. Harriet Alonso, *Peace as a Women's Issue: A History of the US Movement for World Peace and Women's Rights* (Syracuse: Syracuse University Press, 1993); Thomas Borstelmann, *The Cold War and the Color Line: American Race Relations in the Global Arena* (Cambridge, MA: Harvard University Press, 2001).

26. Helen Laville, *Cold War Women: The International Activities of American Women's Organisations* (Manchester: University of Manchester Press, 2002).

27. Akira Iriye, *Cultural Internationalism and World Order* (Baltimore: Johns Hopkins University Press, 1997).

28. Iriye, *Cultural Internationalism*, p. 56.

29. Gabrielle Metzler, *Internationale Wissenschaft und Nationale Kultur: Deutsche Physiker in der Internationalen Community, 1900–1960* (Göttingen: Vandenhoeck and Ruprecht, 2000).

30. Volker Berghahn, *America and the Intellectual Cold Wars in Europe* (Princeton, NJ: Princeton University Press, 2001); Ron Robin, *The Making of the Cold War Enemy: Culture and Politics in the Military-Intellectual Complex* (Princeton, NJ: Princeton University Press, 2001).

31. See, among others, Keck and Sikkink, *Activists beyond Borders*; Ann M. Florini (ed.), *The Third Force: The Rise of Transnational Civil Society* (Tokyo: Japan Center for International Exchange, 2000).

32. John R. McNeill, *Something New under the Sun: An Environmental History of the Twentieth-Century World* (New York: Norton, 2000).

33. Lynton Caldwell, *International Environmental Policy*, 3rd edn (Durham: Duke University Press, 1996).

34. Jack Donnelly, *International Human Rights*, 2nd edn (Boulder, CO: Westview Press, 1998); Louis Menand III, 'Human Rights as Global Imperative', in Mazlish and Buultjens, *Conceptualizing Global History*, pp. 173–204.

35. Paul Gordon Lauren, *The Evolution of International Human Rights: Visions Seen*, 2nd edn (Philadelphia: University of Pennsylvania Press, 2003).

36. Among the best studies of the transatlantic slave trade is Hugh Thomas, *The Slave Trade: The History of the Atlantic Slave Trade, 1440–1870* (London: Picador, 1997). For the transnational anti-slavery movement, see Keck and Sikkink, *Activists beyond Borders*, ch. 1.

37. William McNeill, *Plagues and Peoples* (New York: Anchor, 1976).

38. Leo Tolstoy, *War and Peace*, rev. edn (London: Penguin, 1997); Sebastian Faulks, *Birdsong* (London: Vintage, 1994).

39. Michael Burleigh, *Death and Deliverance: 'Euthanasia' in Germany, c. 1900–1945* (Cambridge: Cambridge University Press, 1994).

40. Among the best analyses of international terrorism is Bruce Hoffman, *Inside Terrorism*, 2nd edn (London: Indigo, 1999). Some of the best essays by historians on the 9/11 attacks may be found in Joanne Meyerowitz (ed.), *History and September 11th* (Philadelphia: Temple University Press, 2003).

41. See, among other recent works, Andrew J. Bacevich, *American Empire: The Realities and Consequences of US Diplomacy* (Cambridge, MA: Harvard University Press, 2002).

42. Samuel Huntington, *The Clash of Civilizations and the Remaking of World Order* (New York: Simon and Schuster, 1996).

43. Koichiro Matsuura, *Building the New UNESCO: Selected Speeches 2001* (Paris: UNESCO, 2003), p. 527.

44. Matsuura, *Building the New UNESCO*, p. 478.

index

compiled by auriol griffith-jones

Note: Bold page numbers refer to Tables. The Notes are indexed only where there is significant additional information.